PSYCHOLOGY, HUMOUR AND CLASS

This challenging book critically examines three forms of contemporary psychology, all displaying various signs of crisis, through analogy with humour associated with three different class perspectives: mainstream psychology; critical psychology; and postpsychology.

By fusing the best of the three psychologies with political and cultural critiques, the book poses the question: what if class conflict and the crises of psychology are related? This is precisely the Gordian Knot which Fozooni tries to untangle. First, the author demonstrates how psychology has traditionally veered towards either an upper-class or a middle-class paradigm. With the demise of these two old paradigms a new understanding of psychology is gradually emerging – a *post-psychology*. Describing how 'mainstream' and 'critical' psychologies are undergoing late-life crisis, and 'postpsychology' is experiencing its birth pangs in an environment hostile to its existence, the book provides an alternative narrative of psychology. The author suggests that while all three forms of psychology have contributed to our self-comprehension, it is only postpsychology that possesses the attributes necessary for a global remaking of humanity.

Tackling the discipline of psychology head-on, Fozooni pits against it a series of scathing yet tongue-in-cheek critiques, making this fascinating and provocative reading for all students and academics interested in psychology, as well as the general reader.

Babak Fozooni is an associate lecturer at the Open University and the author of *What is Critical Social Research?* Volumes 1 and 2 (2012, 2017). He has taught at the University of East London, the University of Westminster, Birkbeck College and the Open University. He writes from a working-class perspective.

CONCEPTS FOR CRITICAL PSYCHOLOGY

Series editor: Ian Parker

Developments inside psychology that question the history of the discipline and the way it functions in society have led many psychologists to look outside the discipline for new ideas. This series draws on cutting edge critiques from just outside psychology in order to complement and question critical arguments emerging inside. The authors provide new perspectives on subjectivity from disciplinary debates and cultural phenomena adjacent to traditional studies of the individual.

The books in the series are useful for advanced level undergraduate and postgraduate students, researchers and lecturers in psychology and other related disciplines such as cultural studies, geography, literary theory, philosophy, psychotherapy, social work and sociology.

Deleuze and Psychology
Philosophical Provocations to Psychological Practices
Maria Nichterlein & John R. Morss

Rethinking Education through Critical Psychology
Cooperative schools, social justice and voice
Gail Davidge

Developing Minds
Psychology, neoliberalism and power
Elise Klein

Marxism and Psychoanalysis
In or against Psychology?
David Pavón-Cuéllar

Psychology, Humour and Class
A Critique of Contemporary Psychology
Babak Fozooni

PSYCHOLOGY, HUMOUR AND CLASS

A Critique of Contemporary Psychology

Babak Fozooni

Routledge
Taylor & Francis Group
LONDON AND NEW YORK

First published 2020
by Routledge
2 Park Square, Milton Park, Abingdon, Oxon OX14 4RN

and by Routledge
52 Vanderbilt Avenue, New York, NY 10017

Routledge is an imprint of the Taylor & Francis Group, an informa business

British Library Cataloguing-in-Publication Data
A catalogue record for this book is available from the British Library

Library of Congress Cataloging-in-Publication Data
A catalog record has been requested for this book

ISBN: 978-1-138-61411-6 (hbk)
ISBN: 978-1-138-61412-3 (pbk)
ISBN: 978-0-429-46418-8 (ebk)

Typeset in Bembo
by Taylor & Francis Books

CONTENTS

FIGURES

PREFACE

If, as George Orwell once opined, every joke is a tiny revolution, and if you like revolutions, then this book is for you. I'm not kidding. The book tackles the discipline of psychology head-on, taking it to task for its middle-class prejudice against collective action, and pitting against it a series of scathing critiques that operate so powerfully because they are geared not only to the content of psychology textbooks but also to the tedious predictable form they so often take. Psychology is so often mind-numbingly bad not only because it reduces social phenomena to the level of individual mental processes – a boring repetition of the lesson that the way to deal with oppression is for us all to adapt to it – but also because it treads its way through an interminable repetitive incantation of the work of the same old founding fathers. If you do not rage against this book, if you are not animated by bitter complaint that it is disrespectful and fails to provide a constructive solution to the problematic assumptions you have made about psychology, then you will laugh out loud.

I'll tell you now so you know what you are in for, and this is as much a recommendation for the book as a warning to the reader, that this guy is trouble. I've had some difficult PhD students, and his thesis that bedazzled his supervisors and examiners fifteen years ago took us almost to the edge of what a respectable academic psychology department in Manchester could bear. I had already suffered at this guy's hands during his time on the critical psychology master's course, but I was a glutton for punishment, for punishing critique of my own timid 'critique' of the discipline; if I wasn't already painfully reflexive enough about my collusion with the discipline, then this encounter pushed me further. Not that there are no limitations to his argument – and this is a clue as to how you might engage in your own thorough-going critique of this book – and you might ask yourself why it is only radical theory boys that are called into the class struggle against psychology? Read this book, work with it, and work against it, to take it further. That would be the best way to take it seriously.

Babak Fozooni breaks radically from the usual format of a psychology (or critical psychology) book, and levels an argument against psychology in such a way that is designed, we might say, to 'outwit' it. In that sense, what you have here in *Psychology, Humour and Class: A Critique of Contemporary Psychology* is a critique that refuses to play the discipline at its own game. That game – one that is usually played on the assumption that there is a level playing field between the old 'mainstream' or 'traditional' or 'old paradigm' psychologists and the outliers, the innovative young paradigm-busters – is rigged against us. What this book must do, then, is to work at the edges, wittily nailing the class-based assumptions of the bourgeois theorists and, this is crucial, not stopping there; the book goes on to subject so-called critical psychology to a like degree of intense scorn. We've had it coming, us would-be reformers, and this book twists the knife. This book works at the margins, stepping into the discipline at one moment only to step back again, 'outwith' psychology; this is a book that insists that you can do without psychology, and that you must do without it if you have a sense of humour.

Ian Parker
University of Manchester

APOLOGIA ADDRESSED TO EDITORS AND ACADEMICS

I have not had the pleasure of meeting my Routledge editors face-to-face. Although they have never been anything but courteous and professional in our communications, I suspect they might be somewhat vexed with me. Not only was I late with the submission of my manuscript, but the final version turned out to be far less funny than I had originally intended. I can only surmise that in the course of researching and writing the text, academia somehow managed to suck the humour out of me. Crafty little monkeys, them academics!

Some humour lingers on, though, and the parallels between humour and social class remain a crucial structuring mechanism throughout. At times, the satire exemplifies 'witcraft'[1] at its finest, while at other times it glides perilously close to the mundane sarcasm, pettiness and sleights that bedevil so much of 'my profession'. However, I have decided to cut out the more vicious instances of buffoonery for fear of causing irrevocable offence. Perhaps the work is better for it, perhaps not. I honestly can no longer tell.

Allow me to be clear, dear reader, for I do not wish to be misunderstood. My assault targets psychology as an ideological institution, a discursive practice and a bourgeois swamp of jealousy and competition. It is not aimed at individual psychologists. Why, some of them I may even consider dear friends! I therefore hope that they can find it within themselves to treat my criticisms with the same generosity of spirit they exhibit when marking student essays.

In relation to academia I have always considered myself an 'insider-outsider'. This hyphenated existence means that one is never fully trusted within the lodge, but it does offer a unique vantage point. The 'insider-outsider' sees it all: the fifth-rate novice teacher who instead of aspiring to become a great pedagogue, settles for the prosaic safety of bureaucracy; the fourth-rate scholar who has to pre- and postfix tired concepts in order to feign post-modern 'originality'; the third-rate researcher who forges an unholy alliance with senior management so as to empower himself; the second-rate celebrity-academic who uses his connections to procure wealth and, finally, the first-rate thinker who … ay, there's the rub!

For, if by 'first-raters' we mean luminaries such as Marx, Luxemburg, Freud, Einstein and Darwin, then frankly academia learned long ago to get along without them. Today's academics are mostly mediocrities, bureaucrats and windbags! And since unlike comics they are incapable of self-deprecating humour, they end up projecting all their shortcomings onto students. Poor, 'rascally, beggarly, b-gg-rly'[2] students, so desperate for any kind of education that they don't even notice that the commodity they cherish is depreciating in use-value, as its market price goes through the roof!

But I do not wish to give the impression that all is doom and gloom in psychology, academia or the world at large. Ironically, the current right-wing, anti-working-class zeitgeist holds one distinct advantage: transparency. The humanising mask, which for so long concealed the warts and blemishes of capital, has finally slipped. Now the real capitalist (politician/news editor/clergy/judge/academic) stands before us: old, decrepit and resentful.

Even psychology, one of academia's brightest protégés, seems bereft of novel ideas. And so it is timely to chart once more psychology's brilliant rise and sudden demise. This is the story of its unexpected findings, its momentary sagacity, its arrogance and its countless follies. Crucially, this account also sketches the contours of what may emerge after its demise: a 'postpsychology' that is truly worthy of humanity. I hope this is more than a book. I hope it ends up being an atheist's attempt to reconstruct Noah's dinghy to save whatever remains salvageable in psychology. May the Great Flood wash away the rest. Amen!

Notes

1 'Witcraft' is a term popularised by, among others, Michael Billig and Jonathan Rée.
2 A phrase attributed to James Justinian Morier (*c.* 1780–1849), a British author and diplomat no less.

ACKNOWLEDGEMENTS

My thanks to Professor Ian Parker who talked me into writing this book, although I would venture to say that now that the work is completed he probably has ambivalent feelings about it. I would like to thank Routledge for not panicking (too much) when confronted by an unusual book. In particular, I found the advice of Alex Howard and Eleanor Taylor very helpful. I would also like to thank my copy-editor, Alison Phillips, whose intelligence has greatly enhanced the writing. I have no idea how much copy-editors get paid, but I am fairly certain it is not enough. Finally, I extend my gratitude to my Open University psychology students, all of whom have promised to purchase a copy of this book, and in the process make me a wealthy man.

INTRODUCTION

One of the minor themes running through the CBS television series *The Big Bang Theory* is the overwhelming superiority of the 'natural sciences' over the 'social sciences'. The central character, Dr Sheldon Cooper, a theoretical physicist, expresses on several occasions his utter disdain for the social sciences and psychology in particular, which is dismissed as the 'doofus' of the sciences! Does Sheldon Cooper have a point? Is psychology really the doofus of the sciences? Sadly, the answer is not as straightforward as the question, and depends entirely on how we choose to perceive 'psychology', 'science' and 'doofusness'. This may seem somewhat pedantic but I am keen to introduce an element of precision into our discussion from the outset.

You see, dear reader, it took me around two years to come up with a possible defence of psychology that does justice to the mockery entailed in Sheldon's accusation. It took me another year to convince myself to set my thoughts on paper. The famous prohibition, 'it is better to remain silent and be thought a fool than to open one's mouth and remove all doubt', acted as a constant refrain. But now that I have opened my mouth, allow me to remove all doubt.

I have chosen a deliberately simple and schematic approach to understanding psychology which is based on three class-bound forms of knowledge: upper-class psychology; middle-class psychology and working-class psychology. Moreover, a deceptively conventional chapter outline adds to the appearance of conventionality. Throughout the volume I have tried to avoid using unnecessary jargon and over-referencing as a cheap form of impressing the audience. Humour is utilised in order to defamiliarise some of the material, and to allow the emergence of an alternative narrative about psychology. I have used academic, literary and cultural resources without demanding feedback from any specialised sector. My aim is not to evidence the nature of contemporary working-class lives, study them in focus groups or reward them with cheddar cheese at the end of a maze quest. Nor am I interested in 'representing' the proletariat, regulating their behaviour, or speaking on their behalf.

I wrote this book primarily for myself and for those workers who still read books. I wrote to laud the *semi*-glorious past and the social struggles to come. I wrote to expose the fragility of bourgeois demagogy. I wrote to escalate and intensify the class struggle, because just like Walter White, I too am *Breaking Bad*. Sadly, unlike Mr White I did not have the good sense to study something useful like chemistry. Instead, I have to make do with turning the base metal of senile social science into alchemical gold.

On psychology

Psychology has always reminded me of an alcoholic in recovery. It seems forever one drink away from falling off the wagon, and turning a mishap into a crisis. Its numerous crises are usually blamed on methodological confusion, or dualistic thinking, or a tendency to reduce complex phenomena to one dimension of analysis. Its epistemology and ontology are charged with criminal intent and brought to justice and yet the crisis ridden nature of psychology persists.

What is ignored in such orthodox narratives is the centrality of social conflict. This book attempts to re-centre class issues and to demonstrate how various crises of psychology have their roots in class struggle. For the sake of convenience, I have sometimes categorised psychology in terms of 'modernist', 'high modernist', and 'postmodernist' paradigms. At other times, I may refer to the clash between 'mainstream' and 'critical' forms of psychology. When sarcasm gets the better of me, I blithely differentiate between 'smart psychology' and 'not so smart psychology'. During moments of rage I may even use terms such as 'revolutionary' or 'reactionary'. And, finally, when I feel particularly cocksure, I divide psychology into 'upper-class', 'middle-class' and 'working-class' variants.

What all these faultlines within psychology reveal is a kingdom that is not at ease with itself – a kingdom that is neither unitary nor united but rather is an 'invented tradition' (Hobsbawm and Ranger [1983] 2012), or if you like, an 'imagined community' (Anderson [1983] 2006). Once this basic element of the narrative is established, certain questions forcibly present themselves: if psychology is an invented tradition, who is doing the inventing and for what purpose? Can the imagined community of psychology be disrupted? Perhaps superseded by something better? Is psychology worth saving? If most forms of psychology serve the ruling class, how can we reinvent it to become an ally of the working class?

The central claim at the heart of this book can thus be expressed in a few simple words: *the social sciences (and in particular psychology) are entrapped in a series of crises caused mainly by class conflict.* Occasionally some of these class-driven crises are partially overcome, resulting in sudden bursts of 'progress' within the field. So, both the crises and the temporary and partial resolution of crises are shaped by class conflict. This is not always easy to see since class struggle has morphed into a complex web of ambiguities and incertitudes. What was once clear and obvious has over the years become mediated, diffused and obscured. But it seems to me both urgent and eminently demonstrable to reclaim what was once common knowledge.

In Part I, I begin by examining upper-class psychology. This does not mean that upper-class people have a different psychology to the rest of us. Nor does it mean that the individual psychologists selected (namely Freud, Hirschfeld, Watson, Maslow and Rogers) were all paid-up members of the ruling elite. In fact, most would probably self-identify as middle class. However, their contributions were taken up and utilised to bolster capitalism, and in this sense they represent an upper-class psychology. Appropriate examples are provided from psychology and the world of humour. In upper-class psychology, style and occasionally form may be undermined but the fundamentals of the status quo are left untouched.

Upper-class (or to simplify things, mainstream or modernist) psychology is epitomised here by psychoanalysis, behaviourism and humanistic psychology. All three began on the margins of orthodoxy but were soon co-opted as a bulwark of conservative capitalism. Each enjoyed its moment in the Sun, until its limitations catalysed not so much a 'paradigm-shift' (Kuhn 1970) but a 'perspective-shift'. This subtle difference suggests that psychoanalysis, behaviourism and humanistic forms of psychology have more in common that is usually admitted by their advocates. All three offered us occasional moments of insight and a rich vocabulary. It would be churlish to deny it. However, they represent a bankrupt approach devoid of originality. Their crisis is manifested ideologically, structurally and even at the personal level. No doubt new technology will breathe some fresh air into their lungs, but these attempts at resurrection are as pointless as digitalising old Monty Python sketches. Once the parrot dies, no amount of trickery can bring it back to life.

The crisis within upper-class psychology compelled some psychologists to interrogate its foundations with renewed rigour. Various currents came together as a middle-class (aka critical) form of psychology in the 1960s, 1970s and 1980s. This phenomenon emerged initially in some 'western' countries, especially the United Kingdom and Germany, and was soon exported elsewhere. Middle-class psychology posed a challenge (of sorts) to the status quo. Within this tradition, *some* further elements of style, formatting and even content are subverted. A number of new fields of inquiry are established. Under the umbrella term, critical psychology, *certain aspects* of individualism, reductionism, positivism, essentialism and empiricism are challenged. All this is explained in Part II of the book by foregrounding the likes of Frankl, R. D. Laing, Foucault, Michael Billig and Ian Parker.

The very best of critical psychology (and some of it is represented in the current Routledge series) remains thought-provoking. But let us be frank with each other. So much of critical psychology today is nothing more than intellectually impoverished, clichéd, middle-class judgementalism. It has become lazy and predictable. I am afraid its crisis is very real. At present, the decline shows itself only ideologically. Critical psychology's structures are still expanding and its personnel are still enhancing their reputations through accumulating prestige. Undoubtedly the application of its theoretical heritage to new fields and subjects will continue to throw up interesting ideas. Nevertheless, the creeping obsolescence of postmodernism will inevitably catch up with critical psychology and expose it at every future turn.

The third, and final, form of psychology is a strange entity, and is given added mystery by the simple fact that it is not yet fully formed (see Part III). It is difficult to know what to call it since linguistic innovation usually lags behind the appearance of a new phenomenon. I don't think 'anti-psychology' is an appropriate nomenclature. I initially wanted to call it 'meta-psychology', or even 'trans-psychology'. I finally settled on the term, 'postpsychology'. This new phenomenon represents a centrifugal tendency that has its roots in psychology but is forever trying to escape the confines of specialism. It is nourished by subversive thinkers working within other social sciences, as well as by radical social movements aiming to reshape humanity. I have chosen to focus on Vico, Dietzgen, Sohn-Rethel, Fromm, Artaud, Vygotsky, Bakhtin and Luria in Part III. Postpsychology is analogous to the working-class humour of Charlie Chaplin and Dario Fo. In postpsychology, form, style and content all undergo radical subversion. It is fair to say that postpsychology is also experiencing a 'crisis' (as with mainstream and critical psychologies), but these are the birth pangs of a new creature fighting for survival in a toxic environment.

Having provided an alternative narrative arc, I will go on to argue that while all three forms of psychology are contributing to our self-comprehension, it is only postpsychology that can aid in the global remaking of humanity. By fusing the best of the three psychologies with accounts from outside psychology, I hope to demonstrate a new way of 'doing' psychology. The discussion will contain specific recommendations for teaching and research.

On class

In many ways class conflict *is* the crisis of psychology. This obvious truism has been suppressed for so long that social class has garnered a distasteful quality. It is not something that decent psychologists discuss in polite company. Even when alluded to, social class is commonly presented as either an afterthought, or as a lingering historical appendage, or worse still, as an independent variable jostling for attention. The reader will soon realise that I have little patience for those thinkers who consider the issue of class 'settled', or who have consigned the class struggle to a bygone age. In short, my central argument is that psychologists either don't *do* class, or when they do, they make a God-awful mess of it! There are, thankfully, a few honourable exceptions and we will come across them in the course of this book.

A shallow reading may adjudge the book 'a history from above'. After all, the eighteen chapters at the core of it seem to correspond to *his*-story, a classic recounting from above by famed male psychologists. Very soon, however, the reader is disinvested of such false notions. I have taken account of the Whig historiography of psychology but countered this with a people's history from below (Thompson [1963] 2013; Hill [1972] 1991). This project has undoubtedly benefited from the autonomist school of historiography (Linebaugh and Rediker 2012) that has recently been making serious inroads into the panegyric accounts of kings and queens. But I have also tried to overcome some of the exaggerated claims of the autonomist school by acknowledging the persistent authority of capitalism.

There have been previous attempts to look at class from a psychological viewpoint (cf. Argyle 1993). The reader will gradually discover that my approach is very different. Part of this difference is due to the use of a more *expansive* definition of class. For me, social class is an entity that should be pursued at different levels simultaneously: at an *abstract* level, class is a set of social relationships that shapes one's productive and reproductive activities; at an *institutional* level we see the visible mechanisms of power and wealth at work; and at the *personal* level we encounter real individuals who are embedded in various social relationships. For example, we can describe the abstract level of relationship under capitalism for most people as being governed by 'wage slavery'. We are compelled to find a buyer for our labour power, otherwise poverty and suffering ensue. For the ruling class, the institutional level may be represented by the World Bank and the International Monetary Fund, while for the proletariat autonomous syndicates and workers' councils are exemplars of institutional power.

The most vital point to convey here is this: in contemporary societies the working class should be defined as those who either directly or indirectly create the wealth – not *some* of the wealth, not even *most* of the wealth, but *all* of the wealth. From my perspective, the working class includes the 'traditional' industrial wing of the proletariat but also (most) office workers, education workers, health workers, firefighters, technicians, scientists, cultural workers, athletes, homeworkers, the unemployed, etc. In short, *the overwhelming majority of people in society are working class*. Both the ruling class and the mainstream media have been exceptionally successful in suppressing this basic truth for far too long.

Without a shadow of a doubt there are always complications. In a society such as Great Britain, for instance, with its somewhat unique history, one could argue there are three (and not one) viable sources of wealth: the labour power of those workers born, educated and trained in Britain; the labour power of those who at some stage of their lives have migrated to Britain; and the labour power of those workers colonised (directly or indirectly) by the British ruling class, who may never see the 'motherland' but who will continue to have surplus value extracted from them, which is then transferred to Britain. In a fair world, the decisions regarding how, when and where to use this immense accumulated wealth would really be up to these three sections of the working class, and yet at present anyone but these workers are the ultimate arbiters of wealth utilisation. Mainstream psychology's insistence on routinely categorising us, not as the overwhelming majority of each and every society, but as a countless myriad of 'minorities', has done untold damage to the anti-capitalist cause. Our united power is diffused and our differences as workers (and there are many) are not seen as yet another source of strength. These provide us with a diverse set of skills, experiences, resilience and abilities but they are viewed as essentialist attributes, and can be used to divide us.

Another complicating factor is this: class has both an 'objective' dimension (e.g. our relationship with the forces of production; which jobs we do; the wages we receive in return for our labour power, etc.), as well as a 'subjective' dimension (e.g. our desires, values, plans, concerns, sources of alienation, etc.). Instead of investigating the objective and subjective side of social class simultaneously, psychology has traditionally taken a dualistic stance and studied one or the other in isolation. This reinforces the artificial divide between quantitative and qualitative methods of research.

On humour

> Some forms of reality are so horrible we refuse to face them, unless we are trapped into it by comedy. To label any subject unsuitable for comedy is to admit defeat.
>
> *Peter Sellers*

I do not remember the first time I laughed but I vividly recall the first time I became aware of the magical power of humour. For me, watching a TV version of Trevor Griffiths' play, *Comedians*, was an eye-opener. It is set in a Manchester evening class for aspiring working-class comedians during the 1970s. The most enjoyable version I have come across boasts Jonathan Pryce and Stephen Rea in the cast.

The play captures the economic desperation of workers who wish to use stand-up comedy to escape the poverty trap. Only one of them cares about the social ability of satire to expose the ills of society, while for the rest it is mostly about making money and breaking into showbusiness. Their teacher (artfully played by Jimmy Jewel) tries to teach them the difference between *laughing at* people and *laughing with* people. During an open mic night the temptation to go for the easier option of laughing at minorities, women and gays, and to give the audience 'what they expect', proves too strong for most of them. Only the Jonathan Pryce character resists the urge and performs a powerful, difficult, avant-garde piece of subversive comedy. Despite being brilliant, he fails to make the grade in showbusiness.

My second lesson in humour came courtesy of the Italian anarchist playwright and actor, Dario Fo, who taught us that different kinds of comedy are associated with different classes. For instance, a *court jester* addresses only the ruling elite. Most court jesters tickle their masters' fancy using safe jokes but a brave minority use the opportunity to inform the absolutist monarch that all is not well in his kingdom. The taxes on peasants may be too high, the latest military recruitment drive might have come just before collecting the harvest, the king's sons have taken too many liberties with married women, etc. No one else may be able to broach these issues openly, not even the king's advisers, but the court jester's unique social status allows him room to manoeuvre (Fo 1991).

On the opposite pole to the court jester is the figure of the *people's clown* who performs for the 'lower' classes. Once again, the majority of these clowns take the easy option and confine themselves to entertaining the audience, but some risk it all by using humour as a cloak for social criticism. This is the most radical type of humour and tends to subvert style, form and content simultaneously. Sandwiched in the middle of the court jester and the people's clown is a third figure that represents a more genteel and refined critical sensibility. This figure, let's call it the *wandering Sufi*, uses subtle criticism not to bring down the system, but to reform and repair it.

These three forms of class-bound comedy have always been with us. The ancient Greeks might have used different terminology to describe them. The upper-class court jester engaged in 'magisterial' humour, the middle-class wandering Sufi specialised in 'Socratic' humour which often featured irony, and the working-class people's clown used 'Menippean' humour which aims for belly laughs. I am sure a few contemporary examples will help to cement this classification.

The examples of court jesters that come immediately to mind include Morecambe and Wise (especially their later work), Brain Manning (who was born working class but introjected the values of the ruling elite), Rolf Harris, Jim Davidson, David Chappell and Michael McIntyre. When Shakespeare and Monty Python were directly addressing the state and recommending various changes in order to modernise its institutions, they too can be included in this group.

Middle-class comedians prefer to stand above it all and poke fun at those above and below them in the social hierarchy. The likes of Woody Allen, Douglas Adams, Mark Twain, Sarah Silverman, Steve Martin, Bill Maher and (some) Stephen Fry represent different shades and styles of this particular group of performers. The Pythons should also be included in this group, as well as the wonderfully inventive *Black Adder* series, and the short-lived TV series *Brass Eye* (Chris Morris).

People's clowns are a more dangerous and critical set of performers/authors. The good ones take risks and push the boundaries of 'decency'. Their cruel jokes usually go to the root of problems that no one else dares to discuss. These are some well-known examples: Richard Prior, David Leary, Russell Brand,

John Belushi, (early) Roseanne Barr, Kathy Burke, (some) Lenny Henry, (some) Sacha Baron Cohen, Joe Brand, (early) Billy Connelly, Grock, Charlie Chaplin and Dario Fo. Some fresher, lesser known British comics might include Sophie Willan, Sian Davies, Adam Rowe and Darren Harriot. The underestimated sci-fi series *Red Dwarf* deserves an honourable mention in this category, as do the more deliciously 'vulgar' plays of Shakespeare.

The point is not to reach a consensus on all these exemplars of class-bound comedy, but to acknowledge that there exist different levels of subversive humour associated with different social classes. Furthermore, there is a rough and ready correlation between these three types of humour and the three classes of psychology mentioned above. Criss-crossing them can help us to think through many of the issues related to psychology and class.

If my first lesson in the importance of humour was Trevor Griffiths' *Comedians* and my second lesson the plays and performances of Dario Fo, then I think my third lesson was an academic study by Lesley Griffiths (2010). This is a fascinating investigation into humour as a form of resistance by workers in a community mental health team. 'Humour allows staff', writes Griffiths, 'to raise forbidden topics that would be difficult to discuss in 'serious' discourse' (ibid., p. 213). Specifically, in this ethnographic study, humour allowed the psychiatric nurse and social worker to 'gang up' on the more powerful psychiatrist in the team, and to undermine both his diagnosis and the bio-medical model he was employing. Humour can, therefore, become the subject of investigation as well as a critical literary device.

Inspired by this work I carried out a preliminary online survey of the use and misuse of humour during psychotherapy. The results were published as a draft paper in Fozooni (2017b). I found that no major theoretician of humour holds sway among therapists, although there was a slight preference for the works of Albert Ellis, Freud and Rogers. The most frequently utilised type of humour seems to consist of jokes and funny anecdotes, followed by the therapist's spontaneous response to a comment by the client. Therapists prefer 'to avoid humour with those they deem "easily offended" and also those with 'narcissistic personalities'. Humour is most often used in the middle and end phase of therapy, with early humour reserved mainly for "ice-breaking" exercises' (ibid., p. 213). Although most of the respondents are in favour of the judicious use of humour in therapy, some recalled at least one negative example of 'failed humour'. The main reasons for this are related to using the 'wrong type of humour' (for example, using irony instead of banter), or using humour during the wrong phase of therapy (for instance, using it before a 'therapeutic alliance' has been established).

Finally, I cannot end this section without mentioning two major thinkers. First, Bakhtin. No other writer has helped me to think through the potentials and pitfalls of humour as much as him. I find his rich terminology and nuanced elaborations relevant to a whole host of topics including therapy, psychology and social emancipation. I will pick up on his contribution throughout the book, but especially in Chapter 17. Michael Billig (2012) has also been useful, although I sometimes wish he could be more open about the relationship between class and humour.

Final remarks on 'doofusness'

After all that rambling, we return to Sheldon Cooper's original charge against psychology. Is psychology the doofus of the sciences? I would argue that if we utilise restrictive definitions of science and psychology, then it is difficult to defend psychology against the charge. If science is limited to natural science criteria of observable behaviour, simplistic cause-effect relationships and statistically verifiable hypotheses, and if psychology insists on replicating these assumptions, then I am afraid we have to concede the doofusness of psychology.

By contrast, if we use an expansive definition of science, as the accumulated knowledge and practice of billions of faceless and nameless people (Conner 2005), and synthesise the very best of mainstream and critical forms of psychology, and relate all that to the class conflict raging all around us, then psychology can shed its doofusness, and become worthy of attention and respect. In short, *psychology must become postpsychology*!

PART I

Mainstream psychology as upper-class prescriptions

All the psychologists discussed in Part I (Freud, Hirschfeld, Watson, Maslow and Rogers) would probably be classified as middle class by most people. Yet their ideas and research contributions were taken up by capitalism and used instrumentally to boost labour productivity, repair damaged labour power, and ensure command over the working class. In this sense, they embody upper-class prescriptions for the smooth running of the system.

In Part I, I try to convey why psychoanalysis has become a highly fetishised area of psychology with both supporters and detractors habitually over- and under-estimating its achievements. I situate the rise of behaviourism within two capitalist traditions, the USA and the USSR. I argue that the humanistic tradition might have represented a 'perspective-shift' from what went before, but not a wholesale 'paradigm-shift' (Kuhn 1970). Finally, I will show that despite recent refinements, most updated versions of these schools remain anchored in a fictive, decontextualised, bourgeois self.

1

FREUD AND SOCIAL CLASS

> I count religion but a childish toy, and hold there is no sin but ignorance.
>
> *Christopher Marlowe,* The Jew of Malta, *Prologue (c. 1589)*

There is nothing more humdrum than yet another critical account of Freud. As is the case with all celebrity intellectuals, Freud has had the dubious honour of being inspected, measured, weighed, pulled, pushed, debated and painfully probed. I have no intention of sanctifying yet more scholarly necrophilia. And while I have availed myself throughout this book of numerous opportunities to laugh at other psychologists, I have steadfastly refused myself this wonderfully sadistic pleasure in the case of Freud. You see, dear reader, he is simply too easy a target. Freud's follies take all the fun out of *Schadenfreude*!

Here is the man at his loopiest:

> It seems that women have made few contributions to the discoveries and inventions in the history of civilization; there is, however, one technique which they may have invented – that of plaiting and weaving. If that is so, we should be tempted to guess the unconscious motive for the achievement. Nature herself would seem to have given the model which this achievement imitates by causing the growth at maturity of the pubic hair that conceals the genitals. The step that remained to be taken lay in making the threads adhere to one another,

> while on the body they stick into the skin and are only matted together. If you reject this idea as fantastic and regard my belief in the influence of the lack of a penis on the configuration of femininity as an *idée fixe*, I am of course defenceless.
>
> *(Freud [1933] 1953, p. 132)*

So, women invented weaving to replicate their pubic hair and to hide their 'inferior' genitalia! And as if this analogy was not asinine enough, Freud also demonstrated his inadequacy as a sex educator when he declared the clitoris unsuitable for sexual pleasure, being no more than a 'stunted penis' (Freud, quoted in Millet 2000, p. 199). There is sufficient sexual naivety in this one paragraph alone to make one weep for poor Mrs Freud.

Instead of poking fun at his absurdities, or proposing yet another unsustainable Freudo-Marxist contraption, or worst still, offering a tedious re-reading of Freud through his many disciples, what I propose to do in this chapter is something very specific to the needs of 'postpsychology'. I aim to pool together class issues related to Freud (and occasionally, Freudianism). The value of this exercise will become clear later on. No doubt my list of topics is far from complete, and I have omitted many seminal works and some of your favourite 'stories'. I beg your forgiveness and your indulgence at the outset, and once again remind you of the deliberately narrow focus of my investigation.

Historical background

By the time Sigismund Freud (1856–1939) was born in Freiberg, Moravia (now part of the Czech Republic), the achievements of the Hussites, Taborites and Adamites were a distant memory. John Huss (*c.* 1369–1415) and his wandering preachers had called for complete liberation from the petty guardianship of the church. But he was arrested by King Sigismund and executed in Constance in 1415. The Taborites (who represented a more radical faction within the Hussite movement) believed in the abolition of taxes, dues, rents and all other forms of private property. Kenneth Rexroth (1974) describes them as 'extreme millenarians, the most militant so far in the history of dissent', while Murray Bookchin (1982) classifies them as an early example of anarcho-communism, and Raoul Vaneigem (1994) sees them as part of the heretical and millenarian movements that challenged both the church and the state. The Adamites (who constituted a more hedonistic version of the Taborites) experimented with new forms of love and sexuality (ibid., pp. 192–193).

By the time the bourgeois revolutions of 1848 broke out, the lofty dreams of these egalitarian currents had transmuted into an assertive nationalism. According to A. J. P. Taylor,

> in great areas of Eastern Europe, the educated classes, the business classes and sometimes the landed classes spoke German, whereas the majority of the inhabitants, even in the towns and still more the peasants, spoke some other language - Czech, Polish or Croat.
>
> *(1980, p. 102)*

Around the time of Freud's birth, the Czech language and culture were gaining momentum. Musicians such as Antonin Dvorak (1841–1904) further contributed to this revival through their operas, concertos and symphonies. But Freud never became part of this Czech renaissance. The eight languages in which Freud eventually became proficient did *not* include Czech. As a migrant Czech he showed little interest in Czech nationalism, nor did he identify with the radical currents from below that had shaped the ideological contours of his homeland.

By the time Freud and his family moved to Vienna in 1860, 'the Austrian secret police was commonly regarded as the most effective in Europe' (Bukey 2000, p. x). They needed to be since the Austrian proletariat was one of the most restless at that time. No sooner had Freud internalised the national identity of his new surroundings than the Austro-Prussian War of 1866 occurred. Otto van Bismarck expelled Austria from German affairs, resulting in an identity crisis for Austro-Germans who now included Freud (ibid., p. 6).

The turbulence of these formative years left Freud with a healthy contempt for the machinations of the ruling elite but also with a fear of proletarian crowds. This explains the ideological overlap between Freud's theory of the crowd and that of Gustave Le Bon. It is also key to understanding him as the archetypal, sceptic, liberal cosmopolitan.

Ensconced within a petty bourgeois bubble

Freud, I would argue, was *excruciatingly* middle class. By this I mean that some people are born into the middle class, some 'raise' themselves up to it, and yet others 'fall' into the middle class. But Freud, it seems to me, arranged every aspect of his life methodically, in order to become both objectively and subjectively entrenched within the middle class. Once safely ensconced in it, he artificially separated his politics from his psychoanalytic doctrine in an effort to bolster psychoanalysis's scientific respectability and to shield himself from potential political fallout. This manoeuvre was part of a knowing stratagem to sell his middle-class doctrine to the ruling class. But for Freud this campaign was not merely about short-term profit – he was building an empire to conquer our minds.

From time to time Freud would come out of his invisible political shell and make a pronouncement as reactionary as it was ill-informed:

> [T]he psychological premises on which the system [socialism or communism] is based are an untenable illusion. In abolishing private property, we deprive the human love of aggression of one of its instruments, certainly a strong one, though certainly not the strongest.
>
> *(Freud [1930] 2015, p. 87)*

In unguarded moments he displayed open contempt for the working class. Ehrenreich writes,

> In a letter to his fiancée, Martha Bernays, [Freud] agreed with her that the behaviour of the lower-class revellers at the town fair in Wandsbeck was 'neither pleasant nor edifying', especially when compared to the more acceptable and bourgeois pleasures of 'an hour's chat nestling close to one's love' or 'the reading of a book'.
>
> *(2008, p. 14)*

He famously referred to psychoanalysts as a 'handful of people' whose work is restricted to the 'well-to-do classes' (Freud, quoted in Jacoby 1997, p. 126). In a sense this sales pitch has been an integral part of the success story of many pioneering psychologists: Jung sold his soul to the fascist faction of the German ruling class; Watson hustled for liberal US capitalism; Pavlov salivated for Bolsheviki capitalism; Sir Cyril Burt went beyond the call of duty to conjure up 'data' for the British ruling class's (unwarranted) sense of superiority; Hans J. Eysenck lit up a ciggie after delightful coitus with the tobacco industry; and Martin Seligman kneeled in front of neo-liberal capitalism to make it 'happy'!

Freud augmented his middle-class values with a penchant for cosmopolitanism. This cosmopolitanism can be seen in both the range of his places of domicile as well as the variety of scientific and literary sources he drew upon in bringing psychoanalysis to the attention of the world. Social class,

FIGURE 1.1 Freud in *Wikipedia*

which shaped everything Freud ever said or did, had to be concealed under a Harry Potter-like 'invisibility cloak' lest it was noticed by the passing 'Snatchers' and 'Death Eaters'.

In one of the very few texts that directly deals with issues of class and psychoanalysis, Joanna Ryan reminds us that although the class status of patients is sometimes obliquely referred to in clinical descriptions, it is filtered out of theory and clinical interpretation (2017, p. 10). As Benjamin Brody concluded in an earlier study, 'there is no indication in the psychoanalytic writings that Freud ever worked psychoanalytically with a lower-class patient' (1976, p. 197). Eissler referred to one of Freud's patients, Katherina, as 'unquestionably [belonging] to the lower class' (cited in Brody 1976, p. 196). However, closer examination reveals her to be the daughter of an innkeeper and probably a petty bourgeois.[1]

Part of living in a safe and shielded middle-class bubble is about attaining equilibrium,[2] and part of it reflects a need to avoid reality. I find the manner in which Freud suppressed certain uncomfortable truths while ensconced in his bubble quite revealing. Parker informs us how 'Freud deliberately avoided Nietzsche's work, partly because of the very similarity of concepts between the two writers, and [partly because] he found the existence of competing views of the unconscious and the "It" … most discomforting' (1997, p. 19).

Despite the protection of the bubble, Freud lived in turbulent times. It was not always possible to protect himself and his family from the brutal realities surrounding them. After all, he lived during the ascendant phase of capitalism when the growth of privately owned property was shattering the old traditions and long-established taboos. The preponderance of 'hysterics' in this era was, for instance, 'the symptomatic fall-out from flourishing capitalism' (Parker 1997, p. 23) in the same way that the contemporary mental health landscape is characterised by narcissism, eating and 'borderline personality disorders'.

One of Freud's most controversial works, *Beyond the Pleasure Principle* ([1920] 2010), postulated the death instinct within all of us (usually referred to as Thanatos). Death is a constant companion. As Richard Stevens explains:

> [During the war] his own sons were called up and one had gone missing for several weeks. As a therapist, Freud had encountered the problem of soldiers suffering from shell shock and 'war neurosis'. And, in January of the year in which the monograph was published, his daughter Sophie died of influenza.
>
> *(2008, p. 21)*

His own heart complaint and obsession with death further convinced him of the actual existence of Thanatos. His friend and biographer Ernest Jones reports how Freud sometimes followed his goodbye by saying, 'You might never see me again' (1957, p. 301).

The suppression of class

Classical psychoanalysis played a significant role in suppressing class issues and turning working-class identity into a taboo subject, so much so that even today many people are reluctant to discuss class 'personally and interpersonally' (Ryan 2017, p. 12). The upper class find grandstanding about their 'superiority' counter-productive, the sandwiched class hope that by ignoring the issue it will somehow go away, and the working class (who constitute the bulk of the population) are socialised from an early age into viewing their 'lower' class position as a permanent sign of inferiority and shame.

One well-known example of denying class is the classic case of Wolf Man. He was, you probably will not need reminding, an aristocratic Russian with a 'compulsive attraction to working class women' (Ryan 2017, p. 43). Part of this attraction might have been personal and part of it cultural, since in Russia as in the rest of Europe the myth (or some say reality) of the concept of the *droit du seigneur* (aka 'lord's right') lingered on. Aristocratic men felt entitled to possess and have sex with underlings. Yet here is Freud downplaying any significance of power disparity: 'all the girls with whom he subsequently fell in love … were also servants, whose education and intelligence were necessarily inferior to his own' (Freud, quoted in Ryan 2017, p. 43).

Freud rather naively dismisses the importance of class differences during childhood: 'A child pays no regard to social distinctions, which have little meaning for him yet' (Freud, quoted in Ryan 2017, p. 45). On the contrary, we know how astute children are in picking up on the minutest of power imbalances in their surroundings (ibid., p. 105). When he does acknowledge class, the focus is usually on the exaggerated notion of 'class envy'. In 'Family Romances' he describes situations when the working-class child becomes envious of bourgeois privileges to such an extent that s/he daydreams about having parents of higher social standing (Freud, see Ryan 2017, p. 157).

A more mundane method of suppressing class is to make sure that psychology ignores extra-psychological factors of development. Freud's analysis usually oscillated between two levels: the intra-psychology of the individual and the inter-psychology of small groups such as the family. In other words, Freud did dissolve some of the barriers between the private and the public, the individual and social, but only to some extent. Class and society were only referred to tangentially, if at all. A similar point is made by Fromm who argues that this is the reason why Freud never developed a fully fledged social psychology (1982, p. 60).

His oft-maligned concept of the Oedipus complex is also intertwined with class issues. Vološinov claims that by sexualising the family, Freud was making it harder for people to understand its true purpose:

> The Oedipus complex is indeed a magnificent way of making the family unit 'strange'. The father is not the entrepreneur, and the son is not his heir – the father is only the mother's lover, and his son is his rival!
>
> *(1987, p. 91)*

At a more interpersonal level, Freud's memories, sexual fantasies and dreams about his working-class nurse (later identified as Monica Zajic) were instrumental in linking arousal and shame to the Oedipus complex. The fact that Zajic was written out of the account, not even identified by name, is for Ryan a clear example of 'disavowal', a defence mechanism usually defined as 'rejecting the reality of a perception on account of its potentially traumatic associations' (Penot 2005). Our rulers know that they preside over a reality without being its creators and they also are cognisant that it is the proletariat that generates all social wealth. The knowledge is pushed aside or ignored, since its implications are too severe to contemplate. This disavowal may also be related to Freud's tendency to dismiss the huge contribution made through the expenditure of 'emotional labour' by wet nurses and carers in raising bourgeois children (Suchet 2007).

Disavowal is rapidly becoming the chief defence mechanism of our times. The dominance of disavowal is probably the chief reason why irony and the exposure of hypocrisy have lost their subversive edge. Sennet and Cobb ([1972] 1993) in their seminal work on social phenomenology show how disavowal operates within the working class by creating a split between the knowing self who understands the injustice being done to it by capitalism, and the sense of guilt, shame and self-blame that becomes introjected. This disavowal eats away at one's ability to resist and fight back, and makes the working class vulnerable to the bourgeois gaze.

The bourgeois family is mostly treated by Freud as universal and permanent, and yet as Raymond Williams (1973) might have argued, Freud's notion of a bourgeois family also contains 'residual cultural artifacts' from feudalism. The father, for instance, is at times portrayed as a lord protector and a knight all rolled into one. Given Freud's adulation of all things modern, it is possible that he was also disavowing all the residual cultural artifacts in his own upbringing. Whether this supposition is true or not does not alter the real tension between feudal and capitalist components in his work. Perry Meisel puts it thus: 'Feudalism and the unconscious are the scaffolding upon which capitalism and consciousness are respectively propped (2017, p. 21).

By disregarding both the cross-cultural traditional families abroad, as well as the proletarian families living all around him, fundamental errors crept into Freud's thinking. One example is the importance that Freud attached to the 'primal scene' in which the child witnesses, and is supposedly traumatised by, the sexual intercourse of the parents. As Fromm correctly observes:

> It is obvious that the significance of this experience is inflated by the fact that in the bourgeois family children and parents live in different rooms. Had Freud thought of the family life among the poorer classes of his time, where children lived in the same room with their parents and were witnesses to their intercourse routinely, this early experience would not have seemed so important to Freud.
>
> *(1982, p. 61)*

Ah, yes, the good old days when we did not need to be educated by internet pornography because entertainment came in the shape of mummy and daddy's nocturnal shenanigans!

Is psychoanalysis even worthy of the working class?

It is important not to exaggerate Freud's distaste for working-class culture. After all, he was no hateful bigot. In the early years of psychoanalysis, free clinics were established with Freud's blessing in Berlin (1920) and Vienna (1922). These catered mainly to a working-class clientele. His empire might have had its headquarters in the middle class, but it planned to annex territory from the upper and working classes when opportunity presented itself. However, after World War II, the 'notion that working-class people were not "analysable" gained widespread acceptance, confining them to physical and pharmacological treatments' (Ryan 2017, p. 58). Hollingshead and Redlich found that

> those in lower class positions were over-represented in treatment, and were more likely to enter treatment via referral by official agencies such as courts as opposed to choosing to enter treatment themselves. They were also more likely to have physical treatments such as shock therapy rather than organic treatments such as psychotherapy.
>
> *(Quoted in Holman 2017, p. 113)*

While some may see this exclusion from the 'pure gold of analysis' (Freud [1919] 1955) as unjust, others no doubt will hail it as dodging a bullet. Leaving the question of efficacy aside for the moment, it is perfectly fair to ask if psychoanalysis is even capable of dealing with the complexities and harshness of working-class lives. To be working class is to exist in a space pre-structured for exploitation and oppression – a space where different forms of consciousness and unconsciousness engage each other in a dialectical vortex. The psychological plane of this space is constituted by both 'neurotic' and 'psychotic' tendencies (old terms that have fallen out of fashion). However, as Kovel reminds us:

> [Despite] a major effort to widen the scope of psychoanalysis … by and large the treatment remains most clearly suited for neurotic problems, in contrast to psychoses or other kinds of severe impairments, such as alcoholism, where the person's life is, practically speaking, out of control.
>
> *(1987, p. 118)*

The problem is, for much of the time most working-class lives are precisely that: 'out of control'! The everyday cycle of desperate trips to the post office to pay utility bills on time while avoiding the repo man, followed by dashes to pick up the children from school, and then to work to please the boss, leave us with little time for therapeutic reflection.

Most forms of psychotherapy espouse values such as individualism and self-sufficiency, whereas working-class survivability has traditionally depended on solidarity and group decision-making. This and the emphasis on bourgeois linguistic repertoires were the reasons for which Freud (1919) argued that the proletariat was not well suited to psychotherapy. When he did give his support for working-class psychoanalysis, it was a 'watered-down version of psychoanalysis for the poor; a large-scale, state sponsored treatment involving direct suggestion and hypnosis' (Holman 2017, p. 114). One can argue that these prejudices remain with us today. The recent UK-organised Improving Access to Psychological Therapies focuses on large-scale, short-term courses of cognitive behavioural therapy for the working class.

Capitalism's ups and downs

It is reasonable to speculate that if Freud's most productive intellectual years coincided with an era of capitalist assertiveness, his later work captured the decay and disillusionment of bourgeois culture. One world war and an impending second had shaken bourgeois faith in its own permanence, and Freud's early optimism was giving way to something darker and less sanguine. The imperative to whinge and whine in psychoanalysis became so stark that one of his most persistent critics, Sebastiano Timpanaro, has argued that

> with the exception of some inspired but fairly restricted conquests, psychoanalysis is neither a natural nor a human science, but a self-confession by the bourgeoisie of its own misery and perfidy, which blends the bitter insight and ideological blindness of a class in decline.
>
> *(1976, p. 224)*

As Stephen Frosh has correctly argued, 'this is not wrong but it is also not the whole story ... psychoanalysis can be more than a portrayal of "a class in decline"' (1987, p. 11).

Vološinov, an even more astute critic of psychoanalysis, goes further and suggests that psychoanalysis is motivated by an old motif: 'A fear of history, a shift in orientation toward the values of the personal, private life, the primacy of the biological and the sexual in man' (1987, p. 11). He traces psychoanalysis's motif of 'supreme power and wisdom of Nature' to such phenomena as 'epicureanism, stoicism, the literature of the Roman decadence ... the skeptical ratiocination of the French aristocrats in the seventeenth and early eighteenth centuries' (ibid.).

Timpanaro and Vološinov offer harsh judgements that even an ardent anti-Freudian such as myself would have difficulty accepting. Instead I would suggest that, despite its bourgeois heritage, many contributions of Freud and neo-Freudians remain tools waiting to be turned against the ruling class. To deny ourselves this rich treasure trove of ideas, concepts and imaginative speculations would be counterproductive.

Postpsychology's attitude towards Freudianism is not a blanket rejection but an engagement that treats Freudianism as primarily a project in dire need of 'translation'. This act of translation entails, on the one hand, the setting aside of those arcane concepts that are reactionary and time-conditioned (such as Freud's ideas about character structure; his forays into biological determinism; his dream interpretations; and his patriarchal views of the family), and, on the other hand, the re-accentuation of lasting ideas that illuminate workers' misery under capitalism (for instance, the concept of the unconscious; transference; narcissism, especially for our times group narcissism; and defence mechanisms). Fortunately, some of this translation work has already been carried out by various Marxist and anarchist neo-Freudians from within the Freudian empire.

Herbert Marcuse (1898–1979) provides us with a useful re-accentuation of Freud's 'reality principle'. Marcuse shows how the present-day reality principle has become a form of 'performance principle'. This manoeuvre brings it closer to Marx's notion of alienation:

> The performance principle, which is that of an acquisitive and antagonistic society in the process of constant expansion, presupposes a long development during which domination has been increasingly rationalized: control over social labor now reproduces society on a large scale and under improving conditions.
>
> *(Marcuse 1955, p. 45)*

This performance may be imposed by the apparatus of domination, but it also requires voluntary acquiescence with the apparatus.

Having offered this useful translation work, Marcuse then overplays his hand by asserting that the performance reality (the maximisation of competition and production) has created the preconditions of a non-repressive form of life: 'The very progress of civilization under the performance principle has attained a level of productivity at which the social demands upon instinctual energy to be spent in alienated labor could be considerably reduced' (Marcuse 1955, p. 129). He is implying here that the 'affluent society' has co-opted the proletariat and that the class struggle is passé. A convincing counter-argument to Marcuse's exaggerated claims for capitalism can be found in Paul Mattick (1972). Mattick shows convincingly that the capitalist crisis is ongoing and that the need for revolution is as real as ever.

Wet-panning Freud

Sometimes we need to go further than mere translation and indulge in what gold prospectors refer to as 'wet panning'. Erich Fromm (1900–1980) has provided us with an excellent account of how we can scoop into a pan some alluvial Freudian deposits, gently agitate them in (Marxist) water to make the gold nuggets sink to the bottom, and throw away the black sand. One example of this black sand that needs to be decanted is Freud's bourgeois materialism. Under the influence of Germans such as Karl Christoph Vogt (1817–1895), Jacob Moleschott (1822–1893) and Ernst Wilhelm Ritter von Brücke (1819–1892), he refused to 'conceive that there could be strong psychical powers whose specific physiological roots could not be demonstrated' (Fromm 1982, p. 5). Their epistemological influence on Freud notwithstanding these half-forgotten bourgeois materialists are interesting due to Marx's criticisms of them. Marx took Vogt to task in *Herr Vogt* (1860) for both his politics (a bourgeois democrat who gravitated towards 'Napoleon the Little') and his brand of materialism. All three were criticised by Engels for flip-flopping between a pre-Darwinian over-emphasis on natural co-operation to a post-Darwinian belief in struggle for existence everywhere (Engels 1875). Bourgeois materialism is the black sand that needs to be separated from whatever gold is left in the pan.

Another Freudian concept in dire need of 'wet panning' is the unconscious. Vološinov has offered us a neat method of rescuing something worthwhile while discarding the black sand. According to Vološinov (1987, pp. 30–31), there are three periods in the history of its development:

1. The 'Freud-Breuer period', approximately the years 1890–1897, and exemplified by *Studies in Hysteria* (Freud and Breuer [1885] 2004). The women studied in this book are victims of sexually repressed family situations. But instead of holding these patriarchal institutions to account, Freud blames the women themselves (Brown 1974, p. 60). During this period Freud's concept of the unconscious was closely influenced by French psychiatrists and psychologists Charcot, Liébault, Bernheim and Janet. A demonstration of hypnosis by Bernheim in particular seems to have made an impression (ibid., p. 32). On the basis of hypnosis and clinical studies, Freud and Breuer worked out what was called the 'cathartic method of treating hysteria'. Freud still treated the unconscious as an 'incidental phenomenon in the human psyche' at this stage.

2. The positivist period, approximately the years 1897–1914. Vološinov writes, 'Now, in the second period, the unconscious becomes an essential and extremely vital component of the psychical apparatus of every single human being' (1987, p. 35). Moreover, it becomes 'a productive source of psychical forces and energies for all domains of cultural creativity, especially for art' (ibid.).
3. The metaphysical period, 1914–1939. During this period the concept of the unconscious 'has begun to approach the metaphysical doctrines of Schopenhauer and Hartmann. *General issues of Weltanschauung now begin to take precedence over particular, specialized problems*' (Vološinov 1987, p. 31, emphasis in the original).

The point, of course, is not to agree with the exact classification offered by Vološinov but to see that every seminal concept in Freudianism is *dynamic* in terms of the individual human psyche, and also in terms of the concept's historical development. What Freud meant by the 'unconscious' in 1885 is not the same as his use of the term in 1939. Second, and just as importantly, I suggest that perhaps we need to restrict the unconscious as a concept to the first and, at most, the second period cited above. Most unwarranted flights of fantasy seem to emerge when the unconscious crosses the threshold of the metaphysical period, and becomes an all-embracing 'revelation'. Wet panning is a useful technique for saving the nuggets of wisdom Freud has to offer.

Sex ed: Freud or Stormy Daniels?

One of Freud's chief personal contradictions is also a very vivid reflection of unresolved contradictions within capitalism: his attitude towards sex. On the one hand, he sometimes referred quite disparagingly to sexuality as 'the common animal need of mankind' (Freud [1910] 1957, p. 101); on the other hand, he seemed to both his contemporaries and to his followers today to be obsessed with all matters sexual.

Freud's grounding in physiology provides us with a clue to solving the riddle. As Fromm reminds us sexuality was one of just a few fields where the connection between the physiological and psychical was understood by the science of his era. Whenever Freud felt intellectually insecure or confused, he would make a fast getaway towards the terrain of sexual biology. It was his 'get out of jail card'.

Here an important point about Freud needs to be underlined. His physiological psychology is reductionist in the sense that he yielded unwarranted powers of interpretation to the physiology of the individual. This reductionism was aimed at controlling sexuality. For Freud, this was key. Control and rationally utilise sexual urges, and capitalism will prosper. Lose control, and libidinal chaos will engulf us all. The parallels with another controlling doctrine, Weber's 'Protestant work ethic', are self-evident. At the heart of both doctrines we find the concepts of self-control and accumulation. It took future generations of psychoanalysts to realise that out-of-control sexual urges can also be harnessed for capitalist profitability. It took Stormy Daniels to complete Freud!

In addition to his mistaken views on sex, it is also valid to point out that by promoting a form of structuralism, he was producing a disempowered subject, one that was being watched over, 'like a garrison in a conquered city' (Freud [1930] 2015, p. 71). However, and this is what raises Freud above the usual advocates of psycho-biological structuralism, his model was over-saturated with complexity. Fromm goes so far as to claim that

> Freud never simplified, he complicated and overcomplicated to the point that, once in the middle of his interpretations, one almost feels in a labyrinth. Freud's method of thinking led one to discover that a phenomenon means what it seems to mean, but that it also may express its negation. He discovered that every emphasis on love could hide suppressed hate, that insecurity could be covered up by arrogance, fear by aggressiveness, etcetera.
>
> *(1982, pp. 19–20)*

This may well be the secret to the longevity of psychoanalysis: Freud succeeded in building an over-saturated structuralist model with enough variety and nuance to also appeal to post-structuralists, thus extending the sell-by date of his doctrine.

Freud and neuropsychology

Psychoanalysis is able to expose the rosy picture painted by rationalists and pragmatics as a forgery. This explains why Freud remains pivotal in psychological debates, not just among neo-Freudians (who acknowledge him openly) or humanists and behaviourists (who acknowledge while marginalising him), but also in recent neuropsychological research.

Neuropsychology inherently gravitates towards the eighteenth-century bourgeois materialism that privileges 'matter' (usually reduced to brain activity) over 'mind'. However, the best neuropsychologists instinctively recognise this as an ontological error. In *The Man Who Mistook His Wife for a Hat* (1985), Oliver Sacks augments his fascinating neurological case studies with either phenomenology, discursive psychology or psychoanalysis, thus turning case studies into narratives. He points out that we have two 'universes of discourse'; the physical and quantitative on the one hand, and the phenomenal or qualitative on the other (Sacks 1985, p. 135). Neglect of either of these discourses leads to reductionism. The recommendation which follows is simple: 'we must deepen a case history to a narrative or tale: only then do we have a "why" as well as a "what", a real person, a patient, in relation to disease – in relation to the physical' (ibid., p. x).

In this instance Sacks was influenced by Luria's notion of a 'romantic science', an approach that brings together the scientific and the romantic; at the intersection of fact and fable (1985, p. xi). But Sacks is very clear that before Luria, Leontiev and Anokhin attempted to bridge this gap, it was Freud who advocated 'the science of brain/mind' (ibid., p. 4). This synthesis is essential if neuropsychology is to overcome its abstract and mechanical presumptions as seen in the classical neurology of figures such as John Hughlings Jackson (1835–1911), who interpreted the brain as merely a machine and not a component of personal judgement at the same time (ibid., p. 21).

Certain Freudian concepts are utilised throughout *The Man Who Mistook His Wife for a Hat* to turn Sacks' case studies into genuine narratives. One illustration should suffice. In Chapter 15, Sacks presents the tale of Mrs O'C who, following temporal lobe seizures, was experiencing musical 'reminiscences' in the form of Irish songs from her youth. Sacks' narrative fuses the physical Jacksonian side of her reminiscence with the personal Freudian anamnesis:

> Mrs O'C found [her seizures] refreshment to the spirit. They gave her a sense of psychological grounding and reality, the elemental sense which she had lost, in her long decades of cut-offness and 'exile', that she *had* had a real childhood and home, that she *had* been mothered and loved and cared-for.
>
> *(1985, p. 152, emphasis in the original)*

Sacks concludes from this case study that the most trivial and random Freudian free association 'may turn out to have an unexpected depth and resonance', but only if a case study can be turned into a narrative (ibid., p. 148).

The great challenge, of course, will be to fuse neuropsychology and critical psychology in such a way that the resultant perspective becomes capable of adding to our understanding of not only 'organic' problems (such as Huntington's disease, Korsakoff's syndrome, senile dementia, syphilis, etc.), but also 'functional disorders' (such as schizophrenia, depression, personality disorders, eating disorders, etc.). To reiterate, I am not suggesting that 'functional disorders' have biological *causations*, but I am pleading for a more serious consideration of biology when critical psychologists provide an account of human behaviour. I will elaborate on this theme in Chapter 18 when discussing Luria.

Going beyond Freud

One way of overcoming Freud's limitations is to take his ideas out of the office and into the real world of socio-economics. Winslow has demonstrated the close resemblance between Freud's ideas about money and John Maynard Keynes' account of capitalist motivation. Keynes had studied Freud thoroughly and regarded him as 'one of the great disturbing, innovating geniuses of our age' (Keynes, quoted in Winslow 1986, p. 550). As Keynes abandoned his belief in the 'rational economic man', he drew even closer to psychoanalytic thinking, in order to come to grips with the 'insane and irrational springs of wickedness in most men' (ibid., p. 576). Keynes's account of the 'animal spirits' of capitalism is indebted to a Freudian explanation of the love of money and the pursuit of power. When Keynes wrote about the 'cruelty' of capitalists he was inspired by Freud's analysis of the 'anal-sadistic character'.

No one has written about this psycho-economic nexus more persuasively than Joel Kovel. His seminal *The Age of Desire* (1981) is a masterpiece of synthesis, combining the insights of Freud with the rigour of Marx. Frankly, it is as good as Freudo-Marxism can get without distorting the kernel of both Freud and Marx. In line with most of the thinkers I have relied on thus far, Kovel is also an admirer of history: 'The effort to locate the object of psychology within a person's so-called mind must be seen as a particularly strategic attempt to obscure participation in history' (1981, p.33).

One of the semi-fictive case studies described by Kovel has parallels with Winslow's attempt to fuse Freud and Keynes. In Chapter 4 of *The Age of*

Desire, Kovel describes Curtis, a successful executive who 'considers his work a kind of disease or intoxication' (1981, p. 37). He is a very well-paid workaholic, with a yearning for his deceased father that is rooted in unresolved infantile conflicts. Although Curtis cannot enjoy commodities, 'he was fiendishly interested in money for its own sake' (ibid., p. 43). But Kovel gradually comes to the conclusion that Curtis's relationship with his father is not the root of his alienation. It is capitalist society that is the main culprit. At this point, Marx becomes indispensable for Kovel's analysis.

Postpsychology would have little or no qualms with Kovel's views on psychotherapy. He argues, quite correctly, that more and more health workers (including lower- and middle-rank psychiatrists) are becoming proletarianised 'and [capitalism's crisis] forces them into alliances, however uneasy, with those for whom they are supposed to care' (1981, p. 252). It is also useful to emphasise that

> there is no essential contradiction between being with a patient on an individual level, and organizing with fellow workers and clients against the oppressive features of the state. Indeed, the two praxes can enrich each other, for they are both movements towards universality, albeit by different routes.
>
> *(Ibid.)*

If psychotherapy is not to succumb to the capitalist imperatives of profit and command then it must allow itself to be fertilised by the desire lurking behind 'madness' (ibid., p. 253). Desire is a key concept for Kovel. It 'exists within and is transformed by every historical situation' (ibid., p. 69). For Kovel, psychoanalysis is the *discourse of desire*. Capitalism 'has alienated desire itself, has twisted it about, and made it spectral and monstrous. And when desire became enough of a historical problem, psychoanalysis was created to deal with it' (ibid., p. 72). Desire is not just intra-psychological but is also intersubjective, capable of being experienced collectively – in the process of a class emancipating itself from bondage, say.

'Psychotherapy', in Kovel's view, 'must be measured not simply by the care it offers but by its attitude toward desire. The patient brings an alienated desire to the therapist, who is given the privilege of deciding what to do with it' (1981, p. 253). Kovel's language is a little dated but the aim is as laudable now as it was then.

Another way of going beyond Freud is to unearth all those analysts who were deliberately excluded from the official history of psychoanalysis. One such figure is Otto Gross (1877–1920), who is caricatured in David Cronenberg's 2011 movie, *A Dangerous Method*, but ably brought to life in Heuer's 2017 biography of him. Gross was an anarchist and the first psychoanalyst to interpret Freudianism radically. As I wrote in a review of the book,

> At a time when most psychoanalysts restricted investigation to the intra-psychological plane of existence, Gross deliberately expanded the purview to include the inter- and extra-psychological dimensions as well. Like Reich and Fromm after him, Gross was determined to narrate a multi-faceted story. In theoretical terms, Gross strove to overcome the 'will to power' with the 'will to relating'. In practice this meant a more egalitarian therapeutic alliance and experiments with group therapy years before Bion formulated his ideas.
>
> *(Fozooni 2017c)*

Gross found inspiration not in Marx but in Kropotkin. He began 'his short career partially influenced by a "biomedical" paradigm. During this phase he was keen to achieve a linkage between Freud's psychoanalytic theory and Kraepelin's psychiatric concepts' (Heuer 2017, p. 47). Gradually he garnered more social and psychological ideas until the biomedical paradigm transformed into a 'biopsychosocial' one. Later still, he broke with the positivist and mechanical presuppositions of the biopsychosocial approach and embraced 'an artistic and increasingly radically psycho-political orientation' (Fozooni 2017c).

In his biography of Gross,

> Heuer claims a number of firsts on behalf of Gross: it was Gross who first suggested that the 'personal is political' (Heuer 2017, p. 104); he is credited with formulating the notion of a 'super-ego' fourteen years before Freud (ibid., p. 71); and he pioneered the notion of an 'authoritarian personality' before Reich and Adorno (ibid., p. 72); his ideas on 'psychological types' influenced Jung (ibid., p. 96); and, perhaps most importantly, Gross advocated the notion of 'inter-subjectivity', which years later became a bedrock of so many strands of post-Freudianism.
>
> *(Fozooni 2017c)*

Establishing chronological priority is important but less vital than demonstrating whether Gross's ideas are an improvement on Freud and post-Freudians. I tried to 'apply' Grossian therapy to a fictional client in a recent article (Fozooni 2014). I will allow the reader to judge for themselves whether I have been successful in showing the continued relevance of Gross and his anarchist and feminist version of psychoanalysis.

Concluding remarks: Freud and postpsychology

In summing up Freud, Michael Billig writes:

> I now tell my students that when they read Freud, they should not expect well-founded theories, which are carefully laid out and cautiously elaborated. Instead, there is a mixture of wisdom and folly with just enough of the former to excuse the latter.
>
> *(2006, p. 451)*

Well said, sir!

Freud's originality does not lie in his 'discoveries' or his over-elaborated speculations, rather it is to be found in the way he integrated intra- and inter-psychological levels of experience. Stevens (2008) reminds us that most of the central assumptions of psychoanalysis did not originate with Freud. The modern notion of the 'unconscious' had already been philosophically discussed by Schopenhauer and Nietzsche and demonstrated clinically by Charcot, Bernheim and Breuer; the concept of the 'id' was probably invented by Nietzsche; 'instinct' was a continuation of Darwin's evolutionary ideas (unkind commentators might even claim that Freud's theory of instinct was a continuation of the religious notion of instinctual human fallibility); Maudsley and Krafft-Ebing had already suggested that 'sexuality' was the root of social feeling; and, Shakespeare had already provided detailed accounts of the Oedipal myth (ibid., p. 99).

Contemporary followers have observed that 'with the emergence of neuroscience … the subtlety of [Freud's] reflections about the workings of the mind are finding exciting new echoes' (Rock and Fonagy 2006, p. 535). For example,

> the work of Le Doux … indicates two different pathways from stimulus to emotional response, one trough cognition, and the other direct … Such research could be consistent with the notion of the parallel processing of conscious and unconscious thought.
>
> *(Stevens 2008, p. 159)*

Fonagy has also cited suggestive evidence in support of psychoanalysis as a form of therapy, especially long-term intensive analysis (Fonagy 2000). Further investigations are doubtless necessary to concretise these points.

In terms of political philosophy, Freud was at heart a liberal of the nineteenth-century variety. In his own words: 'I remain a liberal of the old school' (Freud, quoted in Jacoby 1997, p. 83). But this was a flexible liberalism which would veer towards radicalism here, reaction there. He also displayed paternalistic tendencies not only in his theorising of the 'female psyche' but in his overprotective control of psychoanalysis. The former is unforgivable but the latter is, to some extent, understandable. After all, he had expended an enormous amount of time, energy and prestige in patenting a 'brand' and now every disciple seemed to want a piece of it. His paternalism also acted as a shield against the professionalisation and domestication of psychoanalysis. Jacoby writes, 'He wanted to preserve psychoanalysis as a theory, not exclusively as a trade' (ibid., p. 123). As we have observed, however, Freud was more driven than that. His was an empire-building enterprise, and as with all empires, its twin aims were profit and command. A paternalistic liberal, then, and a petty bourgeois *flâneur*: this is the best way of describing the politics of our little emperor!

Notes

1 To complete the demographic picture let me quote Brody again: 'Women composed about 2/3 of his published cases. 1/2 of his major cases were diagnosed as hysteria, 3/4 were between 18–20 yr. of age, all were members of the upper class, and a majority were probably married. Similar characteristics were also found with his minor (less extensively reported) cases for the most part' (1970, p. 8).

2 On equilibrium: Freud sought equilibrium, a refuge from excess, as did the ancient Greeks. This is not the same as wanting to resolve contradictions in order to achieve a dialectical synthesis. Freud was, in keeping with his middle-class status, a peacemaker between id, ego and superego, between the life instinct and the death instinct, between Eros and civilisation, between consciousness, unconscious and preconscious, between rulers and plebs. Had he been offered an acting role in Fritz Lang's *Metropolis*, it would have been the role of the foreman bringing capital and labour together for a hearty handshake at the conclusion of the movie.

2

HIRSCHFELD, CLASS AND SEXUALITY

Magnus Hirschfeld: A flabby, unappetising fellow

Like most scholars, Freud was blessed with the ability to be simultaneously rude and obnoxious when he wanted to be. A measure of how much Hirschfeld's resignation from the Psychoanalytic Association had hurt Freud is that the latter chose to dispense with all propriety:

> Magnus Hirschfeld has left our ranks in Berlin … No great loss, he is a flabby, unappetising fellow, absolutely incapable of learning anything. Of course he takes your [Jung's] remark at the Congress as a pretext; homosexual touchiness. Not worth a tear.
>
> *(Freud's letter to Jung, 1911)*

Magnus Hirschfeld (1868–1935) was a complex character. His approach to sexology employs a mix of psychology, sociology and biology. Contemporary advocates of the 'biopsychosocial approach' would find much in Hirschfeld worthy of consideration (cf. Toates 2010). Although he was a firm advocate of the 'scientific method', he was also very open to expanding the parameters of science to include qualitative data. As a keen ethnographer, he observed behaviour and discourse in homosexual bars, swimming pools, hotels and private houses (Fozooni 2012a). His criticisms of naive positivism and empiricism would find an echo in current social science research ethos: 'The natural sciences have always left aside the most important aspect of life, which is love' (Hirschfeld, quoted in Wolff 1986, p. 27).

Hirschfeld's politics

Hirschfeld was a scholar, physician, researcher, publicist and an activist. In 1913 he gave a series of successful lectures in London which inspired the

FIGURE 2.1 Magnus Hirschfeld in 1929

creation of the British Society for the Study of Sexual Psychology. He was also interested to learn more about the Suffragettes while in London and took note of the heavy-handed approach of the British state in dealing with dissent (Fozooni 2012a).

During World War I he worked as a physician for the Red Cross. He called war an 'addictive psychosis' but supported conscription (Wolff 1986, p. 164). After the war and the establishment of a social democratic government, Hirschfeld's ideas took a more radical twist. He began to praise Marx, Engels, Bebel, Liebknecht and Lassalle and his patriotism was shelved for 'internationalism'. It is difficult to ascertain with any degree of certainty whether this turn towards Marxism was sincere or opportunistic. According to one report, August Bebel, the founder of the Social Democratic Party of Germany, found Hirschfeld's campaign 'too apolitical' (Weeks 1975, p. 4). At times, his social democratic policies were presented with genuine gusto and enthusiasm. They were also many decades ahead of their time.

His 1926 visit to the USSR did not lead to a denunciation of Leninism or even (the emerging) Stalinism. He did not seem to have possessed the political nous to diagnose the regime as capitalist. Bolsheviks were not his only 'left-wing' admirers. Even genuine revolutionaries such as Sylvia Pankhurst and Emma Goldman were supportive of Hirschfeld's work, although their support was more qualified.

I think it is fair to say that Hirschfeld was at heart a classic liberal of the nineteenth-century variety, with some social democratic tendencies. It is certainly true that he forged tactical alliances with German social democracy and Russian Bolshevism. Apart from those few who were genuine in their support of his work, he was grudgingly tolerated by the official left during the Weimar Republic (1919–1933). As Germany drifted rightwards, attacks on Hirschfeld (both verbal and physical) increased correspondingly. When the Nazis gained power, they tried to obliterate his work.

Like most liberals he had to struggle with a number of insoluble contradictions at the heart of capitalism. He had inherited a stern patriotism from his father but was also very well aware of the self-delusional nature of nationalism: 'Jews and Germans considered themselves to be the chosen people, and both were the most hated in the world' (Hirschfeld, quoted in Wolff 1986, p. 29). As a liminal character, it would not surprise the reader to hear that he expressed support for German patriotism, Zionism *and* internationalism without seeing any contradictions. To his credit, he foresaw the dangers of both Jewish nationalism and anti-Semitism and welcomed the unity of Arab-Jewish working classes. He also alluded to the similarities between the mechanisms of anti-Semitism and homophobia on more than one occasion (ibid, p. 356). He ended up supporting World War I, despite his own pacifist leanings and the government order that led to the dismissal of homosexual officers from the army.

Eventually Hirschfeld became what we would nowadays term a cosmopolitan or in his own words, a 'Panhumanist' (Hirschfeld 1938a, p. 115). He predicted that the next world war would have a racial element and that the only thing capable of preventing it would be panhumanism:

> When that storm bursts, in extent and in frightfulness it may outdo the World War of 1914–1918. There is only one way of preventing the outbreak. Not Pan-Europa can hinder it, nor Pan-America, nor the League of Nations, nor the Pact of Four, nor any such half-measure; nothing can avert it but Panhumanism ... We must hitch our wagon to a star.
>
> *(Ibid.)*

In some ways his ideals are remarkably close to contemporary multiculturalism. Thankfully his respect for other cultures did not involve selective self-censorship as practised by contemporary cultural relativists. When, for instance, he came across the practice of circumcision among Jews or Muslims he condemned it vociferously. He believed that circumcision for boys was 'not done for hygiene but for sacrificial reasons' (Wolff 1986, p. 347). It was even worse for girls who were terrorised and mutilated by the procedure. In Egypt, he contrasted the ancient power of women with the modern suppression of their rights.

Hirschfeld on sex

In 1897 Hirschfeld became one of the founding fathers of the Association for the Scientific Humanitarian Committee (SHC), principally to fight Paragraph 175 of the Imperial Penal Code. This was a national German law that criminalised homosexuality as well as making homosexuals victims of blackmail. In 1914 the Reichstag Commission narrowly rejected Hirschfeld's petition to repeal the law. The law was reinforced by the Nazis, then liberalised in both West and East Germany after World War II to some extent (but significantly not abolished), and finally repealed in 1994. The history of this law serves once more to foreground the uncomfortable philosophical and political overlap between liberalism, social democracy and fascism.

The purview of the SHC gradually expanded to include other demands such as the fight against Paragraph 218 (a German law prohibiting abortion). Hirschfeld encouraged linkages between lesbians and the wider women's movement. He provided examples of famous, successful women such as Queen Christiana of Sweden in an echo of earlier positive profiling techniques used to enhance the reputation of gay men.

He wrote on the notion of an 'intermediate sex' which had been popularised earlier (using slightly different terminology) by Karl Heinrich Ulrichs (1825–1895) and Edward Carpenter (1844–1929). He was also one of the first to integrate the intermediate sex with the latest discoveries in hormone research (Weeks and Holland 1996, p. 104). He borrowed from animal research into castration and testes transplantation by Eugen Steinach (1861–1944) to validate his writings. Surveys, questionnaires, case studies and interviews provided him with ample data to forge ahead with what we might today consider an overdeveloped classificatory zeal. For instance, he classified male homosexuals according to the direction of their desire into three groups: '*ephebophiles* who are attracted to youths from puberty up to the early twenties; *androphiles*, who love persons between the early twenties and fifty; and *gerontophiles*, who love older men, up to senile old age' (Hirschfeld 1938b, p. 236). This predilection for classification went as far as distinguishing between homosexuals according to their nervous systems. It is only fair to point out that medicinal and psychiatric classification were all the rage among scientists at the beginning of the twentieth century, influenced by a general trend within capitalism for the ever greater social and technical division of labour.

In 1919 he set up the Institute for Sexual Research, an ambitious research enterprise that was thirty years ahead of Alfred Kinsey's. Here, sexology was to be studied through biology, pathology, forensic medicine, sociology, psychology as well as ethnology. Although conservative by Wilhelm Reich's standards, the institute planned to study issues like free love alongside problems of marriage, abstinence and prostitution (Fozooni 2012a).

Although he took on board a great deal of Freud's ideas about psychosexual development, he came to disagree with Freudians who saw transvestites as a variety of homosexuals. Hirschfeld borrowed freely from Freud's ideas on the 'erogenous zones' and 'component impulses', although 'we [Hirschfeld] on our part wish to leave entirely open the question whether or not this infantile sexuality is a true sexuality' (Hirschfeld 1938b, p. 50). Regarding the relationship between children and parents, again

Hirschfeld conceded the possibility of the 'true Oedipal situation' in exceptional cases although he felt that it was not necessary to go as far as Freud in generalising the Oedipal and Electra complexes (ibid, p. 53).

Hirschfeld's approach

Here and there, Hirschfeld was changing minds. One prominent convert, Wilhelm Oswald, confessed that as a Christian he had been prejudiced against homosexuals but after reading *The Homosexuality of Men and Women* (Hirschfeld [1914] 2000), he now understood the need for re-evaluation. The book represents a more nuanced understanding of sexual orientation beyond Hirschfeld's initial crude notion of the 'third sex' and is based on a staggering number of interviews with gays and lesbians (10,000 in all).

Wolff has argued that '[Hirschfeld] tapped at the door of science but could not get it to open' (Wolff 1986, p. 129). I believe that it would be more accurate to say that Hirschfeld vacillated between a *restricted* and an *expansive* definition of science. The restricted definition was based on a naive positivist and empiricist epistemology and a quantitative methodology which prefigured the errors of contemporary essentialism. This mode of investigation is a forerunner of the current dominant 'biomedical paradigm' and perceives the categories and values of science ahistorically. Regrettably, whenever he tried to expand the boundaries of this biomedical approach, a crude version of the 'biopsychosocial model' was the best he could conjure up.

The modern version of the biopsychosocial model is usually accredited to George Engel's (1913–1999) attempt to respond to reductionist and dehumanising tendencies within biomedicine. Engel's imaginary patient asks, 'Do my doctors know who I am, who I have been, who I still want to be? Do they understand what I am going through, my suffering, my pain, my distress?' (Engel 1988). The key to understanding patients is to listen intently and to be genuinely curious about them during interviews. These are precisely the qualities that Hirschfeld tried to foster in practitioners by privileging dialogue over the kind of monologue that is normally preferred in both classical psychoanalysis and medicine (Fozooni 2012a).

Hirschfeld would have been comfortable working within the parameters described by recent advocates:

> The biopsychosocial model is both a philosophy of clinical care and a practical clinical guide. Philosophically, it is a way of understanding how suffering, disease and illness are affected by multiple levels of

> organisation, from the societal to the molecular. At the practical level, it is a way of understanding the patient's subjective experience as an essential contributor to accurate diagnosis, health outcomes, and human care.
>
> (*Borrell-Carrio* et al. *2004, p. 576)*

The biopsychosocial model is also in tune with other aspects of Hirschfeld's practice. He practiced, whenever possible, *formulation* rather than *diagnosis.* In other words, when ascertaining the issues confronting his clients, Hirschfeld preferred to describe their narratives rather than label them.

While the biopsychosocial model is an obvious improvement over the biomedical approach, serious objections have been raised regarding its credentials by, among others, David Pilgrim (2002). Pilgrim traces the model to the pioneering work of the Swiss psychiatrist, Adolf Meyer (1866–1950), who insisted on understanding patients through consideration of detailed case histories. His *ergasiology* (researching and noting all biological, psychological and social factors pertinent to the case) and empowerment through *community medicine* and meaningful activity became influential ideas within psychiatry. Another influence is the general field of systems theory as originally expounded by Ludwig von Bertalanffy and Paul Weiss (Pilgrim 2002, p. 585). The insistence on taking a patient's personal history was at odds with the Kraepelinian method of diagnosis. A similar approach was taken up by Hirschfeld in the nineteenth century and expanded by George Engel in the twentieth century. Pilgrim also sees the modern version of the model as a reaction against the criticism levelled at psychiatry by the 'anti-psychiatry' movement of the 1960s and 1970s.

Perhaps Hirschfeld's most enduring success was in challenging the prevailing sexual discourse which referred to homosexuality as 'abnormal', 'insane' or a 'terrible vice'. On his death from a stroke in 1935, one of his creations, the World League for Sexual Reform (WLSR), fragmented along liberal and radical lines. Its ten demands included equality for women, contraception, prevention of prostitution and venereal disease (Dose 2003, p. 7). By this time, the organisation boasted 190,000 members worldwide. One of its leaders, Jonathan Leunbach (1884–1955), identified the League's failures as 'its unwillingness to join the workers' movement, to integrate the struggle for sex reform into the struggle against fascism and for socialism' (Weeks 1996, p. 186). Leunbach was a follower of Wilhelm Reich. He was arrested and imprisoned for carrying out illegal abortions, but the ensuing political debate led to the Danish parliament passing the country's first abortion legislation, 'which reduced the penalty for induced abortion and gave better opportunities to let a woman have an abortion for health reasons' (*Wikipedia*, 'Jonathan Leunbach'). The other main leader, Norman Haire (1892–1952), adopted an apolitical stance which in practice meant distancing the League from the workers' movement. It may even be the case that the short-lived Spanish section of the WLSR was under the influence of Reich and the anarchists (Dose 2003, p. 3).

Hirschfeld on 'race'

His outstanding contribution in this field is a book entitled *Racism* (Hirschfeld 1938a). It may seem somewhat dated by our twenty-first-century standards but its critique of nationalism and racism is remarkably similar to discourse analysis and social constructionism. Using etymological, historical and cultural evidence, he demonstrates the fictive nature of concepts such as 'race'. He shows convincingly that even Mussolini believed that 'race is a feeling, not a reality' (Mussolini, quoted in ibid., p. 48). Moreover, he argues that 'there was no warrant for transferring to mankind a notion [race] which had a specific sense only in zoology and botany' (ibid., p. 54). In a remarkably current manoeuvre, he puts the term 'race' in inverted commas throughout the book.

I would argue that the opening paragraph of *Racism* displays a superior interpretation of fascism than most contemporary treatments, as the anti-working-class nature of fascism is clearly underlined: '"Race war instead of class war" – such was the pithy formula, such the momentous watchwords, uttered by the rulers of the Third Realm as soon as they had established their power over Germany' (Hirschfeld 1938a, p. 35). Most contemporary interpretations ignore or downplay the anti-working-class essence of fascism, and I think it is perfectly fair to inquire as to the reasons for this (Fozooni 2012b).

German racism is forensically examined in its Protestant, Catholic and secular manifestations by Hirschfeld. He even makes time to look at the Nordic movement which was 'a new Protestantism, superseding the Protestantism of Martin Luther, which never succeeded in wholly discarding its foreign trappings' (Clauss, quoted in Hirschfeld 1938a, p. 41). He establishes the separate basis of this Nordicism from Aryanism and Teutonism, while showing how they can feed into each other. All this is very relevant to the rise of neo-fascism in northern Europe. He also emphasises how much of fervent racism originates from insecurity and a need to prove one's own credentials. Here he quotes Hertz approvingly to argue that 'Race hatred is not a natural feeling. The most ardent nationalists are often of foreign descent, and, like renegades, have no invectives strong enough for stigmatising those who were at one time their comrades' (ibid., p. 67). The prime example of this would be Hitler who was born in Austria, immigrated to Germany in 1913, renounced his Austrian citizenship in 1925, and remained stateless until 1932, when he became a German national, only a year before taking office as German chancellor.

Some of his arguments may seem a tad atavistic but Hirschfeld seems determined to fight racism with every weapon available to him. For instance, he points out that

> not one of the Pleiad of outstanding figures who were predominant among German geniuses at the close of the eighteenth and the beginning of nineteenth century – Goethe, Schiller, Herder, Lessing, Kant, Beethoven, and Alexander von Humboldt – conformed to the Nordic ideal … Not even Wagner … Indeed the famous composer's appearance gave some justification for Nietzsche's mischievous remark that Wagner seemed to be an anticipation of his mother's second marriage to a Jewish actor.
>
> *(1938a, p. 72)*

Further on, he once again quotes Herz approvingly:

> [W]e [Germans] have taken our calendar from Babylon, our writing from Phoenicia, our ciphering from India, our religion from Judea, our law from the 'racial chaos' of ancient Rome, our philosophy from Hellas, and the foundations of our exact science mainly from the Arabs.
>
> *(Herz, quoted in Hirschfeld 1938a, p. 75)*

As if taking on the combined forces of racism and nationalism was not burdensome enough, Hirschfeld next turns his critical faculties towards the Bible. He points out there are two narratives in the Bible about the origins of the human race(s), 'One of these versions is monogenetic, indicating that we have all sprung from one ancestral pair; the other is polygenetic' (Hirschfeld 1938a, pp. 95–96). These inconsistencies allow reactionaries to justify any inequity by quoting those parts of the Bible they agree with and ignoring the rest – a hermeneutics trickery which has its 'scientific' counterpart in social science. The religious reactionary selectively chooses the Bible to justify the institution of slavery in the United States and the scientific reactionary (he uses von Horstig as an example here) classifies humanity into three main groups: Gorilla-Blacks, Chimpanzee-Whites and Orange-Yellows (ibid., p. 99)! Hirschfeld himself is of the opinion that we are monogenetic, basing himself on the argument that 'All known human stocks can interbreed freely and produce fertile offspring' (ibid., p. 102). His Panhumanism confidently asserts that 'Mankind was a unity to begin with, and is destined to become a unity once more' (ibid., p. 101).

In countering the prevalent myth that Africans, Indians and Polynesians are 'bone-idle … and work-shy', he comes close to the thesis put forward in *The Right to be Lazy* (1883) by Paul Lafargue. In this text, Lafargue calls for the abolition of wage-slavery and its replacement by playful activity. Hirschfeld writes in a similar fashion, 'In truth they are not work-shy at all, but they like to do their work in "the play-way", and often do it all the better for that' (Hirschfeld 1938a, p. 112). When he does concede ground, Hirschfeld is careful to provide a sociological rather than a biological argument for it. For instance, he admits that there may be truth in the anecdotal evidence about 'half-breeds' suffering relatively more from 'inferiority complex':

> [I]n Hindustan the offspring of Eurasian marriages are … regarded with contempt both by Hindus, Mahrattas, Canarese, Tamils … and members of the dominant white race … Such inferiority is … of sociological, and not biological causation, and would not exist in a sanely ordered society.
>
> *(Ibid., p. 119)*

Despite not enjoying our vantage point, he developed cogent arguments against Franz Joseph Gall's theory of phrenology, the advocates of 'cranial indexing' as a marker of racial character (Hirschfeld 1938a, pp. 134–135), as well as champions of the 'blood myth' (ibid., p. 147). The 'evil practice of attaching national names to sexual peculiarities', for example, syphilis as 'the French pox' or homosexuality as 'le vice Allemand', are similarly dismissed as 'quite unjustified' but he cautions that 'the error is hard to uproot' (ibid., pp. 149–150). Against these myths, Hirschfeld argues that from a biological viewpoint 'all human beings are hybrids' (ibid., pp. 198) and that 'immigration and racial crossings [are] essential to the improvement of economic life and of race' (ibid., p. 219).

Hirschfeld's faith in psychoanalysis remains undiminished despite falling out with Jung and Freud. When it comes to analysing prejudice, he argues that 'Racial dislikes, like other unmeaning dislikes, groundless but often rationalised … can only be elucidated by "depth psychology", for they are rooted in the unconscious' (1938a, p. 225). In fact, social class (and even the reduced notion of class expressed as occupation) is a far better indicator of commonality than race:

> Occupational types are much more conspicuous than racial types. During my voyage round the world I was particularly struck by the likeness between sea-folk of all nations, not only in respect of their movements and their bronzed tint, but also in their features, intonations and gestures. Even the wives of seamen resemble one another.
>
> *(Ibid., p. 253)*

The realisation of this class commonality is hindered by the ruling elite: 'Thus the capitalists will promote anything they think likely to hinder the growth of anti-capitalist forces' (ibid., p. 263).

The book ends with a quote from Fredrich Nietzsche: 'Where races are mingled, we find the sources of all great civilisations. Maxim: Have nothing to do with anyone who participates in the preposterous race-humbug' (Hirschfeld 1938a, p. 316). In case the reader finds the choice of Nietzsche as closing argument troubling, let me remind you that in the nineteenth century Nietzsche was championed by leftists, feminists and Republicans. At the time he was considered, by and large, to be anti-nationalist. The later association of Nietzsche with twentieth-century fascism distorts his initial reception.

Hirschfeld's errors

I have already pointed out the contradictory nature of Hirschfeld's contribution. Although a sexual pioneer in many ways, he was also capable of prudishness. For example, he was vociferously against alcoholism and prostitution. He advised both workers and pregnant women against drinking and its inimical link to the spread of venereal diseases, especially syphilis. Rather naively, he was in favour of religious morality laying the precondition of a 'hygienic life', even though he was not a religious man himself (Fozooni 2012a).

In many ways Hirschfeld's imagination remained encapsulated within an idealised nuclear family. For him, only a 'normal' bourgeois marriage created the preconditions of childhood bliss. Despite his genuine concern for the poor and underprivileged he would occasionally display disdain for the masses. On a visit to the USSR in 1926 insightful comments about the causes of prostitution sit uneasily alongside derogatory comments about the 'common man' who is deemed corrupt and opportunistic by nature. He even claimed without empirical corroboration that sexual molestation of children was more common among the lower class (Wolff 1986, p. 281). Bourgeois humanism was indeed Hirschfeld's refuge from the realities of class antagonism, and he dismissed class identity as yet another form of selfishness.

Hirschfeld was often asked to provide expert medical testimony in legal cases. One such controversial case was the Harden scandal. Harden, who was editor of *Die Zukunft*, had accused a number of Kaiser Wilhelm II's advisers of homosexuality. In this case, not only was Hirschfeld's defence of homosexuality based on the dubious precepts of biological determinism, but it is alleged that he also engaged in a clumsy attempt at 'outing', with the aim of making homosexuality more acceptable (Bullough 2003, p. 65). These tactics backfired. As a result, his expertise was called into question and, much more significantly, he lost the support of the Kaiser.

One of Hirschfeld's key contributions was his study of sexual mores during the course of World War I (Hirschfeld [1941] 2006). This is in part historical documentation, and in part scientific investigation of the dramatic transformation in people's perspectives on sex and love during the four cataclysmic years that reshaped Europe. Significantly, he placed a request in leading newspapers for soldiers to send him 'whatever material they had relative to the history of morals and war' (ibid., p. vii). However, even here errors abound. The book starts with an explanation of how the war released sexual restraints, spread venereal diseases and eroticised nurses. Some of the descriptions of the crowds on the eve of battle are sadly reminiscent of Gustav Le Bon, although Hirschfeld takes care to qualify most of his more rhetorical flourishes. Regarding the war fever that overtook Europe, Hirschfeld writes that 'The masses poured through the streets jubilantly, aroused to a blazing hatred, an enormous beast ready to hurl itself upon the enemy' (ibid., p. 24). The model employed throughout the book is a biopsychosocial one with Hirschfeld attempting to contextualise the sexual impulse for the war within economic and social conditions. However, occasionally, as for instance in discussing the eroticisation of female nurses during the war, he reduces the biopsychosocial model onto the biomedical terrain of libido sublimation. In short, he accuses nurses of receiving sexual pleasure from healing the wounded (ibid., p. 56).

Another flaw is related to crude, speculative biomedical mapping. Hirschfeld was insistent that psychosexual orientations were presented in specific 'brain centres,' a position that might endear him to present-day advocates of brain localisation. His views on the endocrine glands as the key to sexual orientation would find little support among researchers in the field today. His diagnosis of homosexuality in childhood based on physical appearance or demeanour was justifiably ridiculed. In the early 1900s Hirschfeld also conflated transvestism with trans-sexualism (Hill 2005, p. 318).

Hirschfeld, whose support for gays, lesbians, transvestites was unconditional, condemned 'the androgyne for its supposed lack of harmony' (Mosse 1985, p. 104). Ironically, even his views on sexual equality would sound antiquated to our ears. For example, 'he compared homosexuality with a developmental defect, such as hare-lip or club foot' (Wolff 1986, p. 37). He erroneously insisted that homosexuals were different from 'normals' in certain physical traits. He even expressed fear that 'transvestites, like homosexuals, ran the risk of producing degenerate offspring, but he added that he could not be sure of this eugenic danger in the former' (ibid., p. 109). He suggested that homosexuals tended to enjoy helping and serving rather than giving orders, which made them born peacemakers (Fozooni 2012a). Hirschfeld's humanitarianism was from the outset tinged with an overbearing prescriptivism that meandered its way in and out of Malthusian and eugenic currents.

Whenever the tensions within the biopsychosocial model are collapsed in favour of one element, ontological and epistemological errors tend to creep in. Hirschfeld was sufficiently critical to reject some of the wider claims of women's inferiority based on phrenology. However, he was not critical enough to supersede the more established biologically determined narratives prevalent in his time. For instance, he is on record as supporting the gendered version of the intellect-emotion dualism: 'Woman is more receptive in her love and mental life than man ... But she has not the same gift of abstract thought, nor for real creative activity. Her capacity to produce is focused on relatively simple mental functions' (Hirschfeld, quoted in Wolff 1986, p. 87).

Going beyond Hirschfeld: class and kink

A chief talent of critical psychologists is to develop linguistic landscapes for investigating complex phenomena. So long as this landscape remains a *commons* (i.e. an egalitarian space, owned and utilised collectively), talking, thinking and understanding are facilitated. But when it becomes an *enclosure* (i.e. a fenced-up, privately owned property, complete with border guards, experts and town criers), the ensuing toxicity suppresses genuine dialogue. This is how it came to pass that social class was first marginalised, and then written out of debates surrounding sex, sexuality and gender. This is ironic, since capitalism very deliberately turns sexuality into a labour power and seeks to regulate the reproduction of labour power. All this it tries to do consensually whenever possible, but if met by resistance, then coercion is utilised in order to maintain bourgeois morality.

The last two men in the United Kingdom to be hanged for the 'crime of buggery' were London working men, James Pratt and John Smith, who were executed in 1835 at Newgate Prison. Ryan informs us that neither was allowed to give evidence at their trial, while Charles Dickens, who visited them in prison, wrote that '[they] had nothing to expect from the mercy of the crown, their doom was sealed' (Ryan 2015). James Pratt was a groom and John Smith a labourer (reportedly a servant). Had they been wealthy and well connected they would doubtless have enjoyed different fates.

The personal prejudice and institutional discrimination that homosexuals have experienced in the UK is paralleled by their treatment in the East. Although 'homosexuality was prevalent among all social classes' in sixteenth-century Russia, various tsars attempted to suppress it through harsh punishment (*Wikipedia*, 'LGBT History in Russia'). To a large extent, this attitude persevered even after the so-called 1917 'revolution'. The claim that the Soviet Union was the first government to decriminalise homosexuality is somewhat exaggerated. Scholars are divided on this point, but it seems that the first nation-state to decriminalise sodomy was the French Republic in 1791. In the nineteenth century, Brazil (1830), the Ottoman Empire (1858) and Japan (1872) followed suit.

When the Bolsheviks came to power, the entire old tsarist Constitution, including the code on homosexuality, was repealed (Healey 2001). A specialist in this field, Ira Roldugina, describes it in these terms: 'I think we can talk about the early Soviet period as a time of liberation, although not of liberty' (Roldugina, quoted in Langenburg 2017). There was autonomous self-advocacy from below but little genuine support from above. However, since the new Constitution did not specifically criminalise homosexuality, the myth was created that progressives among the Bolsheviks had decriminalised homosexuality. In reality, they did not pay much attention to this issue and were not actively involved in agitating for gay rights. That distinction should probably go to a group of Cadets (Constitutional Democrats), most importantly Vladimir Nabokov and some anarchists (Reddebrek 2018; *Wikipedia*, 'LGBT History in Russia'). Nabokov's research on gay rights was published by Magnus Hirschfeld.

It is worth noting that these temporary gains were restricted to Russia and homosexuality remained illegal in other former territories of the Russian Empire. There is yet more contradiction at work here. On the one hand, under Lenin's leadership, openly homosexual people were allowed to serve in government (ibid.). In addition, indirectly influenced by Hirschfeld, a few medical experts who were working alongside transgender people began to consider gender as a spectrum and not as a simple binary (Healey 2001), and in some parts of the Soviet Union there was 'a brief window of freedom' (Khoroshilova 2017). On the other hand, Lenin retained prudish ideas about sex, and after his death, things gradually became worse for the 'gay community' culminating in Stalin's anti homosexual purges in the early 1930s. Even in the 1920s many Bolsheviks viewed homosexuality as an example of 'bourgeois degeneracy' and a 'social illness to be cured' (*Wikipedia*, 'LGBT History in Russia').

These contradictory tendencies were evident even among researchers. Vladimir Mikhailovich Bekhterev (1857–1927), the famous Russian neurologist, was credited with pioneering objective psychology. He was a rival of Pavlov and 'spent a great deal of time working on "sexual anomalies", not only studying the field but also giving public lectures' (Khoroshilova 2017). In a sense, he was Russia's less progressive version of Magnus Hirschfeld. Believing homosexuality to be a 'sexual anomaly' and not a crime, he defended Petrograd's gay 'community' in the early 1920s. Like Hirschfeld, he provided expert testimony in support of gays in legal trails.

However, his support was very much qualified. Bekhterev preferred homosexuals to hide their sexuality, since

> the public demonstration of such impulses might attract unstable people into the ambit of perversion. The introduction of homosexual tastes and activities to the broad public … is socially harmful and cannot be permitted. The creation of clubs or dens for such purposes must be punished under the criminal law.
>
> *(Bekhterev, quoted in Hekma* et al. *1995, p. 167)*

Despite this chequered record on homosexuality, he was inundated with letters from gay and transgender people requesting advice or a 'cure' for their 'terrible vice' (Meduza 2017). He would prescribe lupulin (an active ingredient found in hops) and a mix of adonis, bromine and codeine. This medical treatment was to be augmented by a course of 'corresponding suggestions' (Khoroshilova 2017).

Throughout the 1920s and 1930s gay people continued to be divided by social class. Accordingly, the first class comprised the so-called aristocrats; more accurately, they were 'representatives of the intelligentsia, nobles, officials, and officers of the Tsarist army and navy' (Khoroshilova 2017). The other group were derogatorily referred to as the 'simples' and consisted of 'soldiers, sailors, clerks – people who had not been part of the fashionable St Petersburg salons before the revolution and who were not welcome guests of the "aristocrats" after 1917' (ibid.). The two classes rarely mixed, and when in 1933 Stalin recriminalised homosexuality, it became even harder for gay people from different classes to interact.

In more recent times, radicals have argued for reinstating social class into debates about transgender issues (Anarchasteminist 2017). Surveys commissioned by the European Union Agency for Fundamental Rights have shown that in terms of wages, unemployment, workplace discrimination and homelessness, transgenders do considerably worse than cisgenders (FRA 2014). Anarchasteminist conclude their short text by commenting,

> A common means of dismissing trans people's attempts to raise issues that affect us or criticise institutions or public figures that have harmed us as a group is to dismiss us as privileged. [It is claimed that] Trans people are a bunch of middle-class kids or a load of wealthy university students who are just looking for something to complain about.
>
> *(2017)*

In reality, data is beginning to validate what most radicals had long suspected: the majority of transgendered people are not only working class but probably belong to the most 'precarious' section of our class. To my mind, foregrounding class issues in this debate is far more pertinent than pursuing over-publicised pseudo-debates between 'second-wave' feminists such as Germaine Greer and Julie Birchall and their transgendered detractors. However, for those readers who are easily impressed by the razzmatazz and unwarranted arrogance of celebrity politics, I refer you to a short Germaine Greer interview with BBC Newsnight (BBC 2015) and a 'censured' article by Julie Birchall (2013).

Hirschfeld: a summing up

I would like to conclude the chapter by underscoring three points about Hirschfeld: first, his pioneering role in media depictions of homosexuality; second, the considerable array of scientific and political forces mobilised against him; and, third, his switch from a biomedical to an early illustration of the biopsychosocial model.

Hirschfeld was keenly interested in the power of the media to change people's attitudes. In the more liberal climate of the Weimer Republic the first ever films about homosexuality were produced and Hirschfeld supported this trend either through consultation or direct participation. *Different from the Others: Paragraph 175* (Dir. Oswald, 1919, b&w, silent with inter-titles) is often cited as the first film to deal explicitly with the subject of homosexuality (*Wikipedia*, 'Different from the Others'). It focuses on how Paragraph 175 promotes extortion but it also tackles wider anti-homosexual discrimination. *Different from the Others* survives as a fragment with photographs replacing the lost scenes. In his scholarly study of the film, Steakley claims that the plotline was also by Hirschfeld (Steakley 1999). Later the director Richard Oswald (1880–1963) worked closely with Hirschfeld and other sexologists to produce a series of sex ed works which dealt with issues ranging from prostitution and abortion to venereal disease (Fozooni 2012a). I think Hirschfeld's relationship to the media is a salutary lesson in both the potential and dangers of working with the media. If postpsychology is to have a meaningful impact on public debates, it should learn how to bypass mainstream media and discover alternative methods of expressing its discoveries.

Hirschfeld saw his filmic role as an extension of his earlier educational work and many people admired the film and communicated their gratitude to Hirschfeld personally, but he was also the target of vicious attacks by clerics, politicians and proto-fascists. There was even an attempt on his life. The government did little to prevent anti-Semitic outbursts against Hirschfeld and in 1920 censorship was re-established. Steakley has noted that these censorship standards 'were so harsh that they required no revision under the Nazi regime' (1999, p. 191). *Different from the Others* was banned for endangering 'public order and security', as well as for seducing impressionable audience members. Three prominent scientists played a pivotal role in its censorship: Emil Kraepelin (who regarded homosexuality as a disease adopted through 'seduction' and a 'psychopathic' condition); Siegfried Placzek (whose conservative sensibilities had been offended); and Albert Moll (who detested Hirschfeld and the popularisation of science through films).

But this is not all that Hirschfeld had to contend with. Throughout his career, he had to struggle against not only homophobes and but also reactionary trends within the homosexual 'community'. For example, Adolf Bland, the editor of the very first journal of sexuality in Germany, *Der Eigene* (*The Personalist*), used racism to gain respectability for homosexuality. The journal, which photographed naked boys and men against the German landscape, praised a distorted Nietzschean 'Superman' for its manliness and toyed with anti-Semitism (Mosse 1985, p. 42). Another reactionary was the homosexual activist, Friedrich Radszuweit, who used anti-Semitic jibes to criticise Hirschfeld and to curry favour with the nascent fascists. He also welcomed the banning of Hirschfeld's films (Steakley 1999, p. 194). As a rival for the leadership of the gay rights movement, Radszuweit had a great deal to gain by undermining Hirschfeld.

The attacks on Hirschfeld had begun as early as 1907 when he was portrayed as a freak by the liberal *Vossische Zeitung*, while the right-wing *Germania* declared after his appearance as an expert legal witness in a court case that 'We must make an end of people like Dr Hirschfeld' (Wolff 1986, p. 73). A Reichstag member was quoted as saying, 'Homosexuals have the morals of dogs' and leaflets distributed outside Hirschfeld's house read, 'Dr Hirschfeld – a Public Danger. The Jews Are Our Undoing' (ibid, p. 74).

As already mentioned, one of his harshest critics was Kraepelin, who wished to initiate a struggle against 'sexual confusion' and 'primarily against masturbation' by, among other means, the 'toughening of the will through gymnastics' (Kraepelin, quoted in Mildenberger 2007, p. 322). Kraepelin called for a ban on 'every form of information about homosexual intercourse that did not condemn it' (ibid.). Kraepelin followed this up by claiming that homosexuals posed a serious danger to the German people. Freud's criticisms of Hirschfeld as 'a flabby, unappetising fellow' came within such a context.

It is important to note that the limited vocal and financial support that Hirschfeld did receive from the Weimar Republic remained grudging and intermittent. As his friend and collaborator, Max Hodann, reminds us, 'The academic gates were closed to Hirschfeld, and even after the fall of the Hohenzollern Empire in 1918 the Weimar Republic had no chair anywhere for the tireless investigator' (Hodann, quoted in Haeberle 1981, p. 271). A minority of state officials in the executive and judiciary were sympathetic, but the legislative was rarely open to his advances.

As a general rule of thumb, Hirschfeld's breakthroughs were achieved within a biopsychosocial mode of inquiry and his errors committed within a biomedical one. When investigating homosexuality, his utilisation of a rudimentary form of biopsychosocial perspective allowed him to tease out complex issues. The same is true of his critique of racism and advocacy for a modernist Panhumanism. However, the scientific shortcomings of his era meant that there was always room for errors and a potential collapse onto the biomedical terrain.

3

WATSONIAN CAPITALISM

> Sir, 'tis my occupation to be plain.
> I have seen better faces in my time
> Than stands on any shoulder that I see
> Before me at this instant.
> *Shakespeare,* King Lear, *Act 2, Scene 2*

Of Rats (or was it rabbits?) and Men

In our frivolous age, it is much easier to gain a favourable reputation than to lose a bad one. A teenager with a quirk becomes an overnight YouTube 'influencer', and a politician surges ahead in opinion polls following snide remarks about Mexicans, Muslims and women. Meanwhile, pioneering psychologists like Watson can still be derided as 'terrible' and 'dark' sixty years after passing away (Conliffe 2018).

Of course, anyone can see that John Broadus Watson (1878–1958) presents a willing and convenient target for such broadsides. Let's be frank: in many ways, he *was* dark and terrible. An absent, alcoholic father and the bullying he experienced at school as 'the dumb country kid' led to a period of delinquency, involving vicious racist attacks on local black people (Conliffe 2018). This prejudice followed him into adult life. He surgically experimented on rats by depriving them of sight and smell, and advocated the practice of child labour, since he believed that children should be treated as young adults. He offered behaviourist techniques to increase the rate of exploitation of the working class and to ensure bourgeois order in the workplace, while declaring women unfit for outside work. He disapproved of thumb sucking, masturbation and homosexuality (*Wikipedia*, 'John B. Watson'), without informing us if, for him, this constituted a causal chain of events. And finally, even if the rest of the world decides someday to graciously overlook Watson's litany of misdeeds, I personally do not possess sufficient reserves of generosity to forgive him for promoting 'celebrity product endorsements' (ibid.)! To this day, I die a little inside every time I watch Harvey Keitel reprising his Winston Wolfe role from *Pulp Fiction* for the sake of a series of car insurance commercials.

You may very well ask at this junction: why should such a *charming* figure be studied at all? Moreover, is he not considered nowadays to be no more than a historical footnote in psychology? Todd (1994) has indeed reported that by the 1950s figures such as Pavlov, Hull, Tolman and Skinner had eclipsed Watson in textbook discussions about learning and conditioning. Within a decade another group of psychologists (Maslow, Piaget, Harlow and Erikson) had replaced Watson's views of emotions and child development (ibid.). His *Behaviourist Manifesto* (1913) was largely ignored by his colleagues and it was not until the publication of his first major book on behaviourism, *Psychology from the Standpoint of a Behaviourist* (Watson 1919), that people paid him any attention at all (Todd 1994). In fact, Todd argues that the role of classical behaviourism in promoting 'objective' psychology has been exaggerated (ibid.). So, why study Watson?

Four reasons come to mind. The first is that our narrative would be incomplete without him. Watson, for all his faults, was, for a time, the most famous psychologist in the world. His *Behaviourist Manifesto* (1913) was a slow-burning fuse that eventually demolished rival schools and ensured, at least in academic psychology, the hegemony for behaviourism 'over the next fifty years or so' (Moghaddam 2007, p. 79). 'Little Albert' is still the most frequently mentioned experiment in psychology textbooks (Todd 1994). Second, most contemporary textbooks simplify, depoliticise and distort Watson. Nowadays, only three aspects of his work get a hearing: his promotion of objective psychology; his extreme environmentalism; and the 'Little Albert' experiment. But, as I explain below, there is much more to his work. Third, while some reactionaries have the decency to stop burbling after death, others persist in reinforcing capitalism from beyond the grave. I would argue that Watson is still very much with us and continuing to inflict damage through contemporary behaviourism. Finally, it is worth noting that Watson believed in the doctrine of American 'manifest destiny' (Richards 2002, p. 62), an ideology that is being updated by powerful elites in and around Trumpism, as a response to the problems of US capitalism. For all these reasons, it is apt to revisit Watson's contributions.

Situating Johnny boy Watson

> Two behaviourists have sex. One turns to the other and says, 'That was good for you; how was it for me?'
>
> *Anon*

Fascinating characters were shaping the scientific *zeitgeist* at the end of the nineteenth century. There was Jacques Loeb (1859–1924), one of Watson's biology professors, who explained animal behaviour in terms of physical-chemical reactions. He convinced Watson that 'an instinct is a system of chained reflexes' (Watson 1919, p. 234). Moreover, Loeb (and Watson's own harsh religious upbringing) may have been responsible for Watson's strident atheism in adult life, of which more later.

From Ivan Pavlov (1849–1936), who was also doing original research in the 1890s, Watson learned the art of animal experimentation. Pavlov's work on animals is paradoxical. Although many dogs were 'sacrificed' during his experiments, he seems to have genuinely cared for them. According to Harré (2009), he erected a monument 'to the dogs who died in his studies of the mechanism of digestion' and placed great emphasis on healing injuries to his dogs 'as far as the nature of the procedure permits' (ibid., pp. 54 and 151). Years later, Watson would be accused of showing less concern for his human subjects than Pavlov displayed for his dogs.

There were many other intellectual loadstars: Wilhelm Maximillian Wundt (1832–1920), responsible for an artificial separation of philosophy and psychology and one of the key originators of experimental psychology; John Dewey (1859–1952), known as the father of functional psychology, with links to contemporary evolutionary psychology; and Henry Herbert Donaldson (1857–1938), whose pioneering work linked neuroscientific findings with education. Watson learned valuable lessons from all of them.

One key figure in this context is Edward Lee Thorndike (1874–1949), whose theory of connectionism helped to shape educational psychology. Thorndike's early experimental work in animal problem solving showed how learning takes place through what he called 'trial and success'. For Thorndike, mental activity was deemed to be yet another type of behaviour

FIGURE 3.1 John B. Watson

and like overt behaviour it was subject to training (Malone 2014). This position was not extreme enough for Watson who accused Thorndike of mind-body dualism. Although not a fully fledged eugenicist, some of Thorndike's biologically deterministic writings leave a bitter taste: 'One sure service of the able and good is to beget and rear offspring. One sure service (about the only one) which the inferior and vicious can perform is to prevent their genes from survival' (Thorndike, quoted in Malone 2014). As Malone argues, Thorndike's 'mind-body dualism, quasi-biological associationism, and his extreme hereditarianism' suggest that although he was not a behaviourist, nonetheless he was someone who had a decisive impact on Watson's intellectual trajectory.

The existence of this milieu of researchers promoting behavioural analysis and 'objective' psychology at the turn of the twentieth century suggests that we should be cautious in describing Watson as the 'founder of behaviourism'. Remember that he did not make such a claim himself. Perhaps we can follow Malone in referring to him as 'more an exemplar of a movement than a founder' (2014).

Theoretical bravado

The beginning of the twentieth century was marked by a series of flamboyant manifestos. All manner of political adventurists, artistic avant-garde and ne'er-do-wells brought out programmes for the edification of the masses. Another 'terrible' and 'dark' character, Filippo Tommaso Marinetti, wrote the *Futurist Manifesto* in 1909. In it he promised 'to glorify aggressive action, a restive wakefulness, life at the double, the slap and the punching fist' (Marinetti 1909). A left-wing counterpunch was launched by Tristan Tzara in the shape of the *Dada Manifesto* ten years later (Tzara 1918). This was a highly advanced text that prefigures at least some forms of postmodern social science by decades. The following quote underscores subjectivity and empowerment while rejecting universalism and grand narratives:

> A work of art is never beautiful by decree, objectively and for all. Hence criticism is useless, it exists only subjectively, for each man separately, without the slightest character of universality … Dada was born of a need for independence, of a distrust toward unity. Those who are with us preserve their freedom. We recognise no theory.
>
> *(Ibid.)*

I do not know if Johnny boy Watson was stylistically influenced by avant-garde artists but undoubtedly some of the same bravado can be glimpsed in his *Behaviourist Manifesto*. In words that may strike some readers as ominous, he claims: 'Psychology as the behaviourist views it is a purely objective experimental branch of natural science. Its theoretical goal is the prediction and control of behaviour. Introspection forms no essential part of its methods' (Watson 1913). As an aside, and to reinforce one of my central arguments that behaviourism is yet another form of humanistic psychology, let us remember that the phrase 'prediction and control' of behaviour first appeared in an 1892 article by the humanist, William James (Parker 2007, p. 20).

Gradually, Watson's anti-introspectional pronouncements become more explicit:

> [Behaviourism's] elimination of states of consciousness as proper objects of investigation in themselves will remove the barrier from psychology which exists between it and the other sciences. The findings of psychology become the functional correlates of structure and lend themselves to explanation in physico-chemical terms.
>
> *(1913)*

This 'prediction and control' of behaviour was initially to be applied to the fields of education, medicine, law and business (Rakos 2013, p. 99). He later extends the list to include behavioural geography and advertising. In addition, a case has even been made for Watson's continued influence on forensics (Hart and Kritsonis 2006, p. 4). In each field, empirical data were to be applied to solving human and social problems. This amounts to a form of top-down social engineering intended to 'make life better for its citizens' (Rakos 2013, p. 99).

We have to be mindful that Watson's intervention was seen by many at the time as a progressive reaction against 'the eugenic fervor sweeping the United States during the first quarter of the [twentieth] century by espousing an extreme and at times polemical environmentalism' (Rakos 2013). It is in this context that his oft-quoted programmatic boast must be evaluated:

> Give me a dozen healthy infants, well-formed, and my own specified world to bring them up in and I'll guarantee to take any one at random and train him to become any type of specialist I might select – doctor, lawyer, artist, merchant-chief, and yes, even beggar-man and thief, regardless of his talents, penchants, tendencies, abilities, vocations, and

> race of his ancestors. I am going beyond my facts and I admit it, but so have the advocates of the contrary and they have been doing it for many thousands of years.
>
> *(Watson 1924, p. 82)*

I have previously confessed to a weakness for quotes. When compact and rhetorically artful, they tend to demystify issues rather skilfully. But there is a risk inherent in quotology, especially with psychologists like Watson who write for stylistic impact. So, let us take a moment here to clarify his evolving position.

The extreme environmentalism of the above 1924 quote must not obscure the fact that in most of his writings Watson paid close attention to the evolutionary, genetic, biological, instinctual and physiological aspects of behaviour. One of his pupils and a future President of the American Psychological Association, Karl Lashley, goes so far as to claim: 'Anyone who knows American psychology today knows that its value derives from biology and from Watson' (Lashley, quoted in Malone 2014, p. 3).

Watson's basic position was that 'human action as a whole can be divided into *hereditary* modes of response (emotional and instinctive), and *acquired* modes of response (habits)' (Watson, quoted in Rakos 2013, p. 103, emphasis in the original). One quote should suffice:

> Is there nothing then in heredity? How absurd. Certainly, there is. We are born men not kangaroos. We are born with two eyes situated close together, not like fowls and horses where the two eyes, except for a narrow range, never view the same object at the same time.
>
> *(Watson, quoted in Reese 2013, p. 57)*

In today's parlance he was an 'interactionist' (combining biology and environment), with distinct dualistic tendencies (the latter charge would not sit well with Watson who continued to view behaviourism as anti-dualistic).

Another common misunderstanding suggests that Watson denied the existence of mental states. He did not. He merely tried through behaviourism to supersede them, in the same sense that 'chemistry supersedes alchemy' (Watson 1920b, 21 mins). He believed that, as behaviourism broadens and deepens, older concepts such as mental states 'are sucked under, never to reappear' (ibid.). In a rather mechanistic manner, he was drawing attention to an important link between implicit thinking and more explicit talking. However, instead of assessing the complex interplay between thought and language (as, for instance, both Vygotsky and Billig have done), Watson *reduces* thinking to language activity.

What is striking about Watson's analysis and analogies in this 1920 text is how mired he becomes in the principles of Taylorism. He is forever trying to filter out 'useless movements', be it by athletes playing sports, or workers on the assembly line who engage in too many 'inefficient' bodily movements, or individuals who introspectively generate many inexact thoughts before the emergence of precise (and measurable) speech. What he is always searching for is the overt and obvious; everything else including 'meaning' is 'an abstraction, a rationalisation and a speculation serving no useful scientific purpose' (Watson 1920a, section VII). Anyone who resists this behaviourist conclusion is, as far as Watson is concerned, practising mystical self-delusion (ibid., section V).

Laboratory applications: 'Little Albert' and other stories

The 'Little Albert' experiment, as it has become known, is nowadays treated like a long-running detective saga. I am willing to bet my bottom dollar that the type of historian who spends years investigating the unknowns of this case is also an avid reader of Raymond Chandler, James Ellroy and Mickey Spillane. You will be pleased to know that I am more interested in what this case tells us about Watsonian behaviourism and psychology in general, than chasing every lead and uncovering every mystery. Nevertheless, I have tried to validate the minutiae of the case to the best of my ability.

This experiment was first described in Watson and Rayner ([1920] 2000) and there is an audio version of the article available on YouTube. Part of the experiment was even committed to film, again available on YouTube (Watson 1920c).

Watson and Rayner begin with the assumption that in infancy 'the original emotional reaction patterns are few, consisting as far as observed of fear, rage and love' ([1920] 2000, p. 313). What they were really interested in was to show how conditioning increases the range of emotions into adulthood. It is superficial, therefore, to suggest that Watson was not interested in emotions. For him, 'the stimulus-response combinations *are* the emotions and because the combinations are observable, they are *things* called emotions' (Reese 2013, p. 59, italics in original).

However, almost immediately this hypothesis is reduced in scope and ambition to a simple test to see whether they can establish fear in a boy child by making a loud noise whenever he is shown a neutral stimulus (a white rat), and to further study whether this fear could be generalised to other furry objects (such as a rabbit, a dog, a monkey, masks, cotton wool, burning newspaper, etc.), and whether this fear persists in time. They narrate how they wrestled with their conscience before deciding to set up fear reactions experimentally in a child, 'comforting [themselves] by the reflection that such attachments would arise anyway as soon as the child left the sheltered environment of the nursery for the rough and tumble of the home' (Watson and Rayner ([1920] 2000, p. 314).

In the first session of the experiment the rat is presented suddenly but without a loud sound. 'Albert' (as Watson and Rayner call him) tentatively reaches out to touch the rat. Three 'joint stimulation' sessions are conducted when the rat and a loud sound are presented simultaneously. The fifth session is a presentation of the rat alone. Now Albert 'whimpers and withdraws body sharply to the left' (Watson and Rayner ([1920] 2000). Two more joint stimulation sessions are conducted. By the eighth session the rat alone causes Albert to cry and he tries to crawl away. Fear has been established through association. The researchers inform us rather sadistically that they are looking into reducing the necessary number of sessions for successful fear conditioning by increasing the intensity of the noise. The experiment is repeated five days later demonstrating that fear had carried over (ibid., p. 314). Based on this flimsy evidence, Watson and Rayner claim that these conditioned emotional responses 'persist and modify personality throughout life' (ibid., p. 316).

When Albert's mother takes him home prematurely, Watson and Rayner lose the opportunity to study various techniques for removing the conditioned emotional responses (aka 'detachment' or 'reconditioning'). Ironically, this probably worked to Little Albert's advantage, since one technique of reconditioning involved 'showing objects calling out fear responses … and simultaneously stimulating the erogenous zones' (Watson and Rayner ([1920] 2000)! Watson and Rayner speculate that 'We should try first the lips, then the nipples, and as a final resort the sex organs' (ibid.). And if this did not work, the researchers were planning to give Little Albert candies. It is a poignant reflection of both Watson's era of unregulated ethical standards and today's climate of fear and suspicion that what were considered high experimental standards in 1920 might today see the researchers end up in jail.

A meticulous study by James Todd (1994) reveals a wide range of minor and major errors in this experiment as described in psychology textbooks over the years, some of them directly traceable to Watson's misreporting of his own experiments. Minor errors may not alter the narrative too much but one major error conflates the case of Albert 'with a later experiment by Mary Cover Jones (1924) in which a fear response in a child named Peter was removed, thereby producing one study in which Watson and Rayner supposedly conditioned and then deconditioned Albert's fear'. Even prominent psychologists such as Martin Seligman, Joseph Wolpe and Hans Eysenck seem to have 'exaggerated the persistence of the fear reaction established in Albert' (Todd 1994; Harris 1979). Harris has additionally argued that 'one major source of confusion about the Albert story is Watson himself, who altered and deleted important aspects of the study in his many descriptions of it' (ibid., p. 154).

Another line of inquiry has attempted to establish the identity of Little Albert. Beck and Irons (2011) have searched the archives for clues about the real identity of Albert and his mother. Watson burnt a great deal of his notes, thus making the task difficult. After a seven-year search and using census data and interviews with relatives, they traced 'an individual, Douglas Merritte, who shared many characteristics with Little Albert' (ibid., p. 394). If they have identified Albert B. correctly, then Douglas died in 1925 at the age of six as a result of hydrocephalus and convulsions.

Following an even more thorough forensic investigation involving archival research, comparisons of facial similarities, head circumference, body weight and health characteristics, Powell *et al.* (2014) have identified Albert Barger (1919–2007) as a more likely candidate. If they are correct, then Albert Barger did develop 'an aversion to dogs and to animals in general' (ibid., p. 609). His aversion is described more as a dislike of animals than a phobia. His dislike of dogs may be related to having lost a dog in an accident as a child (ibid., p. 610). Relatives described Albert Barger as easy-going individual which suggests that the experiment had no adverse effect on his personality.

Instead of spending so much energy investigating a poorly designed and poorly reported experiment, perhaps we should turn the tables and ask: why do so many psychologists become obsessed with the forensic elements of the Little Albert experiment? Beck and Irons have suggested a few reasons, two of which are noteworthy. They rightly claim that when it comes to this experiment, 'there is a lack of closure' (2011, p. 395). We are, after all, storytelling social animals and seem to have a preference for classical closure, although many of us have adapted to the joys of postmodern non-closure as well. Personally, I am still raging about the mysterious ending of *The*

Sopranos! Additionally, it is also true that 'for many psychologists, the Little Albert study is one of the first investigations that they learn about. We tend to value those early experiences that brought us into the discipline' (ibid.).

These are valid points but insufficient in themselves for explaining the enduring appeal of the study. The top-down engineering of behaviourism requires an equally top-down official origin story to cement it. Ben Harris has referred to this as 'social science folklore', 'myth making' (1979, p. 151), and 'celebratory [Whiggish] history' (ibid. 1997, p. 22). Whiggish histories of psychology present the rise of various bourgeois forms of psychology as inevitable and as part of the trajectory of positivist science. Failures are brushed under the carpet and partial successes are hoisted as proof of epistemological and methodological superiority. But, as Harris reminds us 'Albert's fear was difficult to induce [as well as] transitory ...' (ibid., p. 23). A more serious problem for behaviourists, which often goes under-reported, is 'the failure of Watson's contemporaries to replicate his work' (ibid. 1979, p. 155). For example, 'English (1929) obtained no fear conditioning in more than 50 trials with a loud sound' (Reese 2013, p. 60).

As Samelson has reminded us, this process of myth making arises 'largely as a by-product of pedagogy: as a means to elucidate the *concepts* of a scientific speciality, to establish *its tradition*, and to attract students' (1974, p. 223, emphasis in the original). Again, I feel that this explanation is valid but insufficient. It may partially explain why myths originate in psychology, but it does not tell us why they persist. At the risk of getting myself into further trouble, I propose that in reactionary times, such as those we are living through, an unholy alliance is forged between weaker, reactionary teachers and weaker, reactionary students. Both of these groups have an interest in seeing simple, unencumbered success stories that bring prestige to their profession. Complex storytelling that may expose one's educational shortcomings is therefore shunned and avoided. A capitalist crisis promotes 'fake psychologists' who then set about regurgitating convenient myths to 'Make Psychology Great Again'.

Post-university applications: The Mad Man of advertising

> I had a job drilling holes for water – it was well boring.
>
> *Leo Kearse*

It gives me no satisfaction to note the number of prominent psychologists who have gravitated towards the world of advertising – a profession that plays a pivotal role in the survival of capitalism. Advertising fulfils a number of general and specific functions: it completes the production-distribution-consumption cycle, thus realising value, a process essential for restarting the next phase of capital accumulation; it also discovers and maps human 'needs'; beyond 'needs' for survival and prosperity, advertising attempts to create new 'desires' in order to bolster profit margins and capital's image; finally, advertising regulates competition within the ruling class by ensuring the 'survival of the fittest' or, if not the 'fittest', then at least the 'survival of the most suave'.

To continue with my theme of underscoring the common ground between behaviourism and other major schools of psychology, a brief comparison of Edward Bernays and Watson can be instructive. Both psychoanalysis and behaviourism shared the conviction that 'much of human activity is motivated by forces outside our consciousness' (Frances 2017). However, both were also convinced that a great deal of these seemingly random behaviours could be predicted and even changed.

Edward Louis Bernays (1891–1995) was Freud's nephew. He has become known alternatively as the father of modern propaganda, or public relations or spin (depending on your view). Bernays 'made his fortune combining and applying the psychoanalytic concept of the unconscious, Pavlov's behaviourism, and group psychology to improve corporate balance sheets' ([1928] 2004). He viewed his task as the manipulation of habits and opinions of the masses through an 'invisible government which is the true ruling power of [the] country' (ibid., pp. 9–10). So, for example, in the 1930s Joseph Goebbels took inspiration from Bernays for his propaganda schemes. In 1954 Bernays helped the United Fruit Company to overthrow the legitimate government of Guatemala by creating non-existent fears about Russian influence.

Bernays's daughter recounts how her father viewed the masses as 'stupid' (Curtis 2002, Part 1), and how he set about 'engineering their consent'. One famous example was his rebranding of Lucky Strike cigarettes as Torches of Freedom in order to get around the male-imposed taboo of female smoking (Frances 2017). This rebranding took the form of a prearranged performance during a New York Easter Day Parade. He instructed a group of 'rich debutantes' to light a cigarette at a given signal and informed the media about a supposed group of suffragettes who had planned a protest (Curtis 2002, 12 mins). The media took the bait and publicised the 'protest'. Many years later the Situationist Internationalists would refer to such bourgeois stunts as 'recuperation', the process by which radical ideas are turned upside-down, co-opted and commodified in order to strengthen capitalism (Knabb 2007).

Following what is coyly referred to as an extra-marital affair, Watson was forced to resign from his professorship at Johns Hopkins University at the age of forty-two. In 1920, drummed out of academia, he embarked on a successful advertising career which lasted until his retirement in 1945. Watson extended Bernays's efforts to boost cigarette-smoking among women by persuading them that 'smoking was sexy so long as they used Pebeco toothpaste' (Francis 2017). He is alleged to have said that 'it can be just as thrilling to watch the growth of a sales curve of a new product as to watch the learning curve of animals and men' (Watson, quoted in Larson 1979, p. 3). Watson 'would visit successful retailers and find out what products were selling best and why by personal interviews' (ibid., p. 5). He presented his findings in 'countless lectures to business executives on the application of behaviouristic psychology to business and industry' (ibid.). Realising that customers purchase more items nearer the checkout, he advised that more items should be placed strategically there in order to promote 'impulse buying'.

His advertising techniques skewed facts for early behaviourist formulations around emotions. He used fear, love and, to a lesser extent, anger to sell products. According to Conliffe (2016), Watson's campaign for Johnson's baby powder emphasised that the powder was 'pure' and 'clean' (the love angle), but failure to use it 'exposed children to the risk of infection' (the fear angle). Many of today's adverts aimed at children are influenced by the behaviourist belief in children as 'clean slates'. Other influences can still be seen in the 'drip-drip' philosophy in advertising, in which 'consistent repetition of a message conditions the consumer to buy the product advertised' (Duncan 2007).

Going beyond Watson

> A Russian and an American are sentenced to Hell. The Devil summons them and says: 'Guys, you have two options: an American or a Russian Hell. In the American one you can do what you want, but you'll have to eat a bucket of shit every morning. The Russian one is the same, but it's two buckets.' The Yankee quickly makes up his mind and goes to American Hell, while the Russian eventually chooses the Russian one. In a week or so they meet. The Russian asks: 'So, what's it like out there?' 'Exactly what the Devil said, the Hell itself is OK, but eating a bucket of shit is killing me. And you?' 'Ah, it feels just like home – either the shit doesn't get delivered or there aren't enough buckets for everyone!'
>
> *Old Russian joke*

Dear reader, would you like to become the smartest person in the room? You can ooze smarts in the time it takes you to read and digest this section. Honest! Just follow the crumbs.

QUESTION: Why did behaviourism emerge at more or less the same time (1910s–1920s) in two supposedly different societies, capitalist USA and communist USSR? In other words, why did the Russian Pavlov and Blonsky gain traction at more or less the same time as Watson and Skinner?

(NOT-SO-SMART) ANSWER: Well, that's a very decent question, mate. *Excellente!* You're right, of course. The USA was capitalist at the time and the USSR communist. Good. I'm glad that's sorted!

(SMART) ANSWER: The mainstream narrative we receive from imbecilic politicians, journalists and historians is marked by inconsistencies, omissions and elisions. We are repeatedly told that the USA and USSR were fundamentally different entities, and hence in ideological conflict with each other. Capitalism, we are assured, promotes individuality and communism suppresses individuality in favour of a homogenous collectivity. Capitalism is about freedom and communism is a dictatorship as exemplified by the USSR or present-day China.The abovementioned not-so-smart response is 'common-sense' tautology, as well as being woefully inaccurate. The problem is related to how we characterise entities and it is essential that we get this characterisation right whether we are assessing political ideology or dealing with mental distress. Therapists and counsellors dealing with mental health issues seem to have a choice between the description of the problem (aka formulation), categorisation of the symptoms (aka labelling), or a combination of description and categorisation.

Let's apply the same choices to behaviourism in the USA and the USSR by temporarily suspending labels such as 'capitalist' and 'communist'. If we set these labels aside, and focus instead on formulation, we immediately notice a set of deep-seated commonalities between the USA and the USSR in this time frame:

- Both were class societies (although the USSR ruling class liked to pretend otherwise).
- Both societies operated on the basis of money exchange and private property (although in the USSR entrepreneurial property was confiscated by the state).

- Rulers controlled the 'means of production and distribution' (with the exception of a few weeks in 1917 in some parts of the USSR, and the occasional Industrial Workers of the World agitation in the USA, when workers took control).
- Rulers extracted 'surplus value' from workers (i.e. rural and urban workers were 'exploited').
- There was 'general commodity production' and the 'law of value' in both societies.
- There was 'commodity fetishism' in both.
- There was 'alienation' in both.
- There was sexism, racism and homophobia in both accentuated and elaborated by capitalism.
- There was hierarchy in both.
- There were similar 'social and technical divisions of labour' in both.
- There was massive rural to urban migration in both.
- The state played a decisive role in capital accumulation in both.
- The state was the guarantor of the 'dictatorship of time and space' over its citizens in both.
- The church played a vital role in legitimising the status quo in both.

We seem to have reached a paradox. We have described two fundamentally similar societies which have been given divergent labels by experts and mainstream commentators. How do we proceed? Well, one way would be to assume that our detailed description of the USA and the USSR is accurate and that the labels attached to them are inaccurate. I am suggesting that we assume that the USSR was neither socialist nor communist but, in reality, yet another form of capitalism. If we follow this road, the similar formulations make perfect sense.

But is there any evidence to substantiate all of this? Well, actually yes, plenty of evidence. In fact, I can easily bore you with a list of prominent twentieth-century revolutionaries who classified the USSR as capitalist: Michael Bakunin, Emma Goldman, Sylvia Pankhurst, Anton Pannekoek, Guy Aldred, Karl Korsch, Herman Gorter, Otto Rühle, Paul Mattick, Guy Debord, Cornelius Castoriades, Amadeo Bordiga, Freddy Perlman, C. L R. James, Chattopadhyay, etc.

Come on now, you must have heard of at least one or two of these geezers? If not, through the magic of the Internet, you are a click away from discovering a highly intelligent alternative interpretation. Some of these individuals referred to the USSR as 'state capitalism', some called it 'bureaucratic capitalism' or even 'totalitarian capitalism', and some preferred 'backward capitalism' (Fernandez 1997). But all would agree with most of the commonalities between the USA and the USSR cited above.

What are the implications of all this? Huge, of course. If valid, it makes a nonsense of the propaganda we have been fed by both 'western' and 'eastern' news agencies for decades. The eastern ruling class benefited greatly throughout the twentieth century by pretending to be communist, and on the side of the people. Every shortcoming and flaw in the system could be brushed aside, since a 'communist paradise' was being built. Likewise, western rulers could point to a 'backward' capitalist state such as the USSR, East Germany or 'plucky little Albania' and ask their own citizens: 'Is this utopia? Is this really what you want? Cars that don't run, empty shops without essentials or luxuries, leaky condoms and curtailed public freedoms? If not, then please stop your strikes, protests and rebellions. Please go back to work and remember, *you've never had it so good*'! 'Communist USSR' was a convenient lie for both sets of rulers. The competition that existed between them between the 1910s and the 1980s was the rivalry of two capitalist nation-states vying to outdo one other, and not the rivalry of two fundamentally different belief systems.

Now take another look at the list above and reflect on how behaviourism can be viewed as the perfect ideology for justifying every inequity and for policing every transgression. Behaviourism's predilection for social engineering from above was the perfect mechanism for achieving bourgeois command and control in both societies. It permitted the state to atomise the people and control them like clockwork. Fordism and Taylorism could be introduced as 'progress'. Hierarchies could be legitimised as 'natural'. The division of labour could be entrenched as 'inevitable'. Under the directives of behaviourism, human emotion, discourse and behaviour can be effectively policed for signs of malcontent. These are some of the reasons behind behaviourism's dominance over all other forms of psychology from around the 1910s to the 1950s in both the USA and the USSR.

Now, take a deep breath, have your 'aha moment' and smile smugly – for you are now the smartest person in the room! And way, way smarter than most academics who are still bleating on about 'communist' USSR! Feels good being this smart, don't it?

Concluding thoughts: contemporary Watsonian behaviourism

It is convenient to think of Watsonian behaviourism as passé. It is a convenience that many critical psychologists have made use of for far too long.

The truth is, in the landscape of social science, only the good die young; the bad may take an enforced leave of absence, but they always return with a healthy suntan and a self-satisfied smile.

There are a number of prestigious journals conducting research on 'neo-behaviourism': the *Journal of Applied Behavior Analysis*; the *Journal of Health and Social Behavior*; the *Journal of Behavior Therapy and Experimental Psychiatry*; the *Journal of Early and Intensive Behavior Intervention*; and the *European Journal of Behavior Analysis*. Not all can be called Watsonian, but his influence lingers on.

Most of these journals are based in the USA. However, Watson's influence has been more widespread. For example, I was surprised to find the deep footprints left by behaviourism in China. Huyanfeng (2011) has written about the dissemination of behaviourism in modern China. The key figure was Kuo Zing-Yang (1898–1970). He promoted an extreme form of behaviourism and rejected Watson's concessions to instinct and heredity (Huyanfeng 2011, p. 127). He is on record as boasting: 'There are only one and a half true behaviourists in the word; Watson is the half. I am the only true behaviourist' (Kuo Zing-Yang, quoted in Reese 2013, p. 50). I mention this to emphasise that behaviourism has been a global ideology and its narrative should not be restricted to the USA and the USSR alone.

Watson's early animal experiments have had an enduring impact on comparative psychology. Dewsbury recounts how Watson 'found his rats to be remarkably resilient in their abilities to learn even after he removed one or more senses. Rotation of the maze disrupted performance and Watson concluded that kinesthetic sensations were critical to maze learning' (Dewsbury 2013, p. 17). To his credit, Watson correctly observed how his monkeys displayed a far richer and more spontaneous repertoire of behaviour in the field compared with those in the laboratory (ibid.). The process-oriented animal research, which is also sometimes referred to as neo-behaviourism, was derived from Watson's behaviourism (ibid., p. 22). Even pervasive techniques of childminding such as the 'time out' and the 'naughty step' have their origins in Watson's ground-breaking experiments.

Lack of time and space has prevented me from taking a close look at neo-behaviourism and 'behaviourology'. I would like to take this opportunity, however, to encourage those interested to follow up on these currents. Neo-behaviourism can be pursued in Fredrick Toates's biography of B. F. Skinner (Toates 2009). Toates is an admirer of Skinner rather than a mindless fan, and he has penned a sensible and erudite life story of Skinner. If I had to classify Toates's politics I would hazard a guess that he is a classic nineteenth-century liberal, with distinct twentieth-century social democratic tendencies. He is more of a cognitive-behavioural-biopsychologist than a strict Skinnerean. Reading through this text, it occurs to me that if Watson's classical conditioning represents Taylorist and Fordist mechanisms of efficiency within capitalism, then Skinner's operant conditioning corresponds to a more sophisticated post-Taylorist and post-Fordist upgrade. Behaviourology has been ably defended by Jerome D. Ulman. I remain unconvinced by some of his assertions regarding Marx, Pannekoek, Skinner and Darwin but encourage the reader to make up their own mind (Ulman 1996).

In the end, two factors characterise Watsonian behaviourism above all else: *fear* and *elitism*. Fear is a response to life's unpredictability and the ever-present potential of proletarian non-conformity. This fear acts as a silent motivating factor lurking in the background of Watson's directives. It is a pernicious influence as strong as the fear felt by Gustave Le Bon following the Paris Commune of 1871.

Elitism manifests itself epistemologically as well as moralistically when Watson proposes positivist experimental psychology as the bedrock of his programme to socially engineer society from above. I don't believe that I am exaggerating when I say that he considered this the birthright of scientists. Everything must be simplified, reduced, operationalised, regulated and, when necessary, disciplined so that capitalism can continue to function smoothly and predictably. This explains why he gradually moved from the messiness of field research into the safer, more regulated environment of the laboratory (Reese 2013, p. 57).

The most significant weakness within Watsonian behaviourism remains his definition of 'social'. As a generalisation, for Watson, the social is first reduced to the 'environment' then further reduced to the 'situation' and further still to 'stimuli-response' combinations and finally to 'observable stimuli-response'. By the time this process is completed, hardly anything is left of the social!

4

MASLOW AND PEAK CAPITALISM

Political biography

A few years back I remember searching Google for images relating to Maslow in preparation for a lecture, and being pleasantly surprised to find that he did not resemble a pyramid! Then it hit me that after years of study-teaching psychology, the only thing I really knew about the man was his 'hierarchical pyramid of needs'. In fact, I have not been able to find this pyramid in any of his original published work and must assume that the illustration was created by a friend, student or publisher (Kremer and Hammond 2013 seem to concur).

Anthropologists are fond of asking: what can the ziggurats tell us about Mesopotamian civilisations? What can the pyramids at Giza tell us about the pharaohs? So maybe a good starting point for psychologists would be to ask: what can the 'pyramid of needs' tell us about Maslow and 'humanistic psychology'?

The first thing that strikes one about Abraham Harold Maslow (1908–1970) is his acute need to belong and his preoccupation with finding his place in the scheme of things. Throughout his life, and despite considerable academic achievements, he remained somewhat of an outsider, looking in. I don't think it is fanciful to suggest that this ambivalent position was due mainly to various (invisible) class and (visible) 'race' barriers.

His parents were first-generation working-class 'Jewish immigrants who fled from Czarist persecution in the early 20th century' (*Wikipedia*, 'Abraham Maslow'). His childhood and youth were spent in a working-class neighbourhood in New York. He referred to himself as a 'slum boy' (Zweig and Bennis 1968, 12 mins). He often had to run the gauntlet of anti-Semitic gangs who would throw rocks at him (Hoffman 1988, p. 9). This street racism was augmented by the professional racism of his teachers and professors. Maslow reminisces rather poignantly about this in a documentary (Zweig and Bennis 1968, 14 mins). Quite understandably, books and libraries became a refuge for the young Maslow, and allowed him the space to give shape to his convictions about economic and racial justice. In his own words,

> I grew up on the American revolution, you see … Thomas Jefferson was a hero for me … then one of my teachers introduced me to Upton Sinclair … and thinking of socialism, which was also by the way the Jewish tradition … social justice … there was always the hope that it was never considered unrealistic to work for a better world.
>
> *(Ibid., 24–25 mins)*

Although he thought of the USA as a 'fine culture' and a society to which he was 'perpetually grateful', he was also aware of the limitations of nationalism. In the same documentary, Maslow displays his internationalist credentials when he argues that 'the Good Society now has to be one world, it just has to be or it won't work. Nationalism is dead, although it doesn't know it yet' (Zweig and Bennis 1968, 2 mins).

Ironically, I would argue that the same humanistic urge for a Better Society that he was espousing towards the end of his life motivated his early dalliance with behaviourism. Maslow was impressed not just with behaviourism's experimental rigour, but also its social engineering capabilities. As the historian Jessica Grogan has put it,

> he fell in love with behaviourism in the thirties and he thought of it as the most exciting thing ever … he studied monkeys in Harry Harlow's lab … he had the idea that … behaviourism could solve all the problems of the world.
>
> *(Grogan speaking on Oppenheimer 2013, 1–2 mins)*

Dennis Fox (1985) claims that this Better Society was nourished by Maslow's sympathies for anarchism. If so, this influence was intermittent and was characterised by the usual anaemic interpretation of anarchism popular among swathes of US bohemians – more Henry David Thoreau than Emma Goldman. Let us not forget that Maslow was extremely critical of both Stalinism and the anti-Stalinist New Left. He was keen on big reformist ideas but never became involved in the nitty-gritty of political activism. Once he was famous, many 'enlightened' capitalists and corporations sought his advice on management issues. Following the Soviet Union's launch of Sputnik in 1957, Maslow's views on fostering creativity in education and the workplace became de rigueur (Hoffman 1988, pp. 236–237). He adapted the anthropologist Ruth Benedict's concept of *synergy* for business to show how capital and labour can work together (ibid., p. 270).

I venture that it would be more accurate to describe Maslow's vision as a worldwide social democratic form of governance, with marked liberal, romantic and transcendentalist tendencies. His entire output can be described as an attempt to write a liberal counter-argument to Marx's *The Communist Manifesto*. His break with behaviourism and eventual 'founding' of humanistic psychology should be more meaningfully interpreted as a 'perspective-shift' rather than a 'paradigm-shift', since he retained his early aim of improving humanity through modernist, liberal and social democratic principles.

In some ways Maslow could be described as courageous and non-conformist. However, his insecurities also created a dependency on strong parental figures who aided him throughout his career. He humorously recounts a story about his first 'sugar daddy', Edward Lee Thorndike:

> [He] rescued me … [and] made me feel important because he promised to support me for the rest of my life, even if I couldn't get a job, and he said … 'though I dislike your work' … I was working with sex and dominance [at the time] and what he thought were unpleasant subjects.
>
> *(Maslow speaking on Zweig and Bennis 1968, 9–10 mins)*

The psychotherapist Alfred Adler (1870–1937), the anthropologist Ruth Benedict (1887–1948), and the gestalt psychologist Max Wertheimer (1880–1943) became ego-ideal figures at various stages of Maslow's life.

These figures became more central to his research after he left the University of Wisconsin for New York in 1935. There he became fascinated by 'unusually strong' and 'lofty' people and began taking field notes while hanging around them. Realising the dearth of literature on healthy people and the

FIGURE 4.1 Abraham Maslow

positive aspects of personality, he began to switch his attention from 'abnormal psychology' to what is known today as 'positive psychology'. As he explains it in an interview, one day this 'wonderful click happens when the two descriptions melted into one and there was a theory, there was generalisation. It was no longer a hobby or a casual observation' (Maslow speaking on Shostrom

1971, 1–2 mins). The more he observed these 'lofty' people, the more coherent the patterns became. He then tied in these results with his heroes from the past, Jefferson, Lincoln and Einstein. However, since he did not deem his observations to be 'scientific', he was reluctant to publish the results until 1942. In his own words, 'I wasn't emancipated yet from a certain conception of science that I had learned from my work with animals, with learning and conditioning and so on' (ibid., 6 mins).

Maslow was still being the outsider, but this time he was looking into the lives and phenomenology of the bourgeois and petty bourgeois elites. It is, moreover, conceivable that he believed that by writing about them he would come to exert a measure of control over them.

The development of Maslow's ideas

In one sense Maslow's perspective-shift from behaviourism to humanism was very significant. Under the influence of the Gestaltist Wertheimer, Maslow called for an anti-reductionist psychology which addresses values and meanings (Richards 2002, p. 83). His humanistic approach was laced with existentialism since it equipped individuals with personal choice and self-direction (Thomson 2009, pp. 132–133). At the same time he was aiming to go beyond orthodox Freudianism. In a famous debate with Carl Rogers and Rollo May, Maslow explained his approach in these terms:

> [I]n part [existential psychology] represents a revolt and a dissatisfaction [against behaviourism and Freudianism] … both of these have played themselves out … we've squeezed all the juice out of these two big systems … and there is nothing terribly exciting happening anymore in these two fields.
>
> *(Maslow 1962, 3 mins)*

He still respected Freud but his compliments were becoming decidedly backhanded. In the same debate he claims that '[Freudianism] doesn't give a tall enough picture of the human being, some excellent psychopathology, it gives us a picture of what's wrong with us, it's a very good theology of evil you might say', but it does not make a place for all those human attributes we value most (Maslow 1962, 6–7 mins). In other words, 'it is as if Freud supplied us the sick half of psychology and we must now fill it out with the healthy half' (ibid. 1968, p. 5). Maslow, unlike some existential psychologists, was not rejecting Freudianism *in toto*; rather, he was adding to it and supplementing it. He blames some of Freud's pessimism on his trials and tribulations, including his cancer: 'Freud was a disappointed and unhappy old man ... maybe the cancer did it' (ibid., 18 mins).

What is left out of the picture as far as Freud is concerned is people's desire to realise their full potential, or as Maslow put it, to 'self-actualise'. Once their lower physiological and safety needs have been met, the individual can seek out friendship, sexual intimacy and self-esteem. Maslow's highest level of achievement (self-actualisation) is a list of bourgeois values that most secular and religious members of the elite can sign up to without a solicitor: acceptance of facts, problem-solving, creativity and morality. As one moves up the pyramid, societal restraints become fewer and our 'innate capacity' to be good blossoms. Or, as he puts it in his own enigmatic words, 'How good a society does human nature permit? How good a human nature does society permit?' (Maslow 1971, p. 212). Note that this dilemma is an updated version of the transcendentalist discussion of the inherent goodness of human nature, which is deemed to have become corrupted by social institutions.

In 1938 Maslow joined a small group of colleagues on an anthropological study of the Blackfoot tribe in Alberta, Canada. He learned a great deal from this encounter. His tests of 'ego-security' did not work well with these subjects because, unlike the urbanised American students the tests were calibrated on, the 'Indians' seemed to be very 'ego-secure'. They defined wealth in a radically different way to most 'Westerners'. Instead of seeing it as commodity production, the Blackfoots viewed wealth as generosity and support based on a gift economy (what anthropologists refer to as 'potlatch'). This chimed with Maslow's social democratic beliefs in the redistribution of wealth. He was also deeply impressed by their child-rearing skills and their use of humour to diffuse tension within the tribe (Hoffman 1988, pp. 111–128).

Maslow is to be commended for tackling big philosophical issues, something that most contemporary psychologists try to avoid. Later in his life, and partly under the impact of his experiences with the Blackfoot tribe and the writings of Frankl, he added a sixth level to his hierarchy called 'self-transcendence'. This new level was meant to move us from independent individuals to an interdependent society (Guest 2014). In Maslow's words, 'The fully developed (and very fortunate) human being, working under the best conditions tends to be motivated by values which transcend his self. They are not selfish anymore in the old sense of that term' (Maslow 1969, p. 4). However, this sixth level remained sketchy and 'spiritual'.

Overall, I think it is fair to suggest that most of the time Maslow was turning our attention away from social relations of production and institutions tasked with maintaining the status quo (which throughout this book I have called the 'extra-psychological' dimension), and also away from the convoluted interactions between individuals (the 'inter-psychological' dimension). His own words can clarify things:

> [W]e've had many centuries of looking to external sources, external hopes for our value systems and I think that practically all of them turn out to be failures and now we have no place to turn but inward into human nature, into the individual ... and into experience.
>
> *(Maslow 1962, 8 mins)*

It is this intra-psychological focus that cements Maslow's mainstream modernist credentials, regardless of whether it comes in the shape of the early Maslow (still under the sway of Freudianism and behaviourism), or the mature Maslow (the fully fledged phenomenologist, existentialist and humanist).

Using examples from literature and film, he expresses ideas that chime with Frankl's 'will to meaning' (see Chapter 6 in this volume). Maslow compares Tolstoy's *The Death of Ivan Ilyich* ([1886] 2010) with Akira Kurosawa's film, *Ikiru* (1952), which is partly inspired by Tolstoy's novella, with one crucial difference. For Maslow, the life and death of Ivan Ilyich is meaningless. When Ivan realises that his illness is terminal, he initially blames his family for their lack of sensitivity and rebukes life for dealing him a cruel hand. Although in the last days of his life he comes to distinguish between his own 'artificial life' and the joys of an 'authentic life', he does not get the chance to leave behind a meaningful legacy. By contrast, the protagonist of Kurosawa's film makes a choice to bury his artificial bureaucratic life. He seeks meaning in life by building a playground for the local children. Having accomplished his plans, he dies with good grace (Maslow 1968, 75–77 mins). Maslow argues that these philosophical issues that were once the exclusive domain of religion could nowadays be discussed under the aegis of existential psychology. Warming to his theme, he even goes on to argue that the cleavage which existed between theism and atheism in the USA during the 1920s–1930s is no longer insurmountable (ibid., 78 mins).

Contemporary applications

Maslow sometimes displayed very definite ideas about the purview of psychological investigation. He once wrote, 'But then let us *not* study cripples, but the closest thing we can get to whole, healthy men ... In a certain sense, only the saints *are* mankind. All the rest are cripples' (Maslow, quoted in Hoffman 1988, p. 173, emphasis in the original). When I started investigating the current applications of Maslow's ideas, I was struck by both their breadth and, sadly, also their superficiality. For instance, most forms of humanistic organisational psychology start with Maslow's 'hierarchy of needs' (commonly defined as physiological, safety, love/belonging, esteem and self-actualisation). Business managers seem to be very fond of applying this 'tool' to workplace issues in order to motivate workers. A number of journals of business and management studies with questionable credentials seem to be spearheading Maslow's revival.

The five levels of the pyramid have been redefined by Tanner (2018) in terms of labour-capital points of contention. The sixth level ('intrinsic values') is usually left out of business applications (Guest 2014). The lowest level, 'physiological needs', now becomes survival based on adequate wages and stable employment. Once this need is met, 'security needs' revolve around benefits, pensions and a safe work environment. 'Belongingness' is now understood as cooperation on the job and identifying with the company; 'esteem needs' can be accrued through job titles, nice workspaces and prestigious job assignments. Finally, management must meet 'self-actualisation needs', which allow workers to gain workplace autonomy and expert status.

The enduring popularity of Maslow's model has been explained by Wendy Hollway in these terms:

> Maslow addressed the problem of alienation at a time of affluence … [his] concept of a hierarchy of needs was taken up [within organisational psychology] in contrast to models of economic man which assumed that workers were only interested in money.
>
> *(1998, p. 31)*

This statement needs to be qualified, since the notion of an 'affluent society' is still being exaggerated to this day. I think it may be more germane to say that this affluence was only meaningful in absolute terms (i.e. compared to previous generations of workers), and not relative to the capital amassed by the ruling class. Moreover, it was an 'affluence' restricted in time and space – to the USA and a few other western societies, between World War II and the capitalist crises of the 1960s. Of course, even by the early 1950s managers in some industries were already issuing warnings about falling productivity. Some of these problems were addressed by Douglas McGregor in *The Human Side of Enterprise* ([1960] 2006), 'which contrasted traditional managerial styles with a people-centred approach inspired by Maslow' (Kremer and Hammond 2013). In the 1960s the crisis spread to more sectors of the economy.

To his credit, Maslow had anticipated the flaws of purely modernist methods of production somewhat earlier in 1943. He understood instinctively that in order for motivation (and productivity) to increase, workers must be treated as more than inanimate objects. Workers had to gain satisfaction once more from seeing a product completed. The assembly line had to be abolished in favour of smaller work units. Fordism and Taylorism needed to give way to something else, and this something else came, in time, to be known as post-Fordism and post-Taylorism. As can be seen from Tanner's contribution above and McGregor's book, the hierarchy of needs captures this shift rather well. Post-Taylorism and post-Fordism are better at tapping people's creative potential (Krueger 2013), and creativity is a key component of self-actualisation because as Maslow put it, 'a musician must make music, an artist must paint, a poet must write, if he is to be ultimately happy … what a man can be, he must be' (1943).

The hierarchy has also been operationalised for assessing student needs within the educational sector. The arguments are similar to those of Tanner shown above. First, ensure that all students have sufficient food, clothing and shelter. The 1946 National School Lunch Act, signed by President Truman, was a state-wide intervention aimed at improving the diet of the next generation of American wage-slaves. Next, create a safe space for learning, and encourage social affiliation through teamwork. Promote self-esteem in students through positive feedback. Finally, facilitate self-actualisation by creating students who 'want to be all they can be' and 'give back' to the larger 'community' (Jones, 2017; Hanson, 2018; Kline, 2018). This liberal model of teaching must be seen as both a motivational tool for students as well as feel-good ideology for teachers. Its prescriptions seem sensible enough, when viewed in isolation. Who can possibly argue against well-fed students, clean bathrooms and a safe learning environment? Why shouldn't students aim to develop their full potential?

The problem is not with specifics but how a tick-box approach to teaching sidelines bigger issues such as what exactly are we teaching? Who exactly are we teaching? And why exactly are we teaching? The focus on pragmatics serves to obscure history and telos. Some of these Maslow-inspired pedagogic slogans ('actualise your potential', 'be all that you can be' 'be spontaneous' and 'be creative') are so vague that they can be adapted to serve not just classic liberalism, but almost any ideology. Furthermore, they paint an abstract landscape of individuals free from poverty, class conflict, racism, sexism and homophobia. There are similarities with the *Star Trek* version of capitalism, especially in the early *Original* and *TNG* series. Here, liberal humanism and humanistic psychology work together to develop perfectly rounded experts who endeavour to better themselves while upholding Gene Roddenberry's vision of a shiny, modernist, liberal utopia (Gregory 2000, p. 145).

We can point to a number of recent studies in this regard. Jackson et al. (2014) have applied Maslow's hierarchy to improve patient care in intensive care units, especially with regard to issues surrounding sedation, delirium and early mobility. The pyramid can be further utilised as an organisational tool for bringing together an interdisciplinary team of specialists (physicians, nurses, physical therapists, psychiatrist, social workers, family and patient). This patient-centred approach presents a holistic care programme for patients. It is hoped that it will improve both survival rates and quality of life following patient discharge.

Henwood *et al.* (2015) have developed a similar programme, this time using Maslow's hierarchy to help adults with serious mental health illnesses who have experienced homelessness. Interestingly, Henwood *et al.* question a strict hierarchical interpretation of the pyramid, '[for those enrolled in the programme] … a focus on self-actualisation seems to occur when more basic needs were not met, which supports Maslow's later hypothesis that *being needs may emerge from the frustration, not fulfillment, of basic needs*' (ibid., emphasis added).

Humanistic counselling has also taken advantages of the pyramid's clear guiding protocols. Lonn and Dantzler (2017) have applied Maslow's pyramid to the counselling needs of refugees and asylum seekers in the USA. They claim that the approach is particularly fruitful for dealing with post-migration displacement and acculturation problems with humanistic sensitivity.

The pattern that is emerging in recent research suggests that complicated long-term care situations involving a multidisciplinary approach could benefit from Maslow's framework. It provides a common language and well-established demarcation lines for specialists, allowing each to take the leading role at the appropriate phase of the rehabilitation process. It also facilitates feedback from the client who can see their own progress and make adjustments accordingly.

In passing let me also mention that there has been suggestive evidence from neuroscience and evolutionary biology for Maslow's pyramid of needs.

Kenrick *et al.* (2010) have argued that 'the basic foundational structure of the pyramid is worth preserving, but that it should be buttressed with a few architectural extensions' in order to bring it up to date with the latest thinking in modern evolutionary theory. Others, from a humanistic perspective, have also modified the order of his hierarchy (Neher 1991). The pyramid has become less unidirectional and rigid under the impact of relativism. Furthermore, it has been pointed out that the definition of various needs alters with time, context and culture. In fact, it is fair to say, Maslow foresaw most of these objections. His own writing was far less rigid than the visual metaphor of a pyramid might suggest.

Maslow, positive psychology and the happiness industry

One sunny Sunday afternoon I decided to carry out a piece of research. I would watch two film versions of a famous Roald Dahl story back to back: the 1971 Gene Wilder version entitled *Willy Wonka & the Chocolate Factory*; and the 2005 update, starring Johnny Depp, entitled *Charlie and the Chocolate Factory*. The plan was to compare the treatment of the Oompa Loompas in the films and to see if there is a clear transition from Taylorist to post-Taylorist methods of management. Unfortunately, an extraneous variable in the shape of cheap but delicious Peruvian wine put paid to that experiment. By the time Willy had begun his tour of the chocolate factory, I had chosen to abandon my own research in favour of a catnap. However, in what must be an example of learning while asleep, these lines have forever been seared into my memory: 'Oompa Loompa doompadee dah / If you're not spoiled then you will go far / *You will live in happiness too* / Like the Oompa Loompa doompadee do' (*Willy Wonka & the Chocolate Factory*, 1971, dir. Mel Stuart, emphasis added). Wage-slavery is thus made synonymous with 'happiness'!

Precisely because I am an Oompa Loompa, occupying the lowest ranks within academia, for some time I have been obsessed with certain goals. For example, I yearn for a jacuzzi. I no longer know if this is a basic Maslowian 'need' or a capitalist-induced 'desire' and, frankly, I don't care. A jacuzzi will make me happy!

I have eccentric sexual fantasies involving celebrities I will never meet (there is a particularly disturbing one involving Billie Jean King – go figure)! Of course, I keep all this to myself, and these fantasies make me happy.

There is a certain Premier League football team I support. Sometimes they play gloriously (brining me close to a Maslowian 'peak experience'), and sometimes they become 'spursy'. I tolerate these masochistic moments of agony because, overall, being a football supporter makes me happy.

The point I am trying to make is an obvious one: despite sourpuss, middle-class academics conjuring an atmosphere of doom, gloom and judgmentalism to reinforce the media's agenda of fear, hatred and chaos, I think that most working-class people, given the chance, would embrace happiness. It also seems to me that most of us know exactly what makes us happy. So, the main postulate of positive psychology – that psychology should not restrict itself to mental illness and suffering but should also promote happiness and growth – seems, on the surface, indisputable. But does subscribing to 'happiness' oblige us to sign up to Maslow, Seligman, positive psychology and the 'happiness industry' as well? That's where the story gets complicated.

Let me introduce a historical note since the psychologists promoting happiness have morphed considerably since the beginning of the twentieth century. Maslow's early attempts to work with 'fully functioning and healthy human beings' rather than 'sick ones' towards what he called a 'positive psychology' are nowadays marginalised by historians of happiness (Maslow 1968). The reluctance of Martin Seligman and his posse to share the spotlight with Maslow should not come as a surprise, since we all know how notoriously attention-seeking this selfie-generation of psychologists has become.

Having reinserted Maslow into the 'happiness debate', I need to emphasise that his psychologising of happiness differed from current attempts – Maslow's was basically *artisanal* in nature. Like a skilled ironmonger he went into his workshop every day, observing, designing and experimenting through trial and error with a variety of compounds, until he had forged the perfect 'lofty' group of people consisting of ideal attributes. By the time Seligman had launched the latest incarnation of positive psychology in his APA Presidential Address of 1998, artisanal economics had given way to a *cottage industry* of in-house psychologists working on 'happiness'. This means that the range of issues researched by positive psychologists is not restricted to 'healthy people' but may include '[lighting] the darkness of trauma' (Linley and Joseph 2003, p. 135), and 'making disability into a resource' (Fave and Massimini 2003, p. 133).

Since Seligman's 1998 speech, the cottage industry has evolved further still, and has transformed into a fully fledged *global industry*. Now 'organisational rhetoric' can be enhanced through positive psychology to put a neo-liberal spin on the last twenty years of downsizing (Henry 2003, p. 139).

Meanwhile, suffering due to terminal cancer or HIV can be confronted with a chirpier style of existential psychotherapy (Bretherton and Ørner, 2003, p. 136). Fringe religious elements within the 'survivor's movement' may even refer to cancer as a 'rite of passage' or a 'gift' (Ehrenreich 2009, p. 29).

First, the liberal Maslow gave way to the neo-liberal Seligman, and when Seligman lost control of the smirking monster he helped to create, the happiness industry imposed its delights through the marvels of technological authoritarianism. No wonder that Barbra Ehrenreich called her critique *Smile or Die: How Positive Thinking Fooled America & The World* (2009).

Ehrenreich has placed the rise of positive psychology within the wider US movement for 'positive thinking'. Her position is that 'Americans did not start off as positive thinkers … [however] systematic positive thinking began, in the nineteenth century, among a diverse and fascinating collection of philosophers, mystics, lay healers, and middle-class women' (Ehrenreich 2009, p. 6). Philosophically this was a set of loose ideas reliant on idealism, including belief in magnetism and sympathetic magic. Religiously its adherents were reacting against the gloom and harshness of Calvinism, described acerbically by Ehrenreich as 'a system of socially imposed depression' (ibid., p. 74). One of the most prominent recruits of this early movement for positivity was the famed father of American psychology, William James (1842–1910). James was, of course, too good a scientist not to be sceptical about the movement's wilder pronouncements; he even criticised it for being 'moonstruck with optimism' (James, quoted in Ehrenreich 2009, p. 88). But after being treated successfully for a number of maladies, his pragmatism got the better of his academic scepticism. So, before Seligman, and before Maslow, there was James giving positive psychology a big push off its launch pad.

Positive thinking plays a key role in imagining the nation as exceptional, great and superior which goes a long way in explaining its reluctance to engage with economics, sociology, and class politics. This is true of all nationalistic ideologies but particularly infectious in the USA, where a series of financial disasters and a general lack of serious political discussion have created insecurities among all the social classes. In fact, Ehrenreich claims, 'all the motivators and gurus of positivity agree that it is a mistake to read newspapers or watch the news' (ibid., p. 57). In a further dig, which one assumes is targeting Seligman specifically, she states, 'This retreat from the real drama and tragedy of human events is suggestive of a deep helplessness at the core of positive thinking' (ibid., p. 69).

I have dwelled on Ehrenreich's critique of positive psychology because it strikes me as both astute as well as strategically sound. We must place positive psychology in at least two types of context: a wider context of capitalist crisis with the pressing need to recruit the proletariat to participate more actively in its own exploitation by developing 'positive emotional labour'; and a more specifically American context that shows the way positivity is linking up with religion, business, medicine and psychology as a tool against the US working class.

The only thing I wish to add to Ehrenreich's analysis here relates to a point raised by Colin Campbell (1987), who reminds us that Christianity did not stop evolving after Luther and Calvin. One significant evolution was pietism, a softer version of Calvinism that allowed for the expression of emotions and has even been linked with the rise of experimental science. One strand of pietism influenced the romantic movement. Both pietism and romanticism had a more accepting attitude towards consumerism and hedonism, and the roots of capitalist hedonism, Campbell argues, lie in a combination of pietism and romanticism (ibid.). I realise that I am stretching things here but assuming that Campbell is basically correct in his assumptions, maybe we can also speculate that today's positive psychologists could be mapped into a 'pietist' wing (encompassing all the religious advocates of positivity) and a 'romantic' wing (representing the secular, experimental psychologists).

There are further problems with positive psychology. McDonald and O'Callaghan (2008) have shown how, while pretending to be 'value-free', positive psychology privileges those character strengths and virtues that support a neo-liberal ideology. For example, this new character regime attempts to establish a new citizenship based on the attributes of 'responsibility, nurturance, altruism, civility, moderation, tolerance, and work ethic' (Seligman and Csikszentmihalyi 2000, p. 5). The new citizen must be cheerful, outgoing, goal-driven and a status-seeking extrovert (Miller 2008, p. 591). Stenner and Taylor (2008, p. 415) find positive psychology implicated in the shift from 'welfare to well-being'. When in the 1980s in countries such as the UK, the USA and Chile governments began to curtail welfare to the working class, a corresponding movement began to take shape whereby all the responsibility for self-repair, self-regulation and self-improvement was shifted to the workers. The 'well-being' movement is all about reducing rights and increasing responsibility; in short, it is a dramatic rewriting of the social contract in favour of the bosses.

Despite Seligman's Herculean efforts to present positive psychology as a 'new objective science', Alistair Miller has accused it of 'tautology, failure to clearly define or properly apply terms, the identification of causal relations where none exist, and unjustified generalisation' (2008, p. 591). Miller continues,

> there is for example, a certain tautological inevitability in the assertion that a person categorised as 'pessimistic' to begin with ... is more prone to depression; or that to achieve a particular goal you need the attitudes, inclinations and motivations that are needed to achieve that goal.
>
> *(Ibid., p. 605)*

Most literature on positive psychology recalls 'self-help' pap, rather than the 'objective psychology' Seligman aspires to. Stenner (2017, pp. 100–106) has raised a number of objections about the viability of measuring happiness. Ironically, positive psychology detracts humanistic psychology for not having an empirical base (ibid., p. 7). Seligman's desire to link positive psychology and positivist experimental psychology may explain Seligman's antipathy towards Maslow.

The utopian component of communism has always been about the redefinition and pursuit of happiness. There is nothing wrong with this so long as it does not substitute the actual, ongoing social movement with promises of wish fulfilment in an indeterminate future. This utopian element constitutes a significant proportion of the contributions made by psychologists such as Otto Gross, Wilhelm Reich, Eric Fromm, Lev Vygotsky, A. R. Luria and non-psychologists such as Marx, Paul Lafargue, Kropotkin and Bakhtin. But the vision for happiness put forward by these thinkers was honest enough to admit that (a) happiness is not an individualistic pursuit, and as socialised individuals our happiness depends on the people around us; and (b) that society shapes the limits and possibilities of happiness. Positive psychology steadfastly refuses to engage with these complexities in order to conceal the fact that it is the perfect intra-psychological cover for neo-liberal models of capitalism. Ah, but I hear you ask, what happens when neo-liberalism itself comes to the end of the road? What happens when it fails to solve the 'productivity problem'? What happens when the jig is up?

As I see it, the neo-liberal version of capitalism has no alternative avenues open to it. Every other bourgeois ideology has already been tried and has failed (classic liberalism, social democracy, Stalinism, etc.). Neo-liberalism can only extend its sell-by date by amalgamating with more authoritarian ideologies. As it becomes increasingly coercive, we have witnessed 'pure neo-liberalism' combine with evermore greater dollops of neo-populism here, neo-fascism there. I predict that as this trend becomes entrenched, positive psychology will also become more insistent on its self-righteous mission to turn all of us into 'happy citizens', whether we like it or not. The original academic propagandists of positive psychology (including Seligman) will be marginalised, and the more powerful corporations will take over the enterprise. The next time you hear the words 'smile or die' it may not be a satirical pose but an actual command.

Concluding remarks on Maslow

I hope I have convinced the jaded reader that Maslow was far more fascinating than a geometric oddity. Earlier I described Maslow's political ideology as a fusion of liberalism, social democracy, petty bourgeois 'anarchism', romantic individualism and transcendentalism. It is an interesting enough mix of ideas but it is also an indication that Maslow had no intention of undermining the fundamentals of capitalism. He might have begun as a working-class 'slum boy' with visions of a Better Society, but he soon became willingly embourgeoisfied (always assuming there is such a word)!

In this sense, Russell Jacoby's harsh judgement of Maslow as part of 'conformist psychology' is justified. In his deliciously sardonic tone, Jacoby writes,

> The formula that Maslow follows is an old one: add soul to misery and injustice and they turn soulful and virtuous … Maslow's entire psychology is oriented toward the healthy and toward saving them from contamination by the ill … What Marx once wrote of Bentham, that he was a genius of stupidity, could be said of Maslow – except that Maslow is no genius.
>
> *(1997, pp. 52, 56 and 72)*

Meow and ouch, indeed! I don't know about you, dear reader, but I wouldn't want to get into an alley fight with Professor Jacoby. The man has sharper claws than Wolverine!

So, on pain of being scratched to death, let us all concur with Russell Jacoby that Maslow wished to strengthen capitalism by basing its foundations on meritocracy and 'equal opportunity', instead of the supposed genetic superiority of the elite. Motivational factors and actual achievements begin to replace birthright and inherent intelligence. What Maslow called 'self-actualisers', or the top 2 per cent of the population, turn out to be his preferred choice of grand and petty bourgeois leaders. The individuals on the list changed over time, although he gradually settled on eighteen names as representatives of this ideal group of luminaries, which included Beethoven, Gandhi, Mother Teresa, Franklin, Albert Einstein, Eleanor Roosevelt and, of course, himself. The key distinguishing attribute of these lofty people is the ease and frequency of their 'peak experiences'. If we agree that by 'peak experience' Maslow meant those moments in life when dichotomies (such as intellect and emotion or the duality between the wish-to-know and the fear-to-know) magically disappear and clarity is attained, then I think it is high time for us 98–99 per centers to demand our share of the pie. Don't you agree?

5

CARL ROGERS

The bolo tie 'internationalist'

> A map of the world which does not include Utopia is not worth even glancing at, for it leaves out the one country at which Humanity is always landing.
>
> *Oscar Wilde*

You have probably read a great deal about Carl Rogers (1902–1987), and it would be an exercise in futility for me to recount his compendium of therapeutic ideas. So, let's cut to the chase. The essence of Carl Rogers can be distilled in four minutes, or 3 minutes and 56 seconds to be precise. There is a YouTube clip showing Rogers during a Q&A session at a 1985 conference on psychotherapy (Rogers 1985). Please watch it now, I can wait … (four minutes later) Wonderful clip, isn't it?

There is a fascinating contradiction at the heart of this short video: please note that Rogers is wearing a bolo tie! The history of the bolo tie is somewhat sketchy but it seems that most sartorialists place its origins in late 1940s or early 1950s America. The inventor might be Victor Emanuel Cederstaff or just as likely a nameless Native American craftsman. In both Arizona and New Mexico, the bolo tie is the designated neckwear of state officials. In the 1980s (remember Rogers is wearing his in 1985) bolo ties became fashionable again and were closely associated with rockabilly revivalists (*Wikipedia*, 'Bolo Tie'). The bolo-wearing Rogers reminds us that in many ways he remained the 'quintessential American'.

And yet faced with the following suspiciously punned question, 'what is your worldview and what ties you to the universe?', Rogers responds by denouncing nationalism:

> I suppose I feel much more a citizen of the world than of any one country … one of the most distressing things that I come across travelling about in different countries is the parochialism, the narrow loyalty to individual nations, states, tribes … it seems to me those narrow loyalties are pretty disastrous in their effects … I regret the narrowness of vision in our own government.
>
> *(1985, 2–3 mins)*

He then encourages his fellow panellist to talk about 'planetary citizenship' which was apparently available to all back in 1985 for the very reasonable sum of $25. The clip goes on to claim that some 350,000 individuals have been granted a planetary passport and that fifty-seven countries around the world accept them as official documentation. In fact, there is an internet website called World Government of World Citizens which offers a 'World Passport' whose 'legitimacy' is derived from Article 21(3) of the Universal Declaration of Human Rights of 1948, and whose philosophy is based on Thomas Paine's famous quote, 'My country is the world' (Paine 1792, Chapter 5, Part 3).

From a working-class perspective, it is all too easy to scoff at such petty bourgeoise half-measures. The whole exercise reeks of the type of gesture politics that idiot celebrities engage in on Twitter! A simple comparison with the practical achievements of the US Industrial Workers of the World (IWW) would be sufficient to foreground the limitations of Rogerian 'non-conformity'. After all, the IWW was an organisation that generated *real* solidarity and cooperation across national and ethnic divides (Staughton and Grubacic 2008; Cole *et al.* 2017). By contrast, Roger's vision of 'internationalism' might be perceived as attending conferences at leafy campus universities, exchanging pleasantries with faculty dons, sampling the local cuisine and 'doing workshops'.

But, in truth, I think for Rogers his numerous trips within the USA and elsewhere represented something more substantial. It expressed a yearning for real dialogue and a better world, and yearnings must never be underestimated, even when they come packaged in bolos and psychobabble. 'Yearnings' may very well be the polite complement to what John Holloway has referred to as the 'scream' (Holloway 2002). Younger, working-class rebels tend to *scream* their disgust at capitalism; older, middle-class non-conformists prefer to *yearn* for a world without borders and injustice. One might yearn when, for whatever reason, one is unable or unwilling to scream. Rogers' denunciation of nationalism may not have the oratorial brilliance of Eugene Debs's *Ohio Speech* (1918), or the fiery rhetoric of Rosa Luxemburg's *Junius Pamphlet* (1915), but for an elderly, unassuming, middle-class bolo-gentleman it is quietly accomplished, don't you think?

You mess with Carl, you get Rogered!

The only occasions when this elderly, unassuming, middle-class bolo-gentleman became irate was when he was being misrepresented or when encountering 'inauthenticity'. During another video clip focusing on his concept of 'empathic listening' Rogers assails his critics:

> [A]n even worse caricature was simply that, 'in non-directive therapy you just say back the last words to the client' ... really, I was so shocked and appalled by that complete distortion of our approach that for a number of years I said almost nothing about empathic listening.
>
> *(1974a, 6 mins)*

Ironically, later in the same video he concedes that by focusing too much on the therapist's response he might have been partially responsible for this misunderstanding.

Contemporary discursive psychologists and social workers would appreciate how Rogers developed his concept of empathy. He describes how he learned from Jessie Taft (1882–1960), a pioneering feminist and social worker, that 'the most effective listening was when you were listening for feelings and emotions that were behind the words, that were just a little bit concealed' (Rogers 1974a, 2 mins). His style was perfected following a long and 'microscopic' discourse analysis of therapeutic interviews (ibid., 5 mins). This process taught him a deep-seated respect for the exactitude of words as a receptacle for one's flow of experience, 'the right word, the right label, or the right phrase often taps the exact meaning of the flow that is going on within [the client], that he hasn't been able to label or understand himself' (ibid., 12 mins). The therapist may go through a list of words until the exact word matching the client's flow of experience is uncovered. This word then unlocks a fresh flow of experience for the client.

FIGURE 5.1 Carl Rogers

Applying the same rigorous standards to his own discursive practice, Rogers proceeds to offer an improved definition of 'empathy'. I will quote him at length because this is key to understanding his evolution towards relationality, group and encounter therapy:

> I would no longer term it a state of empathy ... because [now] I believe it to be a process rather than a state ... [being in an empathic relationship] means entering the private, perceptual world of the other and becoming thoroughly at home in it; it involves being sensitive moment to moment to the changing felt meanings which flow in this other person ... it means temporarily living in his life, moving about in it delicately, without making judgments, *sensing meanings of which he is scarcely aware but not trying to uncover feelings of which he is totally unaware, since this would be too threatening* ... [empathy] means frequently checking with him the accuracies of your sensings ... you are a confident companion to him in his world.
>
> *(1974a, 12–14 mins, emphasis added)*

I have highlighted part of the quote to bring out a key difference with Freud. Rogers avoided what we may term the 'unconscious', whose revelations may be too 'threatening', preferring instead to uncover the 'subconscious', which consist of thoughts, feelings, memories and concerns on the tip of the client's tongue. Using old terminology that has fallen somewhat into disuse, the italicised passage explains why Rogerian therapy has been viewed by most of his followers as more appropriate for 'neurotics' than for 'psychotics'.

However, another comparison illustrates that for Rogers himself things were more complicated. In Chapter 7, I will demonstrate how closely Rogers' process resembles the therapeutic style of R. D. Laing, who also saw himself as a companion to the client. Rogers does recall one case when he immersed himself so much into the client's world that 'he almost went into a psychosis' (1983, 20 mins). Laing adopted Rogers' technique of sitting face-to-face with clients, because it offered a real power change from psychoanalysis. Both Rogers and Laing believed that they could establish an 'I-Thou relationship' (Martin Buber) with even the most disturbed individuals, including 'schizophrenics' (Rogers 1983, 24–25 mins).

Before moving on, let me also point out another connection with Laing, this time a negative one. Apparently, Laing felt a certain amount of 'distaste' for Rogers. According to Schulman, 'part of [Laing's] distaste for Rogers was the latter's claim that he personally never experienced evil within himself' (2015, p. 95). In fact, Laing was of the opinion that the entire American humanistic school was guilty of underestimating the deviousness and inauthenticity of human beings. Or, as Kovel would put it, 'there is a drastic minimisation of the demonic and of repressed unconscious factors in general' (1987, pp. 162–163). When we express 'genuine authenticity', Laing argues, it is not due to some essential core value but to a courageous act of defiance against life's existential threats.

Only in retrospect did Rogers become aware that what he was proposing was a new form of doing psychotherapy – not a medical model but 'a growth model [which assumes that] if the individual is in psychological difficulty it must be because of some influences that hamper his or her growth' (1983, 18 mins). Significantly, the client is best placed for identifying these obstacles, on the condition that they have a safe space in which to reflect upon these problems. The tag 'non-directive' was a protest against the therapy of Rogers' day that was entirely directive. The term 'client' was also ridiculed by psychiatrists. Not being overly fond of the term 'client-centred' for his method he eventually changed its description to 'person-centred' therapy (ibid., 11–12 mins).

If Rogers was breaking with the medical model, he was also burning many bridges with psychoanalysis. One of the characteristics of Rogerian therapy is the brevity of the encounter. This choice not only has the advantage of saving time and money for the client, but it also makes long-term entanglements such as transference and counter-transference less likely to occur (Kovel 1987, p. 161). Of course, psychoanalysts may see these entanglements as the very stuff of therapy, but for Rogerians it is an unnecessary complication.

Gloria in session

In 1965 a unique comparative study was conducted. A client, named Gloria, was filmed in therapy with three distinguished therapists. I wish more therapists and clients would agree to make their private sessions open to public – the educational value is considerable. On the other hand, it could expose the therapist to criticism and ridicule, not to mention the possibility of litigation, so I understand the reasons for the dearth of such recordings. In separate sessions, Gloria discusses her problems not only with Rogers but also Fredrick S. Perls (gestalt therapy) and Albert Ellis (rational emotive behavior therapy). For the sake of brevity, I will focus on Rogers' session (Rogers 1965).

Rogers starts by explaining that his first (and most important) aim is to create 'the proper climate, conditions and relationship'. Key to this process is the therapist's 'genuineness'. In a manoeuvre involving considerable risk for Rogers himself, he opens up himself and is happy for the client to 'see through him'. This transparency works both ways. If, for example, Rogers dislikes his client persistently, he feels he should express it (1965, 5 mins). If Rogers successfully enters Gloria's world, he can understand not just the surface meanings, but gain deeper insights. Once this is achieved, a process of therapeutic movement will 'almost inevitably occur in the client' (ibid., 3 mins). The client then quite possibly shifts from being distant and disapproving of her own feelings to being more immediate and approving. Black and white perceptions may transform into more tentative ways of construing her life (ibid., 8 mins). The 'locus of evaluation' moves from an external position to a more internal one.

Gloria then describes some of her experiences. She is a thirty-year-old, white, middle-class woman. A recent divorcée, she feels distant from her nine-year-old daughter and seeks an improved relationship with her. Specifically, she wants to know if she should tell her daughter the truth about her sex life after 'divorcing daddy'. Gloria feels guilty about 'having a man over' and tries to conceal it from her daughter (1965, 13 mins). She wants Rogers to 'get rid of her guilty feelings' (ibid., 14 mins), even though she understands intellectually that there is nothing wrong with her 'natural sexual desires' (ibid., 22 mins). She needs the expert approval of a world-renowned therapist to take the risk and be honest with her daughter and friends.

There are moments during the course of this session when Rogers is tempted to be directive and dish out advice, but he believes that 'it is up to the person to direct themselves' (1953, 49 mins). During the 1950s and 1960s a new kind of citizen-worker was being manufactured by American capitalism. The directive Taylorism of earlier decades expressed in psychoanalysis and behaviourism was being questioned and a new self-regulating, self-directing individual promoted. The impetus is, therefore, towards convincing Gloria that she already knows what she wants to do. She can solve her own problems. At the end of the session a father-daughter relationship is momentarily established between Rogers and Gloria. Rogers is keen to see this as two human beings 'really encountering each other' rather than the mystifying terminology of transference and counter-transference (1965, 42 mins).

Wickman and Campbell (2003) have looked at this session closely. They remind us that for Rogers therapy was not about practising a set of 'microskills' mechanically, which is how some person-centred therapists teach their craft to students (ibid., p. 178). Nevertheless, his discourse does contain certain devices, such as 'non-expert language', 'invitation for repair' (requests by Rogers for Gloria to correct him), 'problem reformulation' (Rogers highlighted problems that are within Gloria's control and are manageable), and 'meta-statements' (interactions between them about the here and now). There is even a pretty triangular model of Rogers' therapeutic model for those readers interested (ibid., p. 179). Their analysis shows that Rogers' conversational style encouraged Gloria to 'talk in more detail and at a more complex level about her problem situation until it became no longer problematic' (ibid., p. 182).

Kathryn A. Moon (2007, p. 277) reminds us that Rogers 'initiated the practice of recording and analysing counseling sessions and left a concrete legacy of at least 158 recordings and transcripts of sessions between 1940 and 1986'. The impact of technology on the course of humanistic psychology is sometimes underplayed. We know about the influence of measuring devices on psychophysics, audio recordings on introspectional psychology, traffic lights and road signs on the emergence of behavioural geography, the impact of computers (both as measuring tools and metaphors) on cognitive psychology, and scanners on neuropsychology. But what about the accessibility of video recorders for Rogerian therapy? For one thing, it changed the role of the therapist from the all-knowing expert to a friendly voice who listens and bears witness to the client's journey (ibid., p. 283). For another, the comparative aspect of the exercise introduced an element of friendly competition between Rogers, Perls and Ellis, which students of psychotherapy have found productive over the years.

Finally, from a more critical therapeutic perspective, a number of observations could be made about the above case study. John Cromby defines depression as 'a form of distress characterised predominantly by profound and enduring unhappiness' (2004, p. 177). His starting point is that depression is always associated with social inequality. Rogers, by contrast, ignores the historical imperatives imposed on Gloria through her class, gender and lifestyle choices. A simple example will suffice:

> [A]t the turn of the century a diagnostic category for the explanation of women's 'distress' was *hysteria*. The symptoms of this 'disorder' included 'eating like a ploughman', 'cussedness', 'erotic tendencies' and

> masturbation. The 'cure' involved the introduction of ice and water into the vagina, the use of leeches on the labia and, in extreme case, clitoridectomy.
>
> *(Nightingale and Cromby 2001, pp. 123–124, emphasis in the original)*

How can therapy be truly transparent if we ignore, as Rogers does, its history and politics? Moreover, there is the problem of individualism. It is Gloria who must find a solution to her problems and not all the Glorias of this world who share the same restrictions. Rogers is promoting the very same individualism that leads 'many people to believe their misery is a product of their own inadequacy' (ibid., p. 118).

Going beyond Rogers

The chief criticism levelled at Rogers contends that his 'discovery' of a more authentic, better human being, with an inner core that is 'basically socialised, forward-looking, rational and realistic' (Rogers 1961, p. 91), is no more than a comforting fairy tale. For Rogers, this was not a mere belief in the goodness of man but a position arrived at through experience.

According to Rogers, the therapist must do more than practise what phenomenologists call *epoché* (a neutral, non-judgemental evaluation). Merely tolerating the client's oddities will not make a dent in the neurotic alienation that they feel. Even immersing oneself in their world and experiencing it with them empathically may not be enough. Ultimately, the therapist must evince 'unconditional positive regard', which in some of Rogers' writings becomes intertwined with *agape*, known as the highest form of Christian love marked by selflessness and pure concern for others (Feltham 2010, p. 15).

The problem with 'unconditional positive regard' in a therapeutic setting is that not everyone wants or (frankly) deserves it and, more importantly, those who seek it might be 'better served by a more intensive evaluation of their total problem' (Kovel 1987, p. 164). It is 'unabashedly inspirational' (ibid., p. 163) and can lend itself to both the 'happy-clappy' evangelicals of religious therapy or to the more secular machinations of 'positive psychology' (see Chapter 4 in this volume on Maslow). Before leaving Kovel, let me say that he is not completely dismissive of Rogerian therapy which, he believes, can be beneficial to those suffering from feelings of inferiority and insecurity (e.g. students adjusting to school), or those experiencing loneliness and isolation (e.g. moderately neurotic middle-class people).

From a similar Freudo-Marxist perspective, Russell Jacoby has accused Rogers of cheerleading a largely fictitious, decontextualised and depoliticised 'individual': 'The more … late capitalism renders obsolete self-fulfilment, and actualisation, the more they are emphasised as if they could spring to life through an act of will alone' (Jacoby 1997, p. 64). This is very true but what about Rogers' 'encounter groups'? Surely they signal a concerted effort to go beyond individuality?

Rogers has written approvingly about groups. This represents an advance on the suspicions many psychologists harbour about the loss of individuality within a group set-up. Rogers states, 'I trust the group, given a reasonably facilitating climate, to develop its own potential and the potential of its members. For me, this capacity of the group is an awesome thing' (1971).

This trust in the group developed gradually. Its core assumption, Rogers insists, is a non-directive approach to facilitating the encounter. This tendency towards creating a healthy group is biologically driven. Rogers describes it mystically as 'the wisdom of the organism' which can exhibit itself at cellular, individualistic and group level (Rogers 1971). The 'wisdom' works out a goal for the group, not for Rogers. An excellent exemplar of these encounter groups can be viewed on YouTube (ibid. 1974b). Here Rogers and fellow-therapist Richard Farson, who wrote a Bill of Rights for Children, facilitate an encounter where one member, 'a Eurasian woman called Lotus-blossom', is taken to task for playing 'roles' and being 'inauthentic' – two of Rogers' bugbears.

The way Rogers listens to each group member may seem similar to what phenomenologists call *horizontalisation* (placing every utterance on the same level, without prioritising them). But this is a deceptive horizontalisation that is performed for the benefit of making the individuals feel 'validated'. In reality, Rogers admits that he is 'selective in [his] listening, and hence "directive"' (1974b). Videos of Rogers counselling clients clearly show how at crucial moments of therapy he encourages them through bodily movement, nodding and facial expression. He may even direct the group to talk from personal experience rather than in general terms.

The empathic listening, the unconditional positive regard and the congruence are all aimed at creating a psychologically safe climate. Within this safe space, members can then express both positive and negative feelings. This rule applies to Rogers himself who can at times be breathtakingly confrontational: 'Never in my life have I been so pissed off at a group as I am at this one' or, to one man in a group, 'I woke up this morning feeling, "I never want to see you again"' (1974b). Bloody Nora and flaming horror! I'm glad I was never one of his 'clients'!

Of course, Rogers is being less naive than his detractors suggest, for he is fully aware that he 'cannot make the experience safe from the pain of new insight or growth, or of the pain of honest feedback from others' (1974b). He can only try to be there for the individual in moments of pain and joy – a 'confident companion' who may unexpectedly roger you for your own good.

Whether working at individual or group level, Rogers is making us sensitised towards the immediate, and indifferent towards the more mediated, distant, extra-psychological forces that define us (Jacoby 1997, p. 67). The problems go deeper since both the intra- and inter-psychological encounters (where Rogerian psychology supposedly excels) end up adding to the confusion. His encounters encourage individuals to constantly monitor and regulate their emotions, find a niche for themselves within the system and become productive members of the 'affluent society' (J. K. Galbraith), without questioning whether 'affluence' is real, imaginary, selective, temporary or at someone else's expense. Mental pain is divorced from the mode of production that generates it. Capitalism is left unchallenged and social class is rarely acknowledged.

To be fair, this is a problem permeating contemporary therapeutic culture and cannot be blamed solely on Rogerian person-centred therapy. In a study of counselling in the USA, Hanon *et al.* (2001) explain that many Americans do not like talking about class and have been taught to be suspicious of those who do (ibid., p. 138). They also provide evidence which shows that 'Classism is institutionalised in counsellor education programmes in the USA' (ibid., p. 143). Furthermore, 'counselling students are often taught that people from lower classes are more psychologically maladjusted and require more manipulative treatments' (ibid., p. 144). What makes things even more complicated is that since there is a general reluctance to discuss class, much class conflict then reappears in a disguised form, under the rubric of race, ethnicity, nationalism, ageism or gender. This is a problem we encounter time and again in psychology.

The knowledge created by Rogers in the 1940s–1960s was situated in a specific time frame and subjected to the capitalist imperatives of its era. That is to be expected. However, it is the ease with which the humanistic psychology movement made itself available to capitalism's advances that is somewhat indecent. Diana Ralph narrates that 'both the Rockefeller and Ford Foundations enthusiastically picked up the counselling idea and generously funded Carl Rogers to refine the technique of non-directive interviewing for general use in industry' (Ralph 1983, p. 80). Rogers' techniques were used in combination with 'Kurt Lewin's concepts of management training, Bion's theories of "work enrichment", and diverse varieties of group-based wage-incentive and profit-sharing schemes [relying] to varying degrees on Mayo's concepts' (ibid.). Management liked their emphasis on 'feelings to the exclusion of practical changes, on its pseudo-equality between therapist and client, and on its concept of positive mental self-actualisation as opposed to curing mental illness' (ibid., p. 81).

I would like to end this section by bringing to the reader's attention a number of additional criticisms levelled at Rogerian therapy. Feltham argues that Rogers' faith in the client being the best person to make decision about his/her problems is misplaced. 'If clients know best', he asks, 'how come so many of them (of us) have messed up large areas of their lives? How come they are so much in need of help from others like counsellors?' (Feltham 2010, p. 156). He offers a neat solution to this dilemma. Perhaps we can acknowledge that '*temporarily* the client *doesn't* know best', but that ultimately 'with sensitive support and trust' they can come to know best (ibid., emphasis in the original). An extension of this critical point argues that we cannot take the client at face value since not only do they engage in deliberate deceit but, at times, they are governed by self-deceptive processes over which they have little or no control (ibid, p. 85).

Is humanistic 'person-centred therapy' (PCT) a form of religion?

There seems to be a very strong, often turbulent, relationship between many psychologists and religion. Some end up secularising concepts that have been around in religious discourse for centuries (e.g. Jung's 'fascist mysticism' or Fromm's 'Marxist-Buddhism'). Some end up playing with religious themes without being fully aware of it (e.g. the unacknowledged Judaeo-Christian themes in Freudianism). Conversely, some manifest a severe reaction against religiosity (e.g. Watson and Skinner's 'authoritarian bourgeois atheism'). Where does Rogers stand on all this?

The consistently reliable Joel Kovel informs us that Carl Rogers' 'first calling was Christian evangelism through the YMCA' (1987, p. 157). Later, when he switched his allegiance to humanistic psychology, he argued that 'our culture has been dominated by the puritanical idea of original sin' (ibid., p. 158). In fact, Rogers saw Freudianism as the main promoter of original sin within psychology. Freud's contradictory position on religion provided these charges with a modicum of validity. For example, he wrote 'the words, "secular pastoral worker", might well serve as a general formula for describing the function which the analyst … has to perform' (Freud [1927] 2005, p. 70). Jung's more open support for religion within psychology viewed therapists as the new priesthood, and advocated the value of confession and forgiveness for psychological health (Todd 1985, p. 47). Trevor Butt has shown how the theme of the Garden of Eden recurs in George Kelly's writings (2012, pp. 250–251). Kelly's father was a Presbyterian minister and he attended a Quaker college in his youth (ibid.). To show the prevalence of the religious scientist we should also recall that Francis Galton and Karl Pearson based their notions of general intelligence on a secularised version of the puritan idea of the soul (White 2006, pp. 360–361). Somewhat exaggeratedly, Thomas Szasz has used these personal and doctrinal ties of continuity to dismiss the entire therapeutic enterprise as no more than a 'scientific-sounding name for what used to be called the "cure of souls"' (1979, p. 26). But what about Rogers himself?

Person-centred therapy commonly claims that it has no predetermined goals for the client other than those that the client chooses to achieve. Williams and Irving consider this disingenuous:

> Rogerian thinking supposes that there is only one way of moving forward, and that is to take the path of self-actualisation; these Rogerian goals are frequently implicit in the work of counsellors in the West regardless of the particular techniques they employ.
>
> *(2001, p. 5)*

More explicitly, Rogers 'wrote about the healing power of the spirit, although most counsellors play down this aspect of his writings' (ibid.). Williams and Irving's parting shot is aimed at counselling in general:

> Although a religion, counselling is not yet a church. In its form it resembles the early days of Christianity with factions vying for the higher ground, nevertheless, ceremonies and rituals are emerging. In training courses and conferences ceremonial hugs, or moments of 'hand holding silence' are common; symbols, candles and aromas are creeping into practice.
>
> *(Ibid., p. 7)*

Concluding remarks

Here is a critical summing up that captures Rogers' complex contribution rather elegantly:

> Rogers sets out a developmental trajectory that leads from a state of initial grace – 'unconditional positive regard' from the mother – to a state of 'incongruence' and unhappiness, until the individual realises that the answers lie inside himself.
>
> *(Parker 2007, p. 126)*

I agree with Parker's conclusion but I feel that there is more to Rogers than this quote suggests. He was, at the end of the day, what I would call a 'bump-smoother'. Despite not being versed in revolutionary literature, he could instinctively sense upcoming bumps on capitalism's road-journey and designate himself as the chief bump-smoother. Specifically, his efforts helped to smooth out four bumps that could have undermined capitalism's pursuit of profit and command:

1. After World War II, US capitalism embarked on a thorough reorganisation of the workplace. One way of describing this period is to look at how manufacturing and production techniques based on Fordism/Taylorism gradually gave way to post-Fordism/post-Taylorism. Rogers understood this change instinctively and realised that the new post-Taylorist worker would need to possess self-regulating abilities. Person-centred therapy is geared towards healing the post-Taylorist worker, and teaching him/her self-monitoring and self-regulating skills. Rogers demystified some aspects of therapy in the same way that post-Fordism was subjecting management to a partial demystification.
2. Another aspect of change was the replacement of classical liberalism, not with neo-liberalism (that would come later in the 1970s–1980s), but with Keynesianism. One aspect of Keynesianism required encouraging producers to become producer-consumers. This meant added responsibilities and learning to function in a new field of competitive behaviour when shopping. PCT was at hand to smooth the bumps.
3. 'Gender battles' became quite heated in the 1960s–1970s. Rogers understood the significance of this and attempted to smooth out relationships between men and women, in order to improve functionality in both the workplace and at home.

4. With the rise of 'black consciousness' and the eruption of various 'race riots' it became imperative for capitalism to discover more efficient ways of integrating the workforce. This meant opening up channels of communication between 'whites' and 'blacks' in order to smooth out racial tensions. Again, in many ways PCT was tailor-made for the task.

My investigation into Carl Rogers has convinced me that he was far more than a popular and gifted therapist. The bolo tie internationalist developed into the smoother-in-chief for psychology in the twentieth century. Ultimately, he came to exert great influence not only on the course of psychology but also on cultural norms in general.

PART II

Critical psychology as middle-class musings

Critical psychology usually describes itself as a reaction against modernist psychology. This is only partially true. In reality, critical psychology was also reacting against high modernism, the caricatured version of modernism. This explains why so much of critical psychology is smug and lazy. It is not going up against the best of modernism but instead it merely challenges the worst delusions of high modernism.

The critical psychologists discussed in Part II (Frankl, Laing, Foucault, Billig and Parker) are the best this tradition has to offer. They are smart and original. They have made us think profoundly about some of the shortcomings of modernist psychology. However, I believe this wave has lost impetus and the lack of recent innovation within critical psychology is testimony to its demise.

6

VIKTOR EMIL FRANKL

The inconvenient existentialist

The simplicity of your character makes you exquisitely incomprehensible to me.
Oscar Wilde, The Importance of Being Earnest

I thoroughly enjoy the illusion that I carry less prejudicial baggage than most members of the human species. Yet I feel obliged to confess to one persistent prejudice which shadows me to this day: the truth is, I have a tendency to walk more briskly when passing the 'pop psychology' section in bookshops and libraries. And as I do, I avert my gaze from its patronising homilies and hold my breath so as not to inhale the stench of crass commercialism. I deplore the manner in which pop psychology targets the vulnerable by offering 'commonsensical' fluff dressed as salvation. A generous reader may view my behaviour as an expression of 'healthy elitism', while a choleric observer may suspect pure jealousy, for which underachieving academic can deny a tinge of envy when the fluff makes the one-million-copies-sold bestseller list?

This is how it came to pass that I ignored Viktor E. Frankl's classic *Man's Search for Meaning* ([1959] 2004) throughout my rather extended student years. I arrogantly assumed that a bestseller, especially one dipped in saccharine pumpkin pie for the American market, could not possibly add anything to *my* criticality. I suspect that this bias also plays a role in the general neglect of Frankl within contemporary psychology programmes. Today, Frankl has been largely relegated to theology courses where he can lend some scientific objectivity to the 'self-transcendent' quality of human experience. Needless to say, if Frankl was a clichéd petty bourgeois who, having come through the one-in-forty lottery of surviving the concentration camps (Längle and Sykes 2006, p. 39), went on to discover the divine at the end of a rainbow, his life story would be of limited value to a project of postpsychology. He is, of course, far more than that. Below I argue that both his contributions and his considerable flaws are worthy of a more serious engagement.

Viktor Frankl is a man who resists generalisation but, if we were to yield to temptation, the following could serve as a useful political summing up: ultimately, his political ideology represents a mystical reaction against two forms of ideology and two corresponding forms of collective trauma. The two ideologies he reacted against were the German 'reactionary modernism' (Jeffrey Herf) of the 1930–1940s and the US 'high modernism' of the 1950–1960s. The two collective forms of trauma that haunted him throughout his life were the Holocaust and the Cold War. He sought solace within the individual and deliberately disregarded historical and social context. Liberalism constituted a political anchor, but it also requires a dose of responsibility. This is accurately captured in his suggestion that 'the Statue of Liberty on the East Coast should be complemented by a Statue of Responsibility on the West Coast' (Frankl [1959] 2004, p. 134). After introducing 'logotherapy' (Frankl's version of existential therapy) to the USA, he was charged with authoritarianism, by Rollo May among others (Pytell 2016). I will revisit this accusation in the discussion below.

Philosophical foundations of Frankl

Before postmodernism got its grubby little hands on quotes and reduced them to mere textual ornaments, they represented an ideal way of accessing a thinker's *Weltanschauung*. Under the aegis of pre-modernism, modernism and even high modernism the thinking human being had a somewhat different relationship to books, and the right quote could encapsulate something profound and meaningful.

Frankl was fond of quoting Nietzsche, especially from *Twilight of the Idols*, to the effect that 'He who has a *why* to live can bear with almost any *how*', and the survivalists' favourite motto, 'That which does not kill me makes me stronger' (Nietzsche [1889] 1997, p. 6, emphasis in the original). If Nietzsche inspired him to resist, Dostoyevsky and Spinoza provided the chief mode of transcendence: 'There is only one thing that I dread: not to be worthy of my sufferings' (Dostoyevsky, quoted in Frankl [1959] 2004, p. 75), and 'Emotion, which is suffering, ceases to be suffering as soon as we form a clear and precise picture of it' (Spinoza, quoted in ibid., p. 82). Finally, there is this quote by Goethe, 'If you treat an individual as he is, he will remain how he is. But if you treat him as if he were what he ought to be and could be, he will become what he ought to be and could be' (Frankl 1972, 2 mins). If these quotations point us to Frankl's general philosophy of life, there are also significant figures with whom he had a more ambivalent relationship.

FIGURE 6.1 Viktor Frankl

Frankl positioned himself against some of Freud's most cherished notions: retrospective analysis, the pleasure principle and pan-sexualism. Frankl favoured a far less retrospective approach, to the almost total exclusion of both personal and collective history. He firmly fixates on the future and the meanings that need to be fulfilled by the patient. He does not see humans as driven by the Freudian 'will to pleasure', or even Adler's alternative 'will to power'. In fact, he was expelled from the Adlerian Society on this very point (Lantz 1998, p. 94). For him, it is the 'will to meaning' that represents the most basic motivational factor that contributes to being human (Frankl 1972, 2 mins). The task of the therapist is to immunise the client against nihilism or, to put it in George A. Sargent's terms, to resist 'learned meaninglessness' (Frankl [1959] 2004, p. 152). As for the usual charge of pan-sexualism levelled against Freudianism, Frankl ups the ante by suggesting that there is something 'even more erroneous and dangerous' and that something is Freudian 'pan-determinism' (ibid., p. 133). Instead, he argues that 'Man is *not* fully conditioned and determined but rather determines himself whether he gives in to conditions or stands up to them … every human being has the freedom to change at any instant' (ibid.).

It is important to note that Frankl does not reject the entire Freudian edifice. He prefers to see himself as adding layers of meaning to it. Similarly, he does not criticise Sartrean philosophy too harshly. Instead, he attempts to secure a niche alongside it by subtly transforming Sartre's pessimistic existentialism into what he calls 'tragic optimism'. Despite the weight of the 'tragic tirade' of pain, guilt and death, Frankl counsels an optimism in the face of insurmountable odds ([1959] 2004, p. 139). Even in an environment as unforgiving as a concentration camp, once the prisoner has passed through the three stages of shock, apathy and disillusionment, it is possible to turn suffering into human achievement – perhaps even an opportunity to change oneself for the better. Given such comments, it is easy to see how American pragmatists came to fall in love with Frankl.

The chances of surviving the camps depended on many factors, including the type of camps prisoners were sent to, the degree of solidarity among the prisoners, and, significantly for our discussion, the prisoners' ability to overcome what Frankl calls 'deformed time' ([1959] 2004, p. 79). This is a form of phenomenological temporality – subjective experiencing of time – that has lost coherence. It is neither cyclical, moving in an orderly rhythm from sunrise to sunset, nor linear, with a clear demarcation between beginning, middle and end. It has become deformed. As Frankl explains, 'In camp, a small time unit, a day, for example, filled with hourly tortures and fatigue, appeared endless. A larger time unit, perhaps a week, seemed to pass very quickly' (ibid.).

What is useful is the way Frankl links deformed time to the closely related concept of 'provisional existence'. Prisoners whose terms of confinement are not clear have some understanding of the deleterious effects of such an existence. If there is no release date from either imprisonment, unemployment or a disease, existence becomes provisional (Frankl [1959] 2004, p. 78).

These two concepts of deformed time and provisional existence were constructed to make sense of dynamics in the unusually hostile environment in Germany under 'reactionary modernism', and the 'high modernist' era of the Cold War. However, I feel that they can prove instructive in making sense of our own times, when post-modernism is ungraciously cursing and crawling towards its grave. The deformed time of Frankl has now permeated every sphere of activity.

Peter Good (2001) has studied deformed time within the landscape of psychiatry by foregrounding its political valence. Disguised as a volunteer pseudopatient at a psychiatric clinic and employing Bakhtinian concepts, Good shows how

> Time, in the Patient Chronotope [time-space], has a much more unstable quality … It is given to sudden accelerations or alarming tangents and its direction can go backwards or downwards or simply resolve in endless repetition … [very often] it has a slowed-downed almost viscous quality to it.
>
> *(ibid., p. 27)*

However, and here is where Good goes beyond Frankl, this Patient Chronotope has arisen in an antagonistic relationship to what he calls the Care Chronotope, psychiatry's official bonding of time and space. What distinguished the Care Chronotope 'is the sheer speed of its time flow' and the constant projection 'of faith onto a future time', so that capitalism can 'deal with the inevitable disappointments of the present and the shame of the past' (ibid., pp. 25–26).

If Good's distinction between the Care and Patient Chronotopes expands on Frankl's description of deformed time, the analytical concept of 'precarity' serves as an improvement on Frankl's 'provisional existence'. Using a more expansive definition of precarity than that which is usually bandied about, Neilson and Rossiter (2008, p. 52) describe a prevalent mode of existence that is characterised by not only a lack of stable jobs, imposed flexibility, part-time, low-paid jobs but also the simultaneous disappearance of welfare provisions and the time required for building affective personal relations. But precariousness also conveys an element of existential threat to the person. While Frankl's attention was focused on the singular threat of Nazism in the 1940s, and the mutual assured destruction of the 1960s, today's precarious workers have to contend with a more diffused series of threats. Some of these threats are very real (e.g. cancer, Ebola, AIDS, financial ruin, etc.), some are exaggerated (e.g. becoming a victim of knife crime or car theft), and some occur so slowly that they are not noticed until it is too late (e.g. Alzheimer's disease or climate change). What is significant is that capitalism has managed to weave all these threats together into a bundle of nerves, and to create anxiety levels every bit as intense as previous eras of capitalism.

Logotherapy

> I like your opera. I think I will set it to music.
>
> *Ludwig van Beethoven*

Frankl was not the first thinker to use the accumulated prestige of Greek to add gravitas to his ideas. He was not even the first to utilise the term Logos psychologically – Jung beat him to it! But when Frankl coined 'logotherapy' (from *Logos* denoting in this context 'meaning'), he did so in the assured knowledge that the term would have far more euphonic appeal than 'meaning-therapy'. Now his ideas can be attractively packaged as the Third Viennese School of Psychotherapy and compete with their Freudian and Adlerian rivals.

The basic assumption of logotherapy is that the individual's 'will to meaning' has been compromised through 'existential frustration', and this may result in 'noögenic neurosis' (from the Greek *noön*, meaning 'mind' or 'spirit'). The task of logotherapy then becomes to confront and reorient the patient towards the meaning of his/her spiritual life (Frankl [1959] 2004, p. 104).

Logotherapy is a humanistic-existential therapy but it also has a great deal in common with other approaches. The perceptual shifting that is encouraged by logotherapy can be seen as a precursor of cognitive psychotherapy (McMullin 2000), and 'the creative, active, and strengths-focused aspects of logotherapy have parallels with constructive therapies, such as solution-focused or narrative-focused therapies' (Schulenberg *et al.* 2008, p. 448). I would also argue that certain features of logotherapy are very similar to

Vygotsky's 'zone of proximal development' (ZPD) as utilised in therapy. For instance, Frankl writes that 'mental health is based on a certain degree of tension, the tension between what someone has already achieved and what one still ought to accomplish, or the gap between what one is and what one should become' ([1959] 2004, p. 110). This is an individualised version of the ZPD. Vygotsky would envisage the ZPD in constituted by pairs or groups, but the philosophy is similar.

Some of Frankl's formulations are very fresh. He writes that 'Not every conflict is necessarily neurotic; some amount of conflict is normal and healthy ... existential frustration is in itself neither pathological nor pathogenic' ([1959] 2004, p. 108). Frankl looks at distress and boredom as two entities occupying the same spectrum. We are doomed to vacillate between the two poles. Boredom can therefore be as big a contributor to neurosis as distress. Frankl also claims that logotherapy is 'neither teaching nor preaching' (ibid., p. 114). Rather, the logotherapist insists that the individual should take responsibility for his/her life. In order to self-actualise patients must transcend themselves, for instance by giving themselves to a cause or serving another person (ibid., p. 115).

It is important to emphasise that as far as Frankl is concerned, tension is indispensable for mental well-being. He correctly understands that psychotherapy's usual fetishisation of equilibrium is misplaced. In his own words, 'What man actually needs is not a tensionless state but rather the striving and struggling for a worthwhile goal, a freely chosen task' (Frankl [1959] 2004). This may not be a dialectical tension as present in the works of Vygotsky, Riegel and Kovel but it is nonetheless a salutary acknowledgment of the dangers of chasing an artificial and unnecessary homeostasis. As we will see later, this rejection of equilibrium is linked to Frankl's risk-taking style of therapy, a refreshing counter-example to our own risk-averse times. What is more, the risk-taking involves the use of humour in therapy. Humour allows for self-detachment from one's neuroses (ibid., p. 127).

Contemporary applications of logotherapy

If longevity is the ultimate test of any idea, then the outside observer would conclude that logotherapy is performing rather well. Contemporary logotherapy treats a reasonably challenging range of mental health issues, utilises various individualistic and group modes of delivery and is still generating new techniques based on Frankl's original philosophical assumptions.

As mentioned above, one of these assumptions was Frankl's admittedly circular argument that 'existential vacuum' causes boredom which in turn leads to lack of meaning in life. This is due partly to the loss of basic animal instincts which told early man what he had to do, and partly to the decline of tradition which told man what he ought to do (Frankl [1959] 2004, p. 111). Progressive automation may lead to increased free time but since people will not know what to do with it, the endpoint will be even more boredom (ibid., p. 112). In fact, Frankl argued that 'boredom is now causing, and certainly bringing to psychiatrists, more problems to solve than distress' (ibid., p. 111).

It is rather difficult to validate this chain of events experimentally. However, setting up a correlational study is relatively straightforward. Melton and Schulenberg (2007) hypothesised that meaning in life and proneness to boredom would be negatively correlated. The first variable was measured using the Purpose in Life Test, and the second was tested with the Boredom Proneness Scale. Both scales are inspired by Frankl's ideas. The Purpose in Life Test comprises twenty items with a five or seven-point Likert-type response format. One item asks how routine or exciting life is to the subject; another enquires about progress in achieving one's life goals; yet another attempts to measure the subject's sense of choice vis-à-vis determinism. A low overall score indicates an 'existential void' and a lack of purpose in life. By contrast, the Boredom Proneness Scale is a twenty-eight-item, true/false questionnaire. Here are a few examples with the 'correct' response indicated in brackets:

Item 3: Time always seems to be passing slowly (T);
Item 8: I find it easy to entertain myself (F);
Item 18: I often wake up with a new idea (F).

The study reports a statistically significant negative correlation between scores for the Purpose of Life Test and the Boredom Proneness Scale ($r = -0.71$, $p < 0.01$). The critical reader may argue that the rather large correlation suggests that these two measures assess the same construct, and that the usual qualification about correlational studies not demonstrating causality adds further scepticism to the findings. Nonetheless, this is a finding I imagine will find confirmation with further research.

Logotherapy has also been used for treating Internet Addiction (IA), and as we will see below this raises a number of problems. Didelot *et al.* (2012) have correctly criticised the simplistic assumption that IA is a maladaptive cognitive coping style that can be treated adequately with cognitive behavioural therapy. They argue that IA can be more anonymous, accessible and lonely than other forms of addiction, making relapse prevention particularly challenging. Perhaps more controversially, they also argue that cyberspace relationships are a 'substitute for a painful, unsatisfying reality' (ibid., p. 21). Online anonymity can 'create a petri dish for deception', leading to existential emptiness. Online relations 'demand nothing, not even the truth' (ibid., p. 22). But when they claim that 'IA is a disease of contemporary society' I fear that reason has become hostage to passion (ibid., p. 20).

A case study is then presented in order to demonstrate logotherapy's ability to treat IA. Nathan is a thirty-seven-year-old single Caucasian gay man who 'attended to his physical, social spiritual and occupational self with great care', before discovering the Internet (Didelot *et al.* (2012, p. 23). After being snared by the Net, he rarely leaves home and becomes disappointed in his non-virtual friends who are 'not interesting enough, creative enough, or aware enough to hold their own in discourse' (ibid., p. 24). He begins missing work to spend more time chatting on the Net and the refurbishing of his home comes to a standstill. Didelot *et al.* use Frankl to argue that this behavioural repertoire indicates 'the existential concept of escaping from the self' (ibid., p. 26). Logotherapy in this case consists of assisting Nathan to find his will to meaning through creative, experiential and attitudinal values. A first step is to empower Nathan through the acknowledgment of a defiant spirit. A sense of humour would allow Nathan to step outside his situation and find meaning in his suffering (ibid., p. 28). In addition, Didelot *et al.* accomplish logotherapy through 'Socratic dialogue and problem solving, although additional techniques such as values clarification, guided imagery, dream analysis, and building a personal story' are also recommend (ibid., p. 29).

If Didelot *et al.* (2012) focus on the intra-psychological aspect of logotherapy, then Schulenberg *et al.* (2010) capture the inter-psychological dimension. They employ a mix of old and new logotherapeutic techniques for couples' therapy. The foundation of the approach would excite the religious therapists among you since it involves 'value clarification' (logotherapists help people to recognise and prioritise their values), and 'self-transcendent growth' (an unselfish love whereby the partner is experienced as unique) (ibid., p. 96). In this case love is an essential aspect of the meaning of life but it is not a disembodied love, since couples are encouraged to think about pleasuring the partner during sexual activity (ibid., p. 97).

I end this section by mentioning two more unusual papers that show the range of subjects to which logotherapy has been applied in recent years. Maurice Kinsella (2014) has applied Frankl to an Irish setting, by showing how the trend towards 'atomistic nihilism' can be reversed when the meaning of life is reimagined within Irish communities. Logotherapy can also be applied to organisational development. Burger *et al.* (2008) have looked at how Frankl's 'meaning seeking' can be used to overcome resistance to organisational change. The problem with this study is that the nature and aim of 'change' are left rather vague.

Going beyond Frankl

When Frankl encountered a patient who suffered a multitude of torments, he would sometimes ask them what contemporary therapists may consider a risk too far: 'Why do you not commit suicide?'

He was, of course, attempting to refocus the patient's attention on everything concrete and specific that maintains their connection to life, in order to enhance their 'will to meaning'. Contemporary therapists call these connections 'protective factors for suicide' – factors that reduce the likelihood of suicide (Reeves and Taylor 2017, p. 274). In Canada, those indigenous communities that have protective factors in place, such as being in charge of their own civil services and high levels of self-determination, report very low suicide rates. But by contrast, Australian indigenous communities suffer from very high rates (Allam 2019).

Frankl's approach was heavily influenced by his experiences under fascism. He recounts how suicide rates during Christmas festivities increased in camps probably due to dashed hopes of an early release, and how 'a very strict camp ruling forbade any efforts to save a man who attempted suicide' (Frankl [1959] 2004, p. 87). This environmental analysis is opposed to Freud's emphasis on the personal (and usually sexual) causes of suicide. Even the neo-Freudian Erich Fromm had to chide the master: 'Hardly anyone commits suicide because of the frustration of his or her sexual desires, but many are ready to give up living because their ambition or their hate has been frustrated' (Fromm 1982, p. 60).

The newspapers seem to be full of acts of suicide these days, individualistic as well as collective pacts. Ray reports that 'eighteen students died by suicide in one week after they failed their exams in India' (2019). Following widespread protests by parent and student groups, the government 'has ordered the test results of over 300,000 failed students to be recounted' (ibid.). In the UK, teenage suicides have acquired a hashtag. Just as anorexics are described as #Anas, and bulimics as #Mias, 'those with suicidal thoughts have been given the name #Sues, validating and glorifying their dark thoughts' (Lauren 2019). In Malaysia, a teenage girl killed herself after asking her followers to choose death or life in an Instagram poll, and 69 per cent voted for death (Fullerton 2019). More recently, a study found 28.9 per cent increase in suicide rates among Americans aged 10–17 years in the month after Netflix's *13 Reasons Why* aired (Lee 2019).

Besides being tragic, every suicide is also an unintentional launchpad for a study in ethnomethodology. By breaking cultural taboos around the sanctity of human life and by forcing society to repair the damage, suicide touches the very heart of what it means to be a culturally embedded social being. This explains why it is such a controversial site of contestation with various state, religious and individual actors using it to promote partisan philosophies. In case we forget, 'suicide (self-murder) had been a punishable crime in England from the mid-thirteenth century until 1961' (Reeve and Taylor 2017, p. 268). The phrase 'self-murder' has its origins in the fifth century when Augustine condemned suicide as a violation of Biblical injunctions. The commonly used phrase 'commit suicide' may be a pale echo of 'self-murder', as it retains the notion of suicide as a crime and suicidal thoughts as sinful.

In the Middle Ages self-murderers were denied burial rites and sometimes further punished by having their assets seized by the emperor (Tierney 2010, p. 365). This contempt for self-murderers was not confined to religious authorities but at times found an echo among liberals. Immanuel Kant is a prime example:

> [Anyone who would take his own life] has no respect for human nature … and we are free to treat him as a beast, as a thing, and to use him for our sport as we do a horse or a dog, for he is no longer a human being.
>
> *(1963, p. 151)*

Overall, however, 'the hostility toward self-murder generally waned as liberalism spread throughout Europe' (Tierney 2010, p. 366). Hume went so far as to suggest that ending one's life can be considered courageous (ibid., p. 367). More recently, Lorentzon has argued along similar lines to Hume and Frankl that 'suicide can also be conceived as an act of taking control amid a life that is experienced as out of control' (Reeves and Taylor 2017, p. 271).

In the UK, despite recent prevention policies, suicide rates are increasing with a male to female ratio of 3:1, particularly in the 35–49 age group (Reeves and Taylor 2017, p. 273). Since the global financial crisis of 2007–2008 there has been a sharp rise in suicide rates of '54 European and American countries studied, particularly in men and in countries with higher levels of job loss' (Chang *et al.* 2013). According to the Samaritans, 6,188 suicides were recorded in the UK in 2017 (Samaritans 2017). The picture is more dire if we take into account 'self-harm' (behaviour with deferred consequences, including eating disorders, smoking, alcohol and drug use, and sexual risk taking), and 'self-injury' (behaviour with immediate consequences such as cutting, burning, ingesting dangerous substances, etc.). In prisons, self-harm behaviour is ten times higher among female prisoners, and with the fact of being under twenty years old, being white, being unsentenced or having a life sentence all adding to the risk factors (Reeves and Taylor 2017).

This gender difference played a key role in the only instance Marx dealt with the subject of suicide (Marx 1846). He explains how depriving a person of free, conscious activity creates alienation and how this alienation can be extended under capitalism to include man/woman relationships (Plaut and Anderson 1999, p. 6). Three of the four case studies Marx uses in this brief article are women who, as a result of combined exploitation and oppression, have committed suicide. So keen was Marx to ground his musings in empirical data that he even took the time to translate a report on suicide by a police functionary named Jacques Peuchet (1758–1830), who is credited with coining the term 'bureaucracy'. Marx agreed with Peuchet that suicide is a symptom of a sick society.

It was left to Durkheim to provide us with a classificatory system. He is a sociologist we must treat with caution since he betrays both anti-working-class and sexist tendencies. However, he has left us a reasonably thoughtful taxonomy of suicide and it would be churlish to ignore it. He divides suicides into four types:

1. *Fatalistic* suicide stems from excessive regulation, as exemplified by the suicide of slaves and wage-salves;
2. *Egocentric* suicide is due to the rise of excessive individualism and isolation;
3. *Anomie* suicide is a product of modernisation and lack of meaning in life;
4. *Altruistic* suicide is associated with pre-modernity and is caused by an 'underdeveloped individuality'.

For this last category, Durkheim cites the practice of *sati*, or widow suicide, in some parts of India. The kamikaze pilot may offer another example.

Based on Durkheim's taxonomy (which no doubt can be improved upon), I would suggest that Marx is most useful in foregrounding the underlying issues surrounding fatalistic and egocentric types of suicide. An implicit criticism of Frankl on the subject of suicide would be that his contribution is limited to what Durkheim calls anomie suicide. To complete the set, Foucault can be called upon to shed light on altruistic forms of suicide and the historical switch from pre-modernity to 'governmentality'. In fact, Thomas F. Tierney (2010) has already developed these ideas. He argues that in the eighteenth and nineteenth centuries there existed a tension in Europe between the police, mercantilism and liberalism that shaped the suicide debate. Gradually, a particular form of rationality developed (what Foucault calls 'governmentality'). This governmentality promotes 'bio-power', a form of power that does not rely on the traditional threat of punishment but instead endeavours to regulate subjects through administration. Both Peuchet and Durkheim contributed to the establishment of governmentality and bio-power, the former mainly through statistics and the latter through modern sociology. They both showed how during those periods in which there was 'a breach of social equilibrium … there was usually a marked increase in suicide' (ibid., p. 379). Significantly, both recognised that people will no longer tolerate severe punishment and therefore only advocated 'moral punishments' for 'self-murderers'.

Another example I would like to share with you is a short text by Tony Mckenna (2015) which provides an analysis of the remarkably high rates of suicide in Japan. Mckenna makes use of Durkheim but more significantly he also employs Trotsky's theory of 'uneven and combined development' to better elucidate the reasons for which Japan's suicide rate is 'roughly 60 percent above the global average' (ibid., p. 293). Previous explanations for this high rate have focused on either the religious culture of the Japanese or the stigmatisation of mental illness. Unlike the Abrahamic religions, 'neither Shinto nor Buddhism places any explicit divine prohibition on the act of suicide' (ibid., p. 294). This is important but it does not explain why China, which 'has a somewhat similar religious makeup', has a much lower suicide rate (ibid.).

The fact that the Japanese are inclined to view mental health sufferers as 'ethically abhorrent or morally weak' also plays a role. The *Japan Times* reports that 'it wasn't until the 1990s that the word *utsu* (depression) received wide currency' (Brasor 2012). The remarkable increase in prescriptions of the antidepressant Paxil and the anti-anxiety drug Zoloft failed to mitigate the crisis during the first decade of the twenty-first century. More recently, a musician named Kyochi Watanabe has been reported playing music into Japan's infamous 'suicide forest', including John Lennon's *Imagine*, in a bid to prevent people taking their own lives (Baynes 2018). These strategies notwithstanding, it was only the gradual improvements in the economy and the promotion of counselling services that since 2010 have seen the rates drop (XinhuaNet 2018).

What is lacking in these explanations, as with so much of Frankl's writings on suicide, is a historical or cultural context. Mckenna fills this gap by reminding us that the 1868 Meiji Revolution which, unlike its European counterparts, was a top-down bourgeois revolution organised by an ancient feudal class and former samurai warriors, is an excellent example of uneven and combined development. This tendency, as formulated by Trotsky, suggests that societies do not pass through a set of pre-designated linear stages, but that some tend to combine old feudal institutions with advanced capitalist relations. Following the Meiji Revolution, the traditions and values of the feudal class were left more or less intact, fostering an intense loyalty to one's bosses mediated through *shafu* or 'company spirit' (Mckenna 2015, p. 299). On the other hand, Japanese workers are also subjected to intense capitalist competition, long working hours, and massive levels of unpaid overtime (ibid., p. 300). In fact, they have coined a specific word to describe death by overwork, *karoshi* (ibid.). So, in a sense, Japanese workers operate under a double bind: experiencing intense capitalist pressure to work harder for less pay, *and* feelings of guilt and inadequacy whenever patrons express displeasure with their performance.

All this does not render Frankl irrelevant. If we look at the more specific case of Internet suicide pacts in Japan, they can be understood largely in terms of lack of *ikigai*, roughly translated as 'purpose' (Mckenna 2015, p. 301). With the rewriting of the social contract in favour of capitalism and the curtailment of job-for-life arrangements, work has become precarious in Japan. The younger generation of workers have all the responsibilities of their parents without many of the benefits, leading to a loss of *ikigai* and the anomie form of suicide Frankl described.

To conclude my discussion of suicide, let me underscore the main points. As with everything else, suicide is a class issue. One of the most recent reports, 'Dying for Inequality', says that there is

> overwhelming evidence of a strong link between socioeconomic disadvantage and suicidal behaviour … [for example] men in the lowest social class, living in the most deprived areas, are up to 10 times more at risk of suicide than those in the highest social class living in the most affluent areas.
>
> *(The Samaritans, quoted in Davies 2017)*

To suggest, as some religious and philosophical figures do, that suicide is unethical is to obfuscate the real conditions that breeds suicidal tendencies. Modern medicine's viewing of suicide as irrational and a sign of mental illness only adds to the problem, without getting to grips with its underlying causes.

To his credit, Frankl had a profound grasp of the mechanisms of suicide. However, by generalising from the extreme environment of the Holocaust and limiting his analysis and solution to an intra-psychological domain, he banished politics, history and sociology to the sidelines. In mobilising Marx, Durkheim and Foucault in the suicide debate, I have attempted to go beyond these shortcomings.

Final remarks on Frankl

After a twenty-year hiatus, I recently took up driving again. On my first trip I drove a tiny rented Fiat 500 all the way from London to Edinburgh. It started to rain, first vertically, then horizontally. As the countryside drew darker, my contact lenses became cloudier. Heavy trucks shot past me tossing my Fiat hither and thither. I came dangerously close to making the acquaintance of the car's airbag on at least two separate occasions. And yet I persisted to my destination. At the hotel, and after partaking of a few stiff White Russians, I finally stopped shaking. It was then that it occurred to me – this is as brave as I have ever been in my life!

By complete contrast to my ordinary trials, Viktor Emil Frankl endured concentration camps. He survived the Nazis but lost most of his family to them. It is important not to lose sight of this piece of information when evaluating Frankl. He refused to allow this experience to beat him down, and he never lost his sense of humour or his capacity for risk-taking. But if he is worthy of our respect, he is, I believe, also primed for some gentle debunking.

A number of writers have pointed out discrepancies and inconsistencies in Frankl's account of his incarceration in concentration camps. I must be honest here and admit that I have no way of ascertaining the validity of these criticisms. However, since the critics are substantial figures, I feel that their work needs to be flagged for the interested reader. Reading *Man's Search for Meaning* one gets the impression that Frankl spent a long portion of his incarceration at Auschwitz. In fact, Timothy Pytell has argued that

> Frankl was held close to the train, in the 'depot prisoner' area of Auschwitz and for no more than a few days. [He] was neither registered there, nor assigned a number before being sent on to a subsidiary work camp of Dachau, known as Kaufering III, the true setting of much of what is described in his book.
>
> (Wikipedia, *'Viktor Frankl'*)

More significant criticisms have been levelled at his overemphasis on 'meaning' as the ultimate goal of life. Lawrence L. Langer has argued that this is an amoral misuse of the concept which could just as easily be applied to the Nazis finding meaning in making the world free from Jews (Langer 1982). On a similar trajectory, Pytell has pointed out that Frankl embraced key ideas of the Nazi psychotherapy movement of the late 1930s, such as 'will and responsibility' (Pytell 2003). More serious charges have been levelled at him for carrying out experimental brain surgeries on suicidal patients at the Rothschild Hospital even after the hospital was taken over by the Nazis in April 1939. Pytell describes this 'as bordering on collaboration with the Nazis' (Pytell 2003).

Another criticism concerns his relationship with institutionalised religion. Much of Frankl's support in the USA came from religious readers and institutions. In turn, he recruited Methodist ministers and pastoral psychologists to study with him (Pytell 2016). Rollo May criticised logotherapy as hovering close to authoritarianism because

> there seems to be clear solutions to all problems, which belies the complexity of actual life. It seems that if the patient cannot find his goal, Frankl supplies him with one. This would seem to take over the patients' responsibility and … diminish the patient as a person.
>
> *(May, quoted in Pytell 2016)*

From a working-class perspective, I think the major problem with Frankl is that he was a middle-class conformist. Here I am in agreement with Russell's harsh criticisms of Frankl (Russell 2016, p. 57). What Frankl lacked was a political understanding of his predicaments based on clear class analysis. I find little or no evidence of Frankl's engagement with radical writers on Zionism (Avineri 1989; Weinstock 1989), Marxism and the 'Jewish question' (Leon 1946; Traverso 1995), or racism and psychology (Kovel [1970] 1984, 1984). Frankl's analysis is thoroughly individualistic, as are his solutions. This leaves no room for collective acts of resistance such as the ghetto fights in Warsaw between 1941–1943 as ably described by Marek Edelman ([1945] 1994). It leaves no room for social struggle!

7

RONALD DAVID LAING

The naughty existentialist

> I desire that we be better strangers.
>
> *William Shakespeare,* As You Like It

The unpopularity of R. D. Laing

You know you are dead, really, really dead, buried without parole, six feet under the ground dead, so lifelessly dead you wouldn't be offered a part as an extra in a zombie movie, when Dr Who himself fails to revive you!

When David Tennant (surely the greatest Dr Who ever) announced that he would be portraying R. D. Laing in a forthcoming movie, I was ecstatic and assumed that this would be the moment when psychology reacquaints itself with the works of a flawed radical. I recommended the movie to friends and students, not a single one of whom has since indicated that they have watched it! *Mad to Be Normal* was released in 2017, garnered a few lukewarm reviews, then faded away (Mullan 2017). Afterwards, Ronald David Laing (1927–1989) returned to being politely patronised as the naughty, vituperative gadfly who aspired to be a celebrity.

So, it is necessary to ask at the outset: why have all the films, documentaries, plays, websites and symposiums dedicated to discussing Laing failed in their purported aim of reanimating him? It could even be argued this unpopularity began when Laing was still alive. A documentary such as

Did You Used to Be R. D. Laing? captures the irony (Tougas and Shandel 1989). How could a man who was considered by some to be the most renowned psychiatrist of the latter part of the twentieth century become *persona non grata* among vast swathes of the fields of psychiatry and psychology?

Laing's intellectual milieu

Let me start this section by dropping a few names and displaying my impressive erudition, an all-too-familiar academic ritual my dear colleagues sometimes over-generously describe as 'contextualisation'.

The teenage Laing was a keen student of Voltaire, Thomas Reid, Freud, Marx and Nietzsche, but in later years he became increasingly shaped by Sartre, Bateson, Goffman and Foucault. Underscoring a few intellectual connections may be useful here. Thomas Reid's common-sense philosophy which sought an alternative to Hume's empiricism and Descartes's rationalism was a constant lodestar. Nietzsche's *Thus Spake Zarathustra* ([1883–1885] 1997) became a key text since it introduced mechanisms of life affirmation and transformation necessary for therapy: the *laugh* (which transmutes suffering into joy); the *dance* (which transmutes the heavy into the light); and the *game* (which transmutes the low into the high). Thus laughing, dancing and gaming became part of Laing's communication style, aimed at empowering the 'patient' and dissolving the patient/therapist hierarchy (Heaton 2015, p. 49).

Erving Goffman's criticisms of institutionalisation allowed the young Laing to bring his vague unease about psychiatric practice into sharper focus. Goffman demonstrates how institutionalisation can objectify the sufferer, create over-dependency, stigmatise mental illness and even, in some extreme cases, 'cause' schizophrenia (Goffman [1961] 1991). He also helps Laing to see how 'social relationships are basically dramatic performances between actors, not only in obvious situations such as waiting at table or giving a party, but in commonplace interactions as well' (Wing 1971, p. 360). Those who criticise Laing's 'showmanship' would do well to remember such influences.

There is also an intense affinity for Sartre, which has been misconstrued by some as 'an uncritical acceptance of the ideas of the French existential philosopher' (Ratna 1994, p. 422). The 'mad' are seen as active agents in the creation of their own misery who may decide at any point to exert the choice to abandon isolation and relate to others (Meisel 1996). In an echo of both Sartre and Frankl, we are assured that all people are free to live 'authentically', although Laing 'shifts the focus of these dilemmas from the intra-psychic to the interpersonal level' (Scott and Thorpe 2006, p. 335). This shift represents an improvement on Frankl and maybe even Sartre! Laing may not have left us a synthesis of Freud and Sartre as advanced as the one conjured up by Jacque Lacan, but at least one can read Laing without dozing off.

De-mythologising Laing

Before going further, we should ponder some of the myths surrounding Laing, the most persistent of which label him as part of the 'anti-psychiatry movement'. Throughout most of the 1940s–1950s 'western' psychiatry exerted absolute social control over the mental health of the 'mad'. Psychoanalysis offered an alternative but since it confined itself to dealing with 'neurosis', it left the field of 'psychosis' wide open to the whim of psychiatrists. Since this was also a class issue with psychoanalysts preferring the convenience of middle-class neurotic clients and leaving psychiatry to police the more violent and unpredictable working-class patients, psychiatry rightly garnered a harsh reputation among the proletariat.

The oppositional voices that were gradually raised against psychiatry's regime of confinement, lobotomisation, electroconvulsive therapy and medicalisation (Richards 2002, pp. 196–197), had their origins both inside and outside psychiatry. These voices represented different degrees of unease and challenged different pillars of the establishment. For our purposes, it is useful to distinguish between those who wished to abolish psychiatry *in toto* (e.g. Laing's friend David Cooper who was responsible for coining the term 'anti-psychiatry'), and those who aimed to humanise it by combining psychiatry with psychoanalysis, phenomenology and existentialism. Although he contradicted himself a number of times, Laing, by and large, belonged to this latter group and it makes sense to describe his position as 'critical psychiatry' and not 'anti-psychiatry'. These disagreements would eventually lead to a break with Cooper in the 1970s. To clarify matters further, I should point out that Laing practised his critical psychiatry both in groups and individualistically (he called the latter 'man-to-man' encounters).

Another theoretician who is often lazily lumped with Laing is the Hungarian-born psychiatrist Thomas Szasz (1920–2012). One can see the temptation; after all, both were qualified psychiatrists who turned against their profession, and both advocated 'libertarianism of sorts'. However, Szasz was a right-wing libertarian and a rather propagandistic advocate of

FIGURE 7.1 R. D. Laing

the rugged individual against the state. He called for the abolition of psychiatry on numerous occasions, but at his most accommodating Szasz was willing to tolerate consensual psychiatry, on condition that psychiatry severed its links with the criminal justice system (Roberts 2010, p. 694). He criticised Laing for not going far enough in denouncing the notion of mental illness, 'which in Szasz's view remains at best a metaphor', as well as for not condemning outright 'the forced incarceration of people against their will on psychiatric grounds' (ibid., p. 695).

The picture that emerges of Laing's relationship to psychiatry is far more nuanced than the caricature we are usually offered. Laing was proud of his medical background and advocated the judicious use of psychoactive drugs for 'patients', a term he redefined as those who patiently bear suffering without complaint (Thompson 2015, p. 33). Had he lived longer, Laing probably would have gravitated further towards the pioneers of neuropsychiatry such as Kurt Goldstein who viewed schizophrenia as a protective mechanism against anxiety, and the more recent school of neurophenomenology proposed by Francisco Varela, Walter Freeman and Antonio Damasio (Capra 2015, p. 46).

Laing's core ideas

> Blessed are the cracked, for they let in the light.
>
> *Spike Milligan*

Historians of psychology have found it difficult to assess Laing's contributions for two reasons: first, a great deal of his success was performative and interactive, rather than cognitive and textual. Basically, you had to be there to understand and benefit! This is a point made forcefully by Andrew Pickering (2015), and I shall return to it below; and second, Laing was not trying to make a name for himself by patenting new therapeutic techniques every other day, preferring instead to focus on establishing an authentic, equal relationship with the sufferer. This was a more immersive version of what we would nowadays call the 'therapeutic alliance'. In fact, a strong argument could be made that today's therapeutic alliance has in most places degenerated into a 'therapeutic contract', since it is a bourgeoise recognition of rights and duties rather than a genuine alliance based on equality, trust and solidarity.

I must credit Laing for being open about politics in a profession in which so many choose to lurk in the shadows. In the preface to *The Divided Self* Laing writes:

> A little girl of seventeen in a mental hospital told me she was terrified because the Atom Bomb was inside her. That is a delusion. The statesmen of the world who boast and threaten that they have Doomsday weapons are far more dangerous, and far more estranged from 'reality', than many of the people on whom the label 'psychotic' is fixed.
>
> *([1960] 2010, p. 12)*

Laing believed that the 'word-salad' of the schizophrenic will reveal its secrets if the therapist is willing to practise phenomenological *epoché* (temporary suspension of judgement), and enter the world of the sufferer. The existential viewpoint sees the person in context, and psychological alienation is located in the world and not solely in the psyche. It may sound innocuous enough to our ears but in the 1950–1960s this sensible stance constituted a decisive break with orthodoxy. However, and this is key to understanding the limitations of Laing, 'context' is usually defined too narrowly in his work (Brown 1974, p. 104; for a counterpoint to Brown, that I personally find unconvincing see Kirsner 2015, p. 74). Laing was hugely interested in the subjective point of view of the sufferer (the intra-psychological domain), and what goes on within small groups such as a family unit (inter-psychological domain), but the wider socio-economic and materialist imperatives (extra-psychological) were nearly always relegated to an indeterminate future.

An exception to this neglect of the extra-psychological is *The Politics of Experience and the Bird of Paradise* (Laing 1967), his most explicitly political work. In our own era of 'fake news' most of this text still feels fresh:

> There is little conjunction of truth and social 'reality'. Around us are pseudo-events, to which we adjust with a false consciousness adapted to see these events as true and real [Love Island, Neymar faking a football injury, any tweet by Donald Trump, etc.] … We are still half alive, living in the often fibrillating heartland of a senescent capitalism.
>
> *(Ibid., p.11)*

Here Laing is combining Marxism and existentialism (with a dash of Winnicott's object relations theory) to suggest that alienation is 'the social product of the violence of human beings on one another' (Kirsner 2015, p. 75). Winnicott had observed in his therapy work with evacuees during World War II 'that those who sat well-behaved in their new environment were in fact traumatised, while those who lashed out showed some faith in their ability to test this new reality' (Noys 2015). The difference between Winnicott and Laing is that the former located this alienation intra-psychologically, whereas the latter gradually came to see 'ontological insecurity' as a result of a 'false-self system' – usually limited to the family system.

Another factor that elevates Laing's discussion of 'madness' is his attention to class issues. Now, let me qualify this by saying that this attention is sometimes explicit and, when it is not, the reader has to force class contours to reveal themselves. And he was by no means the first existentialist philosopher to discuss class: Fromm, Sartre and the sorely neglected Joseph Dietzgen had already paved the way with sterling contributions. But since most Anglo-Saxon therapists were coy on the subject, Laing's discussion of it was refreshing.

Revisiting the case study of Peter in *The Divided Self* with the aid of Benjamin Noys' commentary foregrounds all this very neatly. Accordingly, Peter's case demonstrates that it is not just being working class that traps people in a 'familial false self' but it also forces them to shift up and down the social ladder. Laing tells us:

> Peter was a large man of twenty-five and he looked the picture of health. He came to see me complaining that there was a constant unpleasant smell coming from him … particularly from … the genital region … He likened it to … the smell that comes from broken-down 'closets' of the slum tenements of the district in which he grew up.
>
> *([1960] 2010, pp. 120–122)*

Further into the analysis we discover that

> His own feeling about his birth was that neither his father nor his mother had wanted him and, indeed, that they had never forgiven him for being born … [as for his teacher he] wanted him to 'speak properly' and to wear 'middle-class clothes'. But all this was trying to make him be what he was not.
>
> *(Ibid., pp. 122–123)*

Objectively, Peter is still working class but subjectively he is pushed towards becoming middle class. This tension leads to the emergence of a 'false self' which shields him temporarily from people's gaze. The 'true self' is further diminished due to 'a sense of pointlessness, a lack of direction, of futility' (ibid., p. 125). The overlap with Frankl's 'will to meaning', discussed in

Chapter 6 in this volume, is clear. Laing ends his analysis by showing the critical point at which Peter's 'neurosis' and anxiety transform into 'psychosis'. Nowadays, neurosis, psychosis and critical points are terms one rarely comes across in polite therapeutic conversation and yet, if we were being honest, they still lurk around in the background of each case study. Laing makes one final underdeveloped point which needs underlining. Peter was not only suffering from feelings of inadequacy and impotence but 'at the same time he felt he was someone very special, with a special mission and purpose, sent by God to this earth' (ibid., p. 133). Well, in the olden days this would have been referred to as someone suffering simultaneously from an inferiority and superiority complex. I would argue that we have been too hasty in jettisoning the notion of a 'complex' and that there is an urgent need to revive these terms if only to make sense of the visceral authoritarian passions we witness in so many people today. It is the *simultaneous* embodiment of these two complexes in the same individual that ought to ring alarm bells.

Getting his hands dirty: Laing's experimental therapy

Laing's therapy took the form of a dialogue with the patient and as such was a unique experience each time. However, certain common devices repeat themselves in most of his case studies. In an all too brief review, Mark Aveline has captured one of its central characteristics rather well: 'Compassion, camaraderie and reducing the rift between psychiatrist and patient are his theme-songs. He does not deny the neurological realities of psychiatry; he seeks to radically improve its practice' (1985, p. 220).

Together with his colleague David Cooper, he created a safe environment for severely disturbed patients. For instance,

> the experimental ward, Villa 21, at Shenley Hospital in which Cooper [worked, where] schizophrenic patients could come voluntarily and refuse treatment if they wished. They had a close one-to-one relationship with a member of staff from a multi-disciplinary team. The ward was run democratically with patients holding communal responsibility.
>
> *(David 1986, p. 380)*

This approach may not seem 'revolutionary' today but at the time it was considered very avant-garde. At Kingsley Hall (located in the East End of London)

> there were no locks on the doors and no anti-psychotic drugs were administered [although there was LSD on offer for those who wanted it] … There were all-night therapy and role-reversal sessions, marathon Friday night dinners hosted by Laing and visits from mystics, academics and celebrities, including, famously, Sean Connery, a friend and admirer of Laing's. Play was encouraged as was regression through therapy to childhood.
>
> *(O'Hagan 2012)*

What made the experiment at Kingsley Hall possible was the higher than usual level of class struggle in Britain and Europe generally. Local residents may not have been very fond of being next to a 'loony bin' but the struggles against capitalism and authority had opened up spaces for people like Laing to do things differently.

Contemporary applications of Laing

A small but dedicated group of admirers are still conducting their work influenced by Laing's theoretical legacy. I would like to briefly look at a few of them below.

Using Laing's existential-phenomenology, Nisha Gupta has explored how 'schizoid' and 'closeted gay individuals' suffer similar traumas and employ similar coping defence mechanisms (2015, p. 170). As Gupta observes, 'Like Freud, Laing believed that much psychological suffering was caused by patients' efforts to deceive and deny themselves of lived experiences that were too painful to bear' (ibid., p. 172). The aim of therapy would then be to empower individuals to reclaim their 'personal truths rather than continue to split-off their true selves' (ibid., p. 173). Laing described the schizoid as someone who feels 'persecuted by reality itself' (quoted in ibid., p. 177). This explains the splitting of the self from the world, resulting in isolation, inner deadness and madness. The persecution that gay people are subjected to is not just psychological but also physical. Basic ontological security is thus denied to both the schizoid and the gay individual (ibid., p. 178). According to Gupta, 'Laing explained that schizoid people, to protect their core self from being annihilated by the outer world, begin to detach from their body and identify exclusively with their mind' (ibid., p. 180). In short, they become 'disembodied' (see Chapter 15 in this volume on Artaud). All behaviour becomes calculated and restricted, and spontaneous self-expression is deemed too risky. Their bodies 'mechanically perform the social behaviours expected of [them], while the mind observes from the inside' (ibid., p. 181). The mind (the true self) 'evaluates this performance with hateful self-scrutiny', and this self-hate leads to guilt and feelings of intense worthlessness (ibid., p. 183).

Laing's influence looms large in the wider movement of 'therapeutic communities' (TCs). These can be residential or day units, voluntary or prison-based. The very first TC was established during World War II at Northfield Military Hospital (Birmingham, UK). People such as Wilfred Bion and S. H. Foulkes pioneered group therapy there. It was this trend that was taken up and developed by Laing and Cooper. A contemporary example of TC would be Grendon Prison where the authorities claim to practise 'democratisation', 'communalism' and 'tolerance' as far as circumstances permit.

One of the most fascinating studies of schizophrenia is Nancy Scheper-Hughes' *Saints, Scholars and Schizophrenics* (1982). This is a sensitive portrait of mental problems in rural Irish society. In interpreting her empirical results which show extremely high rates of mental issues, especially among young men, Scheper-Hughes draws on Laing's work. The more Laing is involved with the families of identified psychotics, she asserts, the 'more hard-pressed he is to say exactly who is sick' (ibid., p. 177). For Laing, 'madness is the product of a skewed communication system shared by all members of a disturbed family' (ibid., p. 178). Family myths develop over time and they serve to maintain the family's homeostasis at the expense of one member of the family. Think of the way Meg in the cartoon series *Family Guy* becomes the butt of jokes and a lightning rod for all the tensions and antagonisms generated by the family. If Meg refuses to play the role of victim, the whole edifice of the family crumbles. Scheper-Hughes suggests that something very similar happens in rural Irish families where 'family myths' are developed and then used to label, scapegoat and blame one individual member: 'What most differentiated the "normal" from the "disturbed" young villager, I contend, is the ability of the former to project evil and blame outwards, and the tendency of the latter toward self-blame and paralysing guilt' (ibid.).

The examples of 'closeted gays', 'therapeutic communities' and 'rural schizophrenia' give an indication of the wide range of subjects that can benefit from a Laingian perspective.

Going beyond Laing: schizophrenia, shamanism and carnivalesque

> I can speak Esperanto like a native.
>
> *Spike Milligan*

One common journalistic ploy for denigrating Laing is to refer to him as a shaman, especially since to the uninitiated, shamanism and charlatanism are perceived as synonymous. If by a shaman one is referring to a magician who can converse between the living and the dead, then clearly the man was no shaman! I think, however, it is perfectly reasonable to refer to him as such so long as we re-accentuate the shaman as a journeyman between 'sanity' (schizoid) and 'insanity' (schizophrenia). Now the shaman becomes a great listener and 'a discoverer of profound truths about the human psyche' (Paton 2015).

More importantly, Laing saw himself precisely in these terms as someone qualified, given the right carnivalesque environment, to travel and listen along this spectrum. Perhaps this is the key difference between the shaman and the schizophrenic: the element of volition. When the time is right, Laing would invite the 'insane' to rejoin the rank of the 'sane'. Some individuals may need to be taken to the extremity of schizophrenia first, before being guided back ('Psychiatrically, this would appear as ex-patients helping future patients go mad', Laing 1967, p. 106), and some may already be on their way back to a schizoid state and needing a helping push ('Madness need not be all breakdown. It may also be break-through', ibid., p. 110). The spectrum stretching between schizophrenia and schizoid goes right to the heart of the perennial debate around diagnosis versus formulation. It also provides us with an opportunity to update Laing with the works of the Russian theoretician, Mikhail Bakhtin.

A Bakhtinian interpretation of the case of Mary Barnes is instructive. In 1965 Mary became the first resident of Kingsley Hall and lived there until 1970. She was encouraged by Laing to 'give in to madness'. Soon she regressed into 'a state of helpless infancy … being fed with a baby's bottle … defecating and urinating, covering herself in her own faeces, and sculpting and painting with it' (Torn 2012, p. 722). The triangular relationship that is established between Laing, Mary Barnes and her primary caretaker, the American psychiatrist Joseph Berke, is unorthodox. We do not have the space to go into it here but interested readers should consult Barnes and Berke ([1971] 2002). It may even be worthwhile to investigate parallels between Laing-Berke-Barnes with the earlier therapeutic triad of Jung-Gross-Spielrein.

Barnes' transgressive behaviour exemplifies the Bakhtinian carnivalesque: it is *eccentric*, aiming at the manifestation of latent sensual feelings; it is *profane*, aiming to undermine the medical and social definitions of her experiences; and it is a *suspension of hierarchies*, aiming to create new forms of relationship with her carers. In short, it is behaviour that adapts the environment around her to her pain and her needs instead of regulating body and mind to perform to the rhythms of psychiatry. As Torn observes,

> The positioning of Barnes by both herself and others as a dominant voice in Kingsley Hall culminates in her becoming its star attraction. Her artwork is featured in the national papers, becoming the focus of a BBC documentary. She writes her story with Berke, becoming Laing's only complete case study.
>
> *(2012, p. 723)*

Another patient of Laing who has been interpreted in Bakhtinian terms is Jesse Watkins. Laing tells us that he was a commander and commodore of coastal convoys: 'During his career at sea, he encountered shipwreck, mutiny and murder' (1967, p. 120). Jesse's 'ten-day voyage', or if you prefer his 'psychotic episode', is described in an interview. Jesse experienced time going backwards. While in hospital he felt animalistic, like a rhinoceros. Ordinary tasks such as looking in the mirror became arduous, 'as though [he] was looking at someone who … was familiar … but very strange' (ibid., p. 122). Reading newspapers was just as difficult, since now 'everything that [he] read had a large number of associations' (ibid., p. 124). Jesse begins to feel as if 'he has enhanced powers of control over his body and could affect others' (ibid., p. 125). All this was very painful, like 'something soft [being dropped] into a bag of nails' but nevertheless it was 'a stage that everyone would have to go through one way or another in order to reach a higher stage of evolution' (ibid., pp. 132 and 130). Eventually, as the tension built up in Jesse, he 'felt he couldn't 'take' it anymore [and he] decided to come back' (ibid., p. 130). This return journey is described as an act of will whereby Jesse focuses on 'linking up' with himself and the present by repeating his name (ibid., p. 131).

Jesse's descent is full of 'grotesque' imagery characterised by estrangement, reciprocal ambiguity and the sense of embodied rotation (Good 2001, p. 115). When he looks at himself in the mirror, we are reminded of Bakhtin's claim that 'before the mirror we are never alone. At least one other voice stands by us, as an image is jointly authored' (ibid.). But he sees both the old and the new as grotesque, unfamiliar images. Time stretches and shrinks to provide yet more frightful ideas. In his narrative, 'every doorways, stairways, and entrances enable a body to pass from one time-space to another but their structure contains the potential of transforming hell or paradise into each other in a single instance' (ibid., pp. 14–15). What a wonderful description of this thing we call 'madness'!

Once the therapist immerses herself into the patient's world, the 'inaccessible' and 'disconnected' word-salad, as Kraepelin put it, becomes meaningful. Bakhtin helps us in this framing as he has left us a vivid discursive practice for describing extreme emotions. The precondition for this is the dialogic interaction and tolerance of ambiguity advocated by Bakhtin (Marlowe 2015). The Bakhtinian analysis reminds us that as the 'journey partner' of the patient, a Laingian therapist must share the risks involved in such a venture. Cowards and conservatives need not apply!

Concluding remarks

Despite what you might have heard from the 'false news brigade', Laing was neither a Marxist (à la Reich and Fromm), nor an anarchist (à la Otto Gross), and not even a situationist (like his chum Alex Trocchi). But I think he was 'touched' by all these ideologies and he took on board as much as his petty bourgeois sensibilities would allow. In 1970 he travelled to India and Ceylon, where he studied Buddhism and yoga. When he returned he was 'a changed man. Unlike his former, angrier, radical self, the new R. D. Laing now enjoined a kind of gentle, Buddhist austerity as the best path to liberation, and expressed a great skepticism about the left's agenda and methods' (Burston 2001). His early political learning never left him completely, and I suspect the best description of his overall politics would be 'left-wing libertarianism', a tag which is loose enough to account for most of his ideas yet specific enough to distinguish his contributions from right-wing libertarians such as Thomas Szasz.

Laing's class analysis remained rudimentary and he never developed a rounded critique of capitalism. For me, this constitutes a major deficiency. In terms of the other -isms I have employed throughout the book (modernism, high modernism, postmodernism), Laing clearly displays *some* modernist tendencies: he believes, for example, in the notion of the self, authenticity, love, truth and the unconscious. At the same time, his work was also a reaction against the high-minded and unfaltering confidence displayed by high modernism in science and technology. This comes through very clearly in his lambasting of psychiatry. Interestingly, he also foreshadows postmodernism by rejecting Galilean objectivity, the myth of analytic neutrality and essentialism. In short, Laing tiptoed across the putrefying corpse of high modernism to straddle the gap between modernism and postmodernism. This has left him vulnerable to criticism from all persuasions, most of which I consider unjust.

Take the otherwise outstanding *Not in Our Genes* (Rose *et al.* 1984). Co-written by a biologist, a psychologist and a geneticist at the height of their intellectual powers, this is a book that is greater than the sum of its parts. I cannot recommend it highly enough. And yet it misjudges Laing rather awkwardly as an advocate of 'anti-psychiatry' and 'labelling theory' (ibid., p. 77). Further on, he is accused of being a 'cultural determinist' who sees schizophrenia as 'essentially a family disorder' (ibid., p. 230). It is certainly true that Laing's inconsistencies and rhetorical style of argumentation provide succour to some of these charges. For instance, in *The Politics of the Family* (1971), Laing mischievously proposes a thought experiment in which a group of 'schizophrenics' are treated as sane and a group of 'normals' are treated as schizophrenic. He believed that the results would show that expectation and labelling *cause* the psychosis. Slippages such as this only go to prove that Ronnie is definitely *not* the messiah! And occasionally he is a very naughty boy! Nevertheless, I hope that sufficient evidence has been presented above to counter the remaining charges.

Another brilliant book, *Social Amnesia* (Jacoby 1997), feigns praise for an approach that 'resounds with political radicalism' and 'revolutionary élan', before accusing Laing of dribbling into 'blind therapy and positivism, pop existentialism and mysticism' (ibid., p. 131). No sooner has Jacoby concluded his opening statement than the trial proceeds in earnest, with further charges of 'neo-positivism' and 'confusion between the surface and the essence' and 'reducing the human community to the I-Thou encounter [abstracted] from historical and social reality' piled on (ibid., pp. 135–146). Again, at the risk of repeating myself, some of these charges are valid, some are exaggerated and some are simply wrong-headed. Too many critics of Laing, even profound ones, have confused the man with his *zeitgeist*, or reduced the totality of his contribution to a hackneyed phrase here, a rash statement there.

In conclusion, I instinctively feel that Laing must be extended or else he will be afflicted by the curse of 'footnotism' (the curse of being permanently relegated to a footnote). But how exactly to manage this feat? Well, I think those parts of his contribution that fall under intra-psychology could be expanded through neurophenomenology. It is a natural ally and, frankly, the collaboration will mutually benefit both Laing and neurophenomenology. Laing's insights may be validated by neurophenomenological studies, and the latter's methodological issues overcome through Laingian *social* phenomenology. His inter-psychology should be enhanced through Bakhtinian psychology, a form of psychology that is bursting with novel ideas and vocabulary. Finally, his extra-psychological work should benefit from a fresh synthesis with the best of Marxism, anarchism and situationism; ideologies he dabbled in without ever mastering any of them.

8

FOR FOUCAULT'S SAKE!

> God is dead. Marx is dead. And I don't feel so well myself.
>
> *Eugène Ionesco*

There are numerous iconic intellectuals who mean a great deal to academics: Althusser, Zizek, Lacan, Negri, Badiou and Foucault, to name but a few. Personally, I find them all very middle class and the end result of their politics extremely reactionary. Moreover, I confess that at times I find their pretentiousness quite insufferable. Their stylised obscurity is, at least in part, quite deliberate. An admirer of Michel Foucault (1926–1984), Fons Elders, has said: 'Translating Foucault is a very difficult task because his style of thinking serves two opposite aims: to express and to hide simultaneously' (1971, see notes beneath the video clip). Talking to academics brought up on such traditions is like discussing painting with kindergarten kids who have barely mastered the use of crayons!

It is, however, undeniable that occasionally even these clowns manage to provide a useful insight or line of inquiry that adds to our working-class understanding. During these rare moments they become worthy of our attention. In this chapter, I wish to focus mainly on Foucault's contributions to psychology, and towards the end I will offer parallels with the work of Negri.

The Badiou interview

In 1965 Alan Badiou (1965a) interviewed Foucault. Badiou begins the interview innocuously enough by asking Foucault: 'What is psychology?' We are then subjected to a rhetorical response in keeping with Dr Sheldon Cooper's description of 'psychology as the doofus of the sciences', with which I opened this book (see Introduction). Foucault explains that this simple question is both about the functions of psychology (which he finds less interesting), and about the scientific status of psychology (which he finds more fundamental). He goes on to explain that psychology must be interrogated on the basis of its claims to objectivity and it should also be interrogated 'like any other type of culture' (Badiou 1965a, 2 mins). Moreover, psychology is 'inscribed in the history of other types of culture' such as the Christian confessional (ibid., 4 mins). In Chapter 10 in this volume, I explain how these interrogative themes comprise the essence of Parker's critical psychology.

Psychology can be viewed as either an updating of philosophy (a reflection upon infinity), or of anthropology (a reflection upon the finitude of humans). Foucault prefers the latter assumption and more precisely he sees the origins of modern psychology in the eighteenth-century contributions of Immanuel Kant (1724–1804). According to Foucault, psychology is still trying to answer Kant's four fundamental anthropological questions: 'What can I know?', 'What should I do?', 'What can I expect?' and, most important of all, 'What is man?'

This claim may very well be true of mainstream psychology where psychologists are still attempting to complete the Enlightenment project. However, critical psychology, which was born in the 1970s as a result of class defeats endured in previous decades, reformulates these Kantian explorations negatively: 'Why can't I know?', 'What shouldn't I say or do?', 'Why should I limit my expectations?', and 'Why is humanity ultimately unknowable?' This is a clear instance of the dialectics of thesis (mainstream psychology) coming into conflict with its own anti-thesis (critical psychology), and hopefully one day resolving the ensuing contradictions through a synthesis (postpsychology).

Psychology will continue to remain the most important of the social sciences, according to Foucault, because of its 'disciplining' capabilities (Badiou 1965b, 1 min). The 'discovery of the unconscious' had a profound impact on not only psychology but also physiology and sociology (ibid., 3 mins). Freud 'discovered' the unconscious as one would discover a text (here Foucault follows Lacan's formulations). This text then becomes an analytical method for all the social sciences. In true Foucauldian tradition, no evidence is furnished to prove or at least anchor these propositions. Presumably that would undermine the sublimity of his sermonising.

Foucault and discourse

For many, Foucault's most significant contribution is the notion of 'discourse'. This is ironic, since it is one of the most poorly defined terms in his entire body of work. His use of discourse is so inconsistent that one has to wonder if he is being deliberately obtuse. It is best to think of it as a set of (more or less coherent) statements about an object such as 'madness' or 'sexuality'. These discourses are tied into specific disciplines such as psychiatry and sexology and embedded in certain structures of power. Foucault uses these discourses to reconstruct history and understand the past. So, discourse fills the gap between spontaneously occurring talk and the innately inherited grammar of language, and allows us to talk systematically about specific issues in a culture (Foucault [1972] 2002).

Foucault turned the power of discourse analysis against his own privileged background (a very bourgeois background that he tried to prevent journalists from investigating). His upper-class education included Jesuit schooling and bouts of rebelliousness interspersed with self-harming. His attempted suicide at the age of twenty-two resulted in his first brush with psychiatry. His homosexuality and inclination for sadomasochism met with disapproval from French society, which is one of the reasons he travelled so widely in search of less censorious environments.

One can speculate as to the impact of all this on Foucault's developing critique of medicine and psychiatry. Without denying the achievements accomplished in these fields, he was of the opinion that the professional eighteenth-century physician was a sinister figure who subjected the sufferer to the 'medical gaze' – a gaze that observed symptoms, organs, biological flaws, and dysfunctions, but not a real person. He reminds us of Malthusian debates in England about the 'overbreeding of the poor and about the sexual excesses of the aristocracy contributing to revolutionary collapse' (Weeks 1985, p. 73). There was nothing 'neutral' or 'impartial' about this gaze. On the contrary, the medical gaze (and this also applies to the 'social science gaze') is always ideologically inclined, and aims to regulate the working class.

This is a valid and necessary counterclaim to the mainstream Weberian separation of 'facts' from 'values'. Weber postulates this separation in order to imbue factual evidence with an inherent superiority in all evaluative judgements. According to this viewpoint, social scientists must limit themselves to discovering and presenting facts to the authorities. The facts are then taken up by the state and other institutions to establish 'norms'. These norms gradually develop the notion of the 'normal' through the 'abnormal' (Fillingham 1993, p. 17). In other words, categories such as 'homosexual', 'black', 'unemployable', 'mad' and 'migrant' are constructed, then abnormalised and finally marginalised. But as marginalised categories they remain crucial for maintaining norms around 'heterosexuality', 'white', 'wage-slaver', 'sane' and 'native born'. Finally, the development of norms into discourses confers further power to the upper and middle classes who come to manage the discursive practice.

Resistance to these normalising tendencies emerges in the form of 'reverse discourse'. For example, homosexuality having been constructed as a category by medicine, psychiatry, jurisprudence and literature during the 1870s then begins 'to speak in its own behalf, to demand that its own legitimacy or "naturality" be acknowledged, often in the same vocabulary, using the same categories by which it was medically disqualified' (Spargo 1999, p. 22). A great deal of Hirschfeld's campaigning work (discussed in Chapter 2 in this volume), falls under this description. It is claimed by queer theorists and others that 'reverse discourse' is the germ of what will eventually be called 'identity politics' (ibid.), a term that incidentally Foucault himself found ambivalent. In fact, we should underline this point: when we have full control of our identity and have the space to develop it, an identity might be useful. However, when it becomes allied to 'the prescriptive work of religion, psychiatry, medicine or the law', identity becomes an imposition and a crude tactic of power (Weeks 1985, p. 187). Identity, suggest Weeks, 'may … be no more than a game, a ploy to enjoy particular types of relationships and pleasures. But without it, it seems, the possibilities of sexual choice are not increased but diminished' (ibid., p. 210).

The case of Herculine Barbin dite Alexina B may be instructive here. Barbin was a young hermaphrodite who lived, studied and taught in nineteenth-century France (Lafrance 2005, p. 161). Her story reflects how power uses various tactics to domicile 'those whose bodies defied the rigid two-sex system' (ibid.). Alexina (as she was known) was born a female in 1838. 'Though deemed a female at birth, Barbin quickly realised that she was unlike most of her female peers. As she got older, she developed increasingly "masculine' features"', writes Lafrance (ibid., p. 169). In 1860 'everything changed as Barbin was ordered to abandon her life as female and begin living as male' (ibid., p. 165).

As Foucault shows, this was a period when the 'will to truth' around issues of sex and sexuality was at its most intense. Scientists and bureaucrats became obsessed with collecting and classifying sexualised bodies. Barbin's experiences first in an orphanage and later at school were conditioned by 'disciplinary power' (Foucault 1991). This is a relation rather than an entity that can be possessed: it is not, according to Foucault, owned by the ruling class, 'nor is it exercised through straightforward repression' (Lafrance 2005, p. 166). Through disciplinary power, the orphanage, boarding school, nunnery and other pedagogic institutions she attended regulated her time and space. The overall efficiency of the dictatorship of time and space must be underwritten through surveillance, usually 'panoptic surveillance' (ibid., p. 168).

What is ironic is that the 'homosocial' space of the convent she lived in, and its Christian discourse that denied the body its sex and sexuality, actually helped Barbin 'to live a life of relative peace' (Lafrance 2005, p. 171). She was to some extent protected from the constant panoptic surveillance that was at work outside the convent. Foucault believed that modern power is enabled and sustained through confessionals, and it was precisely Barbin's confessions of her bodily 'abnormalities' to a priest that led to her intrusive medical examination. Now she was scrutinised by the bio-medical gaze. The medical report shows that Barbin had 'just as many male traits as she did female traits', but the doctors involved in Barbin's examination classified her as a man (ibid., p. 177). She was forced to change her gender legally, as a result of which she lost her job as teacher and began working as a low-paid clerk in a railroad office (ibid., p. 178). She also lost her lesbian lover. She committed suicide in 1868 by inhaling gas from her gas stove (*Wikipedia*, 'Herculin Barbin').

Foucault's historical method

Throughout the 1950s and most of 1960s Foucault was under the sway of structuralist thinking, although if Piaget is to be believed Foucault did not really understand structuralism (Trombadori 1991, p. 113). Following Saussure and Lévi-Strauss, he too believed that binaries were paramount; the rules binding these binary oppositions can be best studied by freezing time and looking at a single moment cross-sectionally (the *archaeological*

FIGURE 8.1 Foucault

method); and the most important structure of all is the linguistic one (Fillingham 1993, p. 95). He once defined structuralists as 'people for whom what counts in essence are systems of relations and thus not at all the lived, individual experience of people' (Elders 1971, 9 mins). In the mid-1970s Foucault came to see the limits of this approach, and moved towards what other social scientists would in time call 'post-structuralism'.

In an interview with Trombadori, Foucault once said, 'I happen to write what I would call books of exploration and books of method. Books of exploration: *The History of Madness, The Birth of the Clinic*, etc. Books of method: *The Order of Things, The Archaeology of Knowledge*' (Foucault, quoted in Trombadori 1991, p. 28).

As far as his method is concerned, I feel that too much (far too much) has been made of the distinction between his two main choices: 'archaeology' and 'genealogy'. Foucault himself did not care for such distinctions. However, it is valid to suggest that the first of these, the archaeology method, was employed by him throughout the 1960s. The method focuses on discourses and how they can be examined. It is a useful way of bringing out similarities and differences. In contrast to so much of mainstream history, it is a method that concentrates on a short time frame and investigates it cross-sectionally. As Fendler (2014, p. 38) explains, Foucault 'studied artifacts of eighteenth-century European linguistics, economics, and science. Then he tried to figure out how those artifacts made sense together'.

The genealogical method is quite similar but Foucault's concerns underwent subtle changes in the 1970s. Again, Fendler is a useful guide here: 'While archaeology works to understand how artifacts fit together in a historical moment, genealogy works to figure out what kind of people would fit into that set of artifacts' (2014, p. 39). There is more emphasis on power relations within genealogical analysis, as we just witnessed in the case of Barbin. However, even its adherents are ready to admit that the genealogical method is limited in understanding wider social forces and the class struggle (Henriques *et al.* 1984, p. 109).

Foucault's approach to history sometimes reminds me a little of the Native American character in Dustin Hoffman's *Little Big Man* (1970). The character is called Younger Bear and he is a 'contrary',

> the most dangerous of Chayanne warriors because the way they live drives them half crazy. Except for battle, a contrary does everything backwards. He says goodbye, when he means hello! Yes, when he means no … and washes with dirt and dries with water, and so forth.

Foucault's treatment of history is contrary. Where Whiggish historiography narrates a continuous classical tale of incremental progression, Foucault disrupts it by pointing out differences and contradictions. For instance, his history of madness shows how things became worse, not better, as the physical incarceration of the 'insane' gave way to the humanist method of caring for 'patients'. In those historical methods that foreground discontinuity (e.g. Kuhn's paradigm-shift approach or the belief that Greek and Christian civilisations are two different regimes), Foucault insists on listing similarities and continuities. Younger Bear sure knew how to piss off the rest of the tribe!

Now his major works begin to make more sense. In *Madness and Civilisation* (2001), *Discipline and Punish: The Birth of the Prison* (1991), as well as *The Birth of the Clinic* ([1973] 2003), Foucault argues that the dominant linear interpretation of history which charts 'progress' from dark medieval barbarism to the humanity of the Enlightenment is both self-serving and erroneous. The Middle Ages were not as 'barbaric' and 'ignorant' as mainstream history has suggested, and humanism is not the liberation of humans it claims to be, but is instead a fabrication (Elders 1971, 12 mins). The transition of state violence from a visible expression of punishment carried out in public to a private operation conducted inside prisons entailed not a civilising imperative but a transition to a more efficient judicial machinery. Physical punishment has been transformed into the discipling of the 'soul'. When internalised, this can lead to masochism.

In a radio interview with Deleuze, Foucault suggests that

> modern man has not de-ritualised pain. I only think he has ... distributed the ceremony. One part was transformed by him into administration ... one could call [it] *the police*. Another part he has reproduced in his fantasies, and this the strange sexual perversion that one calls *masochism*.
>
> *(1963, 1 min, emphasis added)*

He notes that the term masochism is associated with an individual (Leopold von Sacher-Masoch, 1836–1895), who lived in an oppressed country (the Austrian Empire), and who was the son of a policeman. He also observes the formal, contractual character of masochism in Sacher-Masoch's novels, when the masochist signs a bourgeois contract promising to conform to the dictates of the sadist.

Against his own interpretation, he also implies that in places and epochs 'where sex becomes too available ... variations are necessary to enhance the pleasure of the act' (Weeks 1985, p. 48). According to Foucault, irrespective of the social origins of sadomasochism we can turn it into a 'strategic game', and we can transform it from a contractual expression of domination to a source of pleasure (Spargo 1999, p. 65).

Significantly, this transition from public punishment by the state to private masochism also makes resistance harder to organise. When punishment was public and involved ritualistic torture, the condemned would sometimes become the subject of pity and mercy. Occasionally riots would erupt and prisoners released by angry crowds. The monarch's judicial sovereignty was thus punctured by a sense of injustice rising from below (Linebaugh 2006).

Today the functioning of the law is still 'spectacularised' (in the Debordian sense of the term), but there is neither glory, nor shame, not even dramatic ruptures. Today the condemned become part of an overcomplicated, bureaucratic, legal machinery that attempts to ascertain the 'truth' dispassionately. Obviously, the system has some benefits over previous regimes, otherwise it would have fallen into disrepute long ago. For instance, the bourgeois notion of 'assumption of innocence until proven guilty' might have been no more than a chimera even at the height of bourgeois law, but it was an attractive ideal. The fact that so many nation-states have decided to do away with even this fig leaf of fairness is an indication of the authoritarian turn capitalism has taken in order to save itself.

Foucault's historical method applied to 'madness'

In a documentary for Dutch TV Foucault recounts how 'western civilisation' (a phrase admittedly overused and loosely defined throughout his work) has been familiar for a long time with the phenomenon of madness (Elders 1971, 1 min). The 'mad' have appeared in plays and literature since at least the Greek era. However, 'madness' only became the subject of scientific discourse in the nineteenth century. What Foucault brings out in his historical investigation is how the ground had to be prepared for this manoeuvre. He shows how from the seventeenth century onwards the 'mad' were 'taken out of society … secluded' (ibid., 2 mins). One seminal moment of this process can be seen in the famous paintings of the Dutch master, Frans Hals (1582–1666), especially *The Women Regents*. 'There around a table are these five old women', says Foucault, 'whose job it is to hold, to run this house of imprisonment where … all socially worthless people, the troublemakers, were imprisoned' (ibid., 2 mins). The emergent rational thinking would, henceforth, deem most eccentricities as expressions of madness and set it apart physically in houses that would later become known as asylums.

In the Middle Ages the image of 'madness invoked that of the vagrant and the sinner' (Henriques *et al.* 1984, p. 136). In the sixteenth and seventeenth centuries the tragic figure of the mad begins to be feared. The symbolic 'ship of fools' proceeds to become the 'lunatic asylum'. Now 'madness becomes something that must be tamed and silenced', a threat that must be 'tracked down and forced to the conformity of the norms of the rational' (ibid., p. 137).

In pursuing this logic, Foucault goes on to question the myths that western civilisation generates about itself; in particular, the myth of tolerance and the myth of humaneness. The road to 'tolerance' is paved first through degradation and then violent exploitation before the 'other' can be 'made tolerable' (Elders 1971, 4 mins). Sexuality, for instance, has to be suppressed by puritanism, before medicine and then psychoanalysis can recognise it in the nineteenth century and make it the subject of their discourse (Henriques *et al.* 1984, p. 220). The recognition is a distorted one whereby women's reproductive capacity and their bodies become, in Foucault's sense, hystericised. This distorted recognition becomes instrumental in reproducing 'mothering' not as the passionate loving of children, but as a 'calculating and monitoring' relationship (ibid., p. 221).

In summary, the universality of western culture has been acquired through suppression, denial and rejection of the marginalised. Foucault's method of inquiry revolves, then, around an attempt to investigate how various fields such as biology, economics and linguistics have suppressed their own origins unconsciously (Henriques *et al.* 1984, p. 221).

The Foucault vs Chomsky debate

Negri claims that during the 1970s Foucault was beginning to question some of his previous structuralist positions and was very gradually moving towards a more nuanced post-structuralist perspective (2017). If this periodisation of Foucault's thought is to be trusted, the 1971 debate between Foucault and Chomsky comes into sharper focus. Foucault was still mainly trying to de-centre humans but was now also beginning to claim a semblance of agency for them. Chomsky was a more politically evolved creature and as such quite content to give much more primacy to the subject, but a subject that has more in common with bourgeois individualism than Marx's 'socialised individual'. Historically, the last waves of proletarian struggles of the late 1960s in France, Italy and the USA were fading and the new wave of struggles (e.g. the British miners' strike of 1972; the Italian autonomous struggles of 1977–1978) had not yet begun. The class struggle in societies most immediately relevant to Foucault and Chomsky was in a state of hibernation.

As Chomsky and Foucault walk down the Dutch TV studio staircase like a pair of ancient Roman gladiators entering a colosseum, or some futuristic Mad Max warriors stepping into the Thunderdome, one half-expects the audience to chant: 'Two men enter, one man leaves'! Thankfully, no blood was spilled and both survived the encounter with minimal damage to their bodies and souls. The facilitator (the Dutch philosopher Elders) begins the discussion by asking Chomsky about the innateness of 'human nature'. Chomsky points out that there is a palpable gap between the small and restricted linguistic 'data' a person is immersed in throughout his/her life, and the 'highly articulated, highly systematic, profoundly organised resulting knowledge that he somehow derives from this data' (Elders 1971, 6 mins). This gap can only be explained by attributing to the individual the ability to bring to the learning process a great innate set of schemas or structures (ibid., 8 mins).

For his part, Foucault expresses scepticism about the concept of 'human nature' but accedes that each scientific era has its own organising principles. For example, in biology 'reflex' has been a well-established core concept. Reflex, therefore, has a high 'degree of elaboration' (Elders 1971, 10 mins). Alongside such core concepts there have also been peripheral concepts without the same descriptive or explanatory powers. As such they are not organising principles but exist merely to point out 'some problems … or certain fields in need of study' (ibid., 11 mins). An example of peripherality is the concept of 'life' in biology. In the seventeenth and eighteenth centuries it was 'hardly used when studying nature; one classified natural beings, whether living or non-living' (ibid.). At the end of the eighteenth century a number of problems arose concomitantly with the invention of new technologies such as the microscope which brought new phenomena into the light. Now it made sense to talk about 'life' in biology because it 'served to point out new fields of study in science' (ibid., 12 mins). In the same way the concept of 'human nature' may be useful as a peripheral and contingent pointer for new fields of investigation.

The debate moves on to the subject of 'creativity'. To what extent is the individual able to create or discover something new? Chomsky gives creativity a central role in not just scientific but everyday living. We all utilise creativity to find an alternative route when stuck in traffic, dealing with a difficult colleague, or learning a new language. Foucault, by contrast, sees creativity within the limitations of epistemological fields. These are unconscious rules that manage the totality of all the separate fields of knowledge. We can think of it in terms of a network or grid that encompasses us and imposes thinking rules on everyone (Elders 1971, 12 mins). Ironically, at this stage of their intellectual development Chomsky's innately inherited linguistic mechanisms seem to provide individuals with more freedom than Foucault's rigid structuralism.

We can see the reasons behind Foucault's fierce rejection of Chomsky's individualistic account. In the history of scientific creativity, the contribution of great individual thinkers 'has been accorded maximum importance' (Elders 1971, 15 mins). The biographical narratives (and genius) of Newton and Mendel become the framing device for understanding 'their discoveries'. However, in each epoch a number of 'obstacles' prevent humanity from seeing the truth. These obstacles may be due to religious dogma, or socio-economic conditions. During moments of scientific transformation and social rupture obstacles are removed and only at this stage do individual thinkers gain the licence to 'discover' gravity or genetics. But, significantly, Foucault also argued that as science provides clarity by removing mouldy grids, so does it create new grids which end up obscuring existing forms of wisdom. So, 'truth is not acquired through a kind of continuous and cumulative creation, but through a set of grids stacked on top of one another' (ibid., 19 mins). The freedom to be scientifically creative and a system of rules are dialectically related.

The problem is that at this junction of the debate, they are talking at cross-purposes (Chomsky, to his credit, sees this). Had they utilised the term 'imagination' instead of 'creativity' the conceptual problems would have been overcome. Foucault is discussing high-level 'creative imagination' in science when Newton and other greats make their discoveries. Chomsky is referring to low-level 'mechanical imagination' used by us lesser mortals on a daily basis to solve problems. Had A. R. Luria been present during this debate all this confusion would have been avoided. For the time being let us conclude that both forms of imagination are essential for scientific, artistic and revolutionary thinking.

Now the discussion takes an explicitly political turn. Chomsky describes himself in favour of direct workers' participation within an anarcho-syndicalist framework. His argument is based on the need to actualise the full 'creative urge' of all, by removing coercive institutions and rules. This implies a series of decentralised and non-hierarchical free associations based on consensual decision-making. Foucault feigns political nativity in a rare moment of humility when he admits that his political ideas are not as advanced as Chomsky's (Elders 1971, 37 mins). What is urgent, according to Foucault, is the realisation that power is exercised not only by the government but also by a series of institutions such as the army, the police and the bureaucracy. Furthermore, some institutions, such as universities, openly favour the ruling (and part of the middling) class and attempt to exclude everyone else. The central political task for Foucault becomes the criticism of these institutions (ibid., 40 mins). Accordingly, to talk about a utopian anarcho-syndicalism at this stage runs the risk of replicating power relations in another form.

Both philosophers are displaying flawed thinking here. Foucault at this stage of his 'political life' has been reduced to a mere unmasker of institutional violence, and Chomsky (whose politics are definitely more advanced) understands the need to retain the dialectical tension between criticisms of the existing order and the projection of a utopian alternative. Where Chomsky errs is in basing this utopia on a fixed and static interpretation of human nature. The Chomskian utopia is characterised by 'fundamental human characteristics such as dignity and creativity'. Under pressure from Foucault, he concedes that this human nature is partly socially constructed but that the universalistic assumptions prevail with Chomsky. Marx (at his very best) understood that communism is both a social struggle against the existing state of affairs and a prefiguring of an alternative way of being and consciousness.

The antagonisms between Foucault and Chomsky become starker still when they debate the rule of law, the notion of illegality, civil disobedience and the proposal to establish people's tribunals for exposing bourgeois law. Chomsky plays a subtle game here, arguing that in both national and international law there exist concepts and precedences that are useful, and should be utilised to empower people, and hold illegal state activity to account. Something strange happens now: suddenly the hitherto social democratic, reformist Foucault transforms into a class warrior and argues that the proletariat does not wage class war 'because it considers such a war to be just' but in order to 'take power' (Elders 1971, 56 mins). Chomsky disagrees: 'the only reason for wanting [the proletariat to take power] … is because one thinks, rightly or wrongly, that some fundamental human values will be achieved [i.e. freedom, dignity, justice, etc.] by that transfer of power' (ibid., 57 mins). On more than one occasion Chomsky describes these human values of the enlightenment as 'absolute' and 'fundamental' entities.

Foucault counters by arguing that a violent, bloody, even dictatorial rule is justified so long as the target remains the ruling class. If the violence turns inward and the proletariat itself becomes the target, that only serves to prove that another force (e.g. the petty bourgeoisie) has taken over the revolution (Elders 1971, 58 mins). Chomsky does not want to give the impression that he is a pacifist. Violence is a relative concept and may very well be necessary under exceptional circumstances, but he insists on the dialectical link between means and ends. Vile means, he seems to be saying in an echo of Wilhelm Reich (1948), promote vile ends. In fact, after the debate, Chomsky criticised Foucault's total rejection of the possibility of a universal morality, in these harsh terms:

> He struck me as completely amoral, I'd never met anyone who was so totally amoral […] I mean, I liked him personally, it's just that I couldn't make sense of him. It's as if he was from a different species, or something.
>
> *(Miller and Miller 1993, pp. 201–203)*

Perhaps Foucault's vision threatened Chomsky and anyone who buys into the Enlightenment ideas of 'progress' and 'purposeful rationality'.

The passage of time, as well as more recent studies, has made some of these formulations dated: Hal Draper's 1989 seminal study of the various interpretations of the phrase, 'dictatorship of the proletariat', has demonstrated the fundamental difference between Marx, on the one hand, and Engels, Lenin, Trotsky, Stalin and Mao on the other. Moreover, we now live in highly depoliticised and dehistoricised times and suffer under the weight of bourgeois assaults that have lasted for decades. The working class does not seem to be able to manage a rudimentary defence of its gains, let alone wage an offensive class war for a classless society. It could even be argued that in the most 'advanced' parts of the world, the working class does not even recognise itself as the historical class tasked with ushering in the classless world human community. For the time being at least, these debates are moot.

Going beyond Foucault

In season 2, episode 1 of *Game of Thrones*, there is a compelling rhetorical exchange between Queen Regent Cersei Lannister and Lord Baelish (Littlefinger), which exemplifies Marx and Foucault's differing concepts of 'power' very well (Taylor 2012). Cersei is a member of the ruling class and an exemplar of monarchical sovereignty. Littlefinger is a shifty, self-serving, senior civil servant who has worked exceedingly hard to get where he is. The Queen Regent relies on a conception of power that is, at least on the surface, absolute and uncontested. Baelish has learned that 'knowledge is power', especially privileged knowledge, and he tries to use the semi-secret incestuous relationship between Cersei and her brother as leverage. The tactic backfires. Cersei orders his guards to grab him and cut his throat. At the last moment she offers Baelish a reprieve and then, staring unnervingly at the flustered bureaucrat, reminds him, 'Power is power'!

In a famous interview, this is how Foucault summed up his career: 'In the end I had only produced a history of power' (quoted in Trombadori 1991, p. 17). Foucault would want to understand both Cersei and Littlefinger's utilisation of power. He never claimed that power was the be all and end all of analysis: 'I have never presumed that "power" was something that could explain everything. It was not my objective to substitute an explanation based on power for one based on economics' (quoted in ibid., p. 148). These points are noteworthy because as I have tried to demonstrate throughout this chapter, it is perfectly possible to synthesise Foucault with Marx.

Against naive positivism and empiricism, Foucault argued that knowledge 'is not a body of truth as science would have it, but a historical product of certain practices' (Hollway 1984, p. 26). Foucauldians are extremely fond of saying that 'power should not automatically connote something negative; something linked with oppressive practices. In a Foucauldian analysis, power is productive of all knowledges, oppressive and liberatory' (ibid.). They claim that power 'produces not so much repression as regularities' (Massumi 2015, p. 19). Power does not just come at us from the outside, but acts intrinsically by creating identities for us (ibid.).

Such claims to originality, repeated ad nauseum by middle-class followers of Foucault, has always made me wonder how familiar they are with the real Marx. I suspect most read a little 'easy Marx' in their youth, and have been working from memory ever since. By saying 'power is not a property but a relationship', some critical psychologists are pretending to be revealing vital new truths (Henriques *et al.* 1984, p. 117).

In addition to getting Marx wrong, many contemporary critical psychologists selectively celebrate the post-structuralist Foucault and ignore the fact that for most of his intellectual life he was a structuralist (see the section above on Foucault and Chomsky). The post-structuralist Foucault is then recruited to undermine the Marxist-anarchist conception of class power, even though for Foucault both extrinsic and intrinsic forms of power created resistance (Massumi 2015, p. 104). All very shabby, all very dishonest, (and sadly) all very academic!

In any event, Foucault was correct in reminding us, for the umpteenth time, that 'the most pernicious and effective strategy of power is to camouflage its own workings' (Henriques *et al.* 1984, p. 57). My point is that Cersei and Baelish (see above), not to mention Guy Debord ([1967] 1977) with his categorisation of various forms of the spectacle, as well as the 'early' and 'mature' Marx, taught us these lessons with a clarity of expression that is far superior to Foucault. Still, let us not be uncharitable in our evaluation and try to salvage what is salvageable in Foucault.

I think it is fair to say that from the mid-1970s until his death in 1984 Foucault was interested in charting the contours of power relations at a more local and individualistic level. Instead of looking at how a group (such as the ruling class) exerts power over another (the working class), Foucault was entertaining a more diffuse, multifocal form of power. In his own words, 'I do not mean "Power" as a group of institutions and mechanisms that ensure the subservience of the citizens of a given state' (Foucault [1978] 1990, p. 92). His remarks on 'power' (with a small 'p') are at times contradictory. If all he was doing was to point out more subtle, micro and contingent illustrations of power dynamics in families, classrooms and hospitals, then no Marxist would deny the importance of his contributions. If, however, he was rejecting the centrality of class struggle (as it appears from *some* of his illusive commentary), then we would depart from his company, having noted that he was collapsing back into his youthful reformism.

In one particular case, his politics deteriorated further still. I am referring here to his ill-fated and uninformed intervention on Iran. The fact that he got Iran so very badly wrong suggests that, for all his florid language and trendy concepts, he lacked any real instinct for politics. The damage he inflicted on the working-class struggle against the authoritarian version of Islam that came to power at the end of the 1970s still arouses rancor in many people, myself included. So instead of a serious critique of his sympathetic position on the Islamic Republic of Iran, allow me to conclude with a suitable quote by Edmund Blackadder: 'Your brain, for example, is so minute Baldrick, that if a hungry cannibal cracked your head open, there wouldn't be enough to cover a small water biscuit!'

Last words on Foucault

The most important criticism of Foucault is the sheer obviousness of so much of his 'discoveries'. Statements such as 'power is everywhere' or 'sex, sexuality and gender are related', or 'human nature is not fixed' or 'justice is experienced differently by different people based on class, race, gender' have been known to numerous thinkers before Foucault. Frankly, I suspect that were he not speaking in melodious French, the banality of some of his arguments would be much easier to fend off.

From our perspective we must start by questioning Foucault's knowledge of psychology. He began his academic career as a philosopher, then became a historian of science and finally specialised in the history of the social sciences. However, I think it is perfectly fair to point out that most of his psychological knowledge is limited to Freudianism. Foucault has been described as 'obsessed' with Rorschach tests, giving them to his students and to many others throughout his life (Fillingham 1993, p. 23). A great deal of what he says about mental illness is patently obvious, to the point of being clichéd.

Foucault's politics oscillated between Stalinism, Maoism, social democracy and low-grade imbecility. We are informed that he

> joined the Communist Party [of France] later than most of his friends, and dropped out earlier (he was probably an official party member from 1950 to 1953). It is hard to tell whether he left the party because he suspected some of the atrocities of Stalin, or because Michel did not like to follow the crowd.
>
> *(Fillingham 1993, p. 99)*

In his own very revealing words, 'without knowing Marx very well, refusing Hegelianism, and feeling dissatisfied with the limitations of existentialism, I decided to join the French Communist Party. That was in 1950. A Nietzschean Communist!' (Foucault, quoted in Trombadori 1991, p. 51). He is also on record regarding the impact of Althusser (known affectionately and accurately among the British working class as 'ale-tosser' or even 'Al, the tosser'!) on the decision he made: 'I followed Louise Althusser, who worked militantly in the PCF. It was also somewhat under his influence that I had decided to join' (Foucault, quoted in ibid., p. 55).

So, assuming that I have done my maths correctly, Foucault was twenty-four years old when he became an official Stalinist. Is it fair to castigate someone so young for political naivety? Well, actually yes, I think it is perfectly fair! By the time I was that age, I had been a decade-long atheist who rejected all forms of Bolshevism as anti-working class, and I was also developing a pretty decent take on the limitations of anarchism, council communism, left communism and libertarian socialism.

Moreover, unlike Foucault, I was very good at sports and had the distraction of football, ping-pong, tennis and kinky sex to contend with! As far as I am concerned, Foucault had no excuse for being a political imbecile. But it wasn't just imbecility, it was partly cowardice:

> A little while before the death of Stalin, the news was spread that a group of Jewish doctors had tried to kill him … No matter how unconvinced we were, we still forced ourselves into believing what they told us.
>
> *(Foucault, quoted in Trombadori 1991, p. 52)*

I am not sure how to respond to the absurdity of believing in the doctors' plot! I am (almost) fucking speechless, mate!

His slow journey from official Stalinism to a kind of 'post-Stalinist Stalinism' began in the 1950s and gathered pace in the 1960s – a process not uncommon in middle-class intellectuals who left the Party without dealing with the root causes of everything that is rotten and reactionary in Stalinism. In 1955 he travelled to Sweden whose social democracy functioned 'well' (Foucault, quoted in Trombadori 1991, p. 132). He presented manuscripts of *Madness and Civilisation* to a certain Professor Sten Lindroth in an attempt to obtain a doctorate but the good professor rejected it as not serious, historically poor and too speculative.

Various ideas from Maoism were then utilised to 'expand' his political thinking. In the Elders interview he asserts that Maoism helps us to ask what knowledge will be possible following liberation from the economic, cultural, moral and political constraints of capitalism (1971). During May 1968 he was in Tunisia, which was experiencing its own political turmoil. In some ways he considered the Tunisian events to be more radical than the French crisis because in Tunisia there was unity of purpose and in France Marxism had fractured into competing splinter groups: 'It wasn't May of '68 in France that changed me; it was March of '68, in a third-world country' (Foucault, quoted in Trombadori 1991, pp. 136 and 139). Graciously he did credit May 1968 with providing opportunities for his investigations into subjects such as prisons and sexuality (ibid., p. 141).

Performing the kind of ritualistic humility that celebrity academics are renowned for, Foucault once claimed: 'I absolutely will not play the part of one who prescribes solutions' (quoted in Trombadori 1991, p. 157). Given how many political errors he committed, we should be grateful that he was not more prescriptive. Occasionally, Foucault is quite brilliant. Most of the time, however, he is pedantically annoying. He has always brought out the sardonic in me, so yes, I need to end this chapter with another quote from Edmund Blackadder: 'The eyes are open, the mouth moves but Mr [political] Brain has long since departed, hasn't he, Percy?' (*Blackadder II*, episode 4, 'Money').

9

BILLIG

The sultan of critical psychology

On Billig

Pity the poor little critical psychologists! For while mainstream psychologists operate under a mere double insecurity bind, their critical counterparts are crushed under a triple whammy: (most) criticals share with (most) mainstreamers the general misfortune of having been born middle class, but nowadays they are also experiencing a downward trend on their wages, specific to this period of all-out assault on academics and practitioners. This assault is demoting most psychologists to an objective proletarian existence, even though the subjective recognition of the fact is lagging behind. As if these insecurities are not dispiriting enough, criticals are also constantly belittled by the more powerfully positioned mainstreamers. Hence the triple nature of their insecurity: being born into a 'sandwiched' class; being consistently pushed downward towards the working class; and being the uninvited, unwanted, unwashed gatecrashers at a psychology ball!

It is hardly surprising, therefore, that criticals have evolved into cantankerous creatures, forever playing the victim and bemoaning their diminishing prospects. So, I hope I am not crushing their fragile spirits still further when I say that, in my opinion, Michael Billig (b. 1947) is so far ahead of the rest of the field that the field would probably never catch up with him. I am not playing favourites here, you understand, since I am not acquainted with the gentleman personally.

Above all, there are two things that impress me about his work. First, Billig has researched a wide spectrum of topics (including group identities, ideology, humour, nationalism, rhetoric, etc.), using a wide array of perspectives (cognitive psychology, psychoanalysis, discursive psychology, history). Second, every time Billig chooses a new topic to investigate, he manages to push the envelope a little bit further. In a discipline generally drowning in mediocrity and bewitched by semantics, Billig's contributions stand out as seminal moments of originality. I hope that by the end of this section the reader will come to agree with my contention that a great deal of Billig's work can be mined for a project of postpsychology.

Throughout this book I have employed various forms of contextualisation. At times I have provided a brief social history of a perspective (e.g. the rise of Watsonian behaviourism as narrated in Chapter 3). At other times I have drawn a more explicit link between class conflict and the evolution of psychology (e.g. attempts by Freud to suppress proletarian struggle; see Chapter 1). And I have also focused on 'material' conditions that shape individual psychologists (e.g. the impact of the Holocaust on the work of Frankl in Chapter 6).

But there is yet another form of contextualisation which demonstrates the development of psychology as a discipline with its own *technical* division of labour (i.e. the way psychology is internally subdivided into social, developmental, clinical, etc.), as well as its *social* division of labour (i.e. the way psychology is demarcated from politics, sociology, economics and biology, etc). I have argued throughout this book that these technical and social divisions of labour, while very productive in capitalist terms in the past, have today become fetters on innovation and progress. Billig's work is an attempt to escape this predicament.

Billig on the philosophy of psychology

> People who lean on logic and philosophy and rational exposition end by starving the best part of the mind.
>
> *William Butler Yeats*

Michael Billig's *The Hidden Roots of Critical Psychology* (2008) is an outstanding exemplar of this last form of contextualisation. He delves in and out of history, sociology and philosophy in order to clarify the origins of both mainstream and critical forms of psychology.

Billig's central point is that both mainstream and critical psychologies have been around for far longer than the last few decades. In this admittedly Anglo-centric retelling of the history of psychology, the philosopher John Locke (1632–1704) is the father-originator of both behaviourism and cognitive psychology. Meanwhile, in a historical oddity dripping with irony, Locke's aristocratic tutee, the third Earl of Shaftesbury (1671–1713) performs the role of the antagonist emphasising 'the social nature of humans … and the importance of language' and chastising Locke for not developing 'a full historical consciousness' (Billig 2008, p. 5). It must appeal to Billig's middle-class sense of humour to trace current Marxist and anarchist critical psychologists back to a member of the British nobility whose politics was as elitist as it was sexist. If the Earl's elitism was a reaction against an increasingly restive peasantry threatening to unite with a nascent urban proletariat, his sexism was probably a reaction 'against a growing tendency for women to enter into, even organise, intellectual conversations in the dining-rooms and salons' (ibid., p. 75).

In most of his psychological writings, Locke viewed the 'mind as passively reflecting the external world, rather than constructing its own version of the external world' (Billig 2008, p. 14). This is a position very similar to that adopted in *early* cognitive psychology. Locke also advocated the empirical exploration of perception and thinking – another commonality with cognitive psychology (ibid., p. 30). In an early echo of George Kelly's (1905–1967) views on development, Locke saw 'the human thinker as an empirical scientist', influenced mainly by nurture rather than nature (ibid., p. 37). The mind of the newborn infant was described as an 'empty cabinet' (ibid., p. 40). The political risks of this argument were clear to all those who had a stake in maintaining ruling-class privilege.

If Locke's use of the term 'ideas' is analogous to what cognitive psychologists would call 'cognitions' (Billig 2008, p. 38), then his usage of the term 'associationism' is reminiscent of behaviourism (ibid, p. 42). Like most cognitive and behavioural psychologists, Locke paid little attention to the longue durée. Because they work with restricted notions of 'social', 'political' and 'historical', these psychologists commonly trace the origins of ideas and behaviour to the birth of the individual and no further (ibid., p. 51).

The third Earl of Shaftesbury (aka Anthony Ashley Cooper) listened to his tutor intently but ultimately decided to forge a profoundly different path. His psychology was 'holistic, social, sceptical … intrinsically rhetorical and … filled with the passions of imagination' (Billig 2008, pp. 73–74). The Earl accused his teacher of separating theory from practice, a dualism that still runs through most of psychology today. By contrast, he believed that we sense patterns (or what today may be called *gestalts*) rather than simple cognitions (ibid., p. 114). What is more, these patterns are generated inter-subjectively and are not isolated within atomised psyches.

Billig argues that a very modern understanding of 'alienation' runs through Shaftesbury's work which is remarkably similar to Marx's interpretation of the term. There are even ideas about playfulness and self-reflexivity that are every bit as advanced as that which postmodernism has to offer (Billig 2008, p. 122). But for me the most interesting connection emerges when Billig links Shaftesbury to Bakhtin. Shaftesbury lived at a time when 'religious fundamentalism' was not of the Islamic variety but was Christian in outlook. The way he describes fundamentalists is similar to what some twentieth-century psychologists would call the 'authoritarian personality' – individuals intolerant of complexity and diversity who seek the solace of a simple, single, monologic doctrine (ibid., p. 136). His solution is to use humour, particularly mockery, to expose the pretentions of religious fundamentalists. For example, 'Shaftesbury took delight in describing how the religious enthusiasts [fundamentalists] had been mocked at Bartholomew's Fair by puppet shows' (ibid., p. 126). Dialogue, especially when it comes from below and is interlaced with humour, can help us to arrive at the 'truth' – a term that has perhaps been subjected to far too much mockery by postmodernism in recent times!

Billig on nationalism

> It is forbidden to kill; therefore, all murderers are punished unless they kill in large numbers and to the sound of trumpets.
>
> *Voltaire*

Three individuals are cited by Billig as influencing his approach to nationalism (Antaki 1999). First and foremost there is Henri Tajfel (1919–1982), Billig's supervisor, who examined the link between cognitive categorisation and prejudice. Tajfel tried to show that prejudice has its roots in everyday cognitive categories and not in an 'authoritarian personality'. Based on the famous 'minimal group' experiments (designed jointly with Billig), Tajfel developed the theory of 'social identity'. These experiments showed how easy it is for individuals to acquire a sense of identity and self-esteem through belonging to a group and subsequently to exaggerate the positive aspects of the ingroup and the negative aspects of the outgroup.

The second influence was Benedict Anderson (1936–2015), the author of the famous book *Imagined Communities* ([1983] 2006), who argued that a nation may consist of millions of people who do not know each other personally, and therefore must be imagined to some degree. According to Anderson, the regular output of the print industry played a crucial role in establishing this national imagination.

The third figure who taught Billig how to think about and investigate nationalism was the anti-fascist activist and journalist, Maurice Ludmer (1926–1981). Visiting the Belsen concentration camp during World War II and witnessing the Notting Hill riots of 1958 forged Ludmer's ideas about the need to combat racism, and in 1975 he launched the magazine *Searchlight*.

How exactly did these three figures impact Billig's political ideology? To my constant irritation, psychologists, even critical ones, are notoriously reticent about their political affiliations. Given how university bureaucracies can destroy careers in a flash, this precaution is perfectly understandable. Nonetheless, it makes our task of getting to grips with major thinkers rather difficult.

I hope I am not being too mischievous in suggesting that all three (Tajfel, Anderson and Ludmer) were leftist thinkers influenced by Leninism. In the case of Anderson and Ludmer, we can further assume that they were mostly under the sway of the Stalinist branch of Leninism, at least temporarily. Billig himself can be described as a leftist who ditched Stalinism as his politics matured and as he became better acquainted with Marx.

His first major book on nationalism is entitled *Fascists: A Social Psychological View of the National Front* (1978). He is dealing here with 'hard' or 'explicit' forms of nationalism. His definition of fascism brings out the racial and statist characteristics of the ideology, but in my view downplays the anti-working-class nature of fascism (Billig 1978, pp. 6–7). This is a very common error among academic treatments of the subject, with only a few honourable exceptions (see Guerin 1973; Ridley 1988; Sohn-Rethel 1987; Vajda 1976).

When it comes to the awkward personal and doctrinal ties of continuity between fascism and psychology, Billig pulls no punches. He shows how in Germany 'Nazism encountered little opposition from German psychology' and how Wilhelm Wundt, Jaensch, Lorenz and Jung either prepared the ground or made common cause with fascism (1978, p. 13). Decades later the British National Front established more productive links with reactionary academics such as Eysenck, Lynn, Garrett and Shuey (ibid., p. 145). Billig is at pains to point out that these links were not always one-way. He then moves on to describe more questionable connections between social psychology and fascism, this time mediated by Freud, Gustav Le Bon, Mussolini and Hitler (ibid., pp. 21–23). These connections are all well documented and there is no need for me to dwell on them here.

He evaluates what is still relevant in previous theories of fascism. Erich Fromm's brilliant *Fear of Freedom* ([1942] 1980) is dismissed rather briskly as being 'essentially a scapegoat theory of prejudice. The psychologically weak, or the angered … seek powerless scapegoats whom they can bully with impunity' (Billig 1978, p. 33). But prejudice, although connected to visceral bigotry, can never account for the intensity of hatred Nazi leaders felt for their victims. The other problem with Fromm and Reich's analysis of fascism is the overemphasis on the Nazi elite and a neglect of their followers (again, this is very ungenerous, especially in Reich's case). Adorno *et al.*'s *The Authoritarian Personality* ([1950] 2019) attempts to correct this shortcoming by studying 'ordinary men and women', writes Billig (1978, p. 37). Remarkably they come to similar conclusions as Fromm, since for Adorno and colleagues a person who is predisposed to fascism has a sadomasochistic character. According to Billig, 'Like Fromm, Adorno et al. saw the potential fascist as a psychological weakling who tries to compensate for his deficiencies by an exaggerated admiration of power and strength' (ibid.). Reich, Fromm and Adorno all concur that fascist supporters are predominantly middle class (ibid., p. 52). Billig shows that the picture is more complicated by showing the 'Nazis attracted votes from all sections of society' (ibid., p. 53).

Underlying the above point is another key consideration. Fascism very deliberately recruits different 'types' of individuals and sets them different tasks within the organisation (Billig 1978, p. 233). Billig criticises previous theories that focus on the inner contradictions of the individual:

> The authoritarian personality as described by Fromm, Adorno *et al.*, and possibly by Reich, is in effect a parodied overcharacterisation of the duty-bound bureaucrat. He is the typification of the cautious and fretful petit bourgeois. Nevertheless, if fascism has commended obedience and exaggerated conventionality in its supporters, it has also mythologised another type. The man of action and the irrational spirit of voluntarism has also been celebrated.
>
> *(Ibid., p. 234)*

To assume that only the authoritarian personality is attracted to fascism may underestimate the true number of potential recruits.

The diverse recruitment policy of fascism may explain the discursive diversity one finds in the rhetoric of fascist leaders; for instance, 'Hitler, in his speeches, valued freedom and independence positively as often as did Roosevelt' (Billig 1978, p. 82). At the same time there was a division of labour between his speeches and his autobiographical book *Mein Kampf*: 'The speeches were full of references to peace, friendship and non-aggression; they contained none of the continual glorification of war to be found in *Mein Kampf*' (ibid., p. 83). So, there is a conscious attempt to appeal to different values and to wrong-foot the opponents of fascism by employing the rhetoric of war *and* peace, pre-modernism *and* modernism, sadism *and* masochism, racism *and* racialism, predator *and* victim, bourgeois *and* proletarian, nationalism *and* internationalism. The organisational division of labour used by fascism (e.g. coteries which act as 'apolitical' carrier groups, pressure groups and leagues which influence politics indirectly, as well as orthodox political parties) facilitates this flexible recruitment policy (ibid., p. 98).

But if fascist elites possess a greater facility with rhetoric than most anti-fascists are willing to admit, then it is also true that the rank-and-file fascist is more nuanced than the caricatures suggest. Billig wants us to stop viewing the adherents of fascism as 'helpless dupes of propaganda, as is implied by the psychoanalytic account', and more as willing '[participants] in their own deception' (1978, p. 85). In short, the rank-and-file understand the con and are willing to suspend disbelief like a filmgoer wishing to enjoy a spectacular sci-fi blockbuster. Furthermore, they also comprehend the semi-secret codes used by their leaders to say the unsayable, and allow themselves to enjoy the political theatre as would the audience of a racist, sexist, stand-up comedian. One telling code is cited from the fascist magazine *Spearhead* which discusses 'the final solution' not in its usual anti-Semitic context but as 'the final solution' to Britain's economic woes (ibid., p. 132).

Amazingly, fascism can openly insult and humiliate the working class and yet there will always be a minority of our class who will still be attracted to its propaganda. As Billig shows with reference to *Spearhead*,

> the contempt for the mass is as strong here as in Le Bon or *Mein Kampf*: 'The vast majority is not studious. It neither studies things deeply nor thinks about them deeply. It requires simple explanations and it's always moved by feeling much more than by intellect'.
>
> (Spearhead, *quoted in Billig 1978, p. 189)*

Given these complications, merely pointing out the irrationality, the illogicality and the inner contradictions of fascist discourse may not have the emancipating impact that some anti-fascists hope for.

Another crucial point concerns the enabling mechanisms for fascism. Oftentimes these enabling mechanisms are transparent, as when a capitalist or an institution is providing funds and platform for fascist groups to peddle their filth. At other times they are opaque, as for instance the discursive ambiguity of mainstream political parties on 'race', which allows fascist lack of ambiguity to appear as a virtue (Billig 1978, p. 139). The inauthenticity of the main liberal and social democratic parties allows fascism to *perform* authenticity. Working-class support is solicited through anti-capitalist rhetoric and middle- and upper-class support is attracted through anti-communist arguments (ibid., p. 162). What is more, fascist ideology has a hidden genocidal core, and a less violent periphery. Most recruits are drawn in from the periphery to the core over time.

The opacity of fascist ideology is a deliberate ploy which allows capitalism and class society to avoid close scrutiny. Conspiracy theories play a crucial role in creating and maintaining this dense fog and Billig is very clear as to what makes conspiracy theories reactionary: 'no real changes in society are called for. It is just a matter of excising a small group of parasitical conspirators' (1978, p. 324). Under modernism the 'small group of parasitical conspirators' were few and constant (Jews, Blacks, Catholics, etc.). Postmodernism multiplies the list of suitable candidates (homosexuals, Muslims, gypsies, Mexicans, etc.), and it ensures a fluid intertextuality, so that one form of conspiracy theory can melt into another and back again.

If Billig's only contribution to studying nationalism was the above analysis of 'hot' or 'extreme' forms of nationalism, that would be impressive enough, but in the 1990s he opened a new front when he turned his attention to 'soft' or 'banal' forms of nationalism (1995). In this work he examined how nationalism is reproduced in a 'banally mundane way, for the world of nations is the everyday world, the familiar terrain of contemporary times … Daily, the nation is indicated, or "flagged", in the lives of its citizenry' (ibid., p. 6). 'Banal nationalism' may have become normalised due to ideological patterns of belief and practice, especially in the 'west', but that does not mean it is 'benign', 'As Hannah Arendt … stressed, banality is not synonymous with harmlessness' (ibid., p. 7). In an oft-quoted sentence Billig explains, 'The metonymic image of banal nationalism is not a flag which is being consciously waved with fervent passion; it is the flag hanging unnoticed on the public building' (ibid., p. 8). This flagging occurs unobtrusively (but systematically) in the 'weather report' (both on TV and the newspapers). The 'weather' is objectified and anchored to the notion of a 'homeland'. Once this is accomplished, the constant juxtaposition between the weather and homeland concretises national identities (ibid., p. 116).

In this reading, 'national identities are forms of social life, rather than internal psychological states' (Billig 1995, p. 24). As with any forms of social life, national identities must be created and maintained. The nineteenth-century Italian nationalist Massimo d'Azeglio (1798–1866) declared: 'We have made Italy, now we have to make Italians' (d'Azeglio, quoted in ibid., p. 25). This identity formation is carried out through rituals and ceremonies acting on collective memory (ibid., p. 42). The US Pledge of Allegiance where school pupils sing the national anthem in front of the American flag felt strange in the 1880s when the ceremony was first established but in most parts of the USA today it feels 'natural'. Billig points out that 'the significance of the ceremony is not diminished if it is treated as routine, rather than as an intense experience. If anything, the significance is enhanced: the sacral has become part of everyday life' (ibid., p. 51).

Historically, the transition from feudalism to capitalism involved altering people's epistemology and ontology in preparation for national identity formation. In an account paralleling Alexander Luria's cross-cultural work with urban and rural dwellers in the central republics of the former Soviet Union, Joshua Fishman recounts a story of peasants in Western Galicia at the turn of the twentieth century: 'They were asked whether they were Poles. "We are quiet folk", they replied. So, are you Germans? "We are decent folk"' (quoted in Billig 1995, p.62). This is a clash of ideological consciousness. The peasants may or may not comprehend abstract notions such as nationalism, but they prefer to look at life from their own concrete perspectives.

This approach helps us to transcend the limitations of social identity theory (SIT) as propounded by Tajfel and others. The examples cited from Luria and Fishman challenge SIT's claim that its categories are universal. The emphasis that SIT places on similarities (what makes individuals identify with the ingroup) is also revealed as a political choice. I, by contrast, may prefer to investigate the dialectics of similarities and differences between groups. Furthermore, as Billig mentions, 'Psychologists, working with Social Identity Theory, tend not to ask what it specifically means to declare oneself to be a member of a national group, or to declare one's group to be a national group' (1995, p. 67).

Many adherents of postmodernism have been writing premature obituaries for nationalism. As Billig puts it, 'The thesis of postmodernism suggests that life in the contemporary world is marked by a banal globalism. Daily the "global village" is flagged, and this banal globalism is supplanting the conditions of banal nationalism' (1995, p. 132). This postmodern thesis has supporters within the ranks of liberals (e.g. Richard Rorty), as well as neo-liberals (e.g. Francis Fukuyama) and postmodern Bolsheviks (e.g. Antonio Negri). The advantage of Billig's approach is that it reminds us of the older and more nuanced complex of nationalism, sub-nationalism, inter-nationalism and supra-nationalism. Today's resurgent nationalism has left postmodernist advocates of the end of nationalism thesis dazed and confused.

Billig's work on 'hot' and 'banal' forms of nationalism is generally well founded and will stand the test of time. However, I feel that it is not yet complete. One weakness is the lack of connectivity between the two forms of nationalism. Not only are they presented separately but the mechanisms by which one may reinforce or transform into the other are not elucidated. Occasionally, a suggestive remark is offered in lieu of explanation. For example, strong emotions such as anger may be implicated in transforming banal into hot nationalism. Shame could pave the way for this anger to emerge. Soft nationalistic discourse is full of shameful utterances such as 'if we fail the past', 'if we abandon our precious national essence', and so on (Billig 1995, p. 101). Once the causes of these feelings of shame are reduced to a suitable (internal or external) target, shame can transmute into righteous anger against those who would force us to abandon our heritage.

Billig on rhetorical psychology

After completing *Fascists*, Billig had time on his hands, and so he began a serious engagement with Aristotle, Plato and the Sophists. He reinterpreted Aristotle's book *Rhetoric* (*c*. fourth century BC) as primarily a study in social psychology. When Billig went to Loughborough University, he added Edwards and Middleton's 'conversational analysis' to this mix. This eventually led to *Ideological Dilemmas* (Billig *et al.* 1988), which foregrounds a more subtle form of prejudice to do with categorisation and rhetorical dilemmas. However, the work I have chosen to emphasise in this section is *Arguing and Thinking* (Billig 1996). If, as we discussed above, *Banal Nationalism* is about what we do routinely and habitually, *Arguing and Thinking* concerns itself with what we are consciously aware of.

Putting further distance between himself and his early inclination towards cognitive psychology, Billig argues here 'against those cognitive theories of thinking, which tend to treat thinking as if it were the silent, internal processing of information' (Billig 1996, p. 2). On the contrary, 'thinking is a form of internal argument, modelled on outward dialogue; attitudes are rhetorical stances in matters of controversy; justification and criticism are key rhetorical activities' (ibid.). Since arguments are full of inconsistencies, it stands to reason that what is commonly referred to as 'common sense' does not 'provide a unitary discourse, for it overflows with numerous bits and pieces, creating and recreating endless "ideological dilemmas"' (ibid., p. 15).

A number of metaphors are employed for understanding rhetoric, such as rhetoric as theatre and rhetoric as game. Both have their uses although Billig is keen to move us past these flawed metaphors. The theatre metaphor has a long history, perhaps reaching an apotheosis in the works of Erving Goffman, who argued that a great deal of human behaviour is performative. We wear masks in order to facilitate these performative interactions. The problem with the theatre metaphor is that it puts too much emphasis on 'the smooth coordination of social life' while relegating 'conflict [to] a rather minor billing in this production' (Billig 1996, p. 43). That is the reason why 'the theatrical metaphor is unable to deal satisfactorily with … class-conflict' (ibid., p. 45). In other words, the metaphor foregrounds the cooperative performance which is happening on stage but ignores the competitive backstage shenanigans.

The game metaphor, Billig argues, improves on the theatrical one. In life we are not given scripts to memorise and enact but rather general rules and guidelines. As Billig argues, 'the players are not tightly constrained by the rules, in the way that an actor is a prisoner within the script' (1996, p. 48). Furthermore, the game metaphor provides a 'perspective in which competition is central' (ibid.). However, even this improved metaphor fails to appreciate the genuinely argumentative element of life. Hence, the necessity for a rhetorical approach to psychology.

Since 'rhetoric' has garnered a poor reputation over the centuries, Billig is fighting an uphill struggle. What is more, this poor reputation is not altogether unjustified. Even Socrates attacked a certain type of rhetoricians for 'jingle-making, maxim-making, image-making' (Phaedrus, quoted in Billig 1996, p. 63). So, it behoves us all to make a distinction between the sullied image of rhetoric (as misappropriated by politicians and advertisers), and the type of rhetoric that Billig is endorsing. He suggests that we call the former 'a rhetoric of adornment' and the latter 'an argumentative rhetoric' (ibid.,

p. 64). When citizens pursue a lawsuit for a property unjustly usurped by a king or when voters argue against a poll tax imposed by politicians, it is this latter argumentative form of rhetoric that is being utilised. Any 'logos' (statement or discourse) has its 'anti-logos' (counter-argument). Class conflict focuses on the social aspect of the logos versus the anti-logos argument. Billig argues that 'any psychological theory of thought which omits the role of the anti-logos will therefore be incomplete' (ibid., p. 79).

Sometimes Billig's writings give the impression that we should merely follow the to-and-fro of arguments to resolve dilemmas. For example, on the one hand he says that 'the flow of social psychological research can be compared to dialogue, oscillating permanently between logos and anti-logos' (Billig 1996, p. 107), while on the other hand he remembers that this simple formula is insufficient and that we should also endeavour to discover 'who says what to whom with what effect' and why (ibid., p. 93). These questions enable us to go beyond the simple-minded machine metaphors of cognitive psychology and show how human thinking is very different from the neat and logical ways in which computers are programmed (ibid., p. 127). Even a concept such as 'schema' is too rigid to encapsulate the dynamism of human thought. Sir Fredrick Bartlett, who is often credited with introducing the term 'schema', eventually 'grew to reject his own word' precisely because of such limitations (ibid., p. 160).

In any case the pre-given and automatically assumed category employed by most cognitive psychologists 'is the negation of thinking … [Because] thinking starts when we argue or deliberate about which categorisation to particularise, or how to categorise a particularisation' (Billig 1996, p. 170). So real critical thinking begins when we 'no longer obey unthinkingly the order of our schema, but we have, to use Bartlett's phrase, turned them around' (ibid.).

The more mature reader might recognise this formulation as the good old Marxist dialects of specific and general. It is precisely because Billig remains faithful to such a dialectical outlook that he avoids some of the pitfalls of both modernism and postmodernism. For instance, some postmodernist linguists insist that there is no 'absolute truth' and that we are forever in the process of constructing and deconstructing phenomena. This extreme relativism is then utilised as an excuse for permanently sitting on the fence. Billig, by contrast, declares that rhetoric foregrounds two aspects of the individual: 'We see the person as the deliberator, uncertainly shuttling between contrary opinions. And then, we see a determined advocate, who has decided upon a single stance and is orating upon the virtues of the chosen position' (1996, p. 186). The dialectics of *advocacy* and *deliberation* contribute towards the creation of a postpsychology.

Billig on humour

> I would challenge you to a battle of wits, but I see you are unarmed!
>
> *Anon*

I know of at least two psychologists who started off as stand-up comedians. There are many others within academia who are partial to a joke. However, I would not necessarily count Professor Michael Billig among them. He has always struck me as someone who is more comfortable writing a treatise on humour than engaging in tomfoolery and thigh-slapping down the pub! Thankfully, being droll is not a prerequisite for providing a profound study of humour and that is precisely what he offers us in *Laughter and Ridicule: Towards a Social Critique of Humour* (2012).

Billig himself might protest, but I believe his attitude towards humour is characterised by a deep-seated suspicion. 'It is easy to praise humour for bringing people together in moments of pure, creative enjoyment', he writes 'But it is not those sorts of moments that constitute the social core of humour, but, instead, it is the darker, less easily admired practice of ridicule' (Billig 2012, p. 2). Under the influence of Freud and Bergson, Billig insists that the core of humour is constituted by ridicule and the purpose of this constant barrage of verbal sadism is to ensure social conformity. Since he has a generous soul, Billig does concede that 'humour can be rebellious' at times, but this non-conformity has been over-studied and exaggerated (ibid.).

Erich Fromm is cited as an example of a post-Freudian who erred by stressing too much the 'positives' of life and overlooking the cruelties of societal repression (Billig 2012, p. 10). Seligman represents an even more extreme case of collusion with capitalism since he has 'switched the focus of his research from attempting to prevent "learned helplessness" to teaching a "learned optimism" that, he claims, will promote psychological health' (ibid., p. 29). To sum up, Billig should not be classed as a 'misogelast' (those who both oppose and despise laughter), nor does he go as far as Freud and Bergson in damning humour. Nevertheless, his lingering suspicion of humour means that he ends up undervaluing its potential to tickle the underbelly of capitalism.

Needless to say, there is a grain of truth in just about everything Billig says about humour and any disagreements I express here are more to do with degree of emphasis, slight omissions and the marginalisation of class, rather than irreconcilable differences. As Billig explains, the policing of humour in favour of the ruling class has a very long history. Plato wanted to reduce laughter in his 'ideal world'. Socrates in *The Republic* 'discussed how laughter can be used to bring order', specifically how to prohibit the 'impertinence of the rank and file against those in authority' (Billig 2012, p. 41). They identified the proletarian carnivalesque as the enemy of class society. Aristotle seems to have had a slightly less prohibitive view of humour. While criticising lower-class buffoonery, Aristotle was open to the rhetorical use of irony by the educated citizen (ibid., p. 44).

When the concept of 'irony' was relaunched in the eighteen century it is precisely this middle-class interpretation that is foregrounded by various philosophers such as Friedrich Schlegel (1772–1829). In contemporary times humour has become a routine mechanism of managerial control with its own hierarchal pattern aimed at dividing the working class (Billig 2012, p. 46). Irony foregrounds the various incongruities that exist in life, many of which may provoke laughter. What this middle-class sensibility calls for is sitting on the fence and pontificating on the incongruities of the upper and working classes from a distance.

Billig is also good at bringing out the contours of spatial humour. The ale house is working class, rough and its sense of humour may be raucous and loud. By contrast, the 'devotees of salons and the coffee-houses needed to determine what was the appropriate sort of laughter that would encourage conviviality without being raucously lower class' (Billig 2012, p. 59). Wit, taste and social rank became the preoccupations of the new eighteenth-century coffee house culture. 'Amiable humour' was linked to moderation and became a feature of middle-class mortality.

Working-class humour, on the other hand, is associated with improper or incompatible *excess* and results not in mirth, but belly laughter. There may even be a preference for the visual over the verbal – think of how difficult it was for Charlie Chaplin's physical humour, created specifically for working-class audiences, to transform itself to the sound era of movies. Billig once again draws parallels between working-class humour and (not so much the social status) but the writings of the third Earl of Shaftesbury. The Earl saw a connection between laughter, ridicule and liberty, whereby 'ridicule was a weapon to be used against the sort of dangerous religious enthusiasm that threatens liberty' (Billig 2012, p. 75).

The observant reader will have noticed that this is precisely how I have attempted to utilise humour throughout this book – as a weapon that exposes the inconsistences and contradictions of bourgeois discourse. As such, my admiration for rebellious humour is more in line with the Earl of Shaftesbury and Michael Bakhtin than Freud, Bergson and Billig.

Going beyond Billig: Is Trump a fascist? Or mad? Do we need to dwell on his tiny mushroom?

> You can fool some of the people all of the time, and all the people some of the time, which is just long enough to be president of the United States.
>
> *Spike Milligan*

How would postpsychology respond to the above questions? Trump's recent attacks on what the media have dubbed 'the Squad' have prompted a reappraisal of his political ideology, and the f-word is being bandied about to describe him more and more often. Is Trump evolving into a fascist?

I think postpsychology would start by pointing out that these are not terribly searching questions since Trump could soon be a sad footnote of history. Far more relevant are the questions: 'Is Trumpism fascist?', 'What can psychology tell us about Trumpism?' Trumpism, after all, represents a movement that paradoxically predates Donald Trump the personage and will no doubt still be around years after he has vacated the presidency.

A group known as Citizen Therapists Against Trumpism (2016) has firmly nailed its colours to the mast by publishing a manifesto warning of Trump's 'narcissism'. Its members see Trumpism as 'an emerging form of American fascism', although they accept that the term may not 'fully fit'. They cite a number of forces that underline Trumpism, such as economic insecurity; fear of terrorism and immigrants; distrust of politicians; and rapid cultural changes that 'have left many people confused and alienated'. For this group, Trumpism is further characterised by scapegoating of the 'other'; degrading and demeaning critics; lack of respect for rational persuasion; and fostering a cult of the Strong Man (Fozooni 2017d).

The most astute psycho-political analysis of Trump thus far comes from Douglas Kellner (2016). Kellner uses Erich Fromm's ideas to characterise Trump as an 'authoritarian populist', who 'like classical fascist leaders, has an underdeveloped Superego … [and who] has had few life-long friends, discards women with abandon … and brags of his ruthlessness in destroying competitors and enemies' (ibid.). According to Kellner, 'for the narcissistically involved person, there is only one reality, that of his own thought, processes, feelings and needs' (ibid.). All this is evident in his obsession 'with putting his name on his buildings or construction sites' and his 'conspicuous consumption' (Thorstein Veblen). Fromm's notion of 'malignant aggression' is used to explain Trump's need to describe his opponents as 'losers' and to sadistically inform contestants on his TV reality show *The Apprentice*, 'You're fired'!

However, while he gives us a pretty decent Freudo-Marxist portrait of Trump, his specialised approach fails to provide a comprehensive critique of Trumpism as a movement and ideology. What remains ambiguous is the specific content of Trumpism.

I would argue that all the evidence marshalled thus far suggests that Trumpism is an amalgamation of four political ideologies. Two of these represent core ideologies and inform most of Trump's discourse and actions, namely neo-liberalism and neo-populism. But he also relies on two peripheral ideologies for various subject positions, and these are neo-social democracy and neo-fascism. This dynamic can be visualised as the diagram shown in Figure 9.1.

Let us take neo-liberalism first. Donald Trump railed against Wall Street and individual bankers during his presidential campaign, 'I know the guys at Goldman Sachs. They have total, total control over [Ted Cruz]. Just like they have total control over Hillary Clinton' (Trump, quoted in Vielma 2016). He once called the Chief Executive Officer of JPMorgan Chase, Jamie Dimon, 'the worst banker in the United States' and complained that hedge fund managers get away with 'murder' (Trump quoted in Merle 2016).

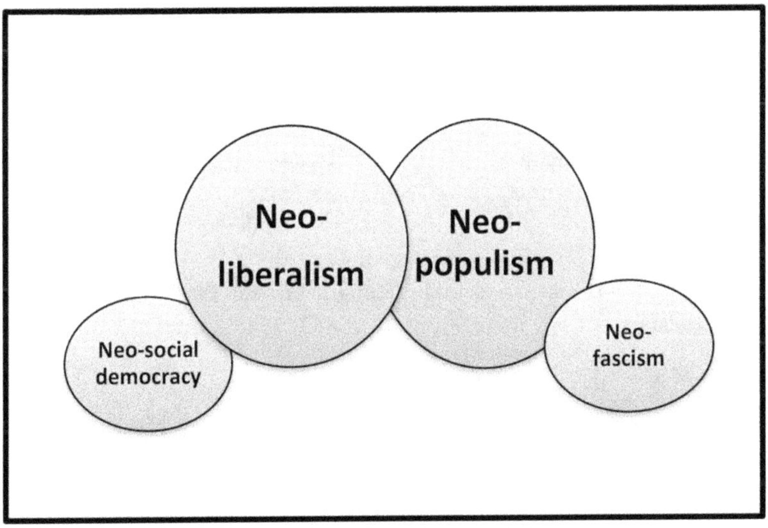

FIGURE 9.1 Political ideologies nourishing Trumpism
Note: For now, neo-liberalism and neo-populism are core ideologies, while neo-social democracy and neo-fascism remain peripheral.

However, as we all know, in office Trump has been eager to appoint multibillionaires who owe their vast wealth to the neo-liberal version of capitalism. Wilbur Ross who became his Secretary of Commerce has an estimated wealth of US $2.5 billion. He used to run Rothschild's bankruptcy advisory business before starting his own private equity firm. Ross has prioritised sweeping deregulation. Trump's Secretary of Education, Betsy Devos, is worth a cool $1 billion (Peterson-Withorn 2017). His Secretary of the Treasury, Steven Mnuchin, is a former Goldman Sachs executive who has jointly created a hedge fund with billionaire financier George Soros. Ben Carson, now in charge of Housing and Urban Development, has been a strong advocate for cutting federal assistance. Even the military men in Trump's cabinet are wealthy. James ('Mad Dog') Mattis is valued at around $7 million. Before becoming Secretary of Defence, he 'sat on the boards of General Dynamics and disgraced blood-testing unicorn Theranos' (ibid.).

The rapid turnover within his cabinet has only accentuated this trend towards recruiting super-rich bankers. Trump has cut the top rate of federal income tax as well as corporation tax. When he met with the corporate executives of the auto industry, the airline industry and Big Pharma he promised to 'free' them of the burden of paying for health, safety and workers' rights.

If most of his ideas about economics are inspired by neo-liberalism, it would be fair to say that the majority of his social views are in tune with right-wing neo-populism. Both the religious and secular adherents of this current display a shallow understanding of social ills and a narrow definition of 'the people', which in this case includes only citizens of European heritage (note how Trump uses every opportunity to foreground his German and Scottish ancestry). As Kazin has reminded us, the classical form of right-wing populism in the early twentieth century 'used xenophobic appeals to lobby Congress to bar all Chinese and most Japanese laborers from immigrating to the United States' (2016). Current US neo-populism is more obsessed with Muslims and Mexicans.

Right-wing evangelical Christians are extremely keen to gain control of this plank of Trumpism (Fozooni 2017a). This is precisely where Trump may run into difficulties. Although he is (probably) neither a classic fascist nor a neo-fascist, his campaign benefited greatly from a plethora of neo-fascist cadres, who are now demanding genuine policy-making clout within the Administration. There are personal and doctrinal ties of continuity between Trump and this neo-fascist support that cannot be so easily severed.

By invoking the term 'fascism', I wish neither to be alarmist nor to trivialise history. However, there are signs that must not go unnoticed. Classical twentieth-century fascism was a capitalist response to social crises that evolved over decades and only towards the end did it morph into full-blown Nazism. What we are witnessing in certain parts of the USA are the off-shoots of an American version of neo-fascism that may or may not gather strength in the coming years.

Trump's ban on Muslims and vitriol against Mexicans is neo-fascistic because it is a pseudo-security device entailing the 'Untermensching' of entire groups of people. His incarceration of refugee children is likewise a neo-fascist tactic. It is a policy that connects personal prejudice to institutional discrimination and even reanimates visceral bigotry. This linkage (prejudice to discrimination to bigotry) is ever-present as a potential within capitalism, but today it is being embedded presidentially. Worryingly, it comes as part of a frontal assault on the left and liberal press. Meanwhile, Trump's regime is also conducting what can only be described as a purge of enemies in the judiciary, the legislature and even the executive.

Furthermore, there is the nefarious influence of Alt-Right, an online network of supporters ranging from neo-Nazis, to fascists to 'men's rights' activists. The demoted Steve Bannon represents the 'responsible' white supremacist faction of Alt-Right, in contrast to the crude neo-Nazi wing (Conatz 2016). 'Responsible' needs to be in quote marks since Bannon is a firm believer in the apocalypse.

The final cluster of Trump's policies has been labelled 'neo-social democracy'. For those readers who associate social democracy with 'leftism', 'welfarism' and 'the redistribution of wealth' this may be controversial. However, classical twentieth-century social democracy was first and foremost a bourgeois ideology that sought to harmonise capital accumulation by negotiating a temporary truce between capital and labour. Trump is not exactly aiming for this, but he is trying to protect certain sectors of the economy, including automobiles, electrical goods, steel, coal and oil, from foreign competition. He has promised to boost growth to an annual average of 3.5 per cent and to create 25 million new jobs in the next decade. He is hoping that this will rebalance US capitalism which in recent decades has allowed the banking and finance sectors to get rich at the expense of the industrial and manufacturing wing of capital.

Other social democratic elements of his ideas can be seen in his attempts to bolster 'military Keynesianism', manage demand and consumption more efficiently and increase investment in science and technology. He has also promised massive funds for new infrastructural and housing projects.

While classical social democracy was about allowing most workers to benefit from boom times, twenty-first century neo-social democracy is mainly about welfarism for the ruling class, with a few crumbs thrown in the general direction of the workforce.

This then is the political ideology of Trumpism. Postpsychology has helped us to pinpoint it as an amalgamation of four distinct but overlapping political ideologies, namely neo-liberalism and neo-populism (operating as core ideologies), in conjunction with neo-fascism and neo-social democracy (constituting his peripheral ideologies). While offering different styles of mystification, these ideologies are united in their fierce hatred of the working class (Fozooni 2017a). We will never be rid of Trumpism until its anti-working-class essence is exposed. Soon the US working class will remember Douglas Adams's acerbic comments:

> It is a well-known fact that those people who most want to rule people are, ipso facto, those least suited to do it. To summarize the summary: anyone who is capable of getting themselves made President should on no account be allowed to do the job.
>
> *(Douglas Adams,* The Hitchhikers' Guide to the Galaxy*)*

Final remarks on Billig

I think that as someone with an underdeveloped sense of humour Billig has provided us with an excellent study of social humour; as someone who is not a nationalist, he has written a profound treatise on nationalism; and as someone who does not really have a thorough class analysis, he has provided us with useful resources for escalating and intensifying the class struggle. Billig and Professor Ian Parker, whom I discuss in the next chapter, have stretched critical psychology as far as possible. My aim, however, is to stretch it beyond breaking point, in anticipation of interesting new mutations.

10

PARKER AND CRITICAL PSYCHOLOGY

OK, now what?

I think I first met Professor Ian Parker in 2004, when I was desperately seeking a PhD supervisor. All my previous attempts at forging a 'career' had reached a humiliating impasse and I found myself with an obsolete skill set and a disconcerting financial balance sheet. I had fallen so low that my new ambition was to transform into George Bernard Shaw's clichéd non-achiever: 'People who are able to do something well can do that thing for a living, while people who are not able to do anything that well make a living by teaching'.

It was to avoid failing even as a teacher that I embarked on a last-ditch effort to obtain a PhD qualification. At this stage, I had read just two articles by Parker: one a 'political text' (which confirmed my suspicions that I was dealing with some sort of Trotskyite), and one 'academic text' (which was a discourse analysis of a children's toothpaste called Punch & Judy). The latter was so original and thought-provoking that I chose to forgive the dodgy wordsmithery of the former. After all, if one of my flawed heroes, Eric Cartman, could defeat Saddam Hussein and Satan in just one scene of *South Park*, surely I could handle a descendant of the 'butcher of Kronstadt'!

Luckily for me, Ian turned out to be much more decent than many of his Bolsheviki brethren, and I soon realised that I had stumbled upon the perfect PhD supervisor. He welcomed me to the department of psychology at Manchester Metropolitan University, opened various hitherto invisible doors, and provided me with ample space to pursue a topic close to my heart. If I have never thanked him properly, allow me to take this opportunity to do so publicly.

For better or worse, he is also directly responsible for this book. Had it not been for his encouragement, I would not have pitched an unusual book about psychology and social class to Routledge. Add to this the fact that as the series editor he was obliged to pen a preface to my book, and you will see that by choosing to write a chapter on Parker I have placed myself in an awkward position. After a number of unsuccessful rewrites, I even contemplated replacing this chapter with one focusing on a less influential critical psychologist, but concluded that it would be too cowardly, even by my dastardly standards.

In what follows, you will be immersed in a debate. On the one hand there is Ian Parker, a Leninist-Trotskyist-Lacanian professor of psychology, who has done more than anyone to establish critical psychology as a viable alternative to mainstream psychology. On the other hand, I am a former student of Parker who shares some of his views about psychology, but who challenges key components of those views from a working-class perspective. I hope the discussion proves fruitful.

Parker and discourse analysis

I remember my sense of incredulity when I first came across Parker's discourse analysis of a children's toothpaste called Punch & Judy. It simply had not occurred to me that the instructions and design logos of a toothpaste are worthy of serious investigative consideration (the intricate design of this particular toothpaste is available on the Internet). Discourse analysis, at its very best, can still shock the reader into looking at life from a completely different vantagepoint.

Parker establishes the epistemological foundations of his approach in these terms:

> Discourse analysis treats the social world … as a system of texts which can be systemically 'read' by a researcher to lay open the psychological processes that lie within them, processes that the discipline of psychology usually attributes to a machine inside the individual head.
>
> *(1994, p. 92)*

This approach is considered an improvement on structuralism, since it deals with a multiplicity of meanings that a system might hold (ibid., p. 93).

In other words, our identities and social relationships are not created by one structure; instead, they are constituted through conflicting discourses (ibid., p. 94).

Parker's definition of discourse is rooted in Foucault who argued that '[discourses] are practices that systematically form the objects of which we speak' (1969, p. 49). This approach acted as a powerful and necessary critique of those previous schools of psychology that viewed language as being merely a reflection of our thoughts. However, it should be pointed out that by surreptitiously allocating language a deterministic role, many discourse analysts have taken things too far. In most forms of discourse analysis, the gaze remains fixated on inter-psychological symbolic activity. This obsession comes at the expense of intra-psychological and extra-psychological dimensions that are either ignored or paid mere lip-service. This is limiting enough but there is, in addition, another flaw at the heart of Foucault to do with his overemphasis on 'difference' at the expense of our shared humanity. In his own words, 'we are difference, that our reason is the difference of discourses, our history the difference of times, our selves the difference of masks' (ibid., p. 131). Parker is mindful of such unbalanced declarations.

It is to the credit of discourse analysis that even when confined to the inter-psychological plain, the exploration can yield substantial discoveries. In the case of the Punch & Judy toothpaste the first task is to turn the package into a written form, while noting how the advertising is reproducing the child as a smaller version of the adult. Parker recommends Freudian 'free association' which he admits might produce some strange connotations. These, he argues, without firm justification, could prove useful later on. Now we systematically itemise the objects that appear in the text and for this Parker suggests we look for nouns, such as 'choices', 'teeth', 'chin', 'mouth', 'fluoride', 'intake', etc. Having identified the objects in the text, the researcher must now find the subjects (the categories of person). He foregrounds the three main ones: 'professionals' (who regulate the treatment); 'parents' (those for whom the instructions are intended); and 'children' (the recipients of dental treatment).

Parker then guides us towards mapping the different versions of the social world which exists in the text, from a 'rational, rule-following discourse' to an assumed 'normative developmental trajectory'. The analyst might speculate as to some early objections to these discourses or, at the very least, consider the 'cultural rules hidden within them' (Parker 1994, p. 100). In addition, the contrasts and commonalities in the various ways of speaking should be identified.

The analyst is then encouraged to move out of the text concerning the chosen toothpaste by drawing comparisons with 'outside' texts. This is an advantage of Parker's method since not all discourse analysts recommend this step. For example, the Punch & Judy texts can be compared to other toothpastes or, better still, to the Plain English Campaign 'which draws attention to and praises clarity and rationality … in official documents' (ibid., p. 101).

If Parker was writing this chapter in the present day, I am sure he would have availed himself of the example of Jacob Rees-Mogg's list of rules for his staff. Apparently, upon his appointment as leader of the House of Commons Rees-Mogg demanded a return to imperial measurements and the use of the suffix 'esquire' for all non-titled males (Rawlinson 2019). Certain terms were to be banned from official communications, such as 'very', 'due to', 'equal', 'lot', 'got', 'I am pleased to learn' and 'unacceptable' (ibid.). Rawlinson points out that the Eton-educated 'honourable member for the eighteenth century', as Rees-Mogg is snidely referred to, has himself used one or another of these banned words in official parliamentary proceedings on at least 700 occasions!

What these puritanical views on language reveal is a deep sense of bourgeois insecurity and intolerance. The policing of language is aimed at reversing the real loss of power and prestige that the ruling class has suffered in recent decades. Ironically, Rees-Mogg's grand bourgeois approach to reclaiming power through grammatical tyranny parallels the petty bourgeois campaign launched by American academics in the 1970s which ultimately became known as 'political correctness'. This is a phrase whose usage began with political conflicts between independent-minded socialists and craven Stalinists who followed the party line dictated by Comintern in the 1930s and 1940s. It was then revived in the 1970s, first genuinely and then in jest by American academics representing the left wing of capitalism. Today, it often carries a derogatory connotation when used by right wingers and the mainstream media. Instructions for the use of a toothpaste and a campaign for linguistic regulation are, therefore, similar in essential ways.

Returning to Parker's step-by-step discourse analysis of the toothpaste, we are now in a position to choose an appropriate label for various discourses. He identifies four: a 'rationalist' discourse which teaches the ability to follow procedures established by professionals; a 'familial' discourse which uses brushing as a way of monitoring the child and is framed by the image of bad parenting as represented by Punch & Judy; a 'developmental-educational' discourse which begins with instructions that later become self-governing, and assumes appropriate age-related activity for various developmental milestones; and, finally, a 'medical' discourse in which the daily use of toothpaste containing 0.8 per cent of sodium monofluorophosphate is associated directly with hygiene, and indirectly with good parenting and perhaps even 'moral fibre' (Parker 1994, p. 102).

We can then investigate when and where these four discourses were developed and how they became normative over time. Furthermore, we could speculate 'who would benefit and who would be disadvantaged by such discourses ... and who would want to discredit these ways of talking' (Parker 1994, p. 103). Finally, the ways in which meaning is reproduced in these seemingly innocuous texts can be linked to power relations in order to complete a Foucauldian-flavoured discourse analysis.

The complexities of qualitative psychology: the case of Fukushima

I started my so-called career in psychology many years ago at Keele University and at that time I was a convinced quantitative and experimental researcher. I still remember having to run the gauntlet of cruel taunts about 'coke gerbilling' when the other students discovered my predilection for colour perception studies with those cute little sand rats! Ironically, I had already begun to feel uncomfortable regarding shortcomings in statistical analysis and experimentation during my undergraduate studies, but a clear break came only after a master's degree in Critical Psychology at Bolton University. This course cleansed the bitter taste left in my mouth after an earlier master's degree in Research Methodology in Psychology at the University of Reading. The Reading course consisted solely of quantitative elements, whereas the course at Bolton was based entirely on qualitative methodology. It is no exaggeration to say that these two camps appear to detest and despise each other (and sometimes, it must be said, with good reason)!

I like to think that I have come a long way since those confused, flip-flopping student days. Nowadays I start from the blatantly obvious assumption that all phenomena are complex, dynamic and multilayered. There is a need to understand them at the intra-, inter- and extra-psychological level simultaneously. As such, both quantitative and qualitative methodologies should be utilised for abstracting various key features. It is not a question of choosing between them; rather, it is a matter of ensuring that both are utilised critically and integrally. Choosing the 'correct' methodology is also shaped by what questions the researcher is interested in and the motivation behind the research in the first place. An example might prove useful in this regard.

In 2011 there was a triple nuclear meltdown at the Fukushima ('happy island') Daiichi ('beautiful') power station (*Wikipedia*, 'Fukushima Daiichi Nuclear Disaster'). A simplified causal explanation of the disaster based on the precepts of positivism and empiricism would note the following sequence of events: an underwater earthquake off the coast of Japan occurred on 11 March 2011 and lasted for six minutes; it was the most powerful earthquake ever recorded in Japan (just above 9.0 on the Richter scale of magnitude), triggering powerful tsunami waves that were estimated to have travelled 40.5 metres inland; the tsunami caused nuclear 'accidents':

> primarily the level 7 meltdowns at three reactors in the Fukushima Daiichi Nuclear Power Plant complex, and the associated evacuation zones affecting hundreds of thousands of residents. Many electrical generators were taken down, and at least three nuclear reactors suffered explosions due to hydrogen gas that had built up within their outer containment buildings after cooling system failure resulting from the loss of electrical power … the World Bank estimated the disaster as the costliest in history at around US$235 billion.
>
> (Wikipedia, *'2011 Tōhoku Earthquake and Tsunami'*)

FIGURE 10.1 IAEA experts at Fukushima, 2013
Source: Greg Webb/IAEA.

I imagine myself as one of the hundreds of thousands of evacuees and ask, 'What would be my immediate reaction to the accident?' Given my almost total lack of knowledge in this field, I would be inclined to find the nearest technician with a Geiger counter, ask him/her where the radiation leak was approaching from, and then get myself and my loved ones in a car and drive like a bat out of hell in the opposite direction. Despite the failure of science and technology to prevent this 'accident' from occurring, I would have little choice but to follow their technical dictates. Once I was safely out of the danger zone, however, I would stop at a hotel, order a cup of Japanese green tea, and reflect on my predicament from a different angle.

Is it really true that only one person is known to have died as a direct result of radiation exposure in Fukushima (*Wikipedia*, 'Fukushima Daiichi Nuclear Disaster')? Is it true that the risk of radiation poisoning has been overblown and that the most common causes of distress are psychological and related to post-traumatic stress, depression and stigmatisation? (Cooper 2015). If 70 per cent of Japan's population is in favour of a nuclear-free future, why is the government ignoring their views and not investing in solar and wind energy? (Rugh 2013). Why was the plant built so close to residential areas? What was the role of 'lax government regulators, a cost-skimming mega-corporation and Japan's powerful mafia, the Yakuza' in the disaster? (ibid.). Why were recommendations about fortifying the plant to withstand waves measuring more than 5.7 metres high not acted upon? Why are around 90 per cent of Japan's nuclear plant contract workers recruited from 'the homeless, the chronically unemployed and members of Japan's outcast Burakumin minority'? (ibid.). How can we prevent future disasters?

The above questions can only be investigated qualitatively. They require a knowledge of political economy, history, culture, sociology and psychology that would help us to peel away layers of mystification and prevarication. In this case, there was so much state-sponsored disinformation relating to Fukushima that a member of the Japanese parliament decided to spill the beans:

> The primary difference between Tepco [the plant owners] and the Yakuza is they have different corporate logos … They both are essentially criminal organisations that place profits above the safety and welfare of the residents where they operate; they both exploit their workers.
>
> *(Rugh, 2013)*

There is another comparative study worth mentioning before I leave Fukushima and return to Parker. Marjolein van der Veen (2013) has compared and contrasted Fukushima with the Chernobyl disaster (1986). It was ultimately the failure of the Soviet capitalist class to complete the transition from a formal phased of capital domination to a real phase of domination that sealed the fate of the USSR. Machinery was introduced too late or too unevenly to increase the rate of profit and the war in Afghanistan took its economic toll. The growth rate slowed to 1.8 per cent between 1980–1985 (ibid., p. 122). Working-class dissent, in the form of strikes, go-slows, work to rule, absenteeism, alcoholism, sabotage and at times open protest, sapped the energy of the ruling class. One factor absent from most analyses of the collapse of the Soviet Union is the economic impact of Chernobyl:

> The Chernobyl disaster put a heavy burden on national budgets, given the need for cleanup, compensation, resettlement, and ongoing health care. To compound the problem, much of the land was now off limits, so investment fell, industry and agriculture declined, unemployment rose, and workers migrated outside the affected areas … A recent study estimated the total economic cost from Chernobyl at about £144 billion.
>
> *(Ibid., p. 126)*

The author claims that the ultimate cost of Fukushima will be worse than Chernobyl 'given the greater number of nuclear reactors and spent fuel pools involved [and] the larger amount of fallout' (van der Veen 2013, p. 128).

Quantitative research is excellent at answering basic questions about what happened at Fukushima and Chernobyl and it is doubtless useful during the process of decommissioning the plants. A simple sequence of events can be drawn up and communicated to all staff for the purpose of clean-up and repair operations. But beyond identifying triggering mechanisms we may wish to understand the underlying causes of such disasters. Key questions regarding why and how they happened can only be tackled through qualitative analysis. Furthermore, qualitative analysis helps us to understand whose interests are served by having a nuclear industry. This is where Parker's radical qualitative approach becomes indispensable.

Parker's contribution to qualitative research

If there is one subject that guarantees tedium in students of psychology, it is research methodology. Frankly, I cannot really blame them since, in general, it is taught rather poorly. Parker's *Qualitative Psychology: Introducing Radical Research* (2005) is one of the very few textbooks on the subject that I have managed to read cover to cover. I think it represents a genuine attempt to foreground the very best approaches to qualitative psychology available to students. It provides guidelines, without being too prescriptive, and the outline is clear. At the core of the book are five methods Parker considers indispensable: ethnography; interviewing; narrative; discourse analysis; and psychoanalysis. There are thought-provoking early chapters on 'ethics' and 'reflexivity' (two concepts that are poorly understood and woefully taught at most universities). The book finishes by showing that all these methods and concepts can be completed through 'action research'. I will pick out just a few of the most fascinating points below.

Ethnography is a research method that seems to be on the wane – a pity since at its most critical it can add immeasurably to our understanding of real and imaginary 'communities' (Taylor 2010). A great deal of time and effort (and at times risk taking) is required of the ethnographer. He or she has to gain entrance to a community, learn its customs and conventions, understand its history and power structure, and all the while remain vigilant against the perils of over-familiarisation and over-identification (Scheper-Hughes 2000). As the geographical contours of the world shrink, the type of 'communities' studied by nineteenth- and twentieth-century ethnographers (far-away 'exoticised' communities in Africa and Asia) could give way to emergent 'communities' in cyberspace. Another key subpopulation that ethnographers can help us to understand is the ruling class itself. Marxists and anarchists have waxed enthusiastically about the wrongs of 'capital' (as a social relationship) and 'capitalism' (as a mode of production), but flesh and blood 'capitalists' are not ethnographically investigated with the same commitment. There is potential for cross-disciplinary future research carried out by critical journalists, ethnographers, and psychologists who would investigate semi-secretive clubs, lodges, homosocial spaces and think tanks in order to analyse the strategising that is being practised by the ruling elites. Our rulers have so many unsavoury methods of subjecting us to surveillance that I feel it is only fair we return the compliment.

One point of disagreement with Parker revolves around ethnomethodology. While I agree with his criticisms of ethnomethodology as it has been imported into psychology, I think the original radical sociological imperative of this field could and should be rediscovered. In psychology (especially conversational analysis) ethnomethodology is reduced in stature to a re-description of conversations. Fancy technical terms and concepts are used to retell the conversation between two subjects from the analyst's point of view. The end result is usually banal and boring. However, ethnomethodology as it was originally put forward was a rather clever method of understanding the rules of the game through breaking them (Garfinkel 1986). The transgression of taboos and conventions was done for two main reasons: first, to see how people would react to having their self-governing rules broken (imagine suddenly talking to strangers in a lift); and two, to see how damage to the webs that bind communities and networks together is repaired.

Down with ethics? Or is it morality? Or is it self-righteous moralism? Ah, confusing!

There are other aspects of Parker's research agenda that are worth dwelling on. He takes 'ethics' in research both more *and* less seriously than the rest of academia. Let me elaborate. His chapter on ethics includes a tightly argued critique of 'ethical committees' as they have been developed by university management over recent years. Although going through the torturous process can occasionally be thought-provoking, 'the ethics committee in a psychology department, hospital or local authority is often a nuisance that seems dedicated to putting obstacles in the way of research' (Parker 2005, p. 18). Ethical committees have an inherent tendency to promote quantitative research and be suspicious of the surprises and outliers that qualitative research frequently uncovers. Subsequently, 'the committee tries to predict and control all the possible outcomes its members are able to anticipate' which means that more complex research is usually rejected (ibid.). The 'checklist' approach of the committee reinforces bureaucratic structures which are already too widespread within universities and researchers end up having to conform to a routine set of rules. To this list we should add the often-neglected point that the primary function of these committees, it seems to me, is not the upholding of 'ethical principles' but the protection of senior management from possible libellous action should things go wrong.

Faced with these obstacles you can either 'play the game' or 'better, you can think through the rules of the game so that your ethical decisions and fidelity

FIGURE 10.2 Ian Andrew Parker

to the research is deeper and even more wide-ranging than they would be able to imagine' (Parker 2005). In other words, expose the performative nature of 'ethical committees' by conducting your research more ethically than they would. This is sound advice (and I hope to make use of it in Chapter 18 in this volume on Luria, when I will argue that critical psychologists should take neuropsychology more seriously than neuropsychologists currently do).

Using Alan Badiou's work, Parker even attempts to reconstruct an alternative set of formulations for ethical research that are intended to overcome traditional accounts of ethics resting on Aristotle, Kant or Bentham.

One thing is missing from Parker's account of ethics, and that is a class perspective. At the risk of inviting charges of reductionism, I would like to suggest that psychologists make a clearer linguistic distinction between externally imposed 'ethics' from above and self-generating 'morality' from below. Ethics is usually bourgeois, individualistic and prescribed by the powerful. Morality, by contrast, is most of the time collectively and consensually arrived at through experience and debate. The distinction becomes murky when we take into account the recent emergence of 'self-righteous moralism' that seems to be as pervasive as it is pernicious. This behaviour is seen in all classes but I suspect that, by and large, it is a middle-class form of power-play that is attempting to win lost prestige through point scoring (Pashukanis [1929] 1989).

What exactly is 'intersectionality'?

> Life is really simple, but we insist on making it complicated.
>
> *Confucius*

This section is partially a response to Parker's short account of 'intersectionality' in *Revolutionary Keywords for A New Left* (2017), which I find troubling. In particular, he seems to be saying that any criticism of intersectionality is a case of sour grapes by 'old male [leftists] who see feminism as an enemy of the class struggle' (Parker 2017, p. 104). By contrast, I feel that it is possible to be a revolutionary, integrate the best of feminism, and still be deeply sceptical about certain models of intersectionality.

To this end, I will describe one particular version of this thing called intersectionality, and then question its limits and shortcomings. What I am trying to understand is whether Kimberlé Crenshaw's intersectionality is yet another sophisticated version of identity politics, and, if so, is it undermining the class struggle against capitalism? I end by suggesting alternative ways of using intersectionality to strengthen the working class.

Kimberlé Williams Crenshaw (born 1959) is a middle-class American lawyer who was appointed as full professor at Columbia Law School in 1995. She self-identifies as a feminist, a critical race theorist and a civil rights lawyer. What sets her apart from similar lawyer-activists is that she is credited with coining the term 'intersectionality' (Crenshaw 1989). In a series of lectures and papers she expounds on how she came up with this notion.

She cites the case of (Emma) *DeGraffenreid v. General Motors* as 'an inspiration'. Emma's application to work at General Motors was rejected. She sued General Motors for discrimination arguing she was qualified to do the job, but was rejected due to being a 'black woman'. But the courts *did not see* Emma as a 'black woman'. They could deal with her lawsuit either in terms of 'race' or 'gender' discrimination but not both! Her claim that she was being discriminated against racially was rejected since the judge argued that General Motors does employ black men on the shop floor, and her suit for gender discrimination was also refused since the company employs many white women in its administrative office. Since Emma stood at the intersection of race and gender discrimination, she 'fell through the cracks' and was not acknowledged by the legal system. The court declined to consider this argument, and dismissed the case (Crenshaw 2016).

Crenshaw devised a legal strategy for countering this decision. In her own words:

> [S]o it occurred to me maybe a simple analogy to an intersection might allow judges to better see Emma's dilemma. So, if we think about this intersection, the roads to the intersection would be the way that the workforce was structured by race and gender. And then the traffic in those roads would be the hiring policies and other policies that ran through those roads.
>
> *(2016)*

Making the disempowered 'invisible' is key to denying them opportunities or appropriate renumeration. Bourgeois law throws an 'invisibility cloak' over vast swathes of the proletariat and it is correct of Crenshaw to try to counter this tendency. Marxist feminists taught us this lesson decades ago when they set up the International Wages for Housework Campaign in order to draw attention to the unacknowledged productive labour carried out by homeworkers (Dalla Costa and James 1975).

Thus, the basic idea behind intersectionality is simple, yet a number of misinterpretations by both sympathisers and critics have prompted this disavowal from Crenshaw:

> [Some] often mistakenly think intersectionality is about multiple identity. I have got 3 [identities] you've got 6. Some colleagues in Germany undertook to count how many intersections there are. Last count there were 17 or something ... there was an attempt to map intersectionality ...

> that's not my articulation of intersectionality. Intersectionality is not primarily about identity. It is about how structures make certain identities … the vehicle for vulnerability.
>
> *(2018)*

In addition, Crenshaw is at pains to show that intersectionality is not a method for quantifying discrimination. For instance, being 'black' and a 'woman' does not mean the axis of discrimination can be added up – it does not necessarily lead to 'double discrimination'. In Crenshaw's words, '[Black women] experience discrimination as Black women – not the sum of race and sex discrimination, but as Black women' (1989, p. 149).

It is very necessary to underline Crenshaw's post-structuralist attempt to update fossilised American legal structures. She is trying to update and modernise bourgeois law rather than to quantify discrimination. She is doing this in order to advocate more effectively on behalf of those who hitherto have been 'invisible' within the legal system. Think of Monty Python's project of modernising antiquated British legal and political structures (minus the humour), and you begin to understand Crenshaw's zest for reformism.

We may agree or disagree with her regarding the relevance and priority of such a project. In my view it is a project aimed at modernising capitalism and not overthrowing it. But at least the project has the distinction of clarity of purpose. Sadly, the same cannot be said about some of her followers who have taken intersectionality to strange places. Figure 10.3 is adapted from Morgan's 1996 mapping of intersectionality.

The above diagram is a kind of 'privilege-o-meter' and is usually accompanied by a set of simple instructions which asks the subject to consider their position on the different dimensions. More importantly, they are encouraged to locate themselves either in the upper (privileged), or lower (oppressed) half of the diagram.

An even more bizarre attempt to 'apply' intersectionality is the 'Intersectionality Score Calculator' (https://intersectionalityscore.com). In fact, it occurred to me as I was navigating though the website that the whole thing could be an attempt at satire. What is it, I hear you ask? Well, according to the website, 'It's an easy and effective way to measure the systematic oppression and discrimination faced by an individual due to their multiple identity factors'. You provide the calculator with sliding scores and the calculator measures your level of oppression. The central aim of such a scoring system is to 'give exclusive opportunities and promotions to people with high intersectionality scores so that they become more represented in positions of power. We also suggest

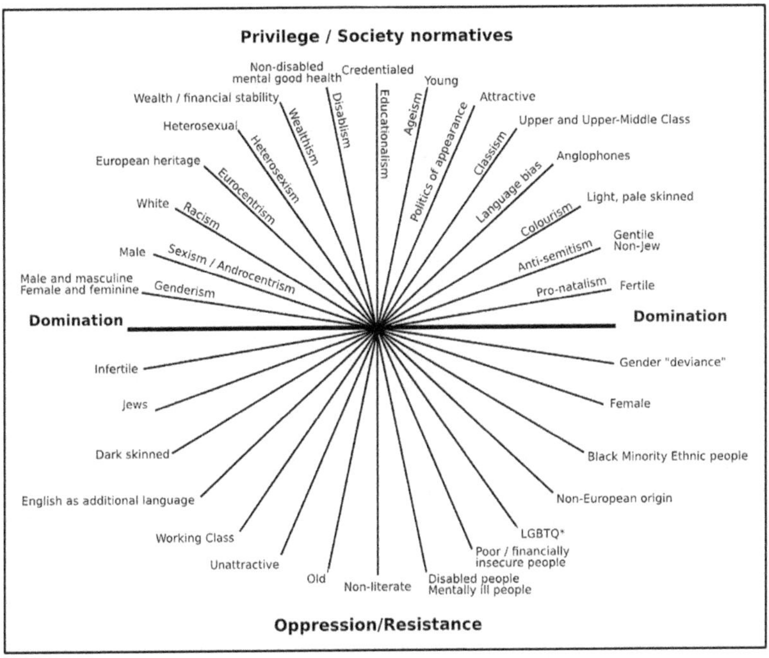

FIGURE 10.3 One view of intersectionality

every group meeting to begin with everyone sharing their intersectionality scores'! You can 'improve' your score. You can even click on the diagram and add your own slider to make the scoring 'more accurate' (Intersectionality Score Calculator, n.d.).

Even if this is a fake website (and I very much suspect it is), imagine the anger and frustration that motivated it. It takes effort to design and maintain such a site. Now, imagine the kind of individual(s) behind such a site. If it is a genuine site, I see a group of atavistic activists who understand little about genuine intersectionality (but are deluded enough to think they are pushing the envelope by operationalising it). Alternatively, if it is fake, I envisage a bunch of angry older reactionaries, who for the time being are expressing their hostility through what passes for social satire among their circle. In either case, I would strongly argue that (a) the existence of such a website tells us something about the age of heightened emotions and miscommunication we are going through, and (b) there may be inherent weaknesses in Crenshaw's original theory which encourage such (deliberate or mischievous) misinterpretations.

I think point (b) is more promising, so let us concentrate on that and scrutinise Crenshaw's original theory more thoroughly. She has written a great deal on the topic, but two seminal articles stand out (Crenshaw 1989 and 1994). An admittedly non-conclusive word checker exercise is suggestive. Using the search engine, I checked for the frequency of certain key terms that I would expect to see in any 'radical' text. The figures express the combined number of occurrences in both texts: capitalism (0); socialism (0); communism (0); Marxism (1); anarchism (0); class struggle (0); wage slavery (0); working class (1). This is strange, I thought. Only one mention of 'Marxism' and that is in the reference section and only one usage of 'working class' and that is in the footnotes! I then checked for the following terms: black (438); women (523); race (130); and community (62).

Could it be that in line with most of her compatriots Kimberlé Crenshaw has been encouraged from birth to develop a racial and gender-based consciousness but not a class consciousness? Is that why she was so enamoured of the myth of a 'black community' or a 'sisterhood' at the start of her intellectual journey? Could it be that it was only when this simplistic intellectual framework was challenged by the brutal realities of the class struggle that she began to seek out a better explanation? If so, good for her! I am pleased that she now takes class issues on board. I am also pleased for her clients, who may be more ably represented in bourgeois courts of law, thanks to Crenshaw's 'discovery' of the class struggle.

Problems with Crenshaw's version of intersectionality

Here I would like to furnish further criticisms of intersectionality, as expounded by Crenshaw and her followers.

1. Crenshaw did not discover 'intersectionality'. She might have coined the term but the idea that various aspects of our existence intersect and shape our social being has very deep roots. During rare flashes of humility she is willing to share the limelight with former pioneers: 'In every generation and in every intellectual sphere and in every political moment, there have been African American women who have articulated the need to think and talk about race through a lens that looks at gender, or think and talk about feminism through a lens that looks at race' (*Wikipedia*, 'Kimberlé Williams Crenshaw'). She specifically mentions nineteenth-century American black feminists, Anna Julia Cooper and Maria Stewart, followed by Angela Davis and

Deborah King in the twentieth century. Even at her most expansive you will note that Crenshaw is limiting herself to two registers: race and gender. For all sorts of reasons, it is necessary to be brutally honest here:

If I want to understand the intersectionality of gender and class, I read Sylvia Pankhurst, Emma Goldman, Rosa Luxemburg, Mariarosa Dalla Costa, Selma James, Raya Dunayevskaya and Leopoldina Fortunati – not necessarily Crenshaw.

If I want to understand the intersectionality of race and class, I read Marx, C. L. R. James, Peter Linebaugh, Marcus Rediker and James Carr.

If I want to understand the intersectionality of race, gender and class, I read Angela Davis and Silvia Federici.

If I want to understand the intersectionality of disability, gender and class I read Helen Keller – not Crenshaw.

One must always seek out the most radical (and they frequently turn out to be the earliest) exponents of an idea, and remain sceptical about any Johnny-come-latelies!

2. Crenshaw's Intersectional Feminism stays firmly focused on 'discrimination'. For instance, she has rebranded workplace segregation as a 'structured intersectional form of discrimination'. To call out discrimination is very useful. However, as I have already mentioned in previous chapters, discrimination does not function alone. Rather, it is embedded in a chain of categories responsible for policing exploitation and oppression: 'bias' (which is usually individualistically and unconsciously expressed); 'prejudice' (which is also individualistically but this time consciously expressed); 'discrimination' (which is imposed structurally on individuals and groups); and 'bigotry' (which is usually a collective and visceral expression of hatred towards the other). Crenshaw is interested in reforming structural discrimination alone. But these categories work collaboratively, reinforcing each other. A radical approach can see this and counter them effectively. Crenshaw's reformist agenda cannot.
3. Following from the point above, Crenshaw fails to provide a radical critique of bourgeois law. Instead, she merely names people not covered by the grace of American law. I can see the attraction of this approach to lawyers, risk assessors, insurance clerks and preachers, but not to anti-capitalists. Naturally, in line with all middle-class reformers, Crenshaw is very keen to share her expertise with the ruling class, 'information has to be made available to people, to stakeholders, to

leaders about the actual dimension of the disparity' (2018). She seems particularly excited about 'informing' that hub of revolutionary subversives, the United Nations!

4. Crenshaw graciously permits the occasional mention of social class, only to 'horizontalise' everything. In abstract terms all registers are considered equal. In reality some (race and gender) are treated more equal than others. In fact, in the 1994 article Crenshaw develops the terrible habit of substituting race for class. It needs to be stated categorically that we, the working class, form the overwhelming majority of the population, exploited in each and every society. Yet Crenshaw's intersectionality downplays this vital fact by fetishising difference. The overwhelming majority suddenly becomes a series of disempowered and fragile minorities, in need of a legal champion. Solidarity and class consciousness are reduced to legal representations of individuals in court, and bearing witness to their suffering in theatrical performances, outside of the courts.

To summarise: if by intersectionality one is referring to the complex network of alliances and contradictions that class struggle structures, then having a model of it is vital. But if this model is to be useful to anticapitalists, we must rediscover the radicals who preceded Crenshaw and recognise her and her followers for what they are: nice, decent, concerned, middle-class people who want a better capitalism!

Final remarks on Parker

Ian Parker is exceptionally productive. In the time it takes me to make some popcorn and sit myself down in front of *Match of the Day*, Ian has completed another text! It is not easy keeping up with him. I have, therefore, left many aspects of his work untouched. I have made no mention of his recently edited book, *Islamic Psychoanalysis and Psychoanalytic Islam* (2018), or his *Slavoj Zizek: A Critical Introduction* (2004), or his *Lacanian Psychoanalysis: Revolutions in Subjectivity* (2010). Oh my God, I just checked his Amazon webpage, and apparently he has published yet another book: *Psychoanalysis, Clinic and Context* (2019). Slow down, man! For *Foucault's* sake, slow down!

But I would like to end on a positive note. To be fair to Ian, he is too anchored in reality to promote extreme relativism of the type expressed in some forms of postmodernism. His work couples the best of modernist thinking, with the most sensible contributions of postmodernism. This means that he is more than capable of self-reflexively gazing upon the shortcomings of postmodernism and discourse analysis. In *Against Postmodernism* (1998) he criticises both branches of postmodernism, the happy, optimistic, celebratory branch which tends to become apolitical and amoral, as well as the pessimistic and fatalistic branch, which ends up embracing scientism, fundamentalism and individualism. 'Postmodernism', he says, 'makes a virtue of its ambiguity and uncertainty' (Parker 1998, p. 611). However, this does not mean we must reject it completely. Rather, we should forge a strategic relationship with it, in order to show that postmodernism sometimes opens up and sometimes closes down 'a dialectical movement of truth and change' (ibid., p. 616).

There is also a wonderful chapter entitled 'Against Discursive Imperialism', co-written with Erica Burman (Parker and Burman 1993), which details not just one or two but 'thirty-two problems with discourse analysis'. These range from lack of opportunity 'for consideration of large-scale political consequences of the repertoires in the material being studied', to 'analysis avoiding the "performative" aspect of language', to discourse analysis's 'clear continuities with empiricism, and this continuity lies in its reductionist tendencies' (ibid., pp. 156–163).

OK, so far, so good. The best of postmodernism has been recruited to chastise universal modernist pretensions, and in turn the extremes of postmodernism have been curtailed with the best of modernism. But, now what? Where do we go from here? This, I am afraid, may very well be the limits of critical psychology. Stretching it any further may result in the elastic band holding it all together to snap! The only solution to this impasse, I would argue, is to return to a better understanding of the class struggle. In Part III, a few stammering working-class voices will try to utter the word *postpsychology*.

PART III

Postpsychology and working-class stutterings

In Part III, I begin to construct an alternative to modernist mainstream psychology and postmodernist critical psychology. I do so by foregrounding figures from psychology and elsewhere, who could furnish us with different pieces of a huge theoretical jigsaw: historians such as Vico, philosophers such as Dietzgen, economists such as Sohn-Rethel, artists such as Artaud, cultural theorists such as Bakhtin, analysts such as Fromm, neuropsychologists such as Luria and psychologists such as Vygotsky.

11

GIAMBATTISTA VICO, IMAGINATION AND POSTPSYCHOLOGY

Giambattista Vico: a short biography

There is a great deal worth admiring in Giambattista Vico (1668–1744). Born to a bookseller in Naples (Southern Italy), this philosopher-rhetorician produced ideas so advanced that centuries later they can be comfortably incorporated into postpsychology. It is true that politically he was conservative and that his philosophical outlook was heavily marked by idealism. In his work, he 'underscores the significance of the role of religion in the civilising process and of divine providence in guiding that process to fulfilment' (Hutton 1983, p. 140). However, as George L. Kline has acutely observed, Vico was ultimately 'closer to Hegel's "objective" idealism than to either the "subjective" idealism of Berkley or the "transcendental" idealism of Kant' (1983, p. 114). He did, after all, explain religious origins 'in terms of man's mythic projection of his feelings of insecurity' (Hutton 1983, p. 141).

It was this more interesting form of idealism that drew the admiration of Karl Marx. Both Vico and Marx viewed consciousness as a social product, 'a set of shared perceptions about the nature and structure of reality' and not simply a state of mind achieved by individuals (Fulco 1983, p. 129). They shared a desire to grasp the 'real world', and by that I mean 'a world quite independent of the observer's perception of it' (Megill 1983, p. 398). In this, they reflected the ideas of Vygotsky and sociocultural psychology rather than cognitive psychology. On a related issue, Vico started out as a Cartesian and gradually became an anti-Cartesian, rejecting reliance on the cogito, ergo sum. He came to believe that 'mere awareness of a result is insufficient for a claim of knowledge if we are not also cognizant of its actual origins' (Rockmore 1983, p. 182). This cognisance was for him an active and social knowing in contrast to Cartesian passivity and individual reasoning. According to Granatella, 'Vico emphasises exactly what Descartes rejects: history, eloquence, poetry, and the human faculties involved in them (memory, sensibility and imagination)' (2015, p. 192).

Contributions to postpsychology

Vico's emphasis on historical analysis is a timely reminder to psychologists. Today, it is fashionable in some quarters to belittle the achievements of the Enlightenment. In this rush to condemn, what is frequently underplayed is the sheer scale of the intellectual effort that had been galvanised. From the late seventeenth to the late eighteenth century, the Enlightenment mustered all of its resources to claim emphatically that 'human beings are endowed with a common nature, a set of mental attributes and powers which remain broadly constant from age to age and milieu to milieu' (Simon 1983, p. 206). Given the dominance of feudal and religious thinking at the time, the Enlightenment constituted a herculean paradigm-shift away from spiritual forces and towards human meaning-making.

What the Enlightenment lacked, however, was a critical self-reflexivity. It needed a non-celebratory history replete with ancestry, origin point and a narrative arc. This is where Vico enters the story. He provided a 'new science' that would 'study the past as a chain of events leading up to the Enlightenment' (Munz 1983, p. 2). He did this without fetishising the nascent concept of 'progress', thereby making his contributions all the more remarkable. In other words, his historicist standpoint relativised the universal features of human life, without collapsing into the kind of extreme relativism with which we are all too familiar courtesy of postmodernism.

Today, gradually the realisation is dawning on isolated individuals within and outside the field of psychology that we too are in dire need of a 'new science'. Not a 'meta-narrative' as caricatured by middle-class postmodernists, i.e. an all-consuming, all-embracing universal narrative for all time. Instead, what is required is a dialectical framework which encourages the removal of artificial boundaries between disciplines and phenomena. I think this is the underlying reason behind the resurgence of interest in Vico's work. A minority of thinkers are reaching the conclusion that both mainstream and critical forms of psychology are coming to an end, and that there is a need for something better. Of course, Vico wanted to synthesise all humanities, through understanding historical development and philology. Our task is somewhat more arduous. We have to synthesise the humanities, social *and* natural sciences in a more ambitious project, fit for more desperate times. Furthermore, we have to achieve all this by creating a politically conscious 'new science' from the viewpoint of the (proletarian) subject.

Another fruitful contribution that sometimes goes unnoticed is his focus on social conflict. He may not use the expression 'class struggle', but he is correctly credited with being one of its modern narrators. The central theme of *The New Science* is how a group of people (the early 'fathers') 'progressively surrender their almost total ownership of their dependents' (Pompa 1983, p. 70). Vico underlines the old axiom that 'the weak want laws; the powerful withhold them' (Barnouw 1983, p. 104). As people become aware of legal injustices (Marx would prefer to use the more precise term 'exploitation'), they fight for greater legal status and citizenship rights. As rights are secured, people become aware of their common humanity (ibid., p. 96).

Vico was not a revolutionary but he wished for the commonwealth to switch 'from an aristocratic to a popular constitution' (Barnouw 1983, p. 105), and for this change to be sanctified in law binding on both plebs and patricians. Otherwise, the gulf between the classes increases not only in terms of wealth but also estrangement (or social alienation) (Hutton 1983, p. 152). Like all non-revolutionary 'middling sorts', Vico was keen to soft-pedal the class struggle, and to establish a harmonious balance between aristocrats and plebeians.

Ricorsi

One of Vico's more useful conceptual inventions was *ricorsi*, which could be defined as cyclical revivals of 'ethical energy and enthusiasm that precede and announce new epochs' (Ball 1983, p. 82). We could very well be living through such a moment in the history of sciences. Vico placed ricorsi in a cyclical pattern of growth and genesis of civilisations. This is a concept that seemed very natural to pre-capitalist modes of production, which is why Vico's Islamic counterpart, Ibn Khaldun (1332–1406) came up with a similar model to explain rural-urban conflicts. According to Vico, throughout this civilising journey, 'man ceaselessly repeats the process of creativity and regeneration in his search for a form of redemption'

FIGURE 11.1 Giambattista Vico

(Hutton 1983, p. 145). We do not have to agree with the religious bent of either Vico or Ibn Khaldun's interpretations to see the usefulness of the concept itself. Sorel would use Vico's cyclical theory of decline and rebirth not only as 'an adequate explanation of the initial emergence of Christianity but also of its continued survival and intermittent rejuvenation' (Jennings 1983, p. 336).

Even if ricorsi has a mythical element to it (and it surely does), it is still a useful analytical mechanism, since myths are 'imaginative building blocks of the structure of perception' (Hutton 1983, p. 146). Vico's *New Science* includes a scientific study of myths, an attempt to translate 'the visual, poetic language of the fables into the abstract, conceptual language of philosophy' (Megill 1983, p. 399). It was through these clearly defined images and myths that Sorel hoped to inspire people and rejuvenate the class struggle (Jennings 1983, p. 341). Needless to say, an over-reliance on mythology obscures its flaws and allows an opportunity to reactionaries such as Stalin, Hitler and Trump to use the same approach for the purpose of political manipulation.

I would suggest that ricorsi (or 'cyclical' revival) is but one route of historical development (there are other patterns, such as the dialectical or 'spiral' route to development). Ricorsi is embedded in the economic 'base', as well as 'structural', and 'superstructural' levels of society. It is when these patterns align at all three levels that a 'regeneration' becomes likely. Take contemporary science. Both the social and technical divisions of mental labour have clearly become fetters on production, which is the reason we hear calls for inter-disciplinary collaboration from so many quarters, especially from within humanities and social sciences. Even the natural sciences are beginning to lag behind the enormous expectations to solve environmental problems, provide clean energy, and roboticise the workplace. The 'base' of science is clearly in trouble. The 'structures' that have traditionally shaped the ricorsi of scientific development are also in crisis, as attested by the constant wave of reorganisation in universities. Finally, at the superstructure level, a general belief is gathering pace that things cannot go on as before and reforming the beast is no longer sufficient for avoiding economic, environmental and military catastrophe. The three levels of ricorsi are synching up and that, I would suggest, represents the 'ethical energies and enthusiasm that precede and announce new epochs' (Ball 1983, p. 82). To call for a postpsychology, therefore, seems to me neither unrealistic nor a divergence. It may very well be an idea whose time has come.

Who was more sensible on 'common sense', Gramsci or Vico?

Critical psychology is deeply suspicious of 'common sense', and rightly so. Most of the time, common sense is merely the reactionary weight of dead tradition or introjected bourgeois ideas normalised through repetition and lack of a counter-argument. Billig studied commonsensical, everyday understandings of the British monarchy and showed its dilemmatic ideological character (Billig 1992). Henriques *et al.* showed how everyday common sense combined with scientific sense reinforce prejudice against black people (1984, pp. 60–89).

The influence of Gramsci looms large on these critiques of common sense. For Gramsci, common sense had no value and must be eliminated: 'Hegemony is but common sense "instrumentalised" so that a minority can, without constant resort to violence, dominate the majority by imposing upon it a common sense' (Jacobitti 1983, p. 370). Rulers prefer to rule through a mixture of coercion and consent. 'This hegemony', Jacobitti continues, 'is a subtle form of domination carried out in the educational system in the art and sciences … so that the definition of an "education", of "success" of "aspiration" is synonymous with the values of the ruling class' (ibid., pp. 370–371). That is why Gramsci placed so much emphasis on 'education' as a mechanism first to defy and then to overcome the rulers. The fundamental error he made was to indulge his own whimsy for elitism by making a false distinction between the fully conscious leaders (and teachers) and the unconscious masses (or learners).

Vico, it seems to me, employs a more expansive definition of common sense. At times he defines common sense as the accumulated wisdom of the past – a wisdom that creates all civil history and all nations (Jacobitti 1983, p. 368). At other times common sense is reduced to the ethical fibre of the nation. He sometimes sees common sense very much in terms of cognitive filters narrowing down human choice to a manageable common denominator. Finally, he seems to be saying that common sense is judgement without reflection: 'Common sense is judgment without reflection, shared by an entire class, an entire people, an entire nation, or the entire human race' (Vico, quoted in ibid.; see also Shotter 1996).

All this provides us with an interesting dilemma as psychologists: which definition is more sensible, Gramsci's or Vico's? I wonder.

Going beyond Vico's concept of imagination

> Working at the Jobcentre has to be a tense job – knowing that if you get fired, you still have to come in the next day.
>
> *Adam Rowe*

> Boredom is counter-revolutionary.
>
> *Situationist International*

In this section I want to address the intellectual paucity in vast swathes of social science writing, which I believe to be related to a lack of political imagination. Some readers may consider this attack unwarranted but I feel it is important to point out that a pedantic writing style is symptomatic of wider problems.

Michael Billig has suggested that there is much 'unnecessary publication' in academia these days (2013). Constant attempts to standardise writing and marking policy merely exacerbate the problem. He argues, 'working in the competitive conditions of academic capitalism, academics feel impelled to keep publishing, whether or not they have anything to say' (ibid.). What makes things worse is that 'academics use a noun-based technical language, which is less precise than ordinary language' (ibid., p. 7). This tedious and confusing style of writing is then made a precondition for success within academia. For example, 'sociologists will explore "reification", rather than people reifying' (ibid., p. 10). Terms such as 'capital', 'capitalism' and 'capitalist' are employed interchangeably. Marx was guilty of this, notwithstanding the heroic attempts by Humphrey McQueen to convince us that the 'unreadable' Marx is a myth created by the bourgeoisie (McQueen 2005). Marx was a genius which means that we are forced to cut the old goat some slack, but that does not mean forgiving him for some of his dreadful verbosity.

In an earlier article Billig has referred to a related issue. He argues that within psychology, especially social psychology, texts are often 'depopulated' and that we must endeavour to 'repopulate' them (1994, p. 307). Textual depopulation occurs through a number of rhetorical devices, 'for instance, "variable vagueness" in describing subjects, unmarked expressions for describing group differences, and the routine absence of individual data' (ibid.). The end result is always the same: real individuals are concealed and made abstract.

Thus, a litany of issues is hampering clear academic writing: the extreme division of labour, reification, capitalist competition, rivalry, the bureaucratization of language, etc. While I agree with everything Billig has argued above, I feel that the problems are more deep-rooted. Could it be that both mainstream and critical forms of psychology have little to tell us these days, because they are gradually coming to the end of their historical usefulness? And could this impoverishment of thought have something to do with the dearth of political imagination?

According to Vico, 'imagination is the cognitive faculty we need in order to construct our world as meaningful for ourselves' (Granatella 2015, p. 186). He argued that imagination is the key higher mental faculty

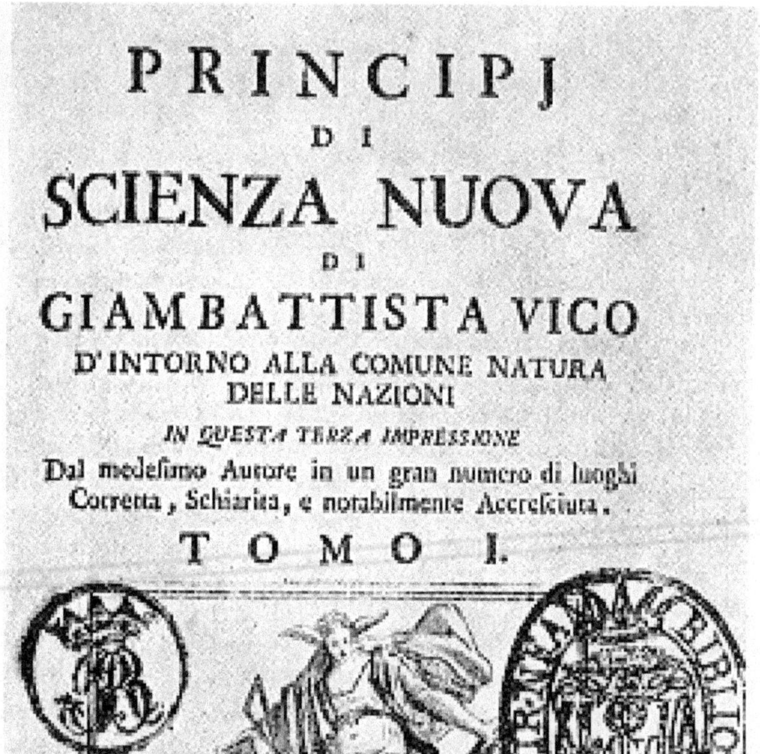

PRINCIPJ
DI
SCIENZA NUOVA
DI
GIAMBATTISTA VICO
D'INTORNO ALLA COMUNE NATURA
DELLE NAZIONI
IN QUESTA TERZA IMPRESSIONE
Dal medesimo Autore in un gran numero di luoghi
Corretta, Schiarita, e notabilmente Accresciuta.
TOMO I.

IN NAPOLI MDCCXLIV.
NELLA STAMPERIA MUZIANA
A spese di Gaetano, e Steffano Elia.
CON LICENZA DE' SUPERIORI.

FIGURE 11.2 Title page of *Principj di Scienza Nuova* (1744) we need in order to make life meaningful for ourselves. Imagination is the 'original manner of concept formation' and thanks to concept formation we are able to rethink human culture (ibid., pp. 186–187 and 190). In tune with many Romantic thinkers, Vico argued that imagination is stronger at the beginning when analytical thought is weak. He believed this to be true of both the first men (who created universal images through the discovery of similarities and differences in perceptual objects) and contemporary children (who are likewise incapable of complex analytical thought) (ibid., p. 190). Without imagination, one of the key ingredients of rationalist thought – abstraction – cannot be conceptualised. Imagination, therefore, is neither purely objective nor subjective, but is instead a gateway between the world and human experience (ibid., p. 194). Vico suggested that we start with language not because of any fidelity to linguistic determinism (as is the case with so many superficial discourse analysts today), but because we can *feel our way* into language and understand its operations. While Marx can *at times* be accused of neglecting language, culture and imagination, Vico's theory continues to shed light on the 'undiminished pull … of religious, national, and ethnic loyalties' that persist today (Kline 1983, p. 125). It is clear that imagination is the 'master key' to his work. How many contemporary social scientists can make a similar claim?

Even some of the established canons of the Renaissance have been accused of lacking imagination. In a recent controversy, Germaine Greer criticised Leonardo da Vinci for being derivative and sloppy (Brown 2019). The Mona Lisa is dismissed as 'The bloody Mona Lisa … this half-dead woman, this strange green-faced female … As for the famous smile, this is what I call the Leonardo smirk. You find it everywhere' (Greer, quoted in ibid.). Greer goes so far as to suggest that da Vinci 'seems to be an experimenter a bit short of imagination' (ibid.). Does Greer have a point? Was da Vinci 'short of imagination'?

It is certainly true that his status as a unique genius of the Renaissance who towered over all others has been exaggerated. As with the rest of us, da Vinci too was a product of his time. A large number of his drawings are imitative and that is only natural since imitation was (and remains) a time-honoured device for mastering craftwork. Once he had mastered his art, his imagination became somewhat freer but even then he produced plenty of derivative and lacklustre drawings.

To understand this paradox, we must go beyond Vico's rather elitist notion that 'imagination is the gift of a few; imitation the lot of the many' (Hutton 1983, p. 144). A better way of making sense of this distinction was later suggested by Luria who talked about two kinds of imagination: *mechanical* and *creative*. Mechanical imagination is far more common and easier to achieve since it involves taking hold of artistic, linguistic, physical and cultural resources already out there, and recombining them in novel ways. It could be argued that da Vinci's designs of tanks, irrigation systems and canals fall into this category. He watched what other designers, engineers and architects had already built and improved upon them through clever reassembly. I am no expert on Renaissance paintings or da Vinci but I would hazard a guess that many elements of the Mona Lisa also fall into this category since there exists a number of similar portraits from the era. However, when da Vinci was brilliantly synthesising science and art, producing designs of what centuries later would be called a helicopter, he was being *creatively* imaginative. Other theoreticians have postulated a similar distinction. Max Wertheimer's classification of thinking into 'reproductive' and 'productive' thinking seems to me very similar to Luria's. Reproductive thinking is associated with repetition, conditioning, habits or familiar intellectual territory. Productive thinking is the product of new ideas and breakthroughs. Productive thinking is insight-based reasoning.

The ratio of creative to mechanical imagination may be a crude indicator but I believe it is something worth bearing in mind when assessing artistic and scientific productions. Different environments, mediums and occupations are characterised by varying ratios. The advent of new technology has a bearing on this ratio. Neuropsychology, for example, is enjoying a renaissance precisely because new scanning techniques have unleashed a burst of imaginative energy. Granted, most of the theoretical connections being made between scans and psychological functioning are mechanical rather than creative, nevertheless they represent a dynamism that is lacking in many other parts of psychology.

The ratio is relevant not only in da Vinci and psychology but in what media critics sometimes derogatorily refer to as the 'low arts'. Two brief examples come to mind. A cursory comparison of the cartoon series *Family Guy* with *South Park* suggests that the former features more instances of mechanical imagination, while the latter achieves more moments of genuine creative imagination. Ironically, at a personal level I still find the more mechanical imagination of *Family Guy* more humorous! Here's another example. A comparison of the original series of *Star Trek* with all the derivatives that came afterwards indicates the same trend. The original series (with Kirk, Spock and McCoy) gave us moments of genuine technological creativity, far more advanced than the actual level of development available in the

1960s. Today science and technology have caught up with some of these ideas: big screen television; personal communicator (mobiles); universal translator; replicators (3D printers); medical scanners; tablet computers; phasers; tricorder; holodeck (virtual reality); hypospray. And from what I can gather even the more outlandish ideas are being worked on: teleportation (tiny particles rather than whole humans!); warp drive; and the famed tractor beam.

In general, most scientific and artistic work is being routinised. When we encounter imaginative work, it is usually of the mechanical variety. Very occasionally do we encounter creative imagination. In order to bring out the stark lack of imagination in academic writing we can briefly compare it with inventive texts from outside academia.

Let's take a book by the great Marxist turned situationist, turned anarchist, turned libertarian socialist, turned neo-primitivist, Fredy Perlman. It is called *Against His-story, Against Leviathan!* (1983). It is written in the form of a story and quite deliberately breaks all the academic rules of 'scientific' writing. No references, footnotes, citations or appendices. Just a story. The narrative takes place across 5,000 years of conflict between the Leviathanic civilisation that aims to subjugate and exploit, and the classless community that attempts to protect humanity. It is written from the viewpoint of civilisation's victims: we, the 'zeks' who are enslaved by Leviathan. The style used by the author makes the familiar Mesopotamian, Greek, Roman, Christian civilisations unfamiliar, and in so doing allows new interpretations to come to the surface. For instance, the book contains the best interpretation of Zoroastrianism I have personally come across. The book narrates how zeks reacted to civilisation in different ways: some ran away, others stood their ground, some infiltrated the Leviathan and attempted to weaken it from within, and some internalised its philosophy. Without boring the reader with the details, Perlman criticises Engels's anthropological writings and what he sees as Marx's stages theory of development.

I read the book years ago and as I browse through its pages to refresh my memory, I am acutely aware of its weaknesses, exaggerations and inconsistencies. And yet, I also remember vividly the thrilling excitement of the initial encounter. Perlman's book was (and for me remains) a breath-taking piece of political storytelling. What made it possible was Perlman's deep-seated knowledge of the class struggle and a determination to be imaginative.

The same qualities are present in the works of the Situationist International, Michael T. Taussig, Barbra Ehrenreich, Nancy Scheper-Hughes, James Bruner, Michael Bakhtin, John Shotter, Joel Kovel, George Orwell,

Kenneth and Mary Gergen, Bruce Lerro, Walter Benjamin and others (see Brockmeier 2009 for more examples). These authors comprehend the human condition better than most, not necessarily because they have amassed vast reservoirs of knowledge but because they know how to feel their way through a body of knowledge, make sense of it and utilise it imaginatively. The lack of political imagination is precisely what is hampering psychology today. Without it we will remain stuck inside 'our specialities' and unable to communicate between disciplines. Postpsychology is a concerted attempt to break out of these restrictions through an act of political imagination.

Final remarks on Vico

Words matter. When static nouns give way to verbs, the processes by which humans engage with the world become clearer. As neo-Vygotskians are fond of reminding us, there is a world of difference between the early translations of Vygotsky's *Thought and Language* (1962) and the more accurately translated *Thinking and Speech* (1987). Reasoning is human; rationalism an ideology with limitations. Empirical sensing makes us who we are; empiricism entraps us within a naive form of psychological thinking. To judge is inevitably human, judgementalism a dis-ease of our times. Vico teaches us to replace 'our rationalistic interest in abstract entities with an interest in origins and processes' (Shotter 2015, p. 231). As our culture evolves, so does our mind and 'nature'. We are, as Shotter puts it, 'still indeterminate' (ibid.). Some forms of psychology find this fluidity a problem, others thrive on it.

Recent work has shown how Vico inspired the 'work of many scholars in psychology, e.g. Wundt, Jung, Cattaneo, Bruner and Moscovici to mention just a few over different historical periods' (Tateo 2015, p. 45). In opposition to Descartes, Vico teaches that 'we cannot know our mind only by observing from "within" the system's logic', rather we must come to understand our mind only in relationship to its products (ibid., p. 52). Every product of human activity is worth being an object of science. This is one of the greatest contributions of Vico to critical psychology – that he expands the range of products that should be studied. In another challenge to Descartes, Vico teaches that verbal language and thinking originate from bodily language (see Chapter 15 in this volume on Antonin Artaud).

Ultimately, what matters to postpsychology where Vico is concerned is not a balance sheet of what he theorised correctly or incorrectly, but the fact that 'Vico seems to be an inspiring and stimulating thinking partner' (Zittoun 2015, p. 252).

12

JOSEPH DIETZGEN

(One of) our philosophers

> To be radical is to grasp things by the root. But for man the root is man himself.
>
> *Karl Marx,* Contribution to the Critique of Hegel's Philosophy of Right *(1843)*

An interesting life

Peter Joseph Dietzgen (1828–1888) was born in Blankenberg in the Rhine Province of Prussia and worked as a tanner and occasionally as a teacher and painter (E. Dietzgen [1894–1895] 1914). His skills as a tanner permitted him to earn his living not only in Prussia but also in Russia and the USA. He was largely self-educated and developed philosophical ideas that can be roughly described as 'phenomenological Marxism'.

Early in life, he befriended three other bushy-bearded Germans called Feuerbach, Marx and Engels. Following his first reading of Dietzgen's work in 1868, Marx forwarded a copy to Engels, remarking,

> My opinion is that J. Dietzgen would do better to condense all his ideas into two printer's sheets and have them published under his own name as a tanner. If he publishes them in the size he is proposing, he will

discredit himself with his lack of dialectical development and his way of going round in circles.

(Marx, quoted in Wikipedia, *'Joseph Dietzgen')*

However, by 1870 Marx had embraced Dietzgen as a friend, and later praised him and his theory of dialectical materialism in the second edition of the first volume of *Das Kapital.* And by 1872 they had become chummy enough for Marx to introduce Dietzgen to the Congress of the First International as 'our philosopher' (Buick 1975, p. 3).

Dietzgen travelled to the USA on three occasions. On one visit to the American South, he witnessed a racist lynching at first hand: 'one morning he found some of his friends strung up in front of their houses, because their sympathy for the North had become inconvenient to their neighbours' (E. Dietzgen [1894–1895] 1914). The American Civil War (1861–1865) eventually drove him back to the Rhine but he returned to set up a tannery (as well as a grocery store and a bakery) in the USA (ibid.). When in 1886 the state and the media framed the Haymarket anarchists, Dietzgen gave the defendants his whole-hearted support. These anarchists were falsely convicted of throwing a bomb at the police during the demonstration. He is buried in Chicago, alongside the murdered Haymarket anarchists.

FIGURE 12.1 Joseph Dietzgen

Ironically, this unorthodox revolutionary who was respected internationally in Germany, the USA and in the mining valleys of South Wales has, today, largely been relegated to historical footnotes. His outlook on life is reminiscent of another marginalised libertarian communist, Guy Alfred Aldred (1886–1963). Both explained the contours of class politics in simple language devoid of partisan affiliations and party politics. Both attempted to reconcile Marxism and anarchism. This is how Dietzgen put it, 'For my part, I lay little stress on the distinction, whether a man is an anarchist or a socialist, because it seems to me that too much weight is attributed to this difference' (*Wikipedia*, 'Joseph Dietzgen'). I hope I have managed to convey in this chapter the reasons why postpsychology should take on board his contributions to the social struggle.

Anton Pannekoek on Dietzgen

Dualistic thinking is not merely an epistemological and ontological error in judgement. It does not simply ooze out of a confused mind and then become fashionable. Dualism is tied up with the class nature of society. The material conditions for its existence simply did not exist prior to the advent of class society. But during ancient slavery, through to serfdom and feudalism, and right up to modern capitalism, the material preconditions for dualism became increasing available. Pannekoek (1902) writes, '[Dualism] is but the expression of the division of mankind into classes and of the uncomprehended nature of social production ever since it became a production of goods for exchange'.

Philosophy, which had itself displaced theology (or at least temporarily paralysed it by giving it a good kick in the groin), was now itself being replaced by what Pannekoek (1902) calls 'a science of human mind'. However, the unpalatable truth for social scientists is that while capitalism has encouraged the natural sciences to progress triumphantly over nature, it has transformed the social sciences into a neutered enterprise, fit only for monitoring and regulating the working class.

Every day genetic engineering, nanotechnology, computer science, physics, medicine and chemistry open our eyes to new configurations and possibilities. True, these potentials are quickly commodified and utilised against the working class, but at least there appears to be real dynamism within the natural sciences.

In the neighbouring field of social sciences, however, there is stagnation, repetition and only occasionally a flickering of originality. This decline is evident in both mainstream and critical strands within the social sciences and is the cause of great regret to me. Pannekoek, who observed the beginning of this demise, would be startled by what passes for scientific psychology today.

According to Pannekoek, bourgeois ideology finds its 'purest expression' in the philosophy of Kant, since a limited, but genuine, notion of freedom is at the epicentre of his system. Pannekoek explains how

> rising capitalism required freedom for the producers of commodities in order to expand its productive forces, it required freedom of competition and freedom of unlimited exploitation … For this reason, freedom became the slogan of the young bourgeoisie aspiring to political power, and Kant's doctrine of the free will, the basis of his ethics, was the echo of the approaching French Revolution. But freedom was not absolute; it was to be dependent on the moral law. It was not to be used in the quest for happiness, but in accord with the moral law, in the service of duty.
>
> *(1902)*

The long-term general interests of capitalism are often violated by individual members of the capitalist class who pursue unrealistically high profits at the expense of the proletariat. Thus, freedom is exposed by the behaviour of the ruling class as a limited, self-serving ideal. Kantian ethics reflects and rationalises this contradiction through its inbuilt dualism: 'Bourgeois ethics and freedom manifested themselves in the form of freedom of exploitation in the interest of the bourgeoisie, as slavery for the working class' (Pannekoek 1902).

'Kant had always separated mind and nature very sharply', but in his defence Pannekoek reminds us that this separation was meant to be a temporary measure for the purpose of investigation (1902). Many contemporary objectivists and post-positivists have conveniently forgotten this injunction and treat the separation as a permanent and natural state of affairs.

There is another aspect of Dietzgen's work with relevance to psychological research and that is ethics. Pannekoek writes that

> Dietzgen in this work indicates the principles of a new ethics. Starting with the understanding that the origin of the ideas of good and bad is found in the needs of man, and designating as really moral that which is generally useful, he logically discovers that the essence of modern morality rests in its class interests.
>
> *(1902)*

Unlike Kantian ethics with its unsubstantiated claims of universality, Dietzgen's ethical guidelines are temporary and contingent. Once class society is abolished, these ethics will also become redundant. I wonder if this type of argument cuts muster with psychology 'ethics committees'? Probably not.

What I admire most about Pannekoek is his clarity of expression. He explains clearly that 'middle-class materialism' in the nineteenth century was the inevitable expression of a nascent bourgeoisie fighting for its emancipation from feudalism and monarchy. However, this nineteenth-century 'middle-class materialism … was somewhat more than a mere repetition of 18th century ideas; the enormous progress of the science of nature in the 19th century was its basis and a source of vigour' (Pannekoek 1975, p. 34). When attacking 'bourgeois materialism', Marx aimed most of his onslaught against eighteenth-century materialists and generally viewed nineteenth-century materialism as 'a back-sliding into obsolete ideas' (ibid.). It took Dietzgen to update the revolutionary critique of bourgeois materialism. Or to put it differently as Herman Gorter might have done: 'Marx pointed out what the world does to the mind, Dietzgen pointed out what the mind does itself' (ibid., p. 35).

According to both Dietzgen and Pannekoek, the separation of mind and matter is not absolute. It is a temporary convenience. The implications are simple enough:

> The entire world, the spiritual as well as the visible and tangible world, is object to our thinking. Things spiritual do exist, they too are really existing, as thoughts; thus they too are materials for our brain activity of forming concepts.
>
> *(Pannekoek 1975, p. 36)*

The manoeuvre conducted by Marx-Dietzgen-Pannekoek first establishes a more expansive definition of 'materialism' and 'idealism' and then shows their inevitable co-mingling. One consequence of this for both psychological research and the class struggle is that thinking is not merely the reflection of matter. Thinking is more than the epiphenomenal superstructure of a determining base. The fact is that matter and ideas, biology and culture, and individual and collective are dialectically intertwined in such a way that ontological priority cannot be determined.

Adam Buick on Dietzgen

Engels is commonly credited with coining the phrase 'dialectical materialism' (the philosophical and biological counterpart to Marx's historical materialism). Scholars as far back as the 1900s believed that Dietzgen discovered dialectical materialism independently of Marx and Engels. The father of Engels-Leninism in Russia, Georgi Plekhanov, lambasted them in no uncertain terms (Plekhanov 1907). But the controversy refused to go away and decades later Adam Buick (1975) reignited the debate by stating that it was indeed Dietzgen who came up with the phrase first. It has even been suggested that credit should go to the English translator of Dietzgen's work who inadvertently created the impression that the phrase originated with Dietzgen.

All this may be fascinating, but it is also nit-picking stuff that frankly we do not have the time for. Instead, let us note with Buick that Dietzgen's most famous work, *The Nature of Human Brain Work* ([1869] 1984), 'presents an empiricist theory of knowledge derived from a rejection of Kantian dualism' (Buick 1975, p. 3). Dietzgen's conception of the universe is both 'materialist (since it posits the existence of a world of reality independent of men's perception of it) and dialectical (since it sees the world of reality as a changing, differentiated unity)' (ibid., p. 4). This is a form of dialectical materialism in opposition to what I insist on calling Engels-Leninism. Dietzgen's conception is superior to Engels-Leninism whether the latter is mediated by Kautsky (in Germany) or by Plekhanov (in Russia).

Dietzgen's dialectical view contrasts with a 'common sense' that sees the world as a collection of separate, fixed objects. In parallel, his view of matter is not confined to the tangible but to everything that occurs including ideas, thoughts, etc. Both mind and matter are abstractions we create in order to make sense of the stream of senses around us, and the rigid distinction between mind and matter does not exist in the world of phenomena (Buick 1975, p. 5). Lenin would obviously disagree with this position, but we need not concern ourselves too much with his notion of dialectical materialism which was poorly conceived and after his death became ossified as Diamat under Stalin.

Tony Burns on Dietzgen

Burns (2002) has provided a useful service by making connections between Dietzgenism and psychology. The key to understanding Dietzgen is his critical account of the 'mechanical' materialism of the eighteenth and nineteenth centuries and the competing Hegelian idealism prevalent in the nineteenth century.

Central to Dietzgen's critique was the rejection of a narrow definition of science and matter which Dietzgen associated 'with physicalism and a belief in universal causal determinism' (Burns 2002, p. 205). Mechanical materialism might have been good at debunking some of the more absurd claims of the monotheistic godhead; however, 'the old materialism takes anti-theological or anti-spiritual arguments so far that it will not countenance the existence of any mind at all – not even in the human mind' (ibid., p. 206). Extreme forms of behaviourism are guilty of this stance, seeing the mind as illusory, irrelevant or sometimes as mere epiphenomenon. Physiological psychology commits a similar error by focusing exclusively on the activity of the brain and the nervous system, whereas it is the human mind, Dietzgen insists, that ought to be the legitimate object of study (ibid., p. 207).

Accordingly, intra-, inter- and extra-psychological relations are both mental and material. Dietzgen even uses the oft-maligned Marxian 'base-structure-superstructure' metaphor to get around the problem of dualism. The body of an individual can be conceived as the material basis upon which the 'mental superstructures' of the individual are reared (ibid., p. 208). In contradistinction to behaviourism and physiological psychology, there is the equally damaging error, committed by some forms of social constructionism and discursive psychology, of ignoring the body entirely. Dietzgen rejects both the 'idealistic' and 'materialistic' forms of one-sidedness, in favour of a worldview which is 'dialectical materialism' in all but name (ibid., p. 210). This version of dialectical materialism is far more humanistic in its outlook and far less dogmatic than Engels's version, even if the differences were not clear to the two thinkers themselves. Retrospectivity allows us the luxury of differentiating between revolution and reaction. We can see demarcation lines when there was only difference of degrees before. Thus, today, we know that Sylvia Pankhurst was a qualitatively superior revolutionary compared to her mother (Emeline) and sister (Christabel); that all Pannekoek's criticisms of Lenin were justified; that Rosa Luxemburg was right to oppose Karl Kautsky as a counter-revolutionary; and that while both Debord and Lefebvre are worth reading, only the former was a genuine friend to the proletariat. Retrospectivity is a wonderfully useful indulgence.

Dietzgen on Dietzgen

Dietzgen quotes Lassalle approvingly about a phenomenon that was causing concern to radical thinkers in the nineteenth century: 'Thinking itself has become a special trade in these days of division of labor, and it has fallen into the worst hands, those of our newspaper writers' ([1869] 1984, p. 2). Luckily, both Dietzgen and Lassalle passed away before the arrogance of newspaper writers finally caught up with their ignorance!

But it would be an error to reduce Dietzgen's observations to the demise of one profession alone. What we are witnessing today is a systematic decline related to the way in which specialism has eroded the ability to think critically. Just look at political elites, bankers, judges, celebrities and academics. The deterioration in competence and integrity has been so rapid that it has taken even the anti-capitalists by surprise. This fundamental weakness was not always there. In the late nineteenth century and up to and including World War II both the social and technical divisions of labour ensured the success of capitalism's productivity. Every capitalist office or factory was attempting to parcel up an area of commodity production as a speciality. This meant expanding the social division of labour. In order to retain their edge, soon capitalists were forced to subject the fields under their control to further intense technical divisions of labour.

Knowledge building was subjected to similar dynamics. Initially, a massive cleavage ripped 'natural science' from 'social science'. Like an unethically conceived twin study of nature versus nurture, the first twin was given shelter, resources and all the love and care it needed for rapid development. The other twin was more or less left to its own devices, before a half-hearted attempt to send it off for adoption into an impoverished environment. Not unsurprisingly, the natural sciences grew and prospered while the social sciences developed a massive inferiority complex. Both camps were then immediately subdivided into new specialisms: biology, chemistry, medicine, mathematics, physics and later computing spearheaded the natural sciences, while history, politics, psychology, sociology and anthropology were left to make sense of the 'human condition' on their own. In order to control their own workers and products, these specialisms created ever increasing technical divisions of labour. Thus, psychology fractured into developmental, cognitive, behavioural, cultural, biological and social forms of psychology.

The thesis I have proposed throughout this book suggests that these social and technical divisions of mental labour were extremely successful in terms of capitalist productivity. Throughout the nineteenth century and most of the twentieth century, natural and even social science achieved impressive landmarks. All disciplines followed a similar evolutionary path, starting with self-identification, then establishing territoriality, and culminating in recognition from the outside world. Guilds were set up to ensure quality control and to police members' conduct according to strict guidelines. Prestige was continuously enhanced through publications, research, teaching and cosying up to the advertising and media industries, as well as funding bodies. Today's natural scientists are still playing the game. But it seems to me that many social scientists are on the verge of denouncing the game and the game-master.

Going beyond Dietzgen: dignity, love and hate

> Many men are loved by their enemies, and hated by their friends, and are the friends of their enemies, and the enemies of their friends.
>
> *Plato*

There have been a number of recent attempts to establish a rapprochement between psychology and phenomenology (cf. Langdridge 2008). However, in this section I prefer to focus on the earlier works of Sennett and Cobb ([1972] 1993), Carl Ratner (1993), and Robert Darnton (1988). These earlier texts can be roughly described as 'social phenomenology with a Marxist twist', and are characterised by a firmer grasp of sociology, history and politics. Moreover, their lineage can be traced back to the pioneering contributions of Dietzgen in a way that Langdridge's more petty bourgeois and individualistic philosophy cannot.

In *The Hidden Injuries of Class* ([1972] 1993) Richard Sennett and Jonathan Cobb remind us that class is not just a question of objective factors (such as occupation, income, socio-economic relations). Social class is also a subjective matter of feelings that are constantly being injured by capitalism. In their own words, 'class is a system for limiting freedom' which leads to loss of dignity (Sennett and Cobb [1972] 1993, p. 28). Accordingly, 'what needs to be understood is how the class structure in America is organized so that *the tools of freedom become sources of indignity*' (ibid., p. 31, emphasis in the original).

Take, for instance, the way in which our values have been restructured to make us feel guilty. No one could blame a worker for losing a job during the Great Depression (*c.* 1929–1939), whereas today the worker will be personally blamed for losing his or her job and letting down the family in the process (ibid., p. 33). What used to be attributed to external social forces is now routinely misattributed to internal individual characteristics.

One way of identifying alienation under capitalism is to carry out cross-cultural observations. The phenomenology of migrants to the USA reveals how in that country there is an absence of rituals for transcending class lines. Sennett and Cobb interview a Greek-American who says: 'Look, in Greece when I saw the janitor of my building at night, we would stop and chat for a moment; here a tenant is doing me a favour by being polite' ([1972] 1993, p. 47). This explains why a politician in jeans appearing at a traditionally working-class gathering, such as a baseball match, shaking hands with one hand while holding onto a conspicuously large hot dog with the other, generates mostly scorn and derision.

Once class lines are reinforced, dignity is dangled in front of the workers. Should they wish to partake of a dignified existence they must display the appropriate abilities as predefined by capitalism. This impulse to determine a person's ability has its roots in the Age of Enlightenment when feudal traditions of patronage and hereditary entitlement gradually gave way to a culture of abilities and expertise. Sennett and Cobb pick up on this dynamic in the 1970s when capitalism was renewing its campaign for more skilled workers:

> Perhaps the most sensitive barometer of the cultural change that is occurring in the lives of the adults with whom we spoke is their feeling that the interdependent relations of extended families are now a source of personal humiliation rather than of collective strength … The family limits their freedom to act in such a way that they lose dignity now by following the old rules of dependence.
>
> *([1972] 1993, p. 107)*

They even link this feeling of powerlessness at home or work to doing poorly on an IQ test. The combined cycle of indignities experienced at school, home and work then becomes self-fulfilling and leads to a lack of trust in one's abilities: 'I just wasn't smart enough to avoid hauling garbage' (ibid., p. 118).

Sometimes regaining one's dignity expresses itself in 'the paradoxical morality of personal sacrifice' (Sennett and Cobb [1972] 1993, p. 121). The sacrifice very quickly becomes everyday and routine, because there exist in capitalism ready-made structures for fostering it. Some of these structures are shaped by what Raymond Williams called 'residual cultural artifacts', leftovers from pre-capitalist modes of production. For example, the man goes out in the job market to hunt and the women stay at home to gather and build a home. These residual cultural artefacts usually wrap themselves around concepts such as 'honour' and 'duty'. Other structures are unique to capitalism and revolve around making a symbolic association between sacrifice for the sake of the nation, family and human progress. These sacrificial obligations become commodified under capitalism and transform the most human of relationships into contracts; for instance, loving as sacrificing becomes a burden which destroys respect within the family (ibid., p. 133).

We begin to see how nodal values such as honour and dignity are context-dependent. This explains Marx's 'contradictory' positions on dignity. Sometimes he was supportive:

> When we have weighed everything, and when our relations in life permit us to choose any given position, we may take that one which guarantees us the greatest dignity, which is based on ideas of whose truth we are completely convinced, which offers the largest field to work for mankind and approach the universal goal for which every position is only a means: perfection.
>
> *(Marx, quoted in Easton and Guddat 1997, p. 38)*

However, when the bourgeoisie uses 'dignity of labour' in order to conceal exploitation, it becomes in Marx's words an 'empty phrase' and a shibboleth for '[taking] refuge from history in morality' (Marx, quoted in Rosen 2012, p. 41). The phenomenology of dignity can only be understood when we have properly contextualised it.

This would be a good place to bring in Carl Ratner's sociohistorical psychology of 'romantic love'. Ratner claims that 'Phenomenology is valuable for illuminating individual intentionality; however, this intentionality bears a cultural character which is only brought to light under the direction of sociohistorical psychology' (1993, p. 503).

Ratner then goes on to demonstrate this synthesis in the case of 'romantic love', which he describes as

> a sensuous, passionate attraction which develops quickly, involves intimate sharing of personal qualities, and is a possessive-exclusive bond. This kind of personal relationship is fostered by an individualised social system which emphasises individual rights and a highly individualistic notion of the self.
>
> *(1993, p. 505)*

Historical studies have explained how the meaning of love is not fixed or permanent; rather, it is constantly shaped by changing socio-economic and cultural dynamics. Mary Ryan (1983 p. 42), for example, has shown how American women in colonial times had neither the time nor the inclination to indulge in romantic love. As she explains, 'A woman's love for her husband, and his in return, became a "duty", a "performance", not a rarefied emotion' (ibid., p. 47). However, by the turn of the nineteenth century romantic love was becoming introjected by middle-class women as 'both a cultural ideal and an individual expectation' (Ratner 1991, p. 80).

What gives romantic love its 'intense, irrational, almost magical quality' is its embeddedness in a developing capitalist system which is prestructured based on two contrasting domains of existence: the private and the public. Under nineteenth-century capitalism, the private realm is imbued with notions of 'honesty, commitment, support, concern and expression', while the public realm has to remain 'impersonal, calculating, unpredictable, competitive ... unstable, [and] alienated' (Ratner 1993, p. 505). As twenty-first-century capitalism and digital technology dissolve the division between private and public, there has been a corresponding decline in the frequency and intensity of romantic love; a decline that Valentine's Day promotionals and Hollywood romcoms can no longer disguise.

A different kind of love could until recently be experienced in most parts of a society such as that of Great Britain. We can describe it as 'familial love' or 'neighbourly love' or even 'class love'. The deliberate destruction of the industrial and manufacturing sector, as well as of small family-operated farms in the 1980s and 1990s by the governments of both Conservative and Labour parties has loosened those bonds and replaced it with apathy and insensitivity, sometimes even cruelty. Northern industrial towns seem to bear the full brunt of these forceful ruptures from 'industrial' to 'post-industrial' societies.

We now come to an example of blatant cruelty which those of you with a kinder disposition should eschew. I am referring to a study in cultural history by Robert Darnton commonly known as 'The Great Cat Massacre of the Rue Saint-Severin' (1988). It is, to my mind, the best illustration of conducting a phenomenological study of subjects long dead and buried. I can only provide a gist of it here. The events occurred in the printing shop of Jacques Vincent, rue Saint-Severin, Paris, during the late 1730s. One of the workers involved, Nicolas Contat, has left us a detailed description of the events. Contat tells us that the apprentice printers slept in a filthy, freezing room, dodged abuse from the master all day, and 'received nothing but slops to eat' (ibid., p. 79). Sometimes the cook sold the leftover food and gave the apprentices cat food. It had become fashionable for the bourgeois masters to keep cats which were very well looked after, while the workers had to deal with howling, wild alley cats all night long.

Eventually the daily regime of wage-less toil, starvation and indignities becomes so intense that the workers decide to massacre both the alley cats and the masters' house cats. A gruesome and detailed description of the massacre is then provided, which involved catching the cats, putting them on trial, and then bludgeoning or hanging them (ibid., pp. 80–81). It is noteworthy that similar massacres were carried out in other parts of France and even in Germany around the same time. Darnton then explains that elements of the 'trial' were similar to Bakhtin's notion of the carnivalesque with laughter, disorder and a symbolic assault on the masters. It may even have been a case of sympathetic magic. As Darnton puts it, 'to kill a cat was to bring misfortune upon its owner or its house' (ibid., p. 94). Darnton also explains that the apprentices were caught in a bind due to the intensification of social conflict. Mastership had become a hereditary privilege which meant opportunities for advancement were rare, and they also felt threatened from below because the masters tended increasingly to hire unqualified printers in order to save costs (ibid., pp. 83–84).

One does not have to agree with the actions of these workers to appreciate the power of social phenomenology in bringing out the salient factors in a complex social event. When carried out by a skilled researcher, social phenomenology can provide not only a subjective narrative from the standpoint of the people, but also an objective explanatory model.

Last words

According to Dietzgen,

> We shall not arrive at the new society without serious struggles. I even think that we shall not get along without disorderly uproar, without 'anarchy'. I believe in 'anarchy' as a stage in transition. Dyed in the wool anarchists pretend that anarchism is the final stage of society. To that extent they are madcaps, who think they are the most radical people. But we are the real radicals who work for the communist order. The final aim is socialist order, not anarchist disorder.
>
> *(Quoted in Gorman 1992)*

His attempt at reconciling anarchism and Marxism may employ jaded language and, if his youthful poetry is to be taken at face value, his perception of the proletariat may be tainted by romanticism. However, his general aim was as valid then as it is today. His writings, taken up by the Dutch Council communists in Europe and by the Industrial Workers of the World in the USA, became part of the long tradition of independent working-class self-education. Dietzgen encouraged us all to do away with the division of intellectual and mental labour, and it was only years later when the philosophical works of the 'young Marx' finally became available to the English-speaking readership that the commonalities with Dietzgen became incontrovertible. The Bolsheviks (both Lenin and the British Stalinised Bolsheviks of the 1930s such as Maurice Dobb, Raymond Postgate and Morgan Philips Price) rightly viewed the 'early Marx', Dietzgen and Pannekoek as a threat and opposed them, sometimes by hook, mostly by crook. Thus, middle-class 'materialism' swallowed up proletarian materialism, and behold the monstrosity known as Diamat was born! It is to Dietzgen's credit that his work can still be used today as a healthy alternative to Diamat.

13

ALFRED SOHN-RETHEL AND RABID CAPITALISM

I am so clever that sometimes I don't understand a single word of what I am saying.

Oscar Wilde

Alfred Sohn-Rethel's character flaws

When he was seventeen years old, Alfred Sohn-Rethel (1899–1990) asked for all three volumes of Marx's *Capital* as a Christmas present. Poor boy – I am guessing he did not have much of a sex life or a PlayStation! Life soon provided him with some excitement, however. His first experience of class struggle came during the Spartacist uprising in Berlin (1919). This general strike and armed workers' revolt took place in post-war Germany and led to the brief establishment of workers' councils. The social democratic government of Friedrich Ebert ordered *Freikorps* soldiers to attack the workers. Hundreds of rebels were killed. After the failure of the revolt, its leaders Karl Liebknecht (1871–1919) and Rosa Luxemburg (1871–1919) were executed. While at university, Sohn-Rethel associated with Walter Benjamin and Theodor Adorno. In 1932 he lived for a time on a housing estate in Berlin, which was built by artists and writers (*Wikipedia*, 'Künstlerkolonie Berlin'). Wilhelm Reich and Arthur Koestler were also residents at this colony around the same time, although it is impossible to know whether these two figures ever met Sohn-Rethel. With a political education such as this, it is hard to understand his future lapses of political judgement. I suggest we get the awkward character flaws out of the way so that we can settle down and enjoy the fruits of Alfred Sohn-Rethel's radical contributions to postpsychology without guilt or remorse.

Despite being an anti-capitalist, after fleeing the Nazis and migrating to England Sohn-Rethel 'wrote economic analyses for a circle close to Winston Churchill which were used against Neville Chamberlain's appeasement policy' (*Wikipedia*, 'Alfred Sohn-Rethel'). Whether this was an early example of the kind of fake research contemporaries associate with the infamous Blair-Campbell 'dodgy dossier' that justified the Iraq war I leave to historians obsessed with detective stories. We can only note that for someone so full of insight about 'intellectual labour' Sohn-Rethel bargained away his own rather cheaply.

The second source of shame is that he joined the 'Communist' Party of Great Britain (the 'C'PGB being in reality a Stalinist outfit and in no shape or form communist), and remained a member until 1972, despite his claim to being an 'independent' Marxist thinker (ibid.). The 'C'PGB repaid the compliment by steadfastly refusing to publish him (Black 2009).

Rediscovery

Sohn-Rethel was eventually rediscovered and brought to a wider public, not by his Stalinist chums, or the Frankfurt School who made use of him while keeping him at arm's length, but by the 1968 protest movements across Europe. More recently his work has attracted renewed interest through the writings of Postone, Virno, Zizek, Alberto Toscano and Anselm Japp. I swear I have seen old 'Marxian philosophers' becoming almost sexually aroused during conferences at the mere mention of Sohn-Rethel's work on 'real abstraction'. This is odd since, for me, his real value lies in his outstanding analysis of fascism and not in his 'neo-Kantian Marxist' critique of political economy. A chief problem with classical neo-Kantianism has been its proponents' determination to show that philosophy is independent of psychology – a position from which I have been at some pains to dissociate myself throughout this book. However, Sohn-Rethel's Kantian-laced Marxism is obviously more sophisticated, since Kant only looked into the nature of the human mind for an answer (Sohn-Rethel 1978, p. 17). I will attempt to briefly contextualise Sohn-Rethel's philosophical work in the hope that critical readers do not feel short-changed.

FIGURE 13.1 Alfred Sohn-Rethel

In *Intellectual and Manual Labour* (1978), Sohn-Rethel discusses commodity fetishism and the relationship between philosophy and money circulation. He argues that the 'real abstraction' of exchange is the true origin of abstract (mathematical) thinking. He makes a distinction between societies of production and societies of appropriation, and relates this to manual and intellectual labour. Before transcending the distinction between intellectual and manual labour, it is necessary to understand why it arose in the first place, and the remainder of Sohn-Rethel's book is an attempt to do precisely that. Towards the end of the book, there are very useful critiques of Taylorism and also empiricism.

More interestingly for psychologists, we can learn from Sohn-Rethel's discussion of 'necessary false consciousness'. He defined it in these terms:

> Necessary false consciousness, then, is not faulty consciousness. It is, on the contrary, logically correct, inherently incorrigible consciousness. It is called false, not against its own standards of truth, but as against social existence … necessary false consciousness is the consciousness needed by the ruling class to maintain their rule.
>
> *(1978, pp. 197–198)*

So, necessary false consciousness is not about people making errors in judgement, nor about having the correct critique of capitalism, nor being duped by ideology. It is about the falsehood that things cannot change – that the status quo is the only alternative. But significantly, it is a falsehood that is *necessary* for survival under capitalism.

Mead and Sohn-Rethel: kindred spirits

For both Sohn-Rethel and George Herbert Mead (1863–1931), the formation of the self and its relationship to mind and society was the crucial locus of investigation. Mead approached it from the perspective of social psychology (and in particular 'symbolic interactionism'), while Sohn-Rethel came to similar conclusions starting from a Marxist epistemology (and one interlaced with Kantian philosophy).

Mead starts his investigations from an 'intersubjective circuit' (Granberg 2019, p. 36) and by and large stays within this circuit. Everything that is good and limiting in Mead stems from this choice. Mead subverts the myth of a pure self that can 'be reached by way of introspection; it is always bound up with others' (ibid.). We can start the cycle shown in Figure 13.2 from the top where the self ventures outside itself and moves to the *object* (this is the object of a social act). Here the individual takes the view of a *generalised* other towards itself. The self allows meaning to become *universal* which then returns in the form of self-consciousness, thus completing the intersubjective circuit. In Mead's own words, 'it is only by taking the roles of others that we are able to come back to ourselves' (Mead, quoted in ibid., p. 37). Granberg shows how Mead's intersubjective account of exchange 'is modelled on barter, and relies on a supposed smooth passage from barter to monetary exchange' (ibid., p. 39), an interesting side-issue that we do not need to dwell on here.

For Sohn-Rethel, the capitalist situation is a variant of Mead's account in that self-regulation bypasses consciousness and becomes 'automatic' (Granberg 2019, p. 40). Mead's intersubjective circuit undergoes subtle changes and is suitably modified for our times. This is diagrammatically depicted in Figure 13.3.

For our purposes we need to remember that under capitalism, objects and others are reified (thingified, or in other words, conventions are disguised as things). Subsequently, individuals are denied the opportunity to recognise themselves as social, as selves who are interrelated to others (Granberg 2019, p. 41). Generalised commodity exchange creates an artificial separation between intellectual and manual labour, which exacerbates this process of reification. From capital's standpoint the separation was beneficial because it 'allowed for the rise of science and "scientific management", as forces directing and configuring the labour process' (ibid., p. 42).

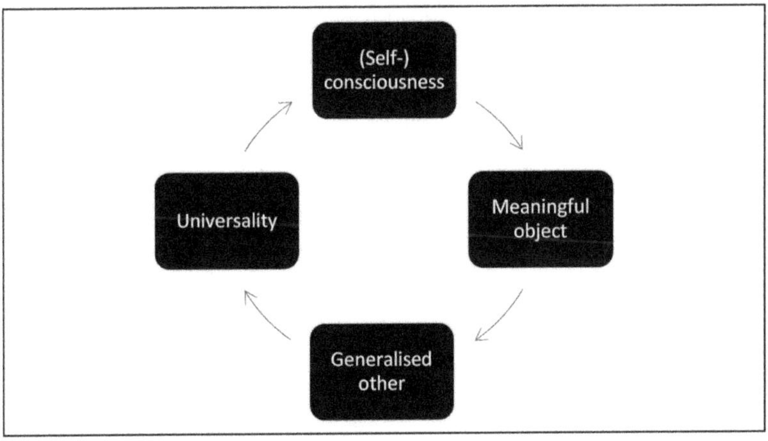

FIGURE 13.2 Mead's intersubjective circuit
Source: Granberg (2019, p. 41).

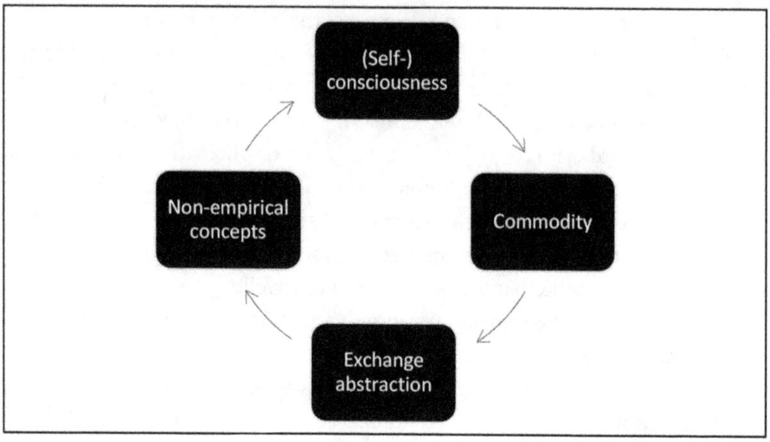

FIGURE 13.3 Sohn-Rethel's practical circuit
Source: Granberg (2019, p. 41).

To summarise, both Mead and Sohn-Rethel tried to understand a socialised self through 'conduct' (Mead) or 'practice' (Sohn-Rethel). Both postulated a circular movement which allows consciousness to displace onto the object of social activity and return to itself as self-consciousness. But Sohn-Rethel in a sense completes Mead by showing how commodity exchange interjects itself into this circular movement, resulting in an insular self (ibid., p. 44). Basically, he is demonstrating how changes in commodity exchange are altering our cognition, which in turn modify our experience of self. This 'objective phenomenology' is very similar to Dietzgen's approach, which is outlined in Chapter 12 in this volume.

On a similar trajectory to Granberg, George Tsogas has suggested that 'Sohn-Rethel's thought finds new relevance nowadays, under the prevalence of a cognitive capitalism' (2012, p. 377). This is a form of capitalism that emerges from the growth of knowledge-based production, which is only possible since manual and intellectual labour have already been sufficiently separated. Cognitive capitalism is part of the neo-liberal assault on workers as well as a response to the failures of post-Fordist reorganisation of the assembly line. The commodity form depicted in Figure 13.3 is fundamental to our ability to think in abstract terms. This abstractness which operates in exchange mechanism is 'the cognitive source of scientific knowledge' (Sohn-Rethel 1978, p. 34). Sohn-Rethel's approach reminds us that it is not just social phenomena such as consciousness that are time-bound and dialectic. Logic, mathematics and the natural sciences are also subjected to the same laws (see Chapter 18 in this volume on Luria). They do not represent 'universal' and 'objective' truths. The division between intellect and manual labour is a reflection of the class structure of society and will be eliminated under communism. Amen!

Sohn-Rethel's contribution to anti-fascism

Now I want you, dear reader, to completely forget the previous section. Get an analyst to hypnotise it out of you, if you have to! It was boring stuff anyway. This, by contrast, is the *good* stuff. Sohn-Rethel's critique of fascism is a timely intervention for our own times, and a crucial resource for comprehending the emergence of neo-fascism globally.

Sohn-Rethel worked as research assistant for a major interest group of German big business, the Mitteleuropäischer Wirtschaftstag. This position allowed him to study the highest echelons of German capitalism between 1931–1936, especially the finance branch. His work, naturally enough, combines theory, empirical data and personal impressions. It shows how the 'urbane and cultivated ruling-class of Germany, with great heart-searching and after all the options had closed, turned to the politics of fascism to preserve their place in the sun' (Edgar, Introduction to Sohn-Rethel 1987, p. 9).

His analysis explains how during 1930–1933 'the unity of monopoly capital was torn by rifts between the leading corporations such as the Steel Trust, I. G. Farben, Krupp, Siemens and the agricultural interest. Out of the bridging of these rifts was born the Hitler regime' (Sohn-Rethel 1987, p. 16). Even before the ascendency of Hitler, many of these enterprises were demanding 'dictatorial government directed against the organised working class' (ibid., p. 32). The state was failing to protect both the isolationist and expansionist branches of German capitalism. Soon a consensus was forged among the top businesses that the solution to most of these problems was simple: the lowering of working-class wages; the extension of the working day; increasing work tempo and intensity; the re-employment of millions of unemployed people on rates of pay no higher than their unemployment benefit; and the cutting of the social wage (ibid., p. 38). In short, the temporary suspension of *relative* surplus value extraction in the most advanced sectors of the economy, and a return to *absolute* surplus value extraction (Marx, [1867] 1990). By this method German capital could be saved. Ironically, this meant that, at least temporarily, the more 'developed' parts of the economy would be ruled by the less 'developed' parts. Since neither the liberals nor the social democrats could fulfil this plan, it was left to the most brutal faction of the ruling class, the fascists, to carry it out. In return for this favour, German capitalism allowed the fascist state relative autonomy in running the show. This meant that Hitler could now foreground his anti-Semitic and militaristic obsessions with impunity. It also meant that the gloves were off and the state would terroristically assault autonomous working-class organisations (ibid., pp. 69–70).

Today, many developing countries are going through a capitalist crisis similar to the one experienced by German in the 1930s. Their transition from *formal* capital domination (and the extraction of mostly absolute surplus value) to *real* domination (and the extraction of mostly relative surplus value) has stalled. In order to complete the transition and re-valorise their systems, they must resort to the brutal control of the working class. Countries like Iran, Turkey, the People's Republic of China and India fall into this category. More advanced parts of the world such as the USA, (Western) Europe and Canada are going through a more 'advanced' version of this where real capital domination over labour has failed. This is sometimes and inaccurately referred to as the crisis of post-Fordism. Here the solution involves a more intricate series of reorganisations involving the application of cybernetics, machinery, digitalisation, etc. But significantly this transition too must be inaugurated with force which explains the rise of right-wing authoritarian regimes interlaced with neo-populist and neo-fascist tendencies, such as the Trump regime.

Going beyond Sohn-Rethel

All rather jolly so far, you might say, but what exactly is the contribution of Sohn-Rethel to postpsychology? Well, I think, his critique of the political economy of rabid capitalism can help us to think through the complicated and at times contradictory lexicons of 'self', 'subjectivity' and 'identity'. He can also aid our understanding of changing social and technical divisions of labour and their impact on individuals. Finally, by utilising his work on fascism, we can understand the authoritarian turn in twenty-first-century capitalism and the rise of neo-fascism. All these have tremendous implications for who we are. Below I attempt to explain all this through a set of diagrams.

Under modernist psychology life had a simple machinic charm to it. We were in possession of these entities called 'personalities' that we wore like masks, and eventually personalities became embedded in our psyche. We did not have many masks back then; most individuals possessed two masks, one for private and one for public. Some thought that personality was innate; others credited the environment or habit. But both camps assumed personality to be more or less permanent once it is forged.

Nowadays, under equally simple-minded postmodern imperatives, most social scientists have ditched the concept of 'personality'. Instead, a confusing and at times interchangeable array of terms like 'self', 'subjectivity' and 'identity' have come to stand for what was once singular. Some postmodernists may deny the existence of the 'self' altogether, while others focus on its fluidity. And yet our everyday interactions still rely implicitly on taken-for-granted self-like attributes. How can we go beyond both the modernist and postmodernist paradigms of the individual?

I start with what I hope is a fairly non-controversial distinction between two contrasting concepts of the self: the *divided bourgeois self* and the *social dialogic self*. The 'divided bourgeois self' emerged with industrialisation and urbanisation around the seventeenth century, first in Great Britain and then elsewhere. It is, therefore, both a product of early capitalist competition and an imagined spectre created by thinkers such as Locke, Hobbes and Descartes. The divided bourgeois self posited a series of demarcation lines within the individual, as well as between the individual and society. Freud, for instance, divided the self into the ego, id and superego. This denoted an imaginary rational personality (ego) balanced against subterranean urges (id) and shiny moral armour (superego). From a social perspective this fiction amounted to a precarious middle-class wish to guarantee its own survival, squashed as it is between aggressive working-class desire for emancipation and upper-class resistance to change.[1]

The 'social dialogic self' was also present at the birth pangs of capitalism, but precariously so. It made fleeting appearances only in moments of upheaval and chaos. As soon as the rupture was sealed and the workers' revolt neutralised, the social dialogic self would vacate the seat to its bourgeois counterpart and hibernate until the next crisis. We have already looked at some of the earliest theoreticians of this social dialogic self: the likes of Vico, the third Earl of Shaftesbury and Dietzgen. They all conceived ideas about the social dialogic self that would only be given theoretical coherence many years later by the likes of Vygotsky and Bakhtin.

Figure 13.4 is a schematic representation of this conflict. I have employed a rough historical periodisation based on Marx's distinction between the formal phase of capital domination over labour (*c.* seventeenth century–1850) and the real phase of domination (*c.* 1850–present day) (Marx [1867] 1990, pp. 943–1084). The divided bourgeois self was envisaged, constructed and reinforced during the formal phase of domination, while the social dialogic self has been gaining ground and recognition during the real phase.

I concede that the process has been far more contested than the simplified representation depicted in Figure 13.4. The critical reader could justifiably object that the scheme is too crude to account for reverses, tangential trajectories and local contingencies. It may even underestimate the heterogeneity of the bourgeois self since some scholars argue that there is considerable divergence between the European conception of individuality and its North American counterpart (Sennett and Cobb 1993, p. 56). Nevertheless, I consider Figure 13.4 to be a useful starting point for a historical reconstruction of the notion of selfhood.

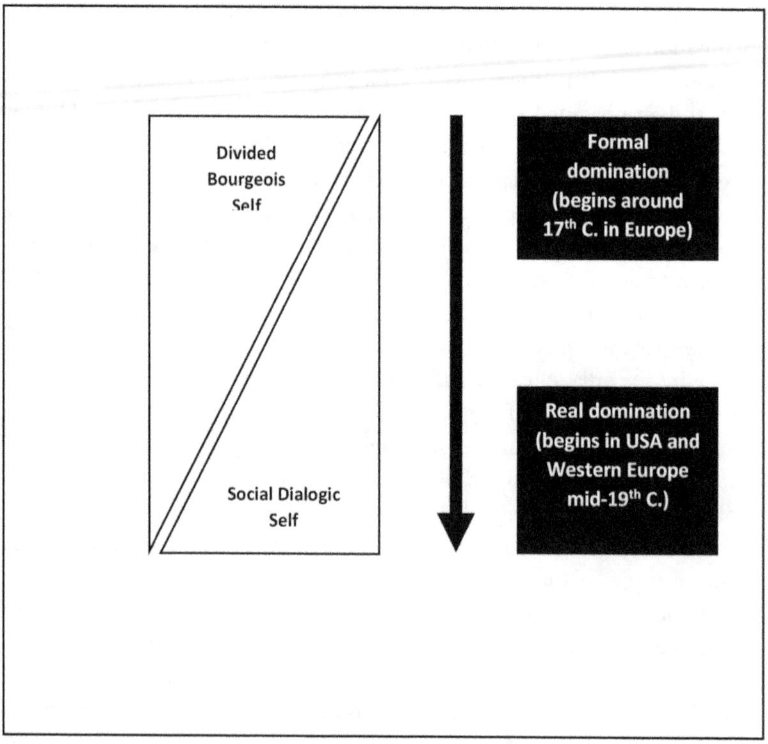

FIGURE 13.4 A simplified depiction of the historical development of two forms of selfhood.

Concomitant with the emergence of the self, capitalism was also entrenching the duality between public and private spheres of activity inherited from earlier modes of production. Thus, the bourgeois self was divided from the outset. I argued earlier that the self is partly real and partly fiction. The same is true of the public and private divide. It predates capitalism but was solidified with the generalisation of wage slavery, urbanisation, normative tendencies within capitalism and the division of labour based on gender. Male wage earners were conditioned into accepting the discipline of the factory, while the house was turned into an unacknowledged prison-factory for the female whose labour was refused value recognition (Fortunati 1995).

Sohn-Rethel talked about this in terms of the division between manual and intellectual labour. Sennett and Cobb (1993, p. 194) have articulated this phenomenon succinctly: '[The male worker] alienates the active, performing self, seeking recognition from others as a distinctive individual, from the passive self that just wants to be, to enjoy family and friends, to love them'. Sennett and Cobb go on to explain that this process of division is not always imposed externally. The individual may also be complicit in this process as a form of avoiding pain: 'Dividing the self defends against the pain a person would otherwise feel, if he had to submit the whole of himself to a society which makes his position a vulnerable and anxiety-laden one' (ibid., p. 208).

I do not think it would be too contrived to go a step further and suggest that the public performing self is what most social scientists usually refer to as 'identity' while the private self is most commonly referred to as 'subjectivity'. Since an element of the private-public divide is fictive and since both identity and subjectivity refuse to be restrained in their allotted compartments the fit cannot be said to be an exact one, but it is, nonetheless, a useful demarcation. Now we are in a position to add details to the diagram above (Figure 13.4) by showing what goes on within the bourgeois self.

Figure 13.5 depicts the divisions within the bourgeois self. The public sphere refers to a spatial arena where an idealised (and by and large fictive), rational dialogue between equals takes place over matters of mutual concern. These public spaces could be bars, coffee shops, salons, newspapers, the Internet or almost any other public forum not financially dependent on the church or the state. The public sphere requires time and a common vocabulary (Habermas, 1989). More pertinently to our discussion, the public sphere is where people perform a theatre of everyday life through adopting various identities.

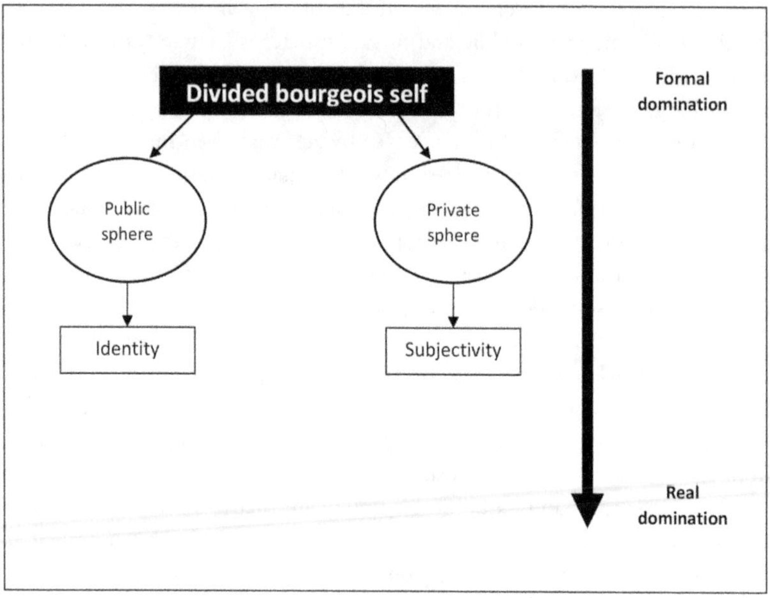

FIGURE 13.5 The 'fictive' division within

By contrast the private sphere is usually defined as patriarchal family, relationships and home. Autonomy within the private domain is a fictive autonomy concealing its economic and ideological origins. The most useful function of the myth of privacy was the denial of the housewife's wealth producing activities (Fortunati 1995). This ensures that a huge chunk of the working class never receives the wages to which it is entitled to. We can now examine more closely the formation of 'identity' and 'subjectivity'.

The public domain excels in providing opportunities for role play and identity formation. Some consider identity formation to be not only inevitable but useful. Erikson (1980) for instance talked about three interrelated forms of identity: the ego identity (a relatively stable and continuous form of identity); personal identity (what distinguishes one person from the rest); and social identity (a collection of social roles that a person might perform through his or her lifespan). His approach sees identity formation as intrinsically linked to development. From a more radical perspective, the work of social identity theoreticians has endeavoured to understand discrimination and conflict based on group identity perceptions (Tajfel 1982). A more nuanced version of this theory, known as the Elaborated Social Identity Model (Drury and Reicher 1999), uses social identity formation to understand the dynamics of crowd psychology, including riots. If Erikson (1980), Tajfel (1982) and Drury and Reicher (1999) represent a positive recognition of identity within the public realm, we also have the works of Holloway (2002), McLaughlin (2003) and Foucault ([1978] 1990) who resist the use of identity as a category.

It may be more useful to think of identity in terms of an entity with both positive and negative components. This aligns my position with a neo-Vygotskian perspective as put forward by Penuel and Wertsch (1995). They seek to 'examine the cultural and historical resources for identity formation as empowering and constraining tools for identity formation' (ibid., p. 83). They do so by examining 'identity as a self-chosen description of the person [taking] place within action' (ibid., p. 84). By looking at action, Vygotskians provide us with a coherent account of identity formation and not identity as a static, inflexible structure of self. This action has a rhetorical element of persuasion attached to it (Billig 1996) which is why studying radical politics, with its rhetorical mechanisms of meaning-making and negotiated consensus between performer and audience, is a fitting approach to the problem of identity formation. At its best identity formation is not 'just a matter of belonging to a particular group, that is reaching consent with others. It is also a matter of being recognised as a unique member of one's community' (Stam 2006, p. 112).

We can now turn our attention to the other key term in Figure 13.5, namely 'subjectivity'. In the early 1980s subjectivity was introduced to the social sciences as an alternative to individuality in a number of key texts including *Changing the Subject* (Henriques *et al.* 1984). There they describe it as follows: 'We use subjectivity to refer to individuality and self-awareness – the conditions of being subject – but understand in this usage that subjects are dynamic and multiple, always positioned in relation to discourses and practices and produced by these' (ibid., p. 3).

Following Nikolas Rose (1985), I feel it is reasonable to associate this subjectivity with the private realm even though the discourses shaping it may emanate from either the private or public spheres. He argues that:

> [O]ur intimate lives, our feelings, desires and aspirations seem quintessentially personal … There is, no doubt, much comfort to be

> afforded by such a belief. But it is profoundly misleading. Our personalities, subjectivities, and 'relationships' are not private matters, if this implies that they are not the objects of power. On the contrary, they are intensely governed.
>
> *(Ibid., p. 1)*

Subjectivity, therefore, is closer to the experience of being subjected, whether by an all-conquering state or through the power/knowledge networks that Foucault discussed (see Chapter 8 in this volume). However, subjectivity can also become an agentic force promoting social transformation. The situationists employed this reading to excellent effect. Autonomists have continued this work by demonstrating both old and new forms of social selves that are not merely subjected to domination but instead act to undermine capitalism.

I am now in a position to offer a more nuanced model of self-development, from the divided bourgeois self at the beginning of the formal phase of capital domination to the dialogic social self, appearing towards the end of the real phase of domination. Figure 13.6 shows how the divided bourgeois self gradually gives way to the dialogic and social as it reaches contemporary times. The public sphere has now invaded the private realm in line with the erosion of privacy in everyday life. We can now see clearly that both identity and subjectivity possess positive as well as negative attributes when looked at from the perspective of emancipation from capitalism.

Figure 13.6 shows how the self undergoes radical change as capitalism's formal phase of domination over labour in the seventeenth century gradually gives way to a more complex real phase of domination. The 'divided bourgeois self', initially predominant, is now reluctantly giving way to a 'dialogic social self'. It needs to be emphasised that this is a contested process, with the bourgeois self resisting its decline tooth and nail. The public sphere (which is expanding disproportionately partly because of new technology) is still moulding our identities, while the diminished private sphere is still relevant in shaping our subjectivities. It is for the social movement to ascertain which elements of identity and subjectivity are positive (and therefore worth preserving), and which elements are in need of supersession.

Figure 13.6 shows something else. The final strategy for rescuing the bourgeois self is the creation of false attempts by capital to overcome its inner contradictions. I have designated these as 'inter-identitarian' and 'inter-subjective' relations. Inter-identitarianism perpetuates the myth of the 'autonomous self' and uses various fictional identities to divided the working class: the 'white supremacy' identity movement in the USA and parts of

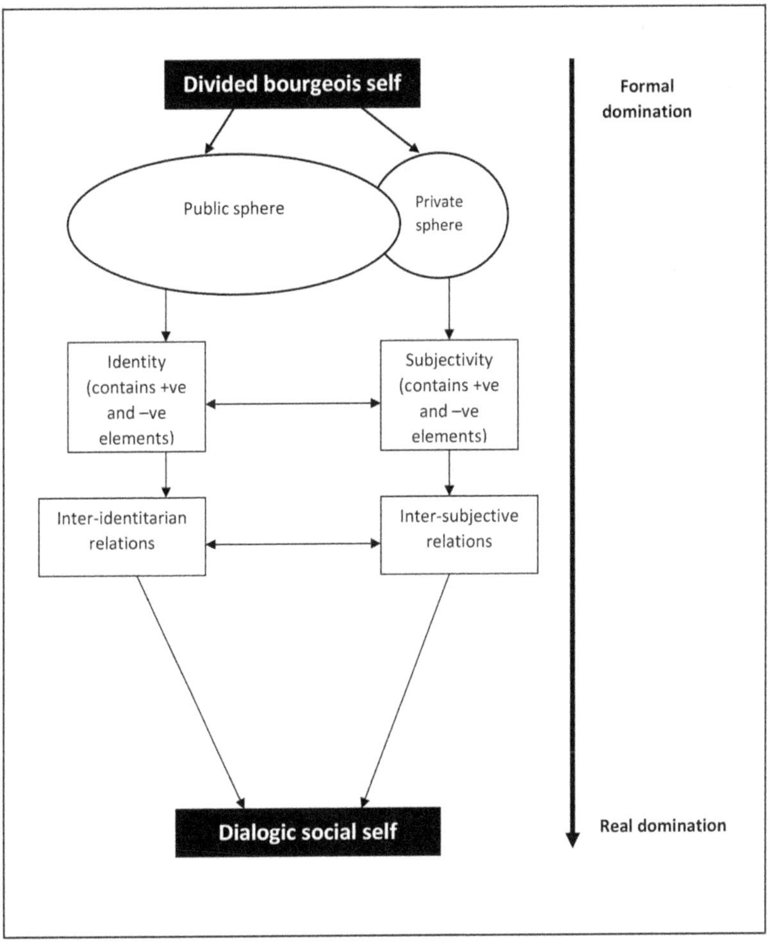

FIGURE 13.6 A more elaborated depiction of self-development from the viewpoint of social emancipation

Europe, and its Islamic counterpoint in the east are clear examples of this counter-revolutionary tendency. Inter-subjectivism attempts to govern our intimate lives, our feelings, desires, frustrations and fears: examples include the new assault on abortion rights, and the intensification of anxiety and fear-mongering by the media.

Inter-identitarianism and inter-subjectivism represent the last stage in capital's attempt to salvage the divided bourgeois self. Once they fail (as I think they must), the movement towards dialogic social selves will gather pace.

Final remarks on Sohn-Rethel

I hope I have managed to demonstrate through all these lovely diagrams that Alfred Sohn-Rethel's work is inspiring. He has helped me to think through the development of self more profoundly than perhaps any other thinker, with the exception of Vygotsky. OK, so his politics were a bit dodgy, and I wish that he had managed to break completely with Bolshevism and become a genuine communist. Well, nobody's perfect!

Note

1 I am mindful that a social interpretation is only one of many options. The compartmentalisation of the mind into id, ego and superego is a structural model of Freud that was preceded by the dynamic model, the economic/hydraulic model and the topographic model (whereby the main distinction is between consciousness and unconscious) (Parker 1997, p. 15). There is also mileage in interpreting these aspects of the mind as a Catholic Trinity (ibid., p 14). However, all these interpretations tend to obscure the specifically class nature of Freud's work.

14

ERICH FROMM AND POSTPSYCHOLOGY

> A man was walking in the street one day when he was brutally beaten and robbed. As he lay unconscious and bleeding, a psychologist, who happened to be passing by, rushed up to him and exclaimed, 'My God! Whoever did this really needs help!'
>
> *An old joke*

The foolhardy analyst

Most contemporary psychologists find it difficult to move out of their comfort zone and engage with those areas of life 'outside their expertise'. Instead, they choose to become specialists in order to enjoy the prestige and safety that the position confers. In many ways, this is the chief defect of non-dialectical times, when the link between specific and general has been disrupted: too many specialists and not enough dialecticians!

Erich Fromm (1900–1980) bucks the trend because he was courageous enough to analyse any topic he deemed worthy of humanity's attention. Occasionally, this strategy resulted in over-reaching himself or falling down the rabbit hole, but he would eventually regain his bearings and continue producing insightful material. Fromm was unceasingly 'foolhardy', and I believe this is the main reason I respect him so much.

Early theorist of 'eco-socialism', 'emotional labour' and 'manufacturing consent'

Unlike Freud who did not leave behind that many video-recordings, the Internet is awash with clips of Fromm expounding his ideas through lectures and interviews. In an early 1958 interview with Mike Wallace, Fromm discusses the dialectics of production and consumption in terms of our relationship to 'nature':

> In our enthusiasm to dominate nature and to produce more material goods we have transformed means into ends. We wanted to produce more in the nineteenth and twentieth centuries in order to give [human beings] the possibility of a more dignified life, but actually what has happened is that production and consumption have ceased to be means and have become ends. And we are production crazy and consumption crazy.
>
> *(Fromm 1958, 3 mins)*

The use of 'dignity' in the above quotation is key. Fromm understands how the promise of dignity played a significant role in encouraging many workers to accede to US capitalism's programme during the nineteenth and twentieth centuries. Poverty, unemployment, homelessness, forced migration from country to the city, and the discipline of the factory are all harbingers of indignity. The tremendous increase in productivity that finally came about from the 1940s onwards restored some dignity to some workers. However, attacks on the working class is relentless, whether capitalism is expanding or in recession. Fromm was one of the first to emphasise how assaults on workers and nature go hand in hand, and how they can both produce indignities.

In the same interview Fromm switches his attention from eco-socialism to what nowadays is referred to as 'emotional labour':

> We want to exchange our own personality package for something. Now this is not so true for the manual worker, [he] does not have to sell his personality, he does not have to sell his smile. But what you might call the symbol-pushers, that is to say all the people who deal with figures, with paper and with men, [those] who manipulate men and science and words … [all those] have not only to sell their service but in the bargain their personality.
>
> *(1958, 6 mins)*

This brilliant observation completes the earlier writings of Sohn-Rethel on intellectual and manual labour (see Chapter 13 in this volume) and foreshadows Arlie Hochschild's seminal 1983 book, *The Managed Heart: Commercialization of Human Feeling*. Hochschild argues in this book that, as economies move from manufacturing and industrialisation to providing services, we are forced to manage our feelings and expressions in order to fulfil the emotional requirements of the job.

Fromm is then asked about the process of political decision-making in the USA. Despite his abiding and genuine respect for American society, his judgement is rather severe:

> [T]he average American … is really concerned only with private affairs – that is to say his health, his money and family affairs … he is not concerned with his society, [although] he talks about it … he has separated his private life from his existence as a member of this society and leaves that to the [government] specialist to take care of.
>
> *(1958, 7 mins)*

He goes on to explain how American citizens have delegated political decision-making to specialists and how democracy is no longer a contract forged by the people themselves but with 'the help of Madison Avenue' it has become a manipulated contract (ibid., 19 mins).

So, there we have it: Erich Fromm, a Marxist psychoanalyst who laid the first foundations of eco-socialism years before Joel Kovel; who theorised emotional labour before Arlie Hochschild; and who critiqued the role of the media and advertising in manufacturing consent before Noam Chomsky. Smart cookie, that Erich!

Fromm on nationalism and western society

> Modern academic and experimental psychology is to a large extent a science dealing with alienated man, studied by alienated investigators with alienated and alienating methods.
>
> *(Fromm 1973, p. 69)*

Smart he might have been but, to my knowledge, no one has ever accused Fromm of being an exhilarating speaker. Nevertheless, his rather ponderous lecturing style should not deter us from a serious engagement with his ideas.

In 1962 Fromm gave a talk entitled 'The Psychology of Nationalism', which I think bears close scrutiny.

He starts by proposing a rather conventional definition of the nation-state in terms of a common language; a distinct economic framework; and political sovereignty (Fromm 1962, 4 mins). He concedes that there is a great deal of positive value in nationalism, if it is seen as 'a feeling of love, or interest or concern for one's nation' (ibid., 6 mins). However, Fromm prefers to talk about negative aspects of the psychology of nationalism, i.e. 'nationalism as something for which jingoism would be an extreme expression' (ibid., 7 mins). This distinction between positive and negative forms of nationalism echoes Lenin's earlier classification between 'oppressed nationalism' and 'oppressor nationalism' (Lenin 1916).

Fromm then steps back into psychology and explains how for the narcissist individual 'there is only one thing that is real, and that is his subjective experience' (1962, 11 mins). Others are seen but for the narcissist 'they have no weight' (ibid.). In parallel to the distinction made between oppressor and oppressed nationalism, Fromm distinguishes between 'malignant' and 'benign' forms of narcissism (ibid., 25 mins). The benign narcissist retains links to the real world through what he produces (e.g. an artist, a scientist, a Kardashian, etc.), while a malignant narcissist celebrates himself despite not having made any real achievements (e.g. someone who has inherited vast wealth without endeavour). Furthermore, malignant narcissism usually includes comorbid features such as paranoia, anti-social behaviour, aggression and sadism (ibid. 1964, p. 77).

To take a convenient contemporary example, someone like Donald Trump oscillates between benign and malignant forms of narcissism. He has enjoyed some real achievements including becoming the president of the USA and many achievements have been handed to him on a silver platter, for which he shamelessly takes credit. His benign narcissism has its roots in real achievements while his malignant narcissism is shaped by imaginary or fictive successes. Crucially, in those moments when his paranoia and sadism get the better of him, his narcissism takes a malignant turn, and his support-base then takes this malignant discourse and makes a 'conspiracy theory' out of it. The belief that the 'deep state' is out to get him and that 'fake news' constantly distort his position are examples of paranoid thinking with just enough elements of truth to make them believable to the shallow-minded. The reason paranoid thinking is so oblivious to the therapist's arguments is that 'paranoia is the only form of insanity that does not conflict with the laws of logic' (Fromm 1962, 16 mins).

In other words, paranoia has a logic of its own, it may be restrictively based on naive forms of empiricism and positivism but it is, nonetheless, based on its own internal line of logic.

As I stated in Chapter 9 on Billig, what is far more dangerous than Trump is Trumpism, a movement and ideology that will continue to damage the working class long after Trump has gone. I like to think that Fromm would have concurred since the rest of his talk is given to examining how individual narcissism transforms into social (or group) narcissism. 'Today you might say', expounds Fromm, '[that] the main objects of group narcissism are the nation, race and political creed. In the seventeenth century the main object of narcissism was religion' (1962, 29 mins). Since Fromm is concerned here solely with Christianity, he might have some justification in claiming that open hostilities between Christian sects have declined. However, group narcissism between Shia and Sunni sects within Islam and between Islam, Christianity and an increasingly intolerant Buddhism suggest that religious narcissism is far from being a spent force.

FIGURE 14.1 Erich Fromm

Fromm then goes on to make a controversial statement about the poorest sectors of society: 'What you find in fact is that the groups that are the poorest ones, economically and culturally, in any country are the ones showing the … most intense group narcissism' (1962, 30 mins). He is referring here to a relative and subjective conception of poverty, because moments later he clarifies his position by saying that in Germany the group that supported Hitler 'was neither the middle class nor the working class but was the old, dying and decaying *lower* middle class' who had been destroyed partly as a consequence of economic changes, and partly as a result of losing the values of the empire (ibid., 31 mins, emphasis added).

In a passage with remarkable contemporary resonance he says, 'narcissism is the one great compensation for the cultural and economic poverty of a certain group … "I am great because I belong to the most wonderful group!" whether that is called Whites or Americans or Aryans' (1962, 32 mins). The parallels with the slogan 'Make America Great Again' are too obvious to need underscoring.

From a therapeutic perspective it is exceptionally difficult to dislodge individual and group narcissism once it has embedded itself. It is common for the narcissist to react to criticism with either extreme hostility and rage or through depression. The reaction depends largely on one's power index. If a disempowered worker cannot afford to be hostile to the boss, the rage turns inwards and becomes depression (Fromm 1962, 34 mins). As far as fighting narcissism is concerned Fromm considers only two mechanisms for counteracting it: the first is what he calls a 'true and authentic religious attitude' and the second is 'a critical science in the modern sense', and not what passes as science in the educational system (ibid., 37 mins). The discerning reader will notice that once again Fromm is ignoring the potential of a working-class movement to overcome problems of individual and group narcissism. This, I would contend, is due to Fromm's 'Marxism' having more in common with a top-down social democratic set of precepts and not a dynamic social movement from below.

Fromm on internationalism and eastern society

There is a saying which might be germane to Erich Fromm's life journey: 'A revolutionary is someone who does not feel at home anywhere but wants to feel at home everywhere'. Fromm might have been afflicted with the same dilemma. He certainly travelled a great deal. Born in Frankfurt, Germany, he moved continuously within Europe but in 1934 was forced by the Nazis to emigrate to the USA. In 1950 he took up a post at the National Autonomous University of Mexico. The last decades of his life saw him criss-cross the USA and Europe until he finally settled in Switzerland, where he died of a fourth heart attack in 1980. He was cremated in Bellinzona, Switzerland. Add to this his lifelong interest in Judeo-Christianity, Buddhism and Marxism and it becomes clear how Fromm was by dint of disposition and intellect an 'internationalist' at heart.

In Chapter 3 in this volume, I took the opportunity to puncture one of the most damaging myths about communism by showing how the USSR (and other so-called communist societies of the twentieth century) were in fact capitalist. I cited a number of theoreticians who have analysed the USSR as a variant of capitalism. One figure who I did not draw upon was Erich Fromm. There is a reason for this. Fromm's politics were rather erratic – they had their good days and their bad days!

On good days, he spoke with a clarity of purpose:

> I am a socialist. What I understand by socialism is exactly the opposite of what … most people mean today … [Socialism] is a society in which the aim of production is not for profit but for use, in which individual citizen participates responsibly in his work and the whole social organisation and in which he is not a means who is employed by capitalism.
>
> *(Fromm 1958, 21 mins)*

When criticised by his interviewer, Mike Wallace, for leaving the worker at the disposal of the state, Fromm responds:

> We must clarify one thing: if the Russians claim they are socialists, this is just … a lie. They have no socialism at all. They have what I would call state-capitalism. Their system is the most reactionary, conservative system anywhere in Europe today … [so] actually the ownership of industry by the state, that is not socialism.
>
> *(Ibid., 22 mins)*

His interviewer persists, 'Well if that is not socialism, then what is'? Fromm answers:

> I see socialism as … the management of the enterprise by all who work in [it]. Socialism is a mixture of the minimal centralisation necessary for a modern industrial state and a maximum of decentralisation … socialism is the exact opposite of a bureaucratically managed culture.
>
> *(Ibid., 23–24 mins)*

What is common to the USA and the USSR is that both 'manage' the working class. However,

> the Russians do it by force, and we do it by persuasion … the Russians have succeeded in one thing. They have sold the world the idea that they represent socialism and the ideas of Marx. And we have done the greatest service to their propaganda by agreeing.
>
> (*Ibid.*, *25 mins*)

He ends the interview by emphasising how the two societies are becoming more similar and how as Russia becomes richer it too will add finesse to brute force.

So far, Fromm's critique of bureaucratic state capitalism is reminiscent of that of Cornelius Castoriadis (aka Paul Cardan), the Turkish-Greek-French co-founder of *Socialisme ou Barbarie* (1949–1965). This famous journal played a significant role in the events of May 1968 (Castoriadis 1997) and can be considered alongside the *Situationist International* as a healthy reaction against all forms of capitalism including Bolshevism. Unfortunately, this is where we reach the limits of Fromm's political sophistication.

In another interview, this time with Elionor Fischer, Fromm tries to position himself as a friendly critic of the New Left movement which swept across most of Europe, the USA and Japan at the end of the 1960s. Initially, Fromm ingratiates himself with the movement's principles by arguing that

> I believe that the New Left expresses a very genuine feeling of deep dissatisfaction of the young, thoughtful and feelingful generation [note once again the working classes are not mentioned directly] against the boredom, emptiness, deadliness of life [in] present day society.
>
> (*Fromm 1968, 1 min*)

The movement, Fromm continues, offers 'some sort of vision' of a future, centred on human relationships rather than the machine and bureaucracy. He warns that

> the New Left seems to be little given to objective analysis of the existing forces … large part of our young generation lives by experience of kicks and thrills which seems to have no structure … Every deep experience must have structure.
>
> (*Ibid.*, *2–3 mins*)

This, of course, is the same tired and cliched criticism one periodically hears from Leninists of a certain age as a form of chastisement for 'youthful spontaneity'. It is rather patronising and inaccurate and mistakes a few middle-class gestural political spectacles for the entirety of the movement. Fromm compares the movement of 1968 to a 'shout' or a 'yell' or a 'moment of excitement' that soon fades away unless it is brought under a robust structure (if it wasn't for the time differential one would assume that he is criticising John Holloway's defence of the 'scream')! Fromm even uses the teachings of the 'great revolutionary' Lenin to explain the 'adventurist and phrase-mongering' nature of the New Left (1968, 12 mins). He shows his ignorance by claiming that 'most of the New Left do not want to make a revolution' (ibid., 13 mins), and contrary to Marx's prediction, 'the working class in America is by no means a progressive class but one of the most conservative if not reactionary of classes' (ibid., 21 mins). Wow! Poor Erich clearly does not grasp the seminal importance of these events.

Kevin Anderson (2002) has discussed a previously unpublished review of *Trotsky's Diary in Exile* (1958) by Fromm. In this short text Fromm writes like a devoted fan of Marx, Engels, Lenin and Trotsky which given his criticisms of these figures both in *The Sane Society* (1954) and in later texts and interviews seems surprising. In fact, his analysis of the USSR as 'conservative state capitalism' while defending Lenin and Trotsky is in line with the position of Marxist humanists such C. L. R. James and Raya Dunayevskaya.

So, at the end of our analysis we are left with a contradictory thinker whose politics were a strange mish-mash of humanism (containing Buddhist, bourgeois and Marxist strands); James and Dunayevskaya's critical Leninism; and Castoriadis's libertarian socialism – all served with a generous sprinkling of social democratic reformism.

Fromm beyond Freud

Fromm's criticism of the master came at a heavy price. As Cheliotis (2013) has observed,

> Fromm's sustained critique of Freud's libidinal determinism in light of the historical materialism propounded by Marx soon estranged him from his core [Frankfurt] School colleagues, who viewed libidinal instincts as a built-in form of biological resistance to the repressive role of society. Due in no small part to this conceptual divergence, Fromm's

affiliation with the Frankfurt School ended under bitter circumstances in 1939; so bitter, indeed, that Fromm was gradually written out of the history of the School.

In his last book, *Greatness and Limitations of Freud's Thought*, Fromm (1982) does not mince words. He refers to two major 'roadblocks' beyond which Freud could not progress: one was the theory of bourgeois materialism, especially as that expounded by Freud's most important teacher, von Brücke. This theory claimed that all psychical powers have a physiological root. This explains Freud's 'obsession' with sex. He lived, after all, in an era in which the influence on the psyche of other physiological factors such as hormones was relatively unknown. Sexuality represented perhaps the only 'phenomenon in which the connection between physiological and psychical was well known' (ibid., p. 5). The second major 'roadblock' was 'Freud's bourgeois and authoritarian-patriarchal attitude' (ibid., p. 6). When John Stuart Mill (who was greatly admired by Freud) 'expressed his ideas concerning the equality of women, Freud wrote in a letter, "On this point Mill is simply crazy"' (ibid.).

Fromm then shows how the content and form of many of Freud's ideas were shaped by class. When it comes to the tripartite structure of an individual (id, ego, superego), the key point is the control of instinctual drives by ego and superego (Fromm 1982, p. 7). This whole scheme is 'a hierarchal structure which excludes the possibility that the association of free, i.e. nonexploited, human beings can live harmoniously and without the necessity of controlling sinister forces' (ibid.).

Likewise, Freud's conception of 'love' is based on the bourgeois contractual obligation of having love rather than being in love (Fromm 1982, p. 8). Fromm reminds those of us who are too lazy to actually read Freud that the master used concepts such as 'love-object' (meaning the person one loves) and 'object love' (as opposed to narcissistic love). For Fromm, love 'is precisely the inner activity which unites two people so that they cease to be objects' for each other, whereas for Freud it is 'nothing but a physiological rooted instinct directed toward an object' (ibid., pp. 8–9). This proclivity towards physiological explanations was to limit Freud's ideas on characterology too. In *Three Essays on the Theory of Sexuality* ([1905] 2017) Freud had clearly expressed his position: 'What we call the character of the person is built up to a large extent from the material of sexual excitations; it is composed of impulses fixed since infancy and won through sublimation' (ibid., p. 57).

However, Fromm comes to Freud's rescue time and again. Fromm pleads that it was Freud's greatness that shielded him from indulging in too much reductionism. He was after all a structuralist, who offered us 'one of the earliest examples of System Theory' (Fromm 1982, p. 15). Freud considered the individual as a whole and as more than the sum of his or her parts. But the individual he understood and the structures he privileged were bourgeois ones. For Freud, 'bourgeois society was identical with civilised society', and while he recognised other cultures, 'they remained for him primitive, undeveloped' (ibid., p. 25).

Most of the criticisms Fromm makes of Freud are sound. His suggestions for improving Freud remain largely within the structuralist mode of thinking, but at least Fromm has two structures to draw upon – Freudianism and his own version of Marxism. By juxtaposing these two structures against each other, he fashions a more nuanced interpretation of humanity than his old master ever could.

Going beyond Fromm

Alzo David-West (2013) has applied Frommian concepts to the social psychology of the Democratic Republic of Korea (North Korea). He defines North Korea as 'an eroding totalitarian' system, modelled on Stalinist, Maoist and fascistic forms of totalitarianism. North Korean nationalism is characterised by a 'wounded and traumatized sense of identity'. Fromm's concept of the *patricentric complex* is utilised to identify key traits prevalent in such patriarchal societies centred on the image and authority of the father: (1) a strict superego; (2) guilt feelings; (3) docile love of paternal authority; (4) desire and pleasure in dominating weaker people; and (5) a damaged capacity for happiness (Fromm 1973).

However, the patricentric complex on its own is not sufficient. Women must also be proletarianised and exploited:

> Economic inferiority and vulnerability of women combined with the authority of the husband, or father, indicates that North Korea is a society in which the patricentric complex prevails. But North Korea cannot function on the patricentric principle alone. Thus, the state and ideology exploit the negative aspects of the *matricentric complex*: fixation to blood and soil.
>
> *(David-West 2013)*

Mother substitutes such as notions of the 'motherland', the 'mother party' are promoted to create emotional attachment to the state. The matricentric complex works in tandem with the patricentric complex to divide the genders and weaken all citizens vis-à-vis the state.

Connected to these complexes is the problem of group narcissism discussed earlier. The Korean War (1950–1953) and the human and industrial devastation it brought about 'exacerbated North Korean group narcissism by threatening the vital interests of the political regime and population at large' (David-West 2013). Since the threat of annihilation has never subsided, North Koreans suffer from what Fromm called 'constant anxiety', a feeling of existential anxiety due to threats from the outside world (Fromm [1941] 1994). This explains the racial hostility that numerous visitors to North Korea have observed and is expressed in the 'nation-first policy' (*minjok cheiljuŭi*) promoted by the state (ibid.).

It is noteworthy that the

> ethnonationalist group narcissism in North Korea is not necessarily synonymous with racism, in the sense of an ideology of domination and exploitation based on ideas of biological inferiority and superiority. North Korean group narcissism is, however, a form of chauvinistic, clannish, and xenophobic race-thinking, fearful of the strange and foreign. The narcissistic pathology is not something that emerges from psychology alone, but has a basis in economic, social, and political conditions.
>
> *(David-West 2013)*

For instance, the economic dependency of North Korean capitalism on China and Russia has resulted in the prevalence of the more *malignant* form of narcissism. Fromm is very succinct on this:

> For those who are economically and culturally poor, narcissistic pride in belonging to the group is the only – and often a very effective – source of satisfaction. Precisely because life is not 'interesting' to them, and does not offer them possibilities for developing interests, they develop an extreme form of narcissism.
>
> *(Fromm 1980, p. 78)*

A similar investigation by Aysha (2017) is inspired by Fromm's work on modernity, applied to the more recent problem of Islamic suicide terrorism. 'Modernity', according to Fromm,

> makes one feel small, insignificant and isolated in the larger scheme of things. This demands a violent response, often involving self-sacrifice, to reassert the balance, which allows Islamists to take advantage of death-related anxieties and exaggerate the sense of confrontation with the world through apocalyptic prophecies.
>
> *(Ibid., p. 82)*

Politically motivated Muslim suicide bombers have neither the theological backing of their religion nor do they seem to have the usual markers associated with suicide. They are not fatherless, friendless, jobless or hopeless (ibid., p. 84).

In *The Fear of Freedom* ([1942] 1980), Fromm argues that capitalist modernity dissolves 'medieval ties' such as clan, tribe, sect, guild and neighbourhood ties. It also creates the new individual while 'leaving him (or her) defenceless, alone and alienated' (Aysha 2017, p. 85). Many individuals conform to new realities but those who fear the new changes and who cannot love life may express their 'rebelliousness' through apocalyptic forms of religious extremism. In relation to Christianity, Fromm writes that 'masochistic sacrifice sees the fulfilment of life in its very negation, in the annihilation of the self' (Fromm, quoted in ibid., p. 92). There is an equivalent tendency in Islam known as *fana* (literally, annihilation) which is about losing oneself in the person of God. An extreme form of this tendency (the physical annihilation of the self), the terrorist believes, allows the chosen *ummah* (literally, community) to inherit the Earth. The solution to religious extremism, according to Fromm, is to reconceptualise religion in terms of 'biophilous' or life-loving tendencies. Only then can we move in the direction of *The Sane Society* ([1956] 2002). This explains Fromm's lifelong preoccupation with Judeo-Christianity and Buddhism.

Cheliotis (2013) has applied Fromm's 'materialistic psychoanalysis' to penology. The question he attempts to answer is a very interesting one:

> Why is it that imprisonment has undergone an explosive growth in the USA and Britain over the last three decades against the background of falling crime rates in both countries? And why has this development met with a significant and escalating degree of support among the public?
>
> *(Ibid.)*

In particular, Cheliotis is investigating how perceived working-class street crime is used to induce fear in the middle class, which in turn leads to the 'political production of middle-class support for punitive penal policies under conditions of neoliberal capitalism' (ibid.). It may very well be that as it becomes increasingly sandwiched between a rising working class and a greedy ruling elite, punitiveness becomes more deeply embedded in the middle class (Young 2007).

Fromm's notion of 'social character' becomes relevant here. This is usually defined as 'the sum total of cognitive and psychic traits typical of human beings in a given society or group' (Cheliotis 2013). It is shaped and in turn shapes the typical expectations and functional requirements according to the dominant mode of production. It describes the emotional attitudes common to people in a social class. The social character operates as a mediator between the economic substructure and the ideological superstructure. It is more than a theory of false consciousness since it helps people to 'derive gratification from acting according to social and cultural expectations' (Foster 2017, p. 3). The 'social character' is what is common to most members of a class due to the same cultural and social matrix, while the 'individual character' marks the way in which individuals differ from one another within the same culture. This is similar to ideas introduced by Tajfel under the rubric of 'social identity theory'.

The crucial point for our purposes is this: if 'a social order neglects or suppresses basic human needs beyond a certain point', and in our example this would be the need for middle-class security and prosperity, then either the group will attempt to change the existing order, or failing that, 'pathological forms of destructiveness ... would emerge within the social character' (Foster 2017, p. 5). The typical example Fromm enjoyed working from was the 'hoarding' character orientation which privileges a puritan approach to capital accumulation. This hoarding orientation not only formed the backbone of nineteenth-century capitalism in Great Britain and elsewhere it allowed the pathology of hoarding to be used productively, as the 'combination of a stable world, stable possessions, and a stable ethic gave the members of the middle class a feeling of belonging, self-confidence, and pride' (Fromm 1986, p. 81). From the 1950s onwards this hoarding orientation became counterproductive, gradually creating the need for a new social character, to which Fromm gives the name *homo consumens*.

When capitalism is in crisis or there is a dire need for reorganisation, one common strategy is to displace the ruling elite's anger onto outgroups which are then scapegoated as dangerous. The mechanism for disciplining and reorganising a particular section of the proletariat is already in place and awaiting activation. The push for activation comes when these fears, anxieties and expectations become cemented as part of the social character of the middle class.

This brings us back to penology under neo-liberal capitalism. What happens when the hoarding character is no longer required under capitalism and *homo consumens* has lost the privilege of excessive consumption due to increased financial woes? Then, Fromm argues, the state resorts to the cultivation of the 'authoritarian character'. Legitimate class anger against the ruling class is distorted into hatred of the scapegoated group, and behold the sadomasochistic individual: one who masochistically succumbs to power in lieu of which power permits him to indulge in a sadistic whipping of the stigmatised. The emergence of the 'authoritarian character' explains why personal prejudice and institutionalised discrimination are nowadays constantly on the verge of becoming a visceral expression of bigotry. So far, this bigotry has expressed itself in individual acts of violence towards the despised group (be that street criminals, Muslims, Jews, homosexuals, gypsy travellers, etc.). It does not take a great leap of imagination to envisage how these widespread individual acts of cruelty can degenerate into pogroms of one kind or another, even in 'civilised' Great Britain!

Final thoughts on Fromm

Annette Thomson (2009) has furnished us with a list of contemporary issues where Fromm should be reanimated. One area is cyberpsychology. Fromm made a distinction between 'productive activity' and 'non-productive activity'. The former refers to the 'positive ways in which we can use our human powers. It originates from our own mental and emotional experience and is thus linked to the *being* mode' (ibid., p. 145, emphasis in the original). The being mode is all about use value and activities that benefit and enhance. By contrast the non-productive activity is 'alienated, relentless busy-ness, driven either by external factors and incessant deadlines or else by internal compulsion' (ibid.). Non-productive activity is mostly about *having* (possessing of commodities).

The relevance of this Frommian distinction for Internet activity can be highlighted thus:

> The concept of 'activity' rests upon one of the most widespread of man's illusions in modern industrial society. Our whole culture is geared to activity – activity in the sense of being busy … (the busyness necessary for business). In fact, most people are so 'active' that they cannot stand doing nothing, they even transform their so-called leisure time into another form of activity.
>
> *(Fromm, quoted in Thomson 2009, p. 145)*

Fromm can be useful in understanding how our leisure time is becoming increasingly regimentalised and how the Internet is turning our imagination mechanical, and how both what we consume and produce while engaged in Internet activity is tending more and more towards exchange value and having, rather than use value and being.

I think we have reached the point when we can dispense with previous extreme evaluations of Fromm. Marcuse and Jacoby were being uncharitable in their judgement when they dismissed him as a 'conformist', and Fromm's fans are being wishful when they claim he was a revolutionary. He was neither. He was, in my view, a highly brilliant thinker who in line with most of the key figures promoted in this section tried to go beyond various crippling dualities, including the duality between individual and social, emotion and intellect, and biological and cultural forms of determinisms. I consider his work to be indispensable for the success of postpsychology.

15

ANTONIN ARTAUD, EMBODIMENT AND POSTPSYCHOLOGY

A lot of people say it's a lack of vocabulary that makes you swear. Rubbish. I know thousands of words but I still prefer f***.

Billy Connolly

Thou whoreson zed, thou unnecessary letter!

Shakespeare, King Lear, *Act 2, Scene 2*

Billy Connolly is a comedian from a working-class background. Shakespeare is Shakespeare. Interestingly, both have a similar take on humour (especially when it comes to breaking social taboos), which is at odds with (most) middle-class sensibilities. Shakespeare's humour, on the other hand, oscillated between the 'vulgar' lower class and the 'refined' nobility. Artaud detested Shakespeare's wordplay, his humanism and his investigations of the inner mind. We need to keep both of the above quotations in mind as we journey through the complex world of Antonin Artaud (1896–1948).

I think it is Artaud's transgressive thinking that I find most appealing, although I hasten to add that I no longer have the patience to sit through his *Theatre of Cruelty*, as I once did in my youth. I am still a fan, but not a dedicated fan. I still see the subversive brilliance and insight, but now I also see the flaws and the balderdash. The absence of humour (despite his affinity for the comedies of the Marx Brothers), and the presence of political confusion will forever limit Artaud's radicalism. Despite these shortcomings, his work is still one of the best ways of introducing certain bodily and linguistic topics into our discussion. In this chapter, I attempt to explain Artaud's relevance to the project of postpsychology.

A tragic life?

> I took out a loan to pay for an exorcism. If I don't pay it back, I'm going to get repossessed.
>
> *Olaf Falafel*

A cruel joke was once told at the expense of the American actor, James Franco. It was during a TV 'roasting' by a comedienne called Natasha Leggero: 'James Franco: acting, teaching, directing, writing, producing, photography, soundtracks, editing: is there *anything* you can do?'

I have watched Franco in one or two movies but I am not sufficiently familiar with his *oeuvre* and, therefore, am in no position to judge the veracity of the implied criticism. However, I do know that as capitalist competition became fiercer, the pressure to become a specialist and stay within the bounds of that specialty also grew. Capitalist propaganda in recent decades has promoted labour flexibility (and to some extent may actually *need* flexibility), but the dialectics of flexibility and specialisation are stacked heavily in favour of the latter. Consequently, anyone engaged in more than one field of activity will immediately be considered suspect. This suspicion may explain why Artaud is no longer fashionable. The plank of his strategy involved criss-crossing boundaries: mind-body; spectator-artist; moral-immoral; biology-culture; art-life, etc. Artaud was a dramatist, poet, essayist, actor, theatre director, anti-psychiatry activist and political rebel (whether he liked 'Politics' with a capital 'P' or not), all rolled into one pained and tortured body.

Pain was his constant companion. At four he fell ill and was diagnosed with meningitis. Later biographers have been sceptical about the accuracy of this diagnosis (Shafer 2016), but do not deny his early brush with death. Subsequently, he developed 'neuralgia, stuttering and intense headaches' (Stoppelman 2000, p. 2). His mother 'gave birth to nine children, but four were stillborn and two others died in childhood' (*Wikipedia*, 'Antonin Artaud'). He learned very early on that illness attacked both his body and his soul and that no medicine could counter the pain.

As he grew older, he came across the *enfants terribles* of French literature, the likes of Rimbaud, Nerval and Baudelaire. From them he took both a healthy *non*-conformist attitude towards the established order, and a rather juvenile *anti*-conformist proclivity for temper tantrums. His physical pain caused bouts of depression and intense rage, and a conviction that neither God nor medicine but 'he alone would be capable of finding a solution to his suffering' (Stoppelman 2000, p. 7).

As his artistic principles became more coherent, first due to contact with the surrealists, and later as a reaction against them, he realised that he must do away with the duality of performers and audiences. He experimented with getting rid of the stage. He tried to shock spectators emotionally, psychologically and physically in order to break them from passively consuming 'the art'. He wanted the 'audience to be "plunged into a bath of fire" … to participate "with their soul and their nerves"' (Artaud, quoted in Barber 1993, p. 71). This anti-psychologism forced him to dispense with words for theatre and to find an alternative language more suitable for bodily performance (hence his contempt for Shakespeare and Molière).

An encounter with 'oriental theatre' marked a turning point. In the summer of 1931 Artaud saw Balinese actors performing in Paris and was electrified. He observed how the actors used the physical resources of the set and how signs, gestures, music and movement were intertwined to create a dramatic spectacle. The spoken word which hindered the spontaneous poetry of images was minimised as much as possible. Everything on stage (words and *mise en scène*) must become significant rather than decorative. To this he added the notion that each performance must be unique and unrepeatable (Stoppelman 2000, p. 15).

Artaud's falling out with the surrealists is instructive but takes us too far beyond our remit. Suffice it to say that things came to a head in 1926 when Breton, Péret, Aragon and others published a pamphlet accusing the 'riff-raff' Artaud of lacking political commitment, which was only *partly* true. Artaud was, as are we all, a political creature but, unlike Breton, did not believe in bureaucratic parties, or Bolshevism. The surrealists were selling themselves to the Bolsheviks even after the counter-revolutionary destruction of the Kronstadt rebellion in 1921. Raoul Vaneigem suggests that 'only Artaud, ever sensitive to the merest hint of oppression, now distanced himself in clear awareness of what was at stake' (1977, p. 20). Artaud's alienation had its roots in his illness but also in the social defeats of the time. 'I suffer frightfully from life', writes Artaud, 'and without a doubt I have been dead for a long time already … I have, as it were, been suicided' (Artaud, quoted in ibid., p. 38). For Artaud, the defeat of the Spartacist uprising (Germany, 1919), the strengthening of Stalinism, and the

FIGURE 15.1 Antonin Artaud

compromises of Dada and surrealism, as well as war and poverty meant that the hopes of a classless society were receding.

Artaud missed the action in World War I because his addiction to laudanum and morphine as well as his somnambulism made him unfit for the army, and during World War II he was incarcerated in various psychiatric asylums. He was reluctant to participate in any social movement. Let's just say he was a loner rather than a joiner. And yet he spent his entire life searching for connections. The desire to connect would at times become overwhelming. So much so that in the summer of 1930 he sent Marinetti, the leader of the Futurist movement and the official poet of Mussolini's regime, a set of photographs. He even dedicated a copy of one of his books to Hitler, although by that time he was (probably) suffering from severe mental issues. The surrealists also charged him with enmity towards art (which was not true). He loved art but again his interpretation of artistic endeavour was different to surrealism. His intentional, conscious and controlled work was diametrically opposed to the surrealists' emphasis on the unconscious.

Artaud for his part rightly pointed out that a genuine revolution is not reducible to practical matters of reorganising society, but entails the restructuring of the 'soul' to lessen real suffering (Vaneigem 1977, p. 33). In a slightly confused and obscure way Artaud was repeating the same point made earlier by Marx, Gross, Reich and Fromm. His retraining of his troupe of actors to express their pain through bodily movements and screaming was reminiscent of the primal (scream) therapy of the 1970s that was so beloved by certain celebrities. Artaud was also warning Breton and his pals that pandering to the Bolsheviks would get them nowhere. Again, this was a confused way of affirming Otto Rühle's battle cry that 'Revolution is not a party affair!' (Rühle 1920).

As an artist-anthropologist Artaud discovered the theme of 'primitive communism', when visiting the Tarahumaras Indian tribe who lived in the Sierra Madre region of northern Mexico. 'The Tarahumaras had an utter disregard for material possessions which paralleled Artaud's own austerity … [and consequently they] practised the only kind of communism which Artaud could tolerate', writes Barber (1993, p. 82). Artaud understood a higher definition of 'communism' to the rather stale Bolshevised rendering:

> Communism exists for this race through a feeling of spontaneous solidarity … the Tarhumara Indians live as though they are already dead … They do not see reality, and draw magical powers from the contempt which they hold towards civilisation.
>
> *(Artaud, quoted in ibid.)*

Had Artaud been more politically savvy, had he been better acquainted with the best of Marxism and anarchism, then perhaps he would not have felt so isolated after his break with the surrealists.

Meanwhile, his theatre was becoming increasingly anti-representational. He was firmly against imitating life or representing it. His performances were an expression of 'a unique energy that consumes itself ... the language used is a surrender, a gift that demands no reward' (Stoppelman 2000, p. 51). This may seem bizarre to our sensibilities but only because we have come to consider the fulfilment of our desires and expectations through art a normal affair. We exchange our money for libidinal and intellectual satisfaction every time we go to the theatre. Artaud was not playing this game. He presented the only thing he had – his pain – as a gift. Many years later anthropologists would discuss the 'gift economy' and the *Situationists International* would pick up on it as an alternative way of structuring society.

Artaud was not Jesus. He was not jumping on the cross to pay for 'our sins'. He was not just enduring pain; he was also inflicting pain in order to force body and consciousness together again. His Theatre of Cruelty re-enacted the fear and suffering associated with the plague. Artaud explained how

> when the plague has become established in a city, all normal social order collapses. The streets are choked with death. Vermin prowl amongst corpses. Plague victims wander through the city delirious and screaming. The smells and sights of the city become nauseating!
>
> *(Stoppelman 2000, p. 54)*

Through cruelty and fear Artaud was trying to strip away the inauthentic layers we have constructed for ourselves, and get at the core of our humanity. He wanted to make our gestures extreme and that involved forcing us beyond the constructed bounds of orthodox morality – beyond good and evil.

Artaud's body and psychiatry

> Madness in great ones must not unwatched go.
>
> *Shakespeare,* Hamlet, *Act 3, Scene 1*

In 1937 Artaud was taken to a psychiatric hospital near Rouen. Later he was transferred to the Sainte-Anne Hospital near Paris, where he was subjected to periods of solitary confinement. This is where he came across a certain Jacques Lacan whom he derided as a 'filthy, vile bastard' (Artaud, quoted in Barber 1993, p. 140). He also accused Lacan of 'erotomania' (Wetherington 2016) which I will just throw in without elaboration since I have no intention of spending the rest of my life debating with the 'Lacanian community'! He was then sent to the Ville-Evrard asylum which was notorious for its ill-treatment of 'difficult patients'. A number of psychiatric labels were pinned on him, but the one that stigmatised him the most was the label 'incurably insane'.

When World War II broke out life became much harsher for the patients. His former surrealist friends had him moved to what was considered a more humane hospital at Rodez where he was placed under the care of Dr Gaston Ferdière, a sympathiser of surrealism. Irony of ironies, that is when things took a turn for the worse, since Dr Ferdière was not just a surrealist poet but an ardent believer in the benefits of electro-shock treatment. Artaud underwent the first few sessions consensually but then began to resist. Sadly, patients had fewer rights in those days and psychiatrists more power. Even fracturing his vertebrae during one of the sessions did not disrupt the inevitability of 'treatment'. All in all, he was subjected to fifty-one electro-shock sessions (Stoppelman 2000, pp. 107–115). As a result, he lost all his teeth and (temporarily) his identity too.

Even if he was not 'insane' before entering various hospitals, his psychiatrists' treatment of him caused deep and lasting scars. He began writing strange letters to his friends containing spells to ward off occult powers. He completely rejected carnal love and everything physical. With the help of other patients, he created a new language only meaningful to them (a not uncommon phenomenon, known as 'glossolalia' in psychiatry and 'speaking in tongues' among Pentecostals).

After years of mistreatment he finally left psychiatry's clutches for good. Gradually, his mental well-being improved. In the 1940s he changed many of his youthful views. He 'abandoned his leaning towards esoteric writings, oriental religions, the cabbala and myths' (Stoppelman 2000, p. 127). He came to understand anguish as a form of bodily suffering with social origins and not an act of the soul. As with R. D. Laing and Michel Foucault after him, Artaud came to believe that the real madmen are not inside the asylum, but outside it (ibid., p. 124). Psychiatrists see every artist as an enemy, he claimed. Many of these themes were further developed in his brilliant book *Van Gogh: The Man Suicided by Society* (1947). Artaud argues that Van Gogh committed suicide because society left him no choice. Writing partly about Van Gogh, but actually partly about himself, Artaud argues:

> Psychiatry, challenged by Van Gogh's lucidity at work, is no more than an outpost of gorillas, themselves obsessed and persecuted, who have only a ridiculous terminology to alleviate the most appalling states of anguish and human suffocation: a fitting product of their disreputable brains.
>
> *(Artaud 1947a, p. 46)*

His own lucidity led Artaud to see that 'the body suffers malicious robberies (by society, family and religion) which leave it fixed and futile, smothered to the point of a terminal incoherence' (Barber 1993, p. 3). His own bodily decomposition constantly contradicted the ideologies of perfection. Its excesses, waste and decay railed against the disciplining of the body that more and more people were becoming subjected to. While charging psychiatry with the murder of Van Gogh, he argued for everyone's inalienable right to destroy themselves, if they so desire (ibid., p. 24). This is many years before the emergence of the 'right to die' movement, whose advocates argue that one's body is one's own. Like Reich after him, Artaud fetishised the body but perhaps this was a healthy and necessary reaction against professions such as medicine, psychiatry, psychology and religion that also lay claim to our bodies.

Towards the end of his life he produced a text entitled 'Shit to the Mind', which attacked all artistic groupings whose name ended with the suffix 'ism', ranging from surrealism to lettrism (Artaud 1947b). Maybe this is the reason the *Situationist International* was reluctant for its work to be referred to as 'situationism'. By giving pre-eminence to the mind, all these artistic movements had subordinated (or erased) the body (Barber 1993, p.142). Artaud demands we 'place the body, the fleshy envelope of organs and fluids, at the centre of social order' (Brown and Stenner 2009, p. 89).

This is a fitting resistance against all those forms of psychology (psychoanalytic, discursive, and even cognitive) that try to ostracise the body in favour of the word. As Artaud put it, somewhat ironically since he was using words: 'All writing is pigshit. People who leave the obscure to try to define whatever it is that goes on in their heads, are pigs' (Artaud, quoted in Brown and Stenner 2009, p. 92). For Artaud, consciousness cannot be divorced from embodiment. As Brown and Stenner put it, 'The body *thinks* as it acts. Consciousness is rooted within the flesh' (ibid., p. 94, emphasis in the original).

Towards the end of his life, he broke with all forms of religiosity when in 1945 he declared, 'As for me, Artaud, I have no use for God, and I refuse to countenance anyone's founding a religion on my backbone or on my brain' (Artaud, quoted in Vaneigem 1977, p. 121). In his last interview in 1948, he aimed a parting shot at his tormentors: 'I know I have cancer. What I want to say before dying is that I hate psychiatrists' (Artaud, quoted in Barber 1993, p.160).

Beyond Artaud's bodily pain

Whenever reaction gets the better of working-class consciousness, the most odious, repugnant and nasty currents within psychology resurface with a vengeance. Sir Cyril Burt (1883–1971), who falsified research data in a bid to prove his ideas about genetic heredity, was exposed by Kamin in 1974, and yet Burt is periodically rehabilitated (Gould 1996). Hans Eysenck who was accused of providing a pseudo-scientific facade for fascist ideology is resurrected (for an excellent critique see Rose *et al.*, 1984). The discredited notion of a 'gay gene' or a 'criminal gene' is plastered over the newspapers every now and then to perpetuate the myths of biological determinism. Pop psychology assaults the senses with endless accounts of gender essentialism to reinforce patriarchy. A new toy is designed by neuro-engineers and suddenly phrenology is back in fashion. An archaeological dig discovers ancient artefacts and the occasion is seized upon to dust off old, simple-minded evolutionary fairy tales. Politicians and the mainstream media nearly always greet new technology with a barely concealed desire for increased behavioural modification of the masses. These attempts at behavioural modification have their parallels in experimental crowd psychology, with 'de-individuation' theories enjoying a resurgence following urban riots. During periods of economic downturn new psycho-active drugs construct new mental categories and new mental categories catalyse the search for 'smarter' drugs. The list goes on. Like herpes, syphilis and athlete's foot, keeping these viral ideas at bay is a constant war of attrition.

Another bad idea that has recently made a comeback is electro-shock treatment, or as its advocates have rebranded it, electro-convulsive therapy (ECT). Historians of psychiatry provide ECT with diverse origin points. The first clearly documented case of deliberate seizure induction is (probably) 1785. Early successes for curing 'hysterical' women were claimed. Rom Harré relates how 'in the second half of the eighteenth century systematic studies of electrical phenomena became very popular' (Harré 2009, p. 22). Luigi Galvani played a seminal role in discoveries about electricity. His famous experiment with the hind legs of frogs was conducted in 1791. He was trying to prove the hypothesis that 'animal spirits' (the kind of electricity emitted by eels or the frog's nervous system) was the same as the 'artificial electricity' produced by friction in electrical machines and 'atmospheric electricity' caused by lightning (ibid., p. 23). Although he made a number of false assumptions, his practical work (and that of his critic and rival Alessandro Volta) laid the foundations for electrophysiology, electrochemistry and even the electrical battery (ibid., p. 28). André Parent (2004) has claimed that 'the principles of Luigi Galvani (animal electricity) and Alessandro Volta (bimetallic electricity) were used together for the first time' around 1801 by a physicist called Giovanni Aldini who treated patients with 'personality disorders and recorded completed rehabilitation following transcranial administration of electric current' (ibid.).

As science became better acquainted with the nervous system, 'nerves' became a crucial metaphorical entry point for intervention. Both the body and the body-politic were being constructed anew by the bourgeoisie. Pain was re-described as 'jangled' or 'frazzled' nerves. Accumulated nervous pain would now cause trauma which, if not treated, resulted in a nervous breakdown in the individual or nation. This basically nineteenth-century biomedical model of 'energy' revisions the human body as

> a stockpile of labour power to be deployed and expended … The nervous system was initially mapped in the same way that changing national boundaries and lines of trade and transport (such as railway lines) were plotted, with the same eye to detecting the most efficacious mechanisms for the application of limited stores of energy.
>
> *(Brown 2005, p. 237)*

In the 1930s the Hungarian neuropsychiatrist Ladislas J. Meduna induced seizures by using first camphor and then metrazol. In 1938 the Italian Ugo Cerletti, who just like Galvani, Volta and Aldini mentioned above, had been using electricity in animal experimentation, was the first neurologist to apply it to a patient diagnosed with 'schizophrenia'. The patient was ideal since he was a 'tramp' member of the working class with no family support or recollection of who he was. After many attempts (and much incremental dialling up of the voltage), they finally managed to induce a seizure in him. At one stage he begged Cerletti, 'Not another one! It's murder!' (Johnstone 2003, p. 236). What is vital to remember here is that Cerletti did not know (and today's psychiatrists do not know either) exactly how and why electrical stimulation to the brain 'works' (Wilson 2017). Later in life, Cerletti admitted that the treatment's 'main effect was to produce brain damage', and that the very idea was 'barbaric and dangerous', adding that 'in everyone's mind was the spectre of the electric chair' (Cerletti, quoted in Barker 2003).

The lack of a scientific explanation did not deter the popularity of ECT. Since it was cheap, it soon replaced metrazol therapy, and by the 1940s and 1950s it had become widespread globally. In 1959 a gross misuse of ECT occurred due to an overzealous colonel in charge of a psychiatric unit in Fitzsimons Army Hospital outside Denver. Apparently,

> Soldiers needing admission as inpatients into this ward, would first need to undergo an extremely high amount of unmodified ECT sessions ... around 100 previously physically fit soldiers were left incontinent because of the sessions, while others were unable to feed themselves.
>
> *(Wilson 2017)*

It was not until the 1990s when the 'unmodified' form of ECT (treatment without anaesthesia and muscle relaxant) was replaced by a less severe version.

There is here an unstated but real relationship between treatment and punishment. This is clearly visible in the use of ECT for 'treating' homosexuality. In England it was used on boys as young as 13, 'with some participants even taking home portable shock boxes to use by themselves when aroused by members of the same sex' (Wilson 2017). The great irony, which may be missed by the less sexually adventurous, is that nowadays thanks to the marvels of technology, electric stimulation is used to *enhance* the sexual experience!

In 1999 ECT was administered to 11,340 patients in England, two-thirds of whom were women, '41 per cent were over 65, and 15 per cent had ECT ... without consent' (Johnstone 2003, p. 236). In Australia, in line with the authoritarian turn in governance and political discourse, there were 203 recorded cases of 'ECT treatments on children younger than 14 – including 55 aged 4 and younger' in 2008 alone (Levine 2009). In the USA, it is more of a lottery, since where you live influences whether you might receive ECT. However, most states 'do not prohibit ECT for kids' (ibid.). More worryingly,

> you might think that before any child receives a series of 70 to 170 volts of brain zappings and is thrown into seizures, every other non-traumatic therapy would have been attempted. You might think that

> before using ECT, in addition to trying every type of psychotherapy, there would also be an exhaustive effort to find a therapist with whom a kid might genuinely connect. You might think all this, but you would be wrong.
>
> *(Ibid.)*

This psychological punishment is accompanied by real organic damage to the brain. Neurologist Sidney Sament describes: 'After a few sessions of ECT, the symptoms are those of moderate cerebral contusions … Electroconvulsive therapy in effect may be defined as a controlled type of brain damage produced by electrical means' (Levine 2009). One reason behind the alleged benefits of ECT is that the patient's trauma is 'forgotten' due to damage to memory traces in the brain. The procedure can also produce 'pronounced slowing of reaction time' and 'persisting retrograde amnesia' that continue six months after treatment (ibid.)!

The critical psychiatrist Peter Breggin is scathing about the lack of controlled studies in favour of ECT treatment (1998). He writes, 'That ECT had no positive effect after four weeks confirms the brain-disabling principle, since four weeks is the approximate time for significant recovery from the most obvious mind-numbing or euphoric effects of the ECT-induced acute organic brain syndrome' (ibid., p. 8). In other words, being subjected to ECT coincides 'precisely with the known sequelae of any trauma to the brain, the acute stage of confusion, headache and nausea, followed by a period of emotional shallowness, denial and artificial euphoria that usually wears off after four weeks' (Johnstone 2003, p. 239). Realising that at present too many powerful psychiatrists are utilising ECT for a ban to be effective, Breggin has instead proposed a more realistic package: ban ECT for children; ban involuntary treatment; ban emergency ECT; ban repeated ECT (1998). He has also suggested that there should be tighter monitoring of ECT treatment and a compulsory one-year follow-up on all patients. The fact that even these mild reforms are resisted is an indication of the current strength of 'authoritarian psychiatry'.

Advocates of ECT argue that as a treatment of last resort, it can prevent suicide. But as Johnstone has concluded, 'there is … no hard evidence that ECT prevents suicide' (2003, p. 237). In fact, the idea that ECT may *increase* the risk of suicide has never been investigated, according to Johnstone. This is despite anecdotal evidence from various individuals including

Ernest Hemingway and Sylvia Plath whose suicide was in all probability related to ECT (ibid., p. 238).

How do ECT practitioners rationalise a procedure which goes against their Hippocratic Oath? A discourse analysis study shows how psychiatrists, anaesthetists and psychiatric nurses from a major city in the United Kingdom employed a repertoire that 'constructed the ECT recipient as severally ill' (Stevens and Harper 2007). Distress was reformulated in biological terms and concern was mitigated by retendering ECT 'as a medical procedure with concomitant risks and benefits; downplaying a lack of clarity over its evidence base; and undermining the legitimacy of criticisms' (ibid.).

This intransigent attitude is all the more surprising since there have always been sound alternatives to ECT. Pat Bracken who works as Consultant Psychiatrist and Senior Research Fellow at the University of Bradford and Bradford Community Trust, UK, writes,

> In 5 years of practice, we have never seen ECT as the answer to a client's problems … Admissions are more often driven by social problems and poor housing than by the nature of the psychiatric disturbance as such …. We attempt to encounter depression as a 'site of struggle' rather than as an illness, and offer to struggle for a solution alongside the individual in question.
>
> *(Bracken 2012)*

Bracken, incidentally, promotes 'postpsychiatry', a concept that has more than mere linguistic parallels to postpsychology.

In 1943, following the administration of the first electroshocks, Artaud pleaded with Dr Ferdière to stop the treatment:

> My very dear friend, I have a great service and a great favour to ask of you. This is to cut short the application of electroshocks on me, which my body obviously cannot stand and which are certainly the predominant, revealing cause of my present vertebral displacement.
>
> *(Artaud, quoted in Barber 1993, p. 108)*

Ferdière refused Artaud's request, not because he was an evil man but because, like today's mainstream psychiatrists, he was trapped within a discourse that brooks no argument.

Final remarks

The success of postpsychology as a project is dependent on recognising how to overcome dualities. The mind-body duality has been a particular bane of psychology. Sometimes, in order to find a solution, it is necessary to step back and seek alternative viewpoints. This is what I have tried to do by looking at embodiment through Artaud's eyes. No doubt phenomenological and sociocultural contributions could be added to this perspective in the future.

16

LEV VYGOTSKY *IS* POSTPSYCHOLOGY!

Vygotsky: the Mozart *and* Bob Dylan of psychology

This was a difficult chapter to plan and write, since I felt overwhelmed by how much I know about Vygotsky. Where do I start? … hmm … Perhaps a generic biography of the man? Nope! That would be tedious as well as superfluous. Nowadays brilliant biographies of Vygotsky are available a dime a dozen (Kozulin 1990; Wertsch 1985). Oh, I know! I'll introduce him by way of a video clip. Sadly, having trawled through YouTube, I can only find clichéd five-minute-long comparisons of Vygotsky and Piaget on child development, mostly cobbled together from previous videos of a similar nature. I could engage in a detailed class analysis of the forces that shaped him, but I somehow get the impression from the slow pace at which you are leafing through the last parts of the book that you have had enough of me bleating on about the class struggle!

OK, I think I've got it. I'll begin by heaping praise on Vygotsky, and given the endemic misunderstandings surrounding his work, I'll clarify his position by illustrating the novel ways in which his ideas have been extended by his most astute followers. This will hopefully illustrate my central claim that Vygotsky *is* postpsychology (or at least an indispensable dimension of it).

The obvious fact that most biographers seem to skirt around is that Vygotsky was exceptionally good looking. No, no, no, bear with me, this is important. In psychology we are not blessed with an overabundance of elegant and appealing practitioners. Most are men, and most seem to have been born octogenarians! There is Carl Gustav Jung, of course, but given the shifty nature of his political affiliations (Noll 1997), perhaps we should be wary of turning him into a poster boy for the purposes of twenty-first-century postpsychology.

Alex Kozulin (1990) has famously described Vygotsky as the 'Mozart of psychology', the inference being that Vygotsky was another exceptionally precocious youngster, who grew up in a hostile environment to evolve into a socially acknowledged genius, and who died tragically early. However, given Vygotsky's zeitgeist defining ideas and his quiet way of providing a voice for other like-minded people, I think he has also won the right to be compared to Bob Dylan.

For long periods, history saw fit to either suppress or distort Vygotsky's ideas. In the USSR the Bolsheviki bourgeoisie found his Marxism a danger to their machinations, and in Anglo-Saxon capitalism he was depoliticised and tamed as providing an alternative method for teaching children liberal norms. It took time for the radical potential of his ideas to be realised. Even today I fear that too many Vygotskians intentionally ignore his revolutionary politics and reduce him to a specialist for improving classroom efficiency. Contrary to this conception of him, I prefer to see him as a thinker-doer whose realm encompassed child and developmental psychology as well as cultural, cognitive and social psychology. His work is also exceedingly relevant to sociology and politics. In analysing neo-Vygotskian researchers for this chapter, I have confined myself to brief descriptions of works that I find integral to a project of postpsychology.

There's dialectical materialism and then there's Diamat!

Cyril Smith (2004), Z. A. Jordan (1967) and many other thinkers have pointed out the various interpretations of 'materialism' and 'dialectics' in Marx. Thankfully, this is not the place to go into a detailed analysis of such esoteric debates. However, I would like to use James P. Lantolf's (2017) text to start off our discussion of Vygotsky on a firm foundation. Lantolf reminds us that Marx 'takes the "commodity" as the cell or unit for understanding capitalism. In the same way, Vygotsky proposed 'word meaning' as the unit of analysis for the study of consciousness' (ibid., p. 175). In his later writings Vygotsky proposed the possibility of 'experienced reality' as the perfect unit for capturing the dialectical unity between emotion and reason.

Vygotsky (as with Holzkamp who is discussed later in the chapter) was opposed to the uncritical importation of the experimental method into psychology. While a simple stimulus-response approach may be adequate for basic biochemical analyses of mental functions, it fails miserably to capture the complexities of higher cortical functions. Instead, he proposed the 'functional method of double-stimulation'. As Lantolf explains,

> this is a two-stage procedure in which children of different ages … are given tasks assumed to be difficult and likely beyond their biologically endowed ability, and then are provided with auxiliary artifacts … that could potentially be integrated into the task solution. The researcher then observes if and how the children use the artifacts to support or mediate their solution to the problem. By studying children of different ages, Vygotsky reasoned it would be possible to trace the formation of higher order (i.e., cultural) thinking in adults as it develops over time.
>
> *(2017, p. 180)*

Lantolf adds two contributions to this general investigative approach. The first is to decentre children as the subject of Vygotskian studies:

> Based on how Vygotsky conceptualised the experimental-developmental method, however, I propose that it would be more appropriate to change from 'child history' to 'adult history'. After all, Vygotsky was interested in the historical development of adult thinking, not with children *per se*.
>
> *(2017, pp. 180–181)*

I wholeheartedly agree. For too long the multifaceted, thrilling adult has played second fiddle to the predictably pedantic child in Vygotskian studies. It is time to refocus on adults. We are far more fascinating than our earlier selves!

The second point Lantolf makes is just as vital. So far, we have discussed how Vygotsky studied the past, but history should also be 'studied forward':

> I would like to raise the possibility that in the zone of proximal development (ZPD), Vygotsky attempted to capture elements of the future in the present. Recall that for Marx, studying history forward was about uncovering elements of a socialist or communist future operating in contemporary capitalism … [in the same way] the ZPD is

FIGURE 16.1 Lev Vygotsky

> concerned with uncovering evidence for and, simultaneously, provoking an individual's future mental processing.
>
> *(Ibid. 2017, p. 181)*

Again, I am in total agreement especially if we expand the ZPD to include the development of collectivities, and not just individuals.

The work of Lantolf (2017), Wertsch (1985) and others illustrates how Vygotsky and the Soviet Stalinists could occasionally use common terminology but end up with completely opposing interpretations. Vygotsky studied dialectical and historical materialism as someone well versed in Marx, while reactionary Stalinists created Diamat to suppress the class struggle. If we make the error of conflating the two philosophies, we would be as guilty as those confusing Christ with the Christian Roman Empire or Nietzsche with the Third Reich.

Vygotsky and Bernstein

The socio-linguistic studies of Basil Bernard Bernstein (1924–2000) echo Vygotsky's approach. In an interesting study, Gabrielle Ivinson (2012) has brought these two great thinkers together in order to find better solutions to working-class boys' educational 'failures' in the former mining valleys of South Wales during the post-industrial era.

These mining communities were relatively insulated from each other, cut off by geography and lack of transport. Their importance peaked during the 1890s to 1920s when they became the centre of the Industrial Revolution, exporting coal all over the world (Ivinson 2012, p. 156). During the 1920s 'the political approach was to abandon the place, encourage outward migration and leave areas derelict' (ibid.). Educational opportunities, especially after the age of sixteen when compulsory education ceased, have always been limited.

Utilising Bernstein's sociological writings, Ivinson explains how

> skilled practices have traditionally been learned through apprenticeship curricula involving a joint enterprise, a shared vocabulary, repetition through time … Tensions arise when skilled practices developed outside school are taught in formal educational institutions because they divorce practices from the field of production.
>
> *(2012, p. 158)*

Bernstein, influenced by Vygotsky and Luria, 'sought to characterise the differences between the codes acquired in working-class families and the formal codes of schooling' (ibid.). The concept of 'code' was meant to describe how culture mediates thinking and talking. Codes were further subdivided by Bernstein into 'restricted' working-class codes and 'elaborated' middle-class codes. The choice of terminology is unfortunate because it describes working-class environments in terms of deficiency. Perhaps we could refer to them as 'formal' and 'informal' or 'concrete' and 'abstract' codes, or even 'contextualised' and 'decontextualised' codes.

Ivinson uses the case study method to present four vignettes of youngsters in South Wales. There is Owain who has to be careful where he gets his tattoos from, since they are illegal at his school before the age of sixteen. According to Ivinson, 'the tattoos and body piercing were ways to present himself as older than his actual age and were marks of a working-class identity that he shared with older men' (2012., p. 162). The tattoos were also a link with the past, and an expression of a community under threat and renewing itself (ibid., p. 163).

Sam is a youngster with a love for mountain bikes. He lives to increase his skills in physical activities. 'Corporeality', according to Ivinson, 'afforded him pleasure, independence, purpose and ambition' (2012., p. 166). But he was unlikely to find a sporting academy to attend after leaving school. Dewi is another mountain bike enthusiast. When being interviewed about their BMX activities, Sam and Dewi began by telling stories about working with horses, hunting with their fathers, learning to use guns, breeding ferrets and handling dogs on the farm. These were clearly ritualised bonding activities that many father and sons may no longer carry out in other parts of the British landscape. Parents in these locales are passing on skills to the next generation, although usually these skills are not valued by a capitalist educational system.

Interestingly, these skills are also a mix of modern skills (BMX activities) and older feudal skills (such as hunting). The former provides the boys with status among their peers but the latter may be associated with 'backwardness' and 'shame'. At school the latter skills were not discussed with peers, and it is undoubtedly the case that schools, by and large, do not value informal, everyday skills learned outside of the set curriculum. These 'restricted' codes, as Bernstein might have observed, cannot be used as cultural capital within the educational system.

Ivinson argues that in these 'post-industrial' times, 'by participating in these skilled practices, boys experienced the pleasure and pain of physical work that mimetically referenced the miner's body' (2012, p. 169). They were appropriating the culturally available tools of their environment, and in so doing they 'revitalise the whole system of practice through which the tool was developed'. Relying on Vygotsky's notion of ZPD, Ivinson is saying that the boys were bringing the whole community forward.

Vygotsky and art

Vygotsky's contribution to art analysis does not receive the credit it deserves, probably because it was made quite early on in his research career. Like the rest of the Russian intelligentsia, Vygotsky attached great importance to literature which he 'saw not only as the ultimate embodiment of culture, but as the most concentrated form of life itself' (Kozulin 1990, p. 21).

When Vygotsky became interested in art criticism, Russian art was split between the 'old' realists and the 'new' formalists. The latter group believed that 'We do not experience the familiar, we do not see it' (ibid., p. 25). They set about 'shifting the image' and experimenting with form in order to get away from the 'familiar'. Vygotsky wanted to go beyond the one-sidedness of both realistic (objective) art and formalist art.

Vygotsky famously tried to redefine the subject of study in psychology, instead of merely studying the types of behaviour and cognitions that previous researchers have been interested in. This attitude was probably due to the influence of Boris Eichenbaum, who argued that formalism does not just study literature but questions what the subject matter of literary study should be (Kozulin 1990, p. 27). Throughout this book I have carried out a similar manoeuvre by moving away from both mainstream and critical forms of psychology. I have done this in the hope of convincing the reader that postpsychology should forge its own subject of study, centred around the social conflict.

Many of Vygotsky's mature ideas were initially presented in his PhD thesis, *Psychology of Art*. He wanted to understand art in terms of the conflictual interaction between content and form. This interaction leads to dramatic confrontation and then 'catharsis', a term which owes much to Aristotle's *Poetics* and to a lesser extent Freud's modernised version of it. Catharsis in art 'not only discharges the [build-up] of tension but also transforms human feelings' (ibid., p. 40). Art is 'therefore one of the most complex systems of symbols which helps to transform the original human feelings into what Vygotsky called an esthetic reaction' (Kozulin 1990, p. 43).

He uses this technique coupled with an existential framework to illustrate how the essence of Shakespeare's *Hamlet* is the deliberately in-built obscurity commentators have decried. In other words, 'any tragedy is ineffable, and this is particularly true of *Hamlet*' (Kozulin 1990, p. 55). The central character seems to suffer from both melancholy and indecision. His will is paralysed, just like a mystic's.

In a recent study of Shakespeare's *Henry V*, I have tried to show why existential, Freudian, cognitive and gestalt interpretations of Shakespeare are limiting (Fozooni 2017a). By using a rhetorical form of analysis inspired by Vygotsky, I have tried to shed new light on the text. My findings suggest the co-existence in *Henry V* of three distinct but interrelated discourses (discourses of 'hard' nationalism, 'soft' nationalism, and 'anti-war' opposition). This suggests that the play is overwhelmingly pro-war and pro-state. I invite the interested reader to decide for themselves if I have been successful in my endeavours. At this junction, however, I prefer to switch attention to a neo-Vygotskian study of painting and creativity.

M. Catherene Connery (2010) reminds us that during semiotic mediations, painters employ both physical tools (e.g. paint and paintbrushes, etc.) as well as psychological tools (e.g. mnemonic techniques, language, etc.). While Vygotsky focused on verbal and written language, we are also capable of visual, aural, kinesthetic, tactile and olfactory modes of meaning making. Together, these multi-modal ways of meaning making have been referred to as 'cognitive pluralism' (ibid. 2010, p. 86). We use specific modalities when problem solving depending on our cultural background.

Vygotsky developed a stages theory of symbols to show how all signs are acquired through a four-phase interdependent process. These are loose, relative and flexible stages:

1. In the 'Natural' stage, the meaning maker's thought exists apart from the sign.
2. During the 'Naive Psychology' stage meaning makers begin to master the external structure of signs.
3. In the 'External Signs and Operations' stage, meaning makers overtly employ signs to solve problems.
4. In the 'Ingrowth stage', sign operations grow within the meaning maker, having been internalised.

Connery's study is about seeing if these stages make sense in the development of her own painting skills. A vast array of material was collected and analysed including cards, letters, school work, grades, journal entries, sketchbooks, doodles, photographs, and so on. In analysing the first phase when thought and signs are still separate, she was shocked to discover 'the drawing [she] produced between 3 and 7 years old reflected the same semiotic means and meanings for [her] best work some twenty years later' (2010, p. 92). Her primary brushstrokes can be compared to the primary expressions of vocalisations by babies learning language. Her choice of colour schemes reflects closely the solid colours her parents dressed her in at this age. Many of the signs used in this phase go on to develop into 'repetitive signs or leitmotifs' (ibid., p. 94).

During the second phase, which for her lasted from the age of thirteen to twenty-one, she continued to acquire and refine semiotic meanings. Experimenting with different materials and media helped her to 'master the external structure of signs' which one would expect from Vygotsky's elaborations. Her personality was also being forged at this time and she realised a preference for abstract oil paintings as opposed to realistic watercolour paintings. Physical tools were constantly being refashioned as she immersed herself in the psychological world of past masters and role models.

The third phase of her artistic development is characterised by the acquisition of a core visual language. A retrospective of her work led to an epiphany in which she 'consciously discovered the existence of the recurrent signs that had unconsciously emerged in the first two stages' (Connery 2010, p. 98). Signs become internalised, active and intentional which allowed her to communicate her ideas (ibid, p. 100).

The fourth and final phase of her development is hallmarked by an expansion and elaboration of her core visual language. A 'playful tension emerged between abstractionism, representationalism and realism' in her paintings (Connery 2010, p. 102). She concludes, 'In becoming painters, we call on the first muse of oral speech to construct a second, visual language' (ibid., p. 103).

Seance with Vygotsky: *who ya gonna call?*

I have only been able to skim the surface of Vygotskian studies in this chapter. There is a vast amount of research out there under various umbrella terms, such as 'activity theory', or 'cultural-historical psychology', or even 'cultural psychology'. The researchers in each strand have placed the emphasis on a slightly different aspect of Vygotsky's original work. I do not wish to get involved in the minutia of differences that separate them. I do not belong to any of them and, frankly, I find the turf war between them somewhat tedious and irrelevant. Instead, in this concluding section I would like to provide a brief flavour of the most radical studies being carried out in the neo-Vygotskian tradition.

Let us imagine you work in a medical or legal setting and wish to understand some of the organisational problems that are hampering your labour and causing a sense of alienation. *Who ya gonna call? Ghostbusters?* No, of course not, don't be silly. You call Yrjö Engeström. His work is all about understanding tools (physical as well as psychological), and how subjects use them to adapt or change their environment. Presenting his work visually in the form of the famous 'Engeström triangle', he shows how the division of labour and the community rules governing an organisation have a profound impact on its aims and achievements. What is more, his work is very practical – usually it involves an attempt to understand obstacles in an organisational setting and overcome them. In the process of reflecting on all this, the subject (individually, but more often collectively) creates an expansive learning ZPD for everyone involved (Engeström 1995).

Let us imagine you are a teacher working with working-class pupils from a Latino-American background. You wish to help them to improve their computer-mediated learning skills. *Who ya gonna call?* Well, how about Carmen M. Martinez-Roldan and Peter Smagorinsky? They use Vygotsky's observations about play to facilitate learning among their own students: 'In play, a child is always above his average age, above his daily behaviour; in play it is as though he were a head taller than himself' (Vygotsky, quoted in Martínez-Roldán and Smagorinsky 2011, p. 165). In line with many neo-Vygotskians, they also shift the emphasis to a collective ZPD which is a far more realistic and interesting space for investigation. Using Vygotsky, they show how a variety of 'ways of knowing' are built into the best video games and how some 'students used this experience as an opportunity to become producers [and not mere consumers] of their own [digital media] ideological material' (ibid., p. 173). They propose 'interweaving' as a much more accurate metaphor of collective learning rather than the clumsy 'scaffolding' metaphor used by some neo-Vygotskians.

Let us imagine you are a protestor involved in a demonstration. You wish to comprehend better your surroundings and your own activities as part of the collective effort. *Who ya gonna call?* I would suggest calling Mastaneh Shah-Shuja (2008). She applies an overwhelming array of concepts and ideas from Vygotsky, Bakhtin and activity theory to show how the class struggle evolves in a space she calls the 'zone of proletarian development'. In fact, she suggests that in all social movements there is an ongoing struggle between this proletarian zone of development and its bourgeois counterpart. She offers tools for strengthening the former at the expense of the latter.

And finally, let us imagine you are sick and tired of a certain interpretation of developmental psychology based on Piaget's structuralism and his universalist stages theory of learning. You wish to learn about alternative forms of developmental psychology. *Who ya gonna call?* Two authors come to mind. The first is Yuriy V. Karpov who has penned a very useful book expounding a neo-Vygotskian model of child development (Karpov 2005). Starting with some very sound criticisms of Vygotsky's limitations, Karpov has offered us a more nuanced and flexible model based on the mastery of tools and signs. I find his approach very refreshing. A second author working in the same field who deserves a great deal of credit is John R. Morss (1996). Taken together Karpov and Morss have come up with the components of an alternative model of development that could be integrated into postpsychology.

Going beyond Vygotsky?

> You'll never find a rainbow if you're looking down.
>
> *Charlie Chaplin*

One way of extending Vygotsky may be through the contributions of Klaus Holzkamp (1927–1995). Politically, the German student movement of the 1960s–1970s was the bedrock of Holzkamp's approach to critical psychology. Epistemologically, Papadopoulus (2009, p. 164) detects a gradual shift in Holzkamp's thinking over the years from structuralist (and universalist) assumptions to a closer affinity with post-structuralism. It was within this movement that he learned about oppression and the human agency to deliver liberation. This movement was inspired by 'neomarxist critical theory of the Frankfurt School' as well as 'atheoretical anti-authoritarianism' (Tolman 1989, p. 629).

As a lecturer at the Free University of Berlin he participated in protests against the Shah of Iran's visit to Berlin in July 1967. The ensuing police brutality led to a protestor's death and this galvanised the whole movement (Tolman 1994, pp. 3–4). Sociology and psychology were 'particularly criticised for their blind reproduction and legitimation of repressive bourgeois social relations' (ibid.). Similarly, both behaviourism and psychoanalysis begin 'with some assumptions about the nature of the individual psyche, create from those assumptions a theory of society, which [they] then introject back into the individual' (ibid., p. 61). At a famous conference in September 1968 the majority of students argued: 'There is no "critical" or "oppositional" psychology! SMASH PSYCHOLOGY!' (ibid., p. 10). A minority grouping believed that a genuinely critical psychology was still possible. In a very real sense, we are still grappling with the issues foregrounded by this movement.

Holzkamp allied himself to this minority position. He explained that due to the import of a naive form of experimental methodology from the natural sciences, mainstream psychology had become embroiled in a state of permanent crisis (Teo 2000). Naive empiricism, he concluded, 'allows no room for reflection on the question of relevance. Nature is understood as an ontologically given, pre-existing, ordered cosmos of laws, the scientist's task being to gain a foothold on some small piece of it' (Tolman 1994, p. 25). Logical empiricism or positivism is seen by Holzkamp as a retreat from the 'confident expectations of naïve empiricism regarding laws of nature' (ibid., p. 27). Science is reduced by this worldview to a series of statements that form a conceptual pyramid or axiomatic system (ibid.) Karl Popper's falsification theory is viewed as yet another retreat from claims 'to deliver scientific knowledge or truth' (ibid., p. 29). Popper reduced science to methodology and logic and obscured the origins of scientific theories. The issues of relevance and interest were ignored. Holzkamp was also opposed to the schism between the natural and social sciences and tried to overcome it through an interdisciplinary approach, very much in keeping with my position throughout this book (Teo 2014, p. 785). Holzkamp developed a project about the 'historicisation of [the] human psyche on the basis of empirical evidence of various sciences (sociology, history, biology, physiology, ethology, anthropology, archaeology, etc.)' (ibid., p. 1532).

Incapable of imagining potential for change, mainstream psychology mostly serves to cement the power of the ruling class. It views individuals as isolated from concrete circumstances, or in Holzkamp's words, the individual behaviour is rendered de-contextualised or 'worldless' (Teo 2014, p. 1871). The task of critical psychologists follows from this premise: Marxist criticism and emancipation. More specifically, he sought to achieve this by combining natural history, prehistory and the history of human beings: 'Holzkamp considered Darwin's theory of evolution as an adequate framework for the natural historical analyses and Marx's historical materialism as decisive for historical analyses' (ibid., 2000). One distinguishing feature of German critical psychology compared to the Anglo-Saxon variety is the attention paid by the former to matters anthropological. The evolutionary transition from pre-human to human involved at least two qualitative 'leaps': the first leap came when pre-humans started using tools; and the second when the use of tools began to influence the already existing division of functions within social units (Tolman 1989, p. 631).

FIGURE 16.2 Klaus Holzkamp

Critical psychology was to be constructed through the individual subject's mediated perspective. This means that the individual person not only is the subject of activity but also shaped by it (Teo 2014, p. 29). The outlook is, thus, both dialectical and critically phenomenological. As Holzkamp emphasised:

> Reasons for action are … always in the 'first person'. They are always in each case 'my' reasons, i.e., reasons from my standpoint and my perspective. When I ask anyone else about the reasons for her/his actions, I am asking about reasons from her/his standpoint and perspective.
>
> *(2013, p. 285)*

Only human beings possess agency, which is defined as a joint creation and recreation of the world, and this distinguishes us from other living beings (Teo 2014, p. 735). Holzkamp's grasp of dialectics led him to argue that 'traditional psychology did not have any emancipatory relevance; that mainstream psychology is operating with hidden, ideological assumptions; and that the subject-object dichotomy which may make sense in the natural science does not apply to psychology' (ibid., p. 1917).

Holzkamp was also very keen to define subjects within the context of their everyday life (Teo 2014, p. 292). The repetitive and cyclical quality of everyday activities reduces the need for attention and negotiation, enabling people to focus on those problems that require the most effort. Everyday routine also has a comforting quality. Our everyday world is not merely 'social' (as are the worlds of other animals), but distinctly 'societal' (i.e. humans have a cultural experience and a shared history which they use to communicate with each other dialogically). And all this shared culture, history and communication comes about thanks to labour. As Tolman writes,

> It is labour that is new here. Labour is the collective, objectifying alteration of nature … for the purpose of providing in advance for the general welfare. This is what distinguishes a *societal* mode of existence from one that is merely *social*.
>
> *(1994, p. 91, emphasis in the original)*

What formal education sometimes forgets, especially in the natural science disciplines, is that learning and cognition are closely connected to the learner's everyday conduct, personal positions and resources. Studying the *process* of learning is therefore far more informative than a snap-shot testing approach, so beloved by mainstream education. This aspect of Holzkamp's work has not gone unchallenged. According to Haug, 'Holzkamp's account is premised on an all too easy rejection of teaching as such; as if teaching, and the school, cannot but be harmful. This ignores the fact, Haug claims, that Holzkamp himself taught and expected his teaching to have some (emancipatory) effect. Holzkamp's exclusive focus on learning also makes it impossible to ask what teaching entails in practice, and how one can learn how to teach, and teach better' (Painter *et al.* 2009, p. 141).

Some of the concepts created by Holzkamp were meant to be valid for the entire human species in any socio-economic context. For instance, he talked about the 'possibility relation' which 'implies that human action and subjectivity is neither strictly determined nor completely in-determined'

(Teo 2014, p. 785). Through the use of this concept learning comes to be redefined as 'an increase in the action possibilities of the individual as seen by the individual' (Roth *et al.* 2012). Other concepts were designed specifically for understanding capitalist conditions and overcoming them within an emancipatory project. The category of 'restrictive and expansive agency' seeks to formulate the choice we all have as individuals to either accept capitalist norms and follow its dictates (restrictive agency), or to struggle against them collectively (expansive agency). Obviously, this formulation is very similar to Vygotsky's ZPD, whereby 'individuals draw on the potential that arises from their pursuit of common interests' (Teo 2014, p. 2103).

One or two examples may clarify this distinction. In cognition, thinking that merely interprets is referred to as restrictive agency. This kind of agency fails to take into account 'societal mediation', and everything is interpreted in terms of immediate situation: 'thus the frustrated man beats his wife, smashes the machine, or, alternatively, concludes that he is himself constitutionally inadequate' (Tolman 1989, p. 632). By contrast, the kind of thinking that goes beyond mere interpretation and actually comprehends and takes on board the larger picture becomes generalised agency. In this way, Holzkamp 'translated' mainstream psychology's concepts around motivation, need, emotion and cognition into a new vocabulary. This is not merely word play. It is turning psychology upside-down, so that it can be utilised by the proletarian subject.

This distinction can be extended to methodological issues. Holzkamp (following Lewin) sees the statistical variety of mainstream psychology, which abstracts from individual cases and ignores their concrete complexity, as based on Aristotle. This form of psychology often seems irrelevant to the subject who provided the data. The second kind of psychology that is based on Galilean thinking generalises differently and does illuminate somewhat the concrete experience of the subject. Parallel to the outlook of A. R. Luria and Oliver Sacks (see Chapter 18 in this volume), 'the move from the "Aristotelian" to the "Galilean" is clearly reflected in the reduced emphasis upon the statistical analysis of large samples to a more "clinical" form of research in which the research subject becomes a co-researcher' (Tolman 1989, p. 634).

We should also be attentive to those aspects of Holzkamp's analysis that were superior to Vygotsky's. Politically speaking, Holzkamp was more astute than Vygotsky, Bakhtin and Leontiev. Holzkamp understood that it was 'necessary to extend and complement a critique of science with a critique of society' (Papadopoulus 2009, p. 163). Vygotsky and his disciples either did not see the need to criticise Soviet capitalism (since he worked from the assumption that the USSR was either a socialist or communist entity), or refrained from thorough criticism of science and society in order not to risk the wrath of the ruling class. Consequently, Holzkamp was more supportive of autonomous working-class struggles against capital and the state.

His committed political engagement allowed Holzkamp to posit a stronger critique of the role of the expert researcher/clinician. In this regard, Vygotsky and co. seem rather atavistic. Holzkamp denied psychology any 'privileged access to the subject. Psychology cannot engage with subjectivity itself; that is what people can do. Psychology can only engage with the conditions which oppress subjectivity' (Papadopoulus 2009, p. 164). Both German critical psychology and soviet activity theory can be used to interrogate relations of power and social control but the former feels ready-made for the task, whereas the latter, one feels, needs to be cajoled into it.

Last words

I hope I have managed to convince the sceptic reader that Lev Vygotsky is a seminal voice that needs to be heard, cherished and elaborated. Although politically he erred by confusing Bolshevism and communism, his methodological and theoretical contributions are as fresh as they have ever been. He truly is the Mozart *and* Bob Dylan of postpsychology.

17

BAKHTIN COMPLETES VYGOTSKY

> 'Nurse, where are we going?' 'To the morgue'. 'But I haven't died yet!' 'The doc said "to the morgue" – to the morgue it is!' 'But what is wrong with me?' 'The autopsy will show!'
>
> *Old Russian joke*

Bakhtin: from unorthodox Marx to mystic Christ?

In *Star Trek VI: The Undiscovered Country* (1991, dir. Nicholas Meyer) the Klingons are invited aboard the *Enterprise* for dinner. While partaking of a sumptuous feast, nerves jangle and insinuations and veiled threats fly precariously about the table. They discuss everything under the stars including the disputed authorship question in Shakespeare. Personally, I am satisfied with James Shapiro's earthbound treatment of the problem. In *Contested Will: Who Wrote Shakespeare* (2010), Shapiro discusses and dismisses all the major alternative authors for the plays, from Bacon to Marlowe to Oxford to Queen Elizabeth. Once I finished reading Shapiro's definitive work, I stopped worrying about the 'authorship problem' and learned to love the plays. I have now read Hamlet, for example, in three different languages: English (Hamlet), Klingon (Khamlet) and Farsi (هملت). All three versions have their charm, although I must confess an abiding fondness for the original Farsi! As the dinner proceeds, both Captain Kirk (William Shatner) and General Chang (Christopher Plummer) become increasingly possessive about an individual they have never met. They both claim Shakespeare for their respective cultures, and dispute vigorously whether Shakespeare/Shex'pir was an earthling or a Klingon!

In a sense, we have the same problem on our hands with Bakhtin (1895–1975), Vološinov (1895–1936) and Medvedev (1892–1938). Who wrote which book? Did they collaboratively write their earliest books? Was Bakhtin's book published under Vološinov's name in order to confuse the Soviet censors? Were they deliberately promoting the notion of 'collective authorship' as a critique of capitalist commodity production? Was plagiarism involved? Were they just lazy referencers? In all honesty, dear reader, I no longer care! I really don't give a damn! At the end of the day, I prefer headbutting the Klingon General Chang than banging my head against a horde of academic nerds pursuing the authorship problem.

Scholars have charted Bakhtin's intellectual journey from a youthful engagement with Marx to a rejection of the class struggle and the embracing of a mystical Christianity (Vice 1997; Coates 1998). This may or may not be an accurate description of his development. But for me a far more intriguing question is whether Bakhtin was on the side of the working class or that of reaction? No, let me rephrase it more precisely. The ultimate question becomes: can we utilise Bakhtin for a better analysis of class which would 'empower' the working class?

Bakhtin and E. P. Thompson

One possible solution to the above question has been offered by Marc W. Steinberg (1997) who argues that Bakhtin's theory of language should be used to complement (rather than displace) Thompson's class analysis of the English working class in the early nineteenth century (Thompson [1963] 2013). Steinberg starts by reminding us that Thompson did not ignore language as a mediator between class and consciousness. Indeed, Thompson discusses culture throughout his analysis, not just experientially but also linguistically, and as part of identity formation. There is his discourse analysis of John Bunyan's *The Pilgrim's Progress*, (ibid., pp. 34–38), his analysis of the law against Combination (ibid., pp. 543–569), his numerous references to Percy Bysshe Shelley, his description of Lincolnshire ballad singers as propagandists (ibid., p. 145), and so on and so forth. In fact, Thompson is very clear that workers 'created political agency through language' (Steinberg 1997, p. 476). The boundaries of the 'moral economy' of the working class are also set by language (ibid., p. 477). He sketches the development of the language of moral revolt in Chartism and Luddism, etc. Part of this language was created by the workers themselves and part of it was appropriated from the rhetoric of the ruling class and turned against them. In other works, Thompson talks about carnivals, a subject very close to Bakhtin's heart (1993).

Bakhtin's notion of 'dialogism' is not as different from Marx's dialectics as postmodernists have made out. Dialogism is defined as everyday dialogue rendered precise in its social, historical and ideological nature (Roberts 2004, p. 891). In fact, I would argue that dialogics and dialectics are very much complimentary. Steinberg agrees, 'The dialogic perspective underscores that inter-class dialogue often involves clashes of meanings' (1997, p. 479). Every word is contested and this is even more so, Vološinov would argue, in the exercise of class power and resistance. The arguments that social classes expressed in nineteenth-century England over the meaning of 'rights', 'commons' and 'enclosures' are replicated today, sometimes with the same words being utilised, and sometimes in a modified fashion.

Steinberg goes on to illustrate the linguistic struggles within various 'speech genres' among the early nineteenth-century Spitalfields silk weavers of East London. These weavers used the image of 'the honourable artisan' to cultivate a moral economy and to strengthen their negotiating hand in disputes with their masters. The weavers may not have questioned the fundamental legitimacy of private property but developed their moral economy through counter-hegemonic language to protect their trade from foreign competition, low wages and unemployment:

> [I]s not all acquired property protected by law, and is not that just? Why then should it not be just to protect natural property which is labour. Labour is the only property a poor man has, which is the root and riches of the great and mighty, who are able to protect themselves, while the poor have neither the means nor the power of self-defence without the assistance of the law.
>
> *(Anon., quoted in Steinberg 1997, p. 484)*

The weavers used Adam Smith's work to argue that 'labour is the fount of all wealth' (Steinberg 1997, p. 484). Another bourgeois philosopher, John Locke, was drawn upon in order to contest the individuated definition of 'freedom': 'For what is the end of all government? Is it not to balance the inequities of society?' Without this 'balance' they argued, freedom would be 'nothing more nor less, in application to the productive classes, than freedom for the powerful to oppress and defraud the weak' (ibid.).

When the level of class struggle is not sufficiently intense for people to forge their own language, the class enemy's linguistic repertoire is appropriated instead. In Steinberg's words: 'Rather than opposing the manufacturers and free traders with an avowedly socialist language, the weavers and their advocates created a counter-hegemonic strategy that was consonant with their principles of collectivism' (1997, p. 496). As with Bakhtin, these weavers understood that the words in use were half theirs.

I wish to end this section by briefly mentioning one more exemplar of class history from below, being enhanced through Bakhtinian concepts. John Michael Roberts (2004) has looked at plebeian dialogue in the public sphere in London between 1684–1812 (in other words, the period preceding the Spitalfields weavers' revolt cited above). More specifically, Roberts observes how a public space, Tyburn at Hyde Park, that was set aside for public executions by the state, 'aroused not terror and fear in the populace of London, but rather sympathy and compassion towards the condemned' (ibid., p. 885). One dismayed bourgeois observer complains: 'What is most shocking to a thinking Man, is, the Behaviour of the Condemn'd, whom (for the greatest Part) you'll find, either drinking madly, or uttering the vilest Ribaldry, and jeering others, that are less impenitent' (Mandeville, quoted in ibid., p. 897). Dialogue had become dialogic. This was key to Tyburn's disappearance as a public space in 1783 when executions became private affairs, conducted behind closed prison gates. Roberts shows how Hyde Park and Tyburn were taken over by the people and how the monologic discourse of the state was transformed into a dialogic plebeian counter-discourse.

Bakhtin's dialogics and Vygotskian dialectics

> I thought I'd begin by reading a poem by Shakespeare, but then I thought, why should I? He never reads any of mine.
>
> *Spike Milligan*

Following on from our discussion above, Elizabeth Jayne White (2014) has investigated the central notions of Bakhtinian dialogics and Vygotskian dialectics in the classroom. She defines dialogism as 'between-ness', and dialectics as 'one-ness through processes of conflict or contradiction' (ibid., p. 222). She, unlike me, does not see these concepts as natural allies, and I think part of the problem lies in the definitions she employs. She cites a number of irreconcilable differences between Bakhtinian and Vygotskian approaches to education which I will scrutinise below.

White describes Vygotsky's general approach to education in these terms:

> Bringing Marx, Spinoza and Hegelian dialectics to bear, Vygotsky's quest then was to emancipate the learner to higher psychological thought processes through the dialectic of everyday and scientific levels of thought, as a pathway to freedom and by paying attention to social context and history.
>
> *(2014, p. 223)*

She contrasts this with dialogics which is characterised by 'a refusal to close off, finalise or predetermine outcomes (where dialectics seeks a resolution)' (ibid., p. 223).

This is a very crude and liberal interpretation of Bakhtin (tinged with suggestive middle-class anarchism). But it is a viewpoint that is given credibility by virtue of the fact that Bakhtin himself came to reject 'Marxism' late in life. However, what Bakhtin and his contemporary liberal followers such as Elizabeth Jayne White reject is not real Marxism or communism, since neither existed in the USSR, but Bolshevism, Diamat and a bureaucratised form of capitalism. No wonder Bakhtin became critical of official Soviet ideology: 'Take a dialogue and remove the voices … remove the intonations … carve out the abstract concepts and judgments from living words and responses, cram everything into one abstract consciousness – and that's how you get dialectics' (Bakhtin, quoted in White 2014, p. 225). Well, this might be a very necessary rejection of Diamat as expounded by (most forms of) Bolshevism, but had it been levelled at Marx, it would have been met with a swift and uncompromising Tysonesque uppercut!

White goes on to build her sandcastle on ever-receding foundations. For instance, her criticisms of inequality in the teacher-pupil relationship within a zone of proximal development (ZPD) does not take into account years of research by neo-Vygotskians to establish more equal relationships between learners in a ZPD. The teacher role can rotate within a ZPD between participants, especially if the zone consists solely of adults. It is true that in most of his writings Vygotsky postulated development with a clear set of goals in sight. But his developmental scheme was loose, flexible and contingent. And it is also true that Vygotsky did not pay power the attention it deserves. That is where Bakhtin can complete him. As such, a faithful

FIGURE 17.1 Mikhail Bakhtin

synthesiser should have little difficulty in amalgamating the most up-to-date versions of Vygotsky and Bakhtin. Dialogics and dialectics are similar in focusing on the idea of the social and the idea of struggle. They also share the ability to deal with complexity, variety and the analysis of a dynamic process. Both Vygotsky and Bakhtin viewed dialogue as central to human consciousness. Bakhtin described dialectics as 'the very soul of all movement', but by this he meant his own version of it, not the ossified interpretation dominant in official Soviet ideology (Gardiner 2000, p. 12).

A few years back I had the misfortune of having to conduct a discourse analysis of encyclopaedias. The research was slow and ponderous. However, I felt obliged to persevere because my Open University students were constantly quizzing me about the reliability, validity and political credibility of *Wikipedia* as an academic source. In order to make the task manageable I selected three encyclopaedias for comparison: the printed version of the *Encyclopaedia Britannica* was chosen as representative of academically reputable referencing; the online *Encyclopedia of Marxism* as an exemplar of no-holds-barred political referencing; and, finally, *Wikipedia*, the post-modernist, academically derided, project of collective knowledge making.

The choice of what to investigate was dictated by my personal interests and field of knowledge. I ended up analysing three distinct entries for each encyclopaedia: the historical biography of Friedrich Engels; the political interpretation of fascism as a movement and ideology; and the genesis and development of social psychology as a distinct discipline within the social sciences (Fozooni 2012b).

I began by noting that the central classificatory task of encyclopaedias is at the same time an exercise in ideological domination. 'Men of letters' (and the early writers were overwhelmingly men) wrote entries as a way of proving the linear progression of civilisation and their class hegemony. As I observed,

> The philosopher-warriors of the Enlightenment enjoyed a cult status as exalted as anything the contemporary era has to offer Wiki-warriors. Perhaps one could also speculate that both sets of elites had disdain for the unwashed masses equal to their faith in the emancipatory virtues of truth. Here is d'Alembert displaying his class prejudices: 'Doubtless the common people is a stupid animal which lets itself be led into the shadows when nothing better is offered to it. But offer it the truth; if this truth is simple … it will definitely seize on it and will want none other'.
>
> *(D'Alembert, quoted in Fozooni 2012b)*

Part of my findings relate to the different philosophies employed by these three encyclopaedias:

> *Encyclopaedia Britannica*, basing itself on positivist and empiricist epistemologies, pursues data in order to secure an abstract notion of bourgeois truth. *EB* conceals the chaotic, messy process of knowledge

> building and presents the reader with a seemingly unambiguous product consisting of 'objective' units of information … *Encyclopedia of Marxism* by contrast nails its colours to the mast of proletarian struggle. It too seeks a mostly abstract notion of truth but one founded on historical materialism and the dialectical notion of class conflict. It represents a higher form of critical thinking which enhances our ability to perceive things as developing and changing … The epistemological foundation of *Wikipedia* incorporates post-structuralist relativism to critically evaluate subjects. Of the three encyclopaedias discussed here, *Wikipedia* is the most writerly and dialogic source. It may use mostly academic knowledge, but *Wikipedia* does not shirk from everyday knowledge. Truth and political creditability become a matter of protracted negotiation between academic and everyday knowledge.
>
> *(Fozooni 2012b)*

While I was not completely satisfied with any of these sources, I found the *Encyclopaedia Britannica* to be the least politically credible of all. For example, the entry on Engels portrays him as having character flaws, and as both oversensitive to criticism and heartless at the same time. He is reduced to the status of a sidekick of Marx and occasionally a 'hatchetman of the partnership' (ibid.). His editorship of newspapers was a 'guise' whose primary aim was to 'foster some degree of conformity among the faithful' and to sell more copies of *Das Kapital* (ibid.). The *Encyclopaedia Britannica*'s coverage of 'fascism' is even more dismal. It is defined in a slipshod manner. Nowhere in the entry is the reader informed of the anti-working-class, anti-women and homophobic tendencies of fascism. Fascism is not properly demarcated from neo-fascism. When it comes to defining social psychology, the subject matter is delineated narrowly as 'the scientific study of human *behaviour*', validated by a model derived at from the 'hard sciences' (ibid., emphasis in the original).

Compared to the *Encyclopaedia Britannica*, the dialectical approach of the *Encyclopedia of Marxism* and the dialogical perspective of *Wikipedia* seem to be far more sophisticated, especially when the latter two are combined. In opposition to White's views above, I found that dialectics and dialogics can be effectively synthesised in education. Furthermore, these two approaches seem to cover up each other's shortcomings almost instinctively.

Most conveniently for my position, Frank Farmer has pointed out that 'Bakhtin's developmental model of language learning is unmistakeably dialectical in progression' (2005, p. 342). Bakhtin once wrote, 'dialectics was born of dialogue so as to return to dialogue on a higher level' (1986, p. 162).

Bakhtin on the couch

Rachel Pollard has written an excellent book on Bakhtinian psychotherapy (2008). She utilises many concepts and ideas from Bakhtin to enrich therapy. The central aim of therapy, according to Pollard, should be the creation of a safe space where 'internally persuasive discourse' can flourish. Bakhtin defined it in these terms: 'Internally persuasive discourse – as opposed to one that is externally autorotative – is … tightly interwoven with "one's own words". In the everyday rounds of our consciousness, the internally persuasive discourse is half ours and half someone else's' (1981, p. 346). For internally persuasive discourse 'nothing is sacred and everything is open to question and critique, including its own suppositions' (Pollard 2008, p. 4).

The concept of 'dialogism' is also welcomed because it allows for a socialised 'self' which retains its individual creativity and dynamism (Pollard 2008, p. 17). Dialogism encourages the shared creation of meaning between the therapist and client. Being in an intersubjective relationship with others allows us to see those parts of ourselves that are hidden (ibid., p. 57). Dialogism can bring forth those voices of the self that have been suppressed or silenced due to shame or fear. Of course, these voices may have been silenced for good reasons and Bakhtin did not attend to the trauma that may be reignited when long-suppressed voices are released without proper preparation.

Bakhtinian therapists become sensitised to the fact that the client is 'polyphonic' (i.e. they have many voices within them), as well as being within a 'heteroglossia' (i.e. an environment with competing cultures, languages and ideas). Heteroglossia is the 'manifestation in language of the tensions, conflicts and struggles that are endemic in class-ridden societies' (Pollard 2008, p. 77). Recently, some researchers have widened the definition of an 'utterance' to include non-linguistic elements, 'particularly situational factors such as material objects, facial expressions, gestures, and institutional conditions' (ibid., p. 137).

My own minor contribution in this field has been to show how the application of more Bakhtinian and Vygotskian ideas can further strengthen the radical credentials of cognitive analytic therapy (CAT). This is a form of time-limited therapeutic intervention in the UK, which claims success with a variety of psychological problems such as depression, trauma, eating disorders, anxiety-related disorders, borderline personality disorder and histrionic personality disorder (Fozooni 2010). While Leiman (1997) and Ryle

(1994) have already introduced Vygotskian and Bakhtinian ideas into CAT, I feel that a number of concepts have remained underutilised: polyphonic traveller, chronotope, activity and performance, to name be but a few (Fozooni 2010, pp. 134–138). The addition of more Vygotskian and Bakhtinian ideas, I have argued, would turn CAT into an even more effective therapy. Bakhtin's ideas focus on unique events and on 'little, fleeting details', which is precisely the reason they are so useful for understanding therapeutic interactions (Shotter and Billig 1998, p. 14). It moves the problem from inside individual minds into a linguistic interaction between people.

Elvis the pelvis: carnivalesque and bad taste!

The arrogance of the ruling class and those middle-class mandarins who have chosen to side with them knows no bounds. Not content with exploiting and oppressing us, they even insist on formulating our 'identities'. The poorest section of the US working class is often referred to as 'white trash', as a crude form of stigmatisation and division (Wray and Newitz 1997).

I sympathise. For years, I have been asked to identify myself in meaningless 'human resources' forms. For years, I have written 'Klingon warrior'! Not once has a 'human resource' person inquired about the veracity of my claim. For years, I have had people asking me inquisitively: 'Where are you from?' For years, I would tell them: 'I'm from the working class'! A response that never seems to satisfy any of them: 'No, where are you from *really*?', they would insist.

In an attempt to provide a more satisfactory response to the latter question I sought to clarify my identity, and within a week or two of searching I succeeded. I remembered a line uttered in *The Big Bang Theory* by Leonard Hofstadter (Johnny Galecki). He was angry with Sheldon Cooper (Jim Parsons) at the time: 'Mm, Sheldon, you didn't have a personality, you just had some shows you liked' (*The Big Bang Theory*, Series 7, Episode 16). Perfect, I thought, I too will discover my new identities through TV!

Movies such as *Willy Wonka & the Chocolate Factory* (1971, dir. Mel Stuart, starring Gene Wilder) and *Charlie and the Chocolate Factory* (2005, dir. Tim Burton, starring Johnny Depp) taught me clearly that I am not just working class, but the Oompa Loompa of academia. After all, I am short, orange, work harder than my colleagues, and I get paid in chocolate! It all fits. Within days of watching these two movies I came across another, very different movie, called *Casino* (1995, dir. Martin Scorsese, starring Robert

De Niro and Joe Pesci), which introduced me to the derogatory term, 'sand-nigger'. Interesting term, I thought, I wonder what it means. Thankfully, Joe Pesci was on hand to 'ice' a 'sand-nigger' in the next scene, who turned out to look remarkably like ... me! So at least part of the English-speaking world sees me as a negro of the dune variety. Fine, I thought. Happy to use it as a designation, so long as I am allowed to 'reaccentuate' (Bakhtin) it as '*field* sand-nigger' (Fozooni 2006).

The final piece of my identity jigsaw was provided by movies such as *The Wrestler* (2008, dir. Darren Aronofksy, starring Mickey Rourke), *8 Mile* (2002, dir. Curtis Hanson, starring Eminem), and *Monster* (2003, dir. Aileen Wuornos, starring Charlize Theron and Christina Ricci). At this junction I cheated and augmented my TV research with a book, Wray and Newitz's *White Trash: Race and Class in America* (1997). The more I learned about this subsection of the US working class, the more I understood them. The more I understood them, the more I identified with their predicaments. By the time I had finished the book I knew that I am, in terms of ethics and aesthetics at least, part 'white trash' myself!

I was now ready to present myself to the idiot doyens of identity politics. My new identity seems to be as rich as it is convoluted: I am a working-class, Oompa Loompa, Klingon warrior, with distinct field sand-nigger and white trash characteristics. Now try putting that in a flipping human resource form!

The white trash described by Gael Sweeney (1997) seem to have a similar complex story. White trash are described as 'an aesthetic of the flashy, the inappropriate, the garish. Unlike camp, which is a product of an urban, elite, and gay sensibility, White Trash has its roots in the South' (ibid., p. 249). White trash, Sweeney believes, are separated from the rest of the working class by their (almost permanent) lack of employment. Powerless to do anything else, they 'collect junk and show it off' (ibid., p. 250). Dolly Parton and Elvis Presley are icons of white trash culture. Sweeney argues that much of the disdain held for white trash by the dominant society has its roots in 'a fear of miscegenation and contamination from mixing with them' (ibid., p. 253). Rumours about Elvis's 'secret black father' find fertile ground in Memphis precisely because of these anxieties.

Bakhtin's 'carnivalesque' refers to a space that counters authority and promotes unruly, vulgar and undisciplined proletarian pleasures. For white trash, this may be expressed when

> they are gambling in Las Vegas, partying in the streets of New Orleans, buying sombreros in Acapulco, off on package tours to Hawaii and

> Florida. These are also, not coincidentally, the locations of Elvis's movies (*Viva Las Vegas, King Creole, Fun in Acapulco, Blue Hawaii, Paradise, Hawaiian Style, Follow that Dream*).
>
> *(Sweeney 1997, p. 254)*

Carnivalesque allows for belly laughter, bad taste, irreverent music, parody, excess in eating and sex. In Sweeney's words, 'The body is released from surveillance and social control: screaming and yelling, as at an Elvis concert, is not only sanctioned, but encouraged' (ibid., p. 255). This explains why 'the Elvis period most beloved by the White Trash Aesthetic is the seventies: white jumpsuit, overweight, and in your face' (ibid.). Of course, Elvis the political figure was anything but subversive. His collaboration with President Nixon and denunciation of the Beatles as a satanic-communist influence is testimony to his naivety. But as an artist his performances were harbingers of something very different for the white trash. Bakhtin allows us to understand, feel and even communicate with a culture that mainstream US culture can never come to appreciate or respect.

The dancing Bakhtin

> 'If I can't dance to it, it's not my revolution' – Emma Goldman, allegedly!
>
> *Shulman (1991)*

> For where there is a dance, there also is the Devil.
>
> *John Chrysostom, the Archbishop of Constantinople*

For some unfathomable reason, I have the urge to write about a subject I know absolutely nothing about – dancing! And I want to write about it utilising a man who by all accounts was not much of a dancer himself – Bakhtin! And I want to situate this study in a country I have never had the pleasure of visiting – Turkey! This section, I fear, already smacks more of bravado than experimentation. Let's get down to it before I have second thoughts.

There are some very silly people (and I am sorry to say that a few of them are sanctimonious academics) who believe that carnivals are too frivolous to play a role in escalating the class struggle. There is another group of highly elitist connoisseurs who believe that if a thinker has become too famous then he or she cannot possibly be worth taking seriously. 'Bakhtin', they would argue, 'has spawned his own industry, just like Shakespeare and Freud before him. Best stay away. Best select more niche *auteurs*'! Well, I beg to differ.

Let's refresh our memory regarding the protests that took place in Taksim Square in Istanbul, Turkey, on 28 May 2013. It started as a protest against building proposals for a complex with a new mosque in Gezi Park, the last spot of greenery in Taksim, and it soon developed into days of angry carnival against the Turkish ruling class and its embodiment, Recep Tayyip Erdoğan (Sherlock 2013). The initial relatively small demonstrations were soon boosted in number due to the security force's harsh response. The protests spread to at least seventy-eight other cities. Since the economy was doing relatively well at the time, it would be fair to say that most complaints were directed at the regime's authoritarian encroachment on people's personal life choices. The majority of protestors were left-wing, secular working- and middle-class youngsters.

The protests had the feel of carnivalesque as defined by Bakhtin. They were both violent and peaceful. Society and its values were being turned upside-down. Children would play in the wreckage left over from the barricades. Environmental concerns meshed into gender equality demands and criss-crossed with more overt political demands about protecting the commons from privatisation. Football supporters joined the protestors and anarchists, leftist communists, Leninists and liberals mingled (relatively) happily together. The slogans showed a level of political sophistication and humour usually absent from bureaucratic demonstrations. Protestors resisted water cannons, tasers, gas canisters, plastic bullets and baton charges.

As Ömer Şener has observed, for a few days at least Taksim Square became 'the people's second life' (Bakhtin 1984, p. 6) and allowed for restrictions on drinking and public dancing and intermingling to be suspended (Şener 2013, p. 40). In the same way that children were observed by Vygotsky to act ahead of their devolvement during play, carnivalesque allows adults to try things they might not have done before. Şener cites 'graffiti, bowdlerised humour, political cartoons, use of twitter and other social networks, and the use of swearing and inflammatory language through these networks to criticise those in authority' (ibid., p. 41).

Carnivalesque laughter became a chief communication device among the protestors and wider society. Numerous cartoons of penguins went viral (apparently a national channel decided to show a documentary about penguins rather than cover the riots in an amateurish attempt by authorities to contain the spread of rioting). Şener also argues that 'in line with the Bakhtinian notion of "polyphony", there was no central authority among the protesters, nor was there a hierarchical structure to restrict views and silence unwanted voices' (2013, p. 41). The other side of the coin was that demands became blurred and anger was diffused.

FIGURE 17.2 Protests in Taksim Gezi Park, 2013

In her outstanding contribution to the history of dancing, Barbara Ehrenreich reminds us that in ancient times, dance did not 'simply merge the individual into the group' through de-individuation, but individuals also sought to shine for their skills and talents (2008, p. 27). Advocates of the social identity theory of crowds would wholeheartedly agree with this generalisation. What was lost, but is sometimes momentarily regained during moments of social rupture such as the Gezi Park protests, was the sense of love, equality and ecstasy that people of various cultures enjoyed. But with the rise of monotheism, 'nature would be dead, joy would be postponed to an afterlife, and the forests would no longer ring with the sound of pipes and flutes' (ibid., p. 57). An exaggerated stance that Ehrenreich herself corrects a few lines later by discussing ecstatic Judaism and

Christianity. We could add to this the ecstatic version of Islam which has deep roots among the Sufis of Turkey. Nevertheless, in societies which currently sanctify a puritanical perspective of Islam, carnivalesque becomes even more precious in outlining an alternative philosophy of existence (cf. Shah-Shuja 2008, pp. 119–170).

Ehrenreich observes how everything good about carnivals can become spectacularised by reaction and turned into its opposite. For example, in fifteenth-century Europe, 'Church authorities often tried to divert the energies of the revellers from the Feast of Fools to the more uplifting spectacle of the ecclesiastical plays' (Ehrenreich 2008, p. 91). This tendency became intensified in the sixteenth and seventeenth centuries. Many sports came under attack: bull running, bear baiting, boxing, wrestling, football (ibid, p. 98). All this brings us conveniently back where we started with E. P. Thompson. He (and others such as Christopher Hill and Max Weber) explained how the repression of festivities was a by-product of the emergence of capitalism: 'The middle classes had to learn to calculate, save, and "defer gratification"; the lower classes had to be transformed into a disciplined, factory-ready, working class' (ibid., p. 100). The suppression of the Gezi Park protests shows how little the agenda of the ruling class has changed!

Concluding remarks on Bakhtin

I would like to end this section by discussing the 'Shchekino experiment'. This is not the kind of experiment you might come across in a psychology textbook. It refers to a failed attempt, spearheaded by the Bolsheviki bourgeoisie, to increase productivity in the former USSR. The leader of the USSR at the time was Leonid Brezhnev (1906–1982), who was slightly younger than Bakhtin (1895–1975). To refresh your memory, Brezhnev is the one who looked mummified even before his death! He became the General Secretary of the Central Committee in 1964 and retained his post (as General Secretaries invariably do!) until his death in 1982. He realised that labour productivity was declining in the USSR and unless this trend was reversed, it could spell doom and gloom for the ruling class.

The source of this decline was in the rulers' inability to extract sufficient surplus value from the workers and also the underutilisation of what was extracted for further expansion. Workers' resistance, through strikes, sabotage, go-slows, absenteeism, non-communication and alcoholism was defeating all attempts to improve the quality and quantity of the socially produced surplus (Arnot 1981, p. 40). The decline required a new growth strategy and this became quite evident after Stalin's death in 1953. Following Marx, Bob Arnot describes this 'changeover from the extensive expansion of the absolute surplus value to the intensive expansion of the relative surplus' (ibid., p. 41, but see also Chapter 13 in this volume on Sohn-Rethel).

The Shchekino experiment was one such attempt to increase surplus, regain command over labour and transform 'formal' domination over labour to 'real' domination. It was implemented at the Shchekino Chemical Combine in Tula on 1 October 1967. The aim was to reduce absolute surplus value extraction and increase relative extraction instead. In other words, to tie in workers' performance to profits, to give the workers a stake in the Chemical Combines fortunes. Over-employment was tackled through disposing of surplus workers and various tasks were merged in order to achieve a more efficient technical division of labour. Labour and material resources were rationalised within the plant.

Arnot relates that the initial signs were encouraging, 'Between 1967–1974 the volume of production grew 2.5 times … the productivity of labour increased 3.1 times … average wages grew by 44%' (1981, p. 45). But problems began to emerge almost immediately, and in the main they were problems of psychology. 'From the outset,' Arnot explains, 'the experiment was faced with the problem of explaining to workers, in a supposedly socialist society, that they are to be made redundant' (ibid, p. 47). After nearly sixty years of propaganda about a supposedly classless utopia this was difficult. Thus, instead of talking about 'dismissal' they talked about 'the utilisation of resources' (ibid.). It was even harder to move from a monologic discourse (bosses instructing workers what will happen) to a dialogic interaction (where managers and workers solve productivity problems collaboratively). Neither the sacked workers nor the retained ones ever felt comfortable engaging in a genuine dialogue with their masters, and with good reason.

Those workers who remained had to be retrained and made more flexible. Again, in twenty-first-century America or Western Europe, subjected to years of neo-liberal capitalist reorganisation, this may not sound like an insurmountable challenge, but in the capitalist Soviet Union of the 1960s, with its overmanning and inertia, it represented a genuine obstacle. The other problem was one of maintaining the momentum of initial successes. Despite the Politburo's support, only 1,000 enterprises had made the switch by 1977. 'For the experiment to have been successfully generalised', argues Arnot, 'it would have been necessary for the ruling group to reintroduce unemployment on a wide scale and not just on the limited scale of dismissals introduced at Shchekino' (1981, p. 53). This amounted to open class warfare, something Brezhnev was not ready for. His successors also saw the need for a switch from formal to real domination of labour but Andropov and Chernenko failed to deliver this, while Gorbachev's more substantial changes came too late to prevent the break-up of the Soviet Union in 1991.

Brezhnev and Bakhtin both witnessed the same events throughout their lives, but from different sides of the barricade. They were both concerned with issues of labour discipline, authority, communication and freedom, although Brezhnev's standpoint was from the top and Bakhtin's from below. Brezhnev used the dead language of bureaucracy and a depoliticised economy to talk at the people. Bakhtin, by contrast, inhabited a sociological, psychological and cultural domain and preferred to talk with the people. It is my argument that a great deal of the hostility Bakhtin displayed towards communism, the class struggle and dialectics was in fact a healthy response to a capitalist USSR, its bourgeois rulers and the Diamat philosophy that was used to justify their dictatorship over the people.

18

LURIA COMPLETES BAKHTIN WHO COMPLETED VYGOTSKY

> A communist died, and since he was an honest man albeit atheist, he was sentenced to rotate spending one year in Hell and one year in Heaven. One year passed and Satan said to God: 'Take this man as fast as possible. Because he turned all my young demons into Young Pioneers, I have to restore some order.' Another year passed, Satan meets God again and tells him: 'Lord God, it's my turn now.' God replied: 'First of all, don't call me Lord God, but instead Comrade God; second, there is no God; and one more thing – don't distract me or I'll be late to the Party meeting.
>
> *Old Russian joke*

Alexander Romanovich Luria (1902–1977) was content to play second fiddle to Vygotsky, even after the latter's untimely death in 1934. Luria had neither his friend's charisma, nor, frankly, his flights of imagination. He once claimed, 'I divide my career into two periods: the small and insignificant period before my meeting with Vygotsky and the more important and essential one after the meeting' (Levitin 1982, p. 159). Ah, yes, the good old days, when psychologists somehow managed to be both smart *and* humble!

However, if we accept such self-deprecation, we run the risk of depriving ourselves of a truly original line of inquiry that Luria launched post-Vygotsky. It is high time we gave Luria the accolades he deserves, since he is (almost) as important as Vygotsky for a project of post-psychology. So, Alexander Romanovich Luria, this is *your* life! Take a bow, son. Take a bow!

Luria and memory

Towards the end of his life, Luria published *The Mind of a Mnemonist: A Little Book about a Vast Memory* (1987). The book represents thirty years of research into the case of Solomon Shereshevsky (or S.). His was a highly unusual memory which followed neither Ebbinghaus's 'forgetting curve' law, nor Bartlett's insight that we generalise experience into 'schemata' (Wagoner 2012, p. 133). S. had the remarkable ability to remember large numbers, non-sense syllables, and even lines from Dante's *Inferno* (in Italian, which he didn't speak). He even remembered the kind of memories from early childhood that most of us forget. Luria concluded that S.'s 'memory was limitless' (ibid., p. 134), although it is just as fascinating to note that S. eventually discovered that he could occasionally delete facts from his memory with just a little conscious effort.

S.'s abilities were due to his 'innate' capacity to mentally imagine in vivid, colourful patterns everything he saw or heard. Everything 'immediately produced an experience of light and colour, as well as a sense of touch and taste' (Wagoner 2012). Every item was converted to a visual image and each would be remembered perfectly so long as S. was given enough time to encode the images and there was no interference or distraction. His synaesthesia was more connected than that of 'normal' subjects. S. seemed to have four of his senses joined (only his sense of smell was not intertwined with the rest). Over time he developed various cultural strategies to augment his natural talent, somewhat akin to the mediaeval 'art of memory' as explained by Francis Yates (1966). This amounted to a shorthand system for remembering. For example, 'to remember a long list of words he would simply "distribute" them along a street in his hometown' (Wagoner 2012, p. 135). He was even able to control his heartbeat by imagining himself running or resting. What is vital to note in this case, however, is that the dialectical exchange between specific sensory data and generalisation that the rest of us take for granted was distorted in S. (perhaps damaged through the overloading of neural pathways). His remembrance of things was so detailed and specific that it left little room for generalisation (or Bartlett's schemata), and this led to problems in maintaining social relations. This is the reason why information had to be conveyed to him slowly so that he would have the time to process it visually. Skim reading, for instance, was an ability alien to S. His comprehension tended to be literal and the use of metaphor in stories created problems for him. Understanding poetry was also a great challenge.

Luria was to confirm these neurological observations using cognitive experimentation. Ratner explains,

> employing a sophisticated design in which sets of six-year-old identical twins received different training, Luria presented some subjects ... with detailed models of objects and then asked the children to duplicate them from a collection of pieces. Other subjects ... saw only the outlines of models and were instructed to construct them from parts.
> *(1991, p. 34)*

Two months later the latter group 'had learned to be far more imaginative and creative' than the former group. The follow-up at eighteen months confirmed the initial findings. The subjects who were trained to attend to structure rather than to isolated details had greater imagination, creativity, planning, analysis, self-reflection and self-control (ibid., p. 35).

Nowadays we know a little more about people like Solomon Shereshevsky. In common parlance such subjects are described as having 'photographic memories'. This description, as Steven Rose explains, 'is not really accurate, in the sense that the images that are held are creatively manipulable by the memorizer, not simply fixed items to be referred to' (1994, p. 102). The technical term for this, *eidetic* (from the Greek for 'image') is not much better since it 'simply scientizes the same concept' (ibid.). Although eidetic memory is rare in adults, it is much more common in children. Early research suggested that around half of all elementary school children possessed some level of eidetic memory. The capacity seems to be 'widely distributed amongst young children of both sexes, independent of ethnic origin, class or school performance' (ibid., p. 103). Rose suggests that the 'perceptual filtering' that develops in most of us during puberty was underdeveloped or only partially functioning in the case of S.

Rose reminds us that having an eidetic memory may not be a gift. To be able to synthesise from past events and indeed to forget huge chunks of irrelevant information is essential for effective action and even survival. This incidentally expresses very well the dangers of living perpetually in an information bubble where we are bombarded with information without the time and space to reflect upon it and organise it into a coherent narrative. This explains why S. had difficulty retaining human relations and holding down a job. After enjoying some success performing as a mnemonist, the initial public enthusiasm gave way to indifference, and S. found himself drifting from job to job. He ended up as a taxi driver in Moscow.

Luria and neuropsychology

Brady Wagoner has discussed how after Vygotsky's death 'Luria decided to take up medical studies, partly because his interests were moving in that direction and partly to avoid Soviet purges' (2012, p. 133). Not only was his Marxism too unorthodox for the Party bureaucrats, but his Jewish background was also a constant risk in a society with strong anti-Semitic tendencies. Although the purges were conceived and carried out by the authoritarian regime of Joseph Stalin, the seeds of state terror where laid during Lenin's period of leadership between 1917–1924 (Mattick 1978). It was due to Lenin's mechanical interpretation of materialism that so-called idealistic psychology (e.g. psychoanalysis and phenomenology) was discouraged, in preference to the 'hard' sciences of behaviourism, reflexology and physiological psychology (Gray 1979). Had Vygotsky lived longer, his Marxist approach would no doubt have earned him the enmity of a regime whose interpretation of science was becoming increasingly instrumentalist.

Providing a science with paternal figures and origin stories is a process fraught with danger but I think it is fairly safe to say that Luria was one of the pioneers of neuropsychology (or more accurately 'cognitive neuroscience'). His specialities were 'brain dysfunction, aphasia and speech disorders' (Newman and Holzman 1993, p. 19) developed from his work with soldiers injured during World War II (Harré 2012, p. 39). He would look at each brain lesion and the corresponding psychological deficit or disturbance in the patient. From this he would infer that the injured part of the brain 'when intact, played a role in the neurofunctional system with which the higher order cognitive function was performed' (ibid.). The concept of 'neural plasticity' was put forward to hypothesise how higher-level brain functions can compensate for injured lower-level skills.

His approach skewed over-reliance on psychometric testing and encouraged more qualitative neuropsychological diagnosis (Goldberg and Bougakov 2009, p. 20), in an attempt to integrate experimental psychology and what Wilhelm Wundt (1832–1920) called *Völkerpsycholgie* (Cagigas and Bilder 2009, p. 27). Kenneth Podell (2009, p. 124) has argued that the typical negative deficit assessment, such as the Halstead-Reitan Battery, can be easily administered by technicians. However, 'assessing qualitative and productive symptomatology and deficits (via Lurian techniques) requires a high degree of neuropsychological expertise' (ibid.). These Lurian techniques consist of detailed studies of the individual which would then lead to rehabilitation protocols (ibid., p. 125). One important result was Luria's

FIGURE 18.1 Alexander Luria

'realisation that more than one region of the brain is involved in any one motor and cognitive process' (Harré 2012, p. 40).

Luria's dialectical method of integrating the specific and general was formulated in opposition to the localisation/modular view of the brain. Although some basic sensory motor functions may be favoured by certain parts of the brain, higher cortical processes are too complex to be confined to any one region of the brain (or any one hemisphere). As such, his theoretical concepts can provide us with an explanatory framework for a modern neuroimaging discipline that is often too atheoretical and data-driven (Cagigas and Bilder 2009, p. 23). Furthermore, he viewed the 'brain itself [as] part of a functional system, which extended into the cultural-historical world' (ibid., p. 25). In other words, for Luria, 'higher-order neurocognitive functional systems were formed by the brain's engagement of culturally organized activity in the real world' (ibid.). There are parallels between Luria and the German neuropsychiatrist Kurt Goldstein (1878–1965) who proposed in 1942 a holistic model based on the principle of 'self-actualisation'. This concept would later influence Maslow's hierarchy of needs.

A great many of Luria's conclusions are accepted by today's leading contemporary neuropsychologists. Davidson *et al.*'s (2003) point regarding emotion is decidedly Lurian: 'modern research illustrates how there is no single region of the brain dedicated to emotion but, rather, different aspects of emotion processing are distributed in brain circuits' (quoted in Prigatano 2009, p. 65). Luria's insights have been applied to complex tasks such as memory. Barr and Nakhutina note that

> Luria distinguished two types of memorising and suggested that each hemisphere made a unique contribution at a different level of this process. The dominant hemisphere [left] was viewed as responsible for *voluntary* memorising, a form of conscious activity where the material to be memorised was organised through the use of logical and often linguistic codes whereas the role of the nondominant [right] hemisphere was in the *involuntary* or unpremeditated background process of imprinting and sorting of traces.
>
> *(2009, p. 110)*

In other words, 'natural memory and memory as a higher mental process have different origins, involve different mechanisms, and develop in accordance with different laws' (Karpov 2005, p. 26). It was Luria's investigation of patients with unilateral lesions as well as cognitive tests of young children that jointly confirmed this theory, demonstrating how discoveries in cognitive psychology and neuropsychology can be complimentary.

The field of neuropsychology brings out the antagonism between mainstream and critical psychologies. On the one hand, mainstream psychologists tend to accept its findings without any serious reflection, assuming that the wonderous orange and blue colours produced in scans must be Nature's way of painting ancient wisdoms for us. On the other hand, critical psychologists have become so allergic to any biological interpretation that they cannot contemplate biology ever leaving the 'sin bin'! So long as neuropsychology dealt with disorders at the margin of psychology (e.g. brain injuries, genetic abnormalities, deficits, etc.), critical psychology (especially that branch of critical psychology that has always felt more secure within a culturally deterministic bubble) could ignore its findings. But now that neuropsychology is scanning and neuroimaging all and sundry in the course of everyday cognitive and emotional interactions, ignoring it becomes tantamount to wilful ignorance. To denounce neuropsychology as simplistic, reductionist and deterministic is no longer convincing. The fact that there are periodic attempts by mainstream neurologists to rehabilitate the discredited 'localisation of function' thesis of Franz Joseph Gall (1758–1828) and the corresponding pseudoscience of phrenology does not justify undervaluing neuropsychology's real achievements. What is required is an integrative framework that unites sociocultural psychology with biology and evolution. This is where Luria could prove immeasurably useful to postpsychology. He was a deliberate bridge-builder.

One recent bridging effort is Jose Dergan's cultural-historical approach to neuropsychological treatments of Latino patients (2011). He observes that 'most Latino patients are discharged from various programs (e.g., pain management, head injury, and so on) without having even achieved basic therapeutic goals' (ibid., p. 134). By analysing two case studies he concludes that

> symptoms, when only superficially analysed (e.g., overt behavioural system, statistically based hypothesis), are only reflecting the surface of a pathological entity usually misleading the subsequent process of clinical treatment … For example, when evaluating an adult who suffers from attention deficit disorder, we must first analyse how symptoms such as wandering off, forgetfulness, and low academic achievement are all interconnected and affect their social activity, self-appraisal, emotionalism, and self-motivation.
>
> *(Ibid., p. 147)*

I, therefore, find myself in agreement with Harré who argues that 'psychology will only be progressive as a science by acknowledging that both neuroscience and discursive/cultural psychology are respectable scientific disciplines, *with the latter taking conceptual priority over the former*' (2012, p. 55, emphasis in the original). Or, to put it differently, neuropsychology is far too important to be left in the hands of (mainstream) neuropsychologists!

Luria's Central Asian studies

> If we are to preserve culture, we must continue to create it.
>
> *Johan Huizinga*

It is sometimes difficult for western psychologists to understand how Soviet psychologists were encumbered by a security regime that scrutinised their every move. Vladimir I. Lubovsky recounts how in the early 1950s Luria somehow got involved with the notorious doctors' plot (Lubovsky, interviewed by Levitin 2002). This was an anti-Semitic campaign aimed mainly at prominent Jewish doctors and organised in 1952, a year before Stalin's death. Some of the doctors were accused of attempting to assassinate Politburo leaders and were summarily executed. Many other doctors, both Jews and non-Jews, were dismissed from their jobs. Lubovsky recounts how Luria was constantly being followed by security agents and always walked with someone because 'he didn't want to vanish walking along the street'. This someone was usually a postgraduate student like Lubovsky. Luria felt very 'strained, and the situation was psychologically hard for him' (ibid.). The wonderful movie *The Death of Stalin* (2017, dir. Armando Ianucci) has an interesting satirical take on the doctors' plot.

In the early 1930s a different series of state terror campaigns made life difficult for the people. Luria carried out a series of cognitive experiments in Soviet Central Asia between 1931–1932 (Luria 1976), which 'got him into serious political trouble' (Tulviste 1999, p. 66). His collaborator, Vygotsky, was too ill to attend personally. These experiments have been referred to as 'cross-cultural' (since they contrasted city-country differences). Wertsch (1985, p. 34) argues that it would be more accurate to call them 'cross-historical', since two different historical eras were being compared (modern city folk vs pre-modern farmers on the verge being collectivised). The real situation is somewhat more complex.

By the early 1930s most regions of the USSR were under the sway of capitalist relations of production but in some remote areas (and this applies to the Central Asian Republics), there existed, side by side with capitalist exchange, various residual pre-capitalist relations of production, such as feudalism. So, in its simplest version, the experiment ended up contrasting two fairly different groups: one group comprised literate city-dwellers, educated in abstract, de-contextualised thought and subjected to a modern capitalist educational upbringing; and the other group comprised non-literate village-dwelling farmers, whose primary mode of inquiry was observational, empirical and contextualised. This suggests that Luria's study was simultaneously cross-cultural *and* cross-historical.[1]

Luria's results confirmed some major cognitive differences between the two groups. The non-literate pre-modern villagers did not employ abstract or inferential reasoning, generalisation, and positivist logic to the same extent as their literate city counterparts. As Wertsch (1985) and Scribner and Cole (1981) have pointed out, the differences are not just due to the presence or absence of literacy. The knowledge-generating epistemology and data collection methodology of the villagers also differed substantially. They employed more concrete situational thinking. Furthermore, the Uzbekistani villagers showed less self-analysis and self-awareness, since their collective culture did not promote individuation. The observed differences were mostly a case of resistance to a modern-urban formal way of thinking, and not due to cognitive deficiency. For example,

> [W]hen presented with syllogisms with unfamiliar contents ('In the Far North, where there is snow, all bears are white. Novaya Zemlya is in the Far North. What colour are bears there?'), the illiterate subjects refused even more decisively to draw inferences ... declaring that they 'had never been in the North and had never seen bears'.
>
> *(Luria 1976, p. 107)*

We conclude from this that the Uzbekis' cognitive functions and language were not 'primitive', as some early psychologists or 'ethno-centric' anthropologists might have inferred, but different. Modern capitalist education favours logical reasoning and technical concepts, whereas the 'practical wisdom' of 1930s Uzbekistan demanded different semiotic mediations and different cognitive abilities. As Kozulin puts it, 'According to Vygotsky and his followers, only the most basic, "natural" cognitive processes are universal, while all higher mental functions, including those required for problem solving, are formed in the course of sociocultural activities' (2011, p. 68). Kozulin has undertaken an updated version of Luria's studies in relationship to the migration of rural Ethiopian Jews to Israel since the 1980s. He found that 'the mere immersion of immigrant children and adults into formal education does not seem to be sufficient for promoting the full range of cognitive functions expected in modern technological society' (ibid., p. 70). He goes on to conclude that 'A systematic mediation of new symbolic tools and learning strategies appear to be a more efficient method for providing new immigrants with the required set of psychological tools' (ibid., p. 85). What Ethiopian immigrants do not need is being subjected to misleading static psychometric tests. Luria would have concurred wholeheartedly.

Going beyond Luria and the romantic sciences

There is a charming video clip of Jerome Bruner (1915–2016) and Oliver Sacks (1933–2015) talking almost reverentially about Luria. The interviewer is Professor Michael Cole (2002).

Bruner starts off by saying how Luria's 'battle for consciousness' in the USSR was similar to his own endeavours to free psychology of mechanistic imperatives and to re-centre it on the 'mind'. In a sense they were both reacting against capitalist Taylorism, the attempt to regulate human beings through prefigured mechanical movements. Both focused on the process of symbolisation or meta-cognition as it is known more commonly today. Both, according to Bruner, were also fascinated by the process of individuation, which explains Luria's neuropsychological emphasis on the prefrontal lobe. But Luria always placed these studies within a sociocultural framework and in this he was distinguished from other greats such as Piaget.

Oliver Sacks talks excitedly about receiving a letter from Luria one month after Sack's review of *The Man with a Shattered World* (Luria [1972] 2008) had come out. 'It was like getting a letter from Freud', says Sacks. He explains how different Luria's perspective was from the likes of Pavlov. Apparently, Pavlov refused to even read Luria's *The Nature of Human Conflict* (Luria 1932), decrying 'you dare call yourself a scientist'!

When Sacks sent Luria some audio tapes featuring a patient with Tourette's syndrome, Luria saw parallels between him and his own mnemonist. Sadly, Sacks does not elaborate further on this topic in the video. When reading *The Mind of the Mnemonist*, Sacks initially thought it was a novel! Gradually, it dawned on him that it was a 'wonderful case history, with all the accuracy of science but also all the sensibility and drama and structure of a novel' (Cole 2002). This encouraged Sacks to attempt a similar portrait of his own patients which is exactly what he did in *Awakenings!* (1973). 'I was feeling that neurology had become desiccated', says Sacks, 'and in Luria's romantic case histories I had a feeling that the richness of 19th century naturalism was recovered along with a functional analysis which was completely new and could take everything to a higher level' (Cole 2002).

In his bestseller, *The Man Who Mistook His Wife for a Hat* (1985), Sacks observes how 'the entire history of neurology and neuropsychology can be seen as a history of the investigation of the left hemisphere' (Sacks 1985, p. 4). The right hemisphere is considered less distinct, even 'primitive' by neurologists. However, 'it is the right hemisphere which controls the crucial powers of recognising reality which every living creature must have in order to survive' (ibid., p. 10). Interestingly, Luria was fond of showing his students photographs of the great Russian filmmaker Sergei Eisenstein's dissected brain. 'Eisenstein's brain', explains Julia Vassilieva, 'featured a dramatically enlarged right hemisphere, which is responsible for visual images and spatial information processing, while his left hemisphere was of a normal size' (2013).

The patient at the centre of Sacks's book (Dr P.) would at times mistake a hat for his wife. Dr P. was a music teacher whose neurological damage was different and more severe than Luria's patient S. and closer to another patient Luria investigates in *The Man with a Shattered World* ([1972] 2008). In the case of P., his cortex – 'the organic prerequisite for all pictorial imagery' – was damaged (Sacks 1985, p. 17). Sacks describes how 'by and large, [P.] recognised nobody: neither his family, nor his colleagues, nor his pupils, nor himself' (ibid., p. 14). But interestingly, P. also had difficulty understanding 'the scene-as-a-whole. He failed to see the whole, seeing only details' (ibid., p. 11). The dialectical linkage between specific and general was severed in P. in the same way that it was (to a lesser extent) in S.

Even though P. had no body-image, he did have what Sacks calls a 'body-music', which compensated for his lack of body-image. He could move fluently based on rhythm, an 'inner music'. If his 'inner music' was suddenly interrupted, he would fail to complete the move. Dr P. had an inability to interpret intuitively – to make judgement calls.

Sacks notes that although neurology and psychology discuss just about everything else, they 'almost never talk of judgment', which is ironic since 'judgment is the most important faculty we have' (1985, p. 21). He traces this absurdity to the evolution of neurology itself:

> For classical neurology (like classic physics) has always been mechanical – from Hughlings Jackson's mechanical analogies to the computer analogies of today. Of course, the brain *is* a machine and a computer – everything in classical neurology is correct. But our mental processes, which constitute our being and life, are not just abstract and mechanical, but personal, as well.
>
> *(Ibid., emphasis in original)*

Sacks finishes his analysis by making an analogy between P.'s agnosia and the plight of cognitive sciences today:

> Our cognitive sciences are themselves suffering from an agnosia similar to Dr P.'s. Dr P. may therefore serve as a warning and a parable of what happens to science which eschews the judgmental, the particular, the personal, and becomes entirely abstract and computational.
>
> *(Ibid., p. 22)*

A more recent neuropsychologist who has tried to fuse Luria's neuropsychological findings with Freudianism is George P. Prigatano (2009). For him, 'successful neuropsychological rehabilitation is in part determined by the patient's personality' (ibid., p. 62). He notes how Luria redefined higher cortical functions as reflex complexes that are 'social in origin, mediated in structure, and conscious and voluntary in mode of function' (Luria, quoted in ibid., p. 63). Luria, however, did not pay sufficient attention to the 'irrational side of human personality' and consequently Prigatano's aim is to develop a broader model to explain higher cortical functions by integrating Freudianism (ibid., p. 64).

This is, after all, precisely what Luria was aiming for. In Cole's words, '[Luria] sought a new, synthetic method that would reconcile art and science, description and explanation' (1979). Luria achieved this not by denying the validity of past neurological research but by taking whatever made sense in its discoveries and reintegrating it in a new framework. He thus learned from localisation theory (e.g. Franz Gall and Pierre Paul Broca), field theory (Jean Pierre Flourens and Karl Spencer Lashley), and middle-ground theories (John Hughlings Jackson and Kurt Goldstein), without ignoring their methodological shortcomings. His new version of neuropsychology is one of the key building blocks for our project of postpsychology. Luria posits consciousness (and the unconscious) as socially produced, symbolically mediated and supported by flexible neurological connectivity. This approach will help us to go beyond postmodern fragmentation without collapsing back onto a unitary foundationalist perspective. In Luria's own words:

> Classic scholars are those who look upon events in terms of their constituent parts. Step by step they single out important units and elements until they can formulate abstract, general laws … Romanic scholars' traits, attitudes and strategies are just the opposite. They do not follow

> the path of reductionism, which is the leading philosophy of the classical group. Romantics in science want neither to split living reality into its elementary components nor to represent the wealth of life's concrete events as abstract models that lose the properties of the phenomena themselves.
>
> *(1979, p. 174)*

Final words

If neurological and biological findings are to be integrated into psychology more productively, we will need a framework capable of making the necessary linkages. For the time being, let us merely state that biology, for various political reasons, will never offer to make the first move – there is simply too much power and prestige at stake for any move that might be interpreted as concessionary. But as you will see below, some critical minds have already taken the first tentative steps.

Sometimes this move can be a simple case of clarifying terms so that translation work can take place more effectively. For instance, we could make a distinction between three concepts: 'enablers', 'triggers' and 'causes'. I have reached this classification by fusing concepts from Harré and Lewontin. Harré (2012) has shown how our subjectivity – here defined as dreams, values, hopes, frustrations – are enabled/disabled by biological systems. But this does not mean that they are caused by biology. It simply means that biological systems can create the material conditions for behaviour to be enabled or disabled. Lewontin (1991) has further argued how genes as triggers are routinely credited with a power they do not have – that of causality. Triggers are the most immediate and focused antecedent of an event and not the cause. Defective genes may trigger cancer but they do not cause it. Overall, biology mainly acts as enabler and/or trigger and very rarely as cause, unless we have in mind organic impairments such as head injuries. In the case of deep-seated and long-term causes of events and behaviour one must analyse the sociocultural and political dimensions. Perhaps we could go a step further and suggest that corresponding to these three starting moments of the process (enablers, triggers, causes), we could also posit three temporary end points. I would suggest that we call them 'impact', 'induce' and 'consequence'. Thus, enabling mechanisms have an impact on the system. Triggering mechanisms induce an event within that system. And causes lead to consequences for the system. This simple wordplay clarifies the complex set of connections any phenomena entails.

However, translation work on its own is clearly not sufficient. We can rely on the wealth of ideas and suggestions proposed in three fairly recent books that have taken the lead in establishing a 'critical neuropsychology'. The first, *Neuro: The New Brain Sciences and the Management of the Mind*, was written by Rose and Abi-Rached (2013). The authors contemplate the best way of 'doing the history of neurosciences' (ibid., p. 28), how to fuse neuromolecular and brain plasticity (ibid., p. 51), the 'social brain hypothesis' (ibid., p. 143), and the implications of the rise of neuroscience for the human sciences (ibid., p. 232). The second book is an anthology by leading theoreticians and practitioners, which aims to create a 'critical neuroscience' (Choudhury and Slaby 2016). The third is a similar work that attempts to bridge the gap between the social and biological (Meloni *et al.* 2018).

More specifically, John Cromby has suggested the interesting work of the Portuguese-American Antonio R. Damasio (b. 1944) as a bridge between neuroscience and the social sciences (Cromby 2007). Damasio's anti-Cartesian 'Spinozist stance, coupled with an explicit recognition of social influence, arguably makes him the most social-science friendly of the major neuroscientists now writing' (ibid., p. 153). Even here there are deterministic tendencies (Damasio 2003) that make the endeavour risky, but I feel it is riskier still not to make the attempt to synthesise.

I think Luria would have approved (well, mostly anyway)!

Note

1 The distinction between 'cross-cultural' and 'cross-historical' is the only wordplay I have indulged in during the writing of this chapter. Had I been as tedious as most post-Vygotskians working today I might have filled page after useless page with a discussion of the best designation for the new science: 'cultural-historical' versus 'sociocultural' versus 'cultural-historical activity theory' vs …!

19

DISCUSSION

> I can write a book: so can many others who have not even learned to spell. What abortions are these Essays! What errors, what ill-pieced transitions, what crooked reasons, what lame conclusions.
>
> *William Hazlitt,* On the Pleasure of Hating *(1826)*

Ignoring the class struggle won't make it go away, you know!

I do not like long goodbyes, even less so long discussions, therefore I'll make this brief and to the point. I hope I have convinced the sceptic reader who has carefully followed the logic of my argument that psychology's achievements and failures do not occur in a vacuum but in a societal context steeped in class conflict. There is no such thing as 'psychology exceptionalism'. The problems that psychology experiences are shared across the social sciences and humanities. The subjects it interrogates (racism, sexism, homophobia, ageism, disablism, sadness, fear, violence, alienation, etc.), become unfathomable unless one takes into account social class. The happiness and mental well-being it promises are illusionary, unless we supersede class exploitation and oppression.

And yet, the majority of psychologists steadfastly refuse to engage with class issues, and the few who do end up sounding more like Edmund Blackadder's manservant Baldrick, than Marx. OK, OK, I exaggerate of course! I am happy to concede that there are still a few politically astute psychologists out there. More if we add writers from adjacent social sciences to the list. Let me briefly massage a few egos, otherwise I won't hear the last of it, either from them or my own conscience.

I like John Drury's engagement with class (2002), although I am not so keen on the social identity theory (SIT) he draws on (Stott and Reicher 1998). SIT has always struck me as an attempt to twist a bourgeoise enterprise into a pleb-friendly endeavour. I am afraid that SIT's epistemological, ontological and methodological foundations are far too mired in cognitive psychology to make it a genuine contender for liberation. Still, when Drury does not dilute his politics by collaborating with less politically savvy researchers, he manages to produce innovative work that clarifies the contours of the class struggle. I consider not having a chapter on SIT, Tajfel and Drury a major weakness of the present work. What can I say, dear reader? I just ran out of time and patience.

Mihalis Mentinis is another original researcher worthy of attention. Whether he is writing about the Zapatistas (Mentinis 2006), the Greek rebellion (ibid. 2010), or the psychopolitics of food (ibid. 2016), it is always fresh and insightful. The old situationist concept of 'psychogeography' has been utilised effectively in recent years by Alexander J. Bridger (2016). Anthony Marcus and Charles Menzies (2005) have attempted to lay the foundations of what they call a 'class-struggle anthropology'. I consider their work to have many parallels with my own. I cannot leave anthropology without mentioning how impressed I am with the work of Michael T. Taussig, especially *The Devil and Commodity Fetishism in South America.* 'Outstanding, Red Team, outstanding! Get you a case of beer for that one!', as Robert Duvall (Kilgore) might have said in *Apocalypse Now* (1979, dir. Francis Ford Coppola).

Ironically for a tradition that traces its heritage back to Marx and Vygotsky, sociocultural psychology does not often engage directly with class issues. I find this very revealing. In fact, most researchers in this field demonstrate a remarkable talent for skewing politics and the class struggle altogether. Carolyne P. Panofsky's (2003) contribution about the relationship between learning and social class represents a rare exception. Another critical psychologist who never ignores the political dimension of psychology is Dennis Fox (2011, 2012). Gottfried M. Heuer's (2017) reanimation of the anarchist Otto Gross allows us to incorporate the hidden history of radical psychology from a similar vantagepoint to Fox. The wonderfully erudite Bruce Lerro is another gem whose work has been neglected for far too long (2017). The Roses (Nicolas Rose, 1985; Hilary Rose and Steve Rose 2014) remain constant lodestars. Their research has helped me to identify psychology's shortcomings and blind-spots with greater clarity. I have already mentioned the thought-provoking ideas of Michael Billig, Ian Parker, Joanna Ryan and John Cromby throughout the course of the book.

I think what all these writers (and many more besides) demonstrate is the continued relevance of radical critique and praxis. Admittedly, the world is experiencing an anti-working-class 'moment' with a rabid form of capitalism barking threats left, right and centre. But tyrants do not last forever. Bullies will get their comeuppance. What is essential is to have the proper ingredients and framework of a postpsychology in place before the next wave of social struggle against capitalism.

The dire need for a postpsychology

The schematic division of psychologists into three classes has been a deliberate gamble, as well as an act of provocation. But it is also a division I stand by. Thomas Kuhn defined a *paradigm* as a specific theoretical orientation, bound in time and convention to a particular scientific community, with its own epistemology, ontology and methodology (Kuhn 1970). The overuse of the term 'paradigm' is problematic. For instance, the perspectives of psychoanalysis, behaviourism and humanistic psychology present more commonalities than divergences. The changes between them should not be inflated into a 'paradigm-shift'. This becomes even more evident if we slightly modify Kuhn's rather depoliticised description to include class interest. Psychoanalysis, behaviourism and humanistic psychology rose partially as a response to class struggle and were then taken up by the ruling class and the state to subdue working class resistance. Most of their updated versions are fulfilling the same role today.

Freud's fear of crowds and wars has been rather well documented (Pick 1995). Daniel Pick writes, 'Whilst the [first] war-time era does not simply overshadow Freud's thought or determine the terms of his concern and his pessimism, his text [*Group Psychology and the Analysis of the Ego*] certainly bears some traces of its most unforgettable experiences' (ibid., p. 40). The seismic upheavals in Russia around 1905 and 1917 aroused his scepticism, and he refers to socialism as 'the heir to the church, indeed to "the Wars of Religion"' (ibid.). In *Group Psychology and the Analysis of the Ego* ([1921] 2012) he uses Gustave Le Bon and William McDougall's ideas about 'primitive instinct' and the 'gullibility of the masses', but writes the book in relation to his own experiences. Lurking in the background is the spectre of the Paris Commune of 1871. This was no ordinary uprising. Rather, it was a working-class insurrection that transformed Paris into an autonomous commune (Ross 2015). It petrified the French and Prussian ruling classes sufficiently for them to suspend hostilities, join forces and turn their efforts against the Commune. It was not the fear of crowds in general, but the specific fear of an insurrectionary proletarian crowd that attracted the rulers to the ideas of Freud. Psychoanalysis was groomed by the rulers to serve the twin aims of analysis and control, but this grooming was welcomed by Freud and most of his followers.

Behaviourism's fear of the proletarian crowd and its subsequent embrace of a top-down socially engineered capitalism is even more intense. The hibernation of the US working class has lasted for so long (Fraser 2015) that we sometimes forget how truly magnificent it once was (Zinn 1999). The Industrial Workers of the World (also known as the 'Wobblies') remains to this day a rupture like no other. Founded in Chicago in 1905 it soon grew both numerically and politically (Lynd and Grubacic 2008). Unlike contemporary radical grouplets who misuse the term 'international' on the spurious grounds that one of their texts was translated into an exotic language or that one of their members once took a package tour of a 'strike zone', the Wobblies were genuinely internationalist. At their best, maybe even trans-nationalists. They had organic connections with South Asia, Spain, Mexico, Finland, Australia, New Zealand, Ireland and elsewhere (Cole *et al.* 2017). They used a variety of tactics to sabotage capitalism and improve the lot of the workers. Their Russian counterparts had already established autonomous workers' councils in defiance of the Tsar and later on the Bolsheviks (Mattick 1978; Pannekoek [1948] 2003). Behaviourism rose at more or less the same time to address the same anti-capitalist spirit of defiance.

Watson's behaviourism is tailor-made for dealing with this phase of capitalist development. It can offer its services to secure the 'formal' domination of capital over labour (Marx [1867] 1990) or better still, the back end of this phase, which is designated by sociologists and economists as Fordism and Taylorism (Gramsci [1934] 1999). Watson's boast about creating the perfect worker-citizen was an early version of contemporary cybernetic and robotic assertions about enhancing labour productivity. In the USSR the close relationship between Pavlov's conditioned dogs and Stakhanov's (1906–1977) Taylorist reorganisation of his fellow workers from below in order to increase productivity was more obvious (Pocknee

2013). Even behaviourism's so-called progressive components (the emphasis being on 'environmental' factors and the 'social' aspects of personality) were soon operationalised and turned into tools of discipline. This could be done rather easily because 'environment' and 'social' were defined in narrow terms from the start (in fact, narrow definitions are always to be mistrusted, as I have shown in relation to 'class' and 'science'). Once behaviourism's alliance with the 'military-industrial complex' was cemented, there was no going back.

Humanistic psychology is desperate to demarcate itself from psychoanalysis and behaviourism, yet my investigation has uncovered one commonality after another. I am talking here about both personal and doctrinal ties of continuity and not the kind of serendipity that can easily be wished away. Maslow began as a behaviourist and retained a deep-seated respect for both behaviourism's scientific credentials and its social engineering agenda. He worked with Harry Harlow and might have spent the rest of his life observing monkeys. Ultimately, his 'rebellion' was meek and limited. It could be argued that he merely turned 'engineering' into 'humaneering'. Early Rogers was heavily indebted to Freud and even the mature Rogers was still translating and incorporating Freudian concepts into a more person-centred discourse. Both Maslow and Rogers instinctively understood that the worker of the 'formal' phase of domination was being replaced by a new worker who belonged to the 'real' phase of capital's domination. Humanistic psychology had to understand and heal a more complex subjectivity, shaped by the demands of post-Fordism and post-Taylorism.

From a working-class standpoint, therefore, it makes perfect sense to classify Freud, Hirschfeld, Watson, Maslow and Rogers as belonging to the same paradigm. I wish I had the space to include Piaget, Jung, Milgram and Zimbardo in this list but I hope that the argument has been sufficiently robust without them. This historical arc begins as a 'pre-science' (Kuhn) of psychology (remember Freud's early dalliance with hysteria and coke), solidifies in the 1920–1950s through recourse to behaviourism and the experimental method, and finally it becomes a 'normal science' (Kuhn), thanks to the efforts of humanistic psychology – so 'normal' that it becomes embedded in both 'high' and 'low' cultures. The real differences existing between these three schools over data-gathering methods and philosophy should, in my view, be referred to as a 'perspective-shift' rather than a comprehensive 'paradigm-shift'. So, within the same upper-class paradigm there were at least two major perspective-shifts (from psychoanalysis to behaviourism and from behaviourism to humanism).

At the end of the 1950s psychology was riding high. For a brief moment in time all seemed hunky-dory, as Americans would say. Psychology got invited to all the best parties in town and rubbed shoulders with the rich and beautiful. However, when observations and research results failed to conform to the paradigm, doubts began to be raised about psychology. These doubts were expressed by both psychology's pragmatic patrons who demanded results, and, from within, by practitioners who were disappointed by psychology's failed promises. As more and more anomalies emerged, doubts gave way to persistent anxiety and the capitalist crises of the 1960s turned this into a full-fledged panic among the advocates of the paradigm.

Slowly, gingerly and haphazardly the early critical remarks were given coherence by various oppositional clusters: existentialist psychologists in France, Laing and Cooper in Britain, followers of Foucault, phenomenologists in northern Europe and the USA, feminists, qualitative researchers and the occasional Marxist and anarchist psychologist. A new paradigm was taking shape, or at least the pre-science phase of a new paradigm.

These first-wave opposition figures were fearless. Viktor Frankl had survived concentration camps. What could frighten him? A rejection from an editor to publish his work? A cancelled book signing? Laing shook the very foundations of British psychiatry. He wrestled naked with Sean Connery (wait, my memory is not what it used to be. I could be confusing this episode with Oliver Reed and Alan Bates in the movie *Women in Love*). My point is, the grip of upper-class psychology could only be loosened by brave souls who were prepared to take risks. Billig's study of the fascist National Front was daring. Parker's assault on mainstream psychology was not calculated to win him popularity. Even the insecure Foucault was in many ways a tough hombre who pioneered new ideas in the face of fierce resistance from established social science.

All these novel ideas, these new ways of doing research and therapy finally coalesced during the 1970–1980s under the rubric 'critical psychology' (Hepburn 2003; Fox and Prilleltensky 2011) or 'postmodern psychology' (Kvale 1992; Simon and Billig 1994). The main problem is that by the time the paradigm was ready to roll out, the proletariat had already suffered massive defeats. The last reverberations of the May 1968 movement were fading fast, and the hopes of a revolutionary rupture were justifiably shelved. The new paradigm of critical psychology became a 'normal science' (Kuhn) during counter-revolutionary times, when British miners were being baton-charged by thugs in uniform, Italian workers were being threatened by a triumvirate consisting of the state, fascists and organised crime, and most American workers had long given up the Wobblies for the wobble board! Critical psychology was (and remains) a predominantly middle-class paradigm, imbued with pessimism and negativity from the outset. The hopes for a world turned upside-down were replaced by a reformist agenda, and grand narratives lost their lustre and were dismissed in favour of competing local narratives of 'minorities' seeking 'identities'.

While the first wave of critical psychologists are worth reading and admiring, the current batch seem to me very dreary. Most go over the same ground, using the same legalistic language, saying precious little. One gets the impression that the first wave was taking on the most powerful arguments of modernist psychology, whereas the current wave prefers to ambush high modernism, a much more crass and convenient opponent. Where is the radicalism in contemporary critical psychology? Where is the imagination? Research and writing have become a box-ticking exercise for the current generation of 'critical' psychologists. I realise that I am being viciously cruel here, but this needs to be stated categorically: the overwhelming majority of work carried out today under the flag of critical psychology is junk!

Both upper-class modernist psychology and middle-class postmodern psychology are in rapid decline. This reflects a more general decline of capitalism. What are the implications of this demise for the social struggle? Simply that we, the working class, we, the overwhelming majority of people in the world, must create our own alternative. This can only be achieved by ruthlessly truncating the bulk of upper- and middle-class psychologies, salvaging the most profound insights and discoveries they have to offer, and integrating that into a new science that I have provisionally called postpsychology.

Postpsychology is not interdisciplinary; it is trans-disciplinary. There have always been attempts to do interdisciplinary research, with rather limited success. The biopsychosocial perspective is one such effort. One of the earliest projects to try to go beyond inter-disciplinary work and discover a common methodology and language involved a collaboration between the great Marxist Karl Korsch and the famed psychologist Kurt Lewin. Mel van Elteren explains that their effort to synthesise psychology, sociology and history was ultimately unsuccessful due to its focus on 'mathematization' (1992, p. 46). The lesson for postpsychology here is to avoid the pitfall of reductionism and the forced imposition of an interpretative language. Korsch and Lewin made their attempt in the 1930s when neither the forces of production nor the relations of production were conducive to achieving synthesis. The social and technical divisions of labour were still unfolding and disciplines were still being productive for capitalism. We are fast approaching an epoch when a second, more nuanced effort, becomes both viable and indispensable. As Bob Noble Dylan says, *For the times they are a-changin'!*

Postpsychology is, therefore, a phenomenon with three overlapping components: one component relates to a systematic attempt to salvage the very best of upper- and middle-class psychologies; the second component goes beyond psychology into neighbouring disciplines in order to discover and bring back novel ideas; and the final component is developed through being involved with the social movement against capitalism.

To dare is to do

While patiently waiting for postpsychology (or for that matter, post-sociology, postpsychiatry, postbiology, etc.) to emerge out of its cocoon, a more short-term and realistic set of pedagogic goals needs to be considered. These goals have been drawn up for teaching psychology in the context of the arguments developed in this book, and taking into account the current resources available for radical teaching and research. I recommend that psychology programmes should be amended by teaching the following subjects, preferably through 'action research':

- *Teaching rhetoric from the standpoint of the working class*: One of the few genuine gains of critical psychology has been the rediscovery of rhetoric, defined here as the art of argumentation and persuasion. Given the close association between talking and thinking (Billig 1996), any improvements in students' rhetorical abilities should translate into clearer thinking. In an age when even politicians and journalists cannot articulate their thoughts with clarity, teaching students to stand their ground, argue and persuade, becomes an urgent necessity. However, since postpsychology is a project dedicated to the emancipation of the working class, rhetoric must be taught from a radical standpoint, and not as a set of neutral linguistic skills. After all, we are not toga-wearing Sophists! Students of psychology, many of whom eventually move into practising psychotherapy, will particularly benefit from studying rhetoric.
- *Teaching radical history and politics*: At every conceivable level, psychology is intertwined with history and politics (Gergen 1973; Parker 2007; Smith and Haslam 2012). But the history and politics currently taught

alongside some psychology programmes are clearly inadequate to the task. Let me be clear and upfront here: the wishy-washy postmodern mix of neo-liberalism, liberalism, social democracy and Leninism on offer is no substitute for a real understanding of history and politics. The very best of Marxism and anarchism should be harnessed to enhance our participation in a historically embedded and politically oriented psychology.

- *Teaching radical cultural studies*: To be fair this element is already an integral part of some psychology programmes (Cole 2003; Skeggs 2004; Ratner 2012; Andreouli and Taylor 2017). Some of this work, despite being rooted in Vygotsky and Bakhtin, somehow manages to neglect or marginalise class issues. Skeggs' work is an exception and we need more contributions along the same line.
- *Teaching radical media production studies*: There is little point in producing the most wonderful and original research if the results are going to be distorted by a media that is more interested in sensationalism than truth. It is, therefore, paramount that psychologists learn how to present their own work. This means taking control of the pre-production, production and post-production cycle of research. With the advent of new technology, the task is not as arduous as it sounds. Watson, Hirschfeld, Maslow, Rogers, Laing, Foucault, Frankl and Fromm all utilised the media adroitly in their quest to reform psychology.
- *Teaching critical neuroscience and critical biological psychology*: Far too many critical psychologists show an allergic reaction whenever they hear words like, 'genes', 'biology', 'neuro' and 'evolution'. The negativity is partly understandable since mainstream science recruited these terms to promote the idea of 'biology as destiny' a long time ago. However, the ostrich mentality adopted by many psychologists towards all things biological is ultimately self-defeating. There are sufficient resources available these days to make teaching critical neuropsychology a genuine possibility (Rose and Abi-Rached 2013; Meloni *et al.* 2018).
- *Teaching statistics from a critical perspective*: There are three principle ways in which a psychologist can humiliate himself in front of his students; by dancing in public (just say no!), by wearing a waistcoat in lecture theatres (especially before *Peaky Blinders* made them fashionable), and by trying to teach stats. We are just awful at teaching stats, let's be honest. I feel that many psychologists dismiss stats too readily. Sometimes this is justifiable. In his excellent article Sibley (1999) described the subtle ways in which reality could be misrepresented by statistical

analysis. Hacking (1981) suggested alternative ways of *doing* the history of statistics. However, a great deal has happened since these two seminal critiques and it is high time that psychologists developed a critical method of teaching statistics. In this context the online journal *Radical Statistics* could prove enormously helpful.

Last words

It would be gratifying to discover in perhaps ten to twenty years' time that this book has made a genuine contribution to efforts to overcome the limitations of upper- and middle-class psychologies. To paraphrase Marx, 'A spectre is haunting psychology; the spectre of postpsychology. All the powers of old psychology have entered into a holy alliance to exorcise this spectre'.

Ah, who am I kidding? It is a comforting fantasy, but in truth I'll be lucky if my sales reach double figures. Old psychology is far too busy selling itself like a painted whore to the rich and powerful to worry about the criticisms of an uppity Oompa Loompa like me: 'What sad times are these when passing ruffians can say "Ni" at will to old ladies' (Monty Python). I hope you enjoyed my 'Ni'!

REFERENCES

Adorno, T., Frenkel-Brunswik, E., Levinson, D. and Sanford, N. ([1950] 2019). *The Authoritarian Personality*. With a new introduction by Peter E. Gordon. London and New York: Verso.

Allam, L. (2019). 'Unspeakable': How Can Australia Stop the Indigenous Suicide Epidemic? *The Guardian*, 14 May. Available at www.theguardian.com/australia-news/2019/may/14/unspeakable-how-can-australia-stop-the-indigenous-suicide-epidemic (accessed 12 September 2019).

Anarchasteminist (2017). *Transphobia Is a Class Issue*. Available at https://libcom.org/library/transphobia-class-issue (accessed 13 September 2018).

Anderson, B. ([1983] 2006). *Imagined Communities: Reflections on the Origin and Spread of Nationalism*. London and New York: Verso.

Anderson, K. (2002). A Recently Discovered Article by Erich Fromm on Trotsky and the Russian Revolution. *Science & Society*, Vol. 66, No. 2, pp. 266–273.

Andreouli, E. and Taylor, S., Eds (2017). *Advancing Social Psychology, Book 1*. Milton Keynes: The Open University.

Antaki, C. (1999). *DARGchive Special: Charles Antaki Talks with Professor Michael Billig*. Available at www.youtube.com/watch?v=O4dtsXY4RLE (accessed 22 September 2018).

Argyle, M. (1994). *The Psychology of Social Class*. London and New York: Routledge.

Arnot, B. (1981). Soviet Labour Productivity and the Failure of the Shchekino Experiment. *Critique*, Vol. 15, pp. 31–56.

Artaud, A. (1947a). *Van Gogh, the Suicide Provoked by Society*. Available at https://issuu.com/samzdat/docs/artaud_antonin_van_gogh_the_suicide (accessed 21 September 2019).

Artaud, A. (1947b). *Shit to the Mind*. Reprinted in *Tel Quel*, No. 3 (1960), pp. 3–8.

Aveline, M. (1985). A Review of 'Wisdom, Madness and Folly: The Making of a Psychiatrist' by R. D. Laing. *British Journal of Psychiatry*, Vol. 147, No. 2, p. 220.

Avineri, S. (1989). *Arlosoroff*. London: Peter Halban Publishers.

Aysha, E. E-D. (2017). Islamic Suicide Terrorism and Erich Fromm's Social Psychology of Modern Times. *Journal of Social and Political Psychology*, Vol. 5, No. 1, pp. 82–106.

Badiou, A. (1965a). *Badiou Interviews Michel Foucault (1/3)*. Available at www.youtube.com/watch?v=PFyB09FrtaY (accessed 9 August 2019).

Badiou, A. (1965b). *Badiou Interviews Michel Foucault (2/3)*. Available at www.youtube.com/watch?v=GqP2nMuh_wg (accessed 9 August 2019).

Bakhtin, M. (1981). *The Dialogic Imagination: Four Essays*. Translated by C. Emerson and M. Holquist. Austin: University of Texas Press.

Bakhtin, M. (1984). *Rabelais and His World*. Translated by H. Iswolsky. Bloomington: Indiana University Press.

Bakhtin, M. (1986). *Speech Genres and Other Late Essays*. Edited by C. Emerson and M. Holquist, translated by V. W. McGee. Austin: University of Texas Press.

Ball, T. (1983). On 'Making' History in Vico and Marx. In G. Tagliacozzo, Ed., *Vico and Marx: Affinities and Contrasts*. London and Basingstoke: Macmillan, pp. 78–93.

Barber, S. (1993). *Antonin Artaud: Blows and Bombs*. London: Faber and Faber.

Barker, P. (2003). Shock Tactics. *The Guardian*, 9 May. Available at www.theguardian.com/society/2003/may/09/mentalhealth.comment (accessed 20 July 2019).

Barnes, M. and Berke, J. ([1971] 2002). *Two Accounts of a Journey Through Madness*. New York: Other Press.

Barnouw, J. (1983). Man Making History: The Role of the Plebeians in Vico, the Proletariat in Marx. In G. Tagliacozzo, Ed., *Vico and Marx: Affinities and Contrasts*. London and Basingstoke: Macmillan, pp. 94–113.

Barr, W. B. and Nakhutina, L. (2009). The Neuropsychology of Epilepsy: An Application of Luria's Concepts. In A.-L. Christensen, E. Goldberg and D. Bougakov, Eds, *Luria's Legacy in the 21st Century*. New York: Oxford University Press, pp. 103–121.

Baynes, C. (2018). John Lennon's 'Imagine' Being Played at Japan's Suicide Forest to Stop People Taking Own Lives. *The Independent*, 21 December. Available at www.independent.co.uk/news/world/asia/japan-suicide-forest-aokigahara-john-lennon-kyochi-watanabe-a8694446.html (accessed 27 September 2019).

BBC (2015). *Germaine Greer: Trans Women 'Not Women'*. Available at www.bbc.co.uk/news/av/uk-34625512/germaine-greer-transgender-women-are-not-women (accessed 13 September 2018).

Beck, H. P. and Irons, G. (2011). Finding Little Albert. *The Psychologist*, Vol. 24, No. 5, pp. 392–395.

Bernays, E. L. ([1928] 2004). *Propaganda*. New York: IG Publishing.

Billig, M. (1978). *Fascists: A Social Psychological View of the National Front*. London and New York: Harcourt, Brace, Jovanovich.

Billig, M. (1982). *Ideology and Social Psychology*. Oxford: Blackwell

Billig, M. (1992). *Talking of the Royal Family*. London: Routledge.

Billig, M. (1994). Repopulating the Depopulated Pages of Social Psychology. *Theory & Psychology*, Vol. 4, No. 3, pp. 307–335.

Billig, M. (1995). *Banal Nationalism*. London: SAGE.

Billig, M. (1996). *Arguing and Thinking: A Rhetorical Approach to Social Psychology*. European Monographs in Social Psychology. Cambridge: Cambridge University Press.

Billig, M. (2006). The Persistence of Freud. *The Psychologist*, Vol. 19, No. 9, pp. 540–541.

Billig, M. (2008). *The Hidden Roots of Critical Psychology: Understanding the Impact of Locke, Shaftesbury and Reid*. Los Angeles, CA and London: SAGE.

Billig, M. (2012). *Laughter and Ridicule: Towards a Social Critique of Humour*. Los Angeles, CA and London: SAGE.

Billig, M. (2013). Academic Words and Academic Capitalism. *Athenea Digital*, Vol. 13, No. 1, pp. 7–12.

Billig, M., Condor, S., Edwards, D., Gane, M., Middleton, D. and Radley, A. (1988). *Ideological Dilemmas: A Social Psychology of Everyday Thinking*. Thousand Oaks, CA: SAGE.

Birchall, J. (2013). Hey Trans People, Cut it Out. *Spiked*, 15 January. Available at www.spiked-online.com/newsite/article/13264#.W5pkgJiZ3mY (accessed 13 September 2018).

Black, D. (2009). *The Capitalism of Philosophy?*Sohn-Rethel on Intellectual and Manual Labour Reconsidered. A talk organised by Principa Dialectica, 9 January, London. Available at https://enemiesofutopia.wordpress.com/2009/02/21/sohn-rethel-uncovered/ (accessed 18 September 2019).

Bookchin, M. (1982). *The Ecology of Freedom: The Emergence and Discussion of Hierarchy*. Altrincham: Cheshire Books. Available at https://theanarchistlibrary.org/library/murray-bookchin-the-ecology-of-freedom (accessed 3 September 2019).

Borrell-Carrio, F., Suchman, A. L. and Epstein, R. M. (2004). The Biopsychosocial Model 25 Years Later: Principles, Practice and Scientific Inquiry. *Annals of Family Medicine*, No. 2, pp. 576–682.

Bracken, P. (2012). Depression, Psychiatry and the Use of ECT. *Asylum*. Available at https://asylummagazine.org/2012/05/depression-psychiatry-and-the-use-of-ect-by-pat-bracken/ (accessed 21 July 2019).

Brasor, P. (2012). Japan's Depressing Increase in Psychoactive Drugs Use. *Japan Times*, 16 September. Available at www.japantimes.co.jp/news/2012/09/16/national/media-national/japans-depressing-increase-in-psychoactive-drug-use/#.W03MvGjPzmY (accessed 17 July 2018).

Breggin, P. (1998). Electroshock: Scientific, Ethical, and Political Issues. *International Journal of Risk & Safety in Medicine*, Vol. 11, pp. 5–40. Available at www.ectresources.org/ECTscience/Breggin_1998_ECT__Overview.pdf (accessed 21 July 2019).

Bretherton, R. and Ørner, R. (2003). Positive Psychotherapy in Disguise. *The Psychologist*, Vol. 16, No. 3, p. 136.

Bridger, A. J. (2016). Walking the Radical Talk. *The Psychologist*, Vol. 29, pp. 276–279. Available at https://thepsychologist.bps.org.uk/volume-29/april/walking-radical-talk (accessed 29 September 2019).

Brockmeier, J. (2009). Reaching for Meaning: Human Agency and the Narrative Imagination. *Theory & Psychology*, Vol. 19, No. 2, pp. 213–233.

Brody, B. (1970). Freud's Case-Load. *Psychotherapy: Theory, Research & Practice*, Vol. 7, No. 1, pp. 8–12.

Brody, B. (1976). 'Freud's Case-Load' and Social Class: A Rejoinder. *Psychotherapy: Theory, Research and Practice*, Vol. 13, No. 2, pp. 196–197.

Brown, M. (2019). 'Short of Imagination': Germaine Greer Scorns Leonardo da Vinci's Art. *The Guardian*, 27 May. Available at www.theguardian.com/books/2019/may/27/short-of-imagination-germaine-greer-scorns-leonardo-da-vinci-art (accessed 29 August 2019).

Brown, P. (1974). *Towards a Marxist Psychology*. New York: Harper Colophon Books, Harper & Row Publishers.

Brown, S. D. (2005). Collective Emotions: Artaud's Nerves. *Culture and Organization*, Vol. 11, No. 4, pp. 235–247.

Brown, S. D. and Stenner, P. (2009). *Psychology without Foundations: History, Philosophy and Psychosocial Theory*. London: SAGE.

Buick, A. (1975). Joseph Dietzgen. *Radical Philosophy*, Vol. 10, pp. 3–7. Available at www.radicalphilosophyarchive.com/wp-content/files_mf/rp10_article1_josephdietzegen_buick.pdf (accessed 2 February 2019).

Bukey, E. B. (2000). *Hitler's Austria: Popular Sentiment in the Nazi Era, 1938–1945*. Chapel Hill and London: University of North Carolina Press.

Bullough, V. L. (2003). Biographical Notes: Magnus Hirschfeld, An Often Overlooked Pioneer. *Sexuality & Culture*, Vol. 7, No. 1, pp. 62–72.

Burger, D. H., Crous, F. and Roodt, G. (2008). Logo-od: The Applicability of Logotherapy as an Organisational Development Intervention. *South African Journal of Industrial Psychology*, Vol. 34, No. 3, pp. 68–80.

Burns, T. (2002). Joseph Dietzgen and the History of Marxism. *Science & Society*, Vol. 66, No. 2, pp. 202–227.

Burston, D. (2001). R. D. Laing and the Politics of Diagnosis. *Janus Head*. Special Issue: *The Legacy of R. D. Laing*. Available at www.janushead.org/4-1/burstonpol.cfm (accessed 27 September 2019).

Butt, T. (2012). George Kelly and the Garden of Eden. *The Psychologist*, Vol. 25, No. 3, pp. 250–251.

Cagigas, X. E. and Bilder, R. M. (2009). Where Culture Meets Neuroimaging: The Intersection of Luria's Method with Modern Neuroimaging and Cognitive Neurosci Res. In A.-L. Christensen, E. Goldberg and D. Bougakov, Eds, *Luria's Legacy in the 21st Century*. New York: Oxford University Press, pp. 23–29.

Campbell, C. (1987). *The Romantic Ethic and the Spirit of Modern Consumerism*. Oxford: Blackwell.

Capra, F. (2015). Laing's 'The Voice of Experience' and the Emerging Science of Consciousness. In M. G. Thompson, Ed., *The Legacy of R. D. Laing: An Appraisal of his Contemporary Relevance*. London and New York: Routledge.

Castoriadis, C. (1997). *The Castoriadis Reader*. Translated and edited by David Ames Curtis. Oxford: Blackwell Publishers.

Chang, S., Stuckler, D., Yip, P. and Gunnell, D. (2013). Impact of 2008 Global Economic Crisis on Suicide: Time Trend Study in 54 Countries. *British Medical Journal*, Vol. 347. Available at https://doi.org/10.1136/bmj.f5239 (accessed 12 September 2019).

Cheliotis, L. K. (2013). Neoliberal Capitalism and Middle-Class Punitiveness: Bringing Erich Fromm's 'Materialistic Psychoanalysis' to Penology. *Punishment & Society*, Vol. 15, No. 3, pp. 247–273. Available at https://journals.sagepub.com/doi/10.1177/1462474513483692 (accessed 20 September 2019).

Choudhury, S. and Slaby, J., Eds (2016). *Critical Neuroscience: A Handbook of the Social and Cultural Context of Neuroscience*. Chichester: John Wiley & Sons.

Citizen Therapists Against Trumpism (2016). *A Public Manifesto*. Available at http://citizentherapists.com/manifesto/ (accessed 27 February 2017).

Coates, R. (1998). *Christianity in Bakhtin, God and the Exiled Author*. Cambridge: Cambridge University Press.

Cole, M. (1979). Introduction: The Historical Context. Introduction to A. R. Luria's *The Making of the Mind*. Available at www.marxists.org/archive/luria/works/1979/mind/intro.htm (accessed 26 September 2019).

Cole, M. (2002). *Michael Cole Interviews Jerome Bruner and Oliver Sacks*. Available at http://luria.ucsd.edu/AudioVideo/DVD_Luria4.mp4 (accessed 11 July 2019).

Cole, M. (2003). *Cultural Psychology: A Once and Future Discipline*. Cambridge, MA and London: Harvard University Press.

Cole, P., Struthers, D. and Zimmer, K. (2017). *Wobblies of the World: A Global History of the IWW*. London: Pluto Press.

Conatz, J. (2017). *A Popular Front of the Right?* Available at https://libcom.org/blog/popular-front-right-30012017 (accessed 15 September 2019).

Conliffe, C. (2018). John B. Watson, Dark Psychologist. *HeadStuff*. Available at www.headstuff.org/culture/history/terrible-people-from-history/john-b-watson-dark-psychologist/ (accessed 11 August 2018).

Conner, C. D. (2005). *A People's History of Science: Miners, Midwives, and 'Low Mechanicks'*. New York: Nation Books.

Connery, M. C. (2010). The Social Construction of a Visual Language: On Becoming a Painter. In M. C. Connery, V. P. John-Steiner and A. Marjanovic-Shane, Eds, *Vygotsky and Creativity: A Cultural-Historical Approach to Play, Meaning Making, and the Arts*. New York: Peter Lang, pp. 83–105.

Cooper, C. (2015). Psychological Impact of Nuclear Disasters Like Fukushima More Damaging Than the Risk from Radiation, Experts Say, *The Independent*, 31 July. Available at www.independent.co.uk/life-style/health-and-families/health-news/psychological-impact-of-nuclear-disasters-like-fukushima-more-damaging-than-the-risk-from-radiation-10428096.html (accessed 5 August 2019).

Crenshaw, K. (1989). Demarginalising the Intersection of Race and Sex: A Black Feminist Critique of Antidiscrimination Doctrine, Feminist Theory and Antiracist Politics. *University of Chicago Legal Forum*, Vol. 1989, Issue 1, Article 8, pp. 139–167. Available at http://chicagounbound.uchicago.edu/uclf/vol1989/iss1/8 (accessed 24 July 2019).

Crenshaw, K. (1994). Mapping the Margins: Intersectionality, Identity Politics, and Violence Against Women of Colour. In M. A. Fineman and R. Mykitiuk, Eds, *The Public Nature of Private Violence*. New York: Routledge, pp. 93–118.

Crenshaw, K. (2016). *The Urgency of Intersectionality*. Ted Talk. Available at www.youtube.com/watch?v=akOe5-UsQ2o (accessed 15 September 2019).

Crenshaw, K. (2018). *What Is Intersectionality?* National Association of Independent Schools. Available at www.youtube.com/watch?v=ViDtnfQ9FHc (accessed 15 September 2019).

Cromby, J. (2004). Depression: Embodying Social Inequality. *Journal of Critical Psychology, Counselling and Psychotherapy*, Vol. 4, No. 3, pp. 176–186.

Cromby, J. (2007). Integrating Social Science with Neuroscience: Potentials and Problems. *Biosocieties*, No. 2, pp. 149–169.

Curtis, A. (2002). *The Century of the Self.* Part 1: *The Happiness Machine.* A film in four parts, first broadcasted on BBC TV. Available at www.youtube.com/watch?v=DnPmg0R1M04 (accessed 20 August 2018).

Dalla Costa, M. and James, S. (1975). *The Power of Women and the Subversion of the Community*. Bristol: Falling Wall Press.

Damasio, A. (2003). *Looking for Spinoza: Joy, Sorrow and the Feeling Brain*. London: Vintage Books.

Darnton, R. (1988). *The Great Cat Massacre: And Other Stories in French Cultural History*. London: Penguin Books.

David, A. S. (1986). A Review of 'Sanity, Madness and the Family'. By R. D. Laing and A. Esterson. *British Journal of Psychiatry*, Vol. 149, pp. 181–379.

David-West, A. (2013). Erich Fromm and North Korea: Social Psychology and the Political Regime. *Critical Sociology*, 4 March. Available at https://journals.sagepub.com/doi/abs/10.1177/0896920512466275 (accessed 30 June 2019).

Davidson, R. J., Sherer, K. R. and Goldsmiths, H. H., Eds (2003). *Handbook of Affective Sciences*. New York: Oxford University Press.

Davies, C. (2017). Strong Link between Disadvantage and Suicide, Says Samaritans. *The Guardian*, 6 March. Available at www.theguardian.com/society/2017/mar/06/strong-link-between-disadvantage-and-suicide-says-samaritans (accessed 17 July 2018).

Debord, G. ([1967] 1977). *Society of the Spectacle*. Translated by Fredy Perlman and Jon Supak. Detroit, MI: Black & Red. Available at http://library.nothingness.org/articles/SI/en/pub_contents/4 (accessed 14 September 2019).

Debs, E. V. (1918). *The Canton, Ohio Speech, Anti-War Speech*. Available at www.marxists.org/archive/debs/works/1918/canton.htm (accessed 29 August 2018).

Dergan, J. (2011). A Cultural-Historical Approach to Neuropsychological Treatment: Understanding Latino and Other Non-Dominant Groups. In P. R. Portes and S. Salas, Eds, *Vygotsky in the 21st Century Society*. New York: Peter Lang, pp. 131–150.

Dewsbury, D. A. (2013). John B. Watson's Work and Comparative Psychology. *Mexican Journal of Behavior Analysis*, Vol. 38, No. 2, pp. 10–33.

Didelot, M. J., Hollingsworth, L. and Buckenmeyer, J. A. (2012). Internet Addiction: A Logotherapeutic Approach. *Journal of Addictions & Offender Counselling*, Vol. 33, pp. 18–33.

Dietzgen, J. ([1869] 1984). *The Nature of the Human Brain Work: An Introduction to Dialectics*. Translated by Ernest Untermann, with an Introduction by Lawrence Gambone. Vancouver, BC: Red Lion Press.

Dietzgen, E. ([1894–1895] 1914). *Joseph Dietzgen: A Sketch of His Life by Eugene Dietzgen*. Available at https://libcom.org/history/joseph-dietzgen-sketch-his-life-eugene-dietzgen (accessed 5 March 2019).

Dose, R. (2003). The World League for Sexual Reform: Some Possible Approaches. *Journal of the History of Sexuality*, Vol. 12, No. 1, pp. 1–15.

Draper, H. (1989). *The Dictatorship of the Proletariat: From Marx to Lenin*. New York: Monthly Review Press.

Drury, J. (2002). 'When the Mobs Are Looking for Witches to Burn, Nobody's Safe': Talking about the Reactionary Crowd. *Discourse & Society*, Vol. 13, No. 1, pp. 41–73.

Drury, J. and Reicher, S. (1999). The Intergroup Dynamics of Collective Empowerment: Substantiating the Social Identity Model of Crowd Behaviour. *Group Processes and Intergroup Relations*, Vol. 2, No. 4, pp. 381–402.

Duncan, D. (2007). Consumer Research in 1958. *The Psychologist*, Vol. 20. Available at https://thepsychologist.bps.org.uk/volume-20/edition-9/online-only-article-consumer-research-1958 (accessed 20 August 2018).

Easton, L. D. and Guddat, K. H. (1997). *Writings of the Young Marx on Philosophy and Society*. Translated and edited by L. D. Easton and K. H. Guddat. Indianapolis, IN and Cambridge: Hackett.

Edelman, M. ([1945] 1994). *The Ghetto Fights: Warsaw, 1941–43*. London: Bookmarks.

Ehrenreich, B. (2008). *Dancing in the Streets: A History of Collective Joy*. London: Granta Books.

Ehrenreich, B. (2009). *Smile or Die: How Positive Thinking Fooled America & The World*. London: Granta Publications.

Elders, F. (1971). *Michel Foucault*. 15-minute documentary broadcasted on Dutch TV, 28 November. Available at www.youtube.com/watch?v=qzoOhhh4aJg (accessed 12 August 2019).

Engel, G. L. (1988). How Much Longer Must Medicine's Science be Bound by a Seventeenth Century World View? In K. J. White, Ed., *The Task of Medicine*, Menlo Park, CA: Henry J. Kaiser Foundation, pp. 113–136.

Engels, F. (1875). *Engels to Lavrov*, 12 November. Available at www.marxists.org/archive/marx/works/1875/letters/75_11_12.htm (accessed 4 September 2019).

Engeström, Y. (1995). Innovative Organisational Learning in Medical and Legal Settings. In L. Martin, K. Nelson and E. Tobach, Eds, *Sociocultural Psychology: Theory and Practice of Doing and Knowing*. Cambridge: Cambridge University Press, pp. 326–356.

Erikson, E. (1980). *Identity and the Life Cycle*. New York: W. W. Norton.

European Union Agency for Fundamental Rights (FRA) (2014). *Being Trans in the EU: Comparative Analysis of the EU LGBT Survey Data, Summary*. Available at file:///C:/Users/mshah/Downloads/fra-2015-being-trans-eu-comparative-summary_en.pdf (accessed 13 September 2018).

Farmer, F. (2005). On Style and Other Unremarkable Things. *Written Communication*, Vol. 22, No. 3, pp. 339–347.

Fave, A. D. and Massimini, F. (2003). Making Disability into a Resource. *The Psychologist*, Vol. 16, No. 3, p. 133.

Feltham, C. (2010). *Critical Thinking in Counselling and Psychotherapy*. Los Angeles, CA: SAGE.

Fendler, L. (2014). *Michel Foucault*. Los Angeles, CA and London: SAGE.

Fernandez, N. C. (1997). *Capitalism and Class Struggle in the USSR: A Marxist Theory*. Aldershot: Ashgate.

Fillingham, L. A. (1993). *Foucault for Beginners*. Illustrated by Moshe Süsser. New York and London: Writers & Readers.

Fo, D. (1991). *The Tricks of the Trade*. Translated by Joe Farrell. New York: Routledge.

Fonagy, P. (2000). The Outcome of Psychoanalysis: The Hope of a Future. *The Psychologist*, Vol. 13, No. 12, pp. 620–623.

Fortunati, L. (1995). *The Arcane of Reproduction: Housework, Prostitution, Labor and Capital*. Translated by Hilary Creek. New York: Autonomedia.

Foster, R. (2017). Social Character: Erich Fromm and the Ideological Glue of Neoliberalism. *Critical Horizons*, Vol. 18, No. 1, pp. 1–18.

Foucault, M. (1963). *Deleuze on Masochism: An Interview by Foucault*. Broadcasted on 3 April. Available at www.youtube.com/watch?v=gBhb2-VJA1w (accessed 12 August 2019).

Foucault, M. (1969). *Archaeology of Knowledge*. London: Tavistock.

Foucault, M. ([1972] 2002). *Archaeology of Knowledge*. Abingdon: Routledge.

Foucault, M. ([1973] 2003). *The Birth of the Clinic*. Abingdon: Routledge.

Foucault, M. ([1978] 1990). *The History of Sexuality: An Introduction*. Translated by Robert Hurley. London: Penguin.

Foucault, M. (1991). *Discipline and Punish: The Birth of the Prison*. London: Penguin.

Foucault, M. (2001). *Madness and Civilisation*. London and New York: Routledge.

Fox, D. (1985). Psychology, Ideology, Utopia, and the Commons. *American Psychologist*, Vol. 40, pp. 48–58.

Fox, D. (2011). Anarchism and Psychology. *Theory in Action*, Vol. 4, pp. 31–48. Available at www.dennisfox.net/papers/anarchism_and_psychology.html (accessed 28 September 2019).

Fox, D. (2012). Interview: Critical Psychology and Social Struggle. *Meydan*, Vol. 6, pp. 14–15. Available at www.dennisfox.net/papers/meydan_istanbul.html (accessed 28 September 2019).

Fox, D. and Prilleltensky, I., Eds (2011). *Critical Psychology: An Introduction*. London: SAGE.

Fozooni, B. (2006). Towards a Critique of the Iranian Psy-Complex. *Annual Review of Critical Psychology*, Vol. 5, pp. 69–88. Available at https://studylib.net/doc/8483892/toward-a-critique-of-the-iranian-psy-complex (accessed 24 September 2019).

Fozooni, B. (2010). Cognitive Analytic Therapy: A Sympathetic Critique. *Psychotherapy and Politics International*, Vol. 8, No. 2, pp. 128–145.

Fozooni, B. (2012a). *What Is Critical Social Research?* Vol. 1. Peterborough: FastPrint Publishing.

Fozooni, B. (2012b). The Politics of Encyclopaedias. *Journal for Critical Education Policy Studies*, Vol. 10, No. 2, pp. 314–344. Available at http://www.jceps.com/wp-content/uploads/PDFs/10-2-11.pdf (accessed 6 September 2019).

Fozooni, B. (2014). Sexual Dysfunction(s) in Iran: Imaginary Encounters with Otto Gross and Wilhelm Reich. *Psychotherapy and Politics International*, Vol. 12, No. 2, pp. 80–98.

Fozooni, B. (2017a). *What Is Critical Social Research?* Vol. 2. Peterborough: FastPrint Publishing.

Fozooni, B. (2017b). Humour in Therapy: An Online Survey. *What Is Critical Social Research?* Vol. 2. Peterborough: FastPrint Publishing, pp. 191–218.

Fozooni, B. (2017c). *Otto Gross: The Troubadour Analyst. A Review of G. M. Heuer's Freud's 'Outstanding' Colleague/Jung's 'Twin Brother'*. Available at https://ottogross.org/otto-gross-the-troubadour-analyst-babak-fozooni-reviews-gottfried-heuers-upcoming-book/ (accessed 5 September 2019).

Fozooni, B. (2017d). Forms of Knowledge and Trumpism. *What Is Critical Social Science?* Vol. 2. Peterborough: FastPrint Publishing, pp. 1–34.

Fozooni, B. (2017e). A Rhetorical Analysis of Nationalism in Shakespeare's Henry V. *What Is Critical Social Research?* Vol. 2. Peterborough: FastPrint Publishing, pp. 75–119.

Frances, A. J. (2017). How Psychoanalysis and Behaviourism Helped Create Advertising. *Psychology Today*, 9 January. Available at www.psychologytoday.com/gb/blog/saving-normal/201701/how-psychoanalysis-and-behaviorism-helped-create-advertising (accessed 20 August 2018).

Frankl, V. E. ([1959] 2004). *Man's Search for Meaning: The Classic Tribute to Hope from The Holocaust*. London: Rider.

Frankl, V. E. (1972). *Why Idealists Are the Real Realists*. Available at www.youtube.com/watch?v=loay2imHq5E (accessed 11 September 2019).

Fraser, S. (2015). *The Age of Acquiescence: The Life and Death of American Resistance to Organised Wealth and Power*. New York: Little, Brown and Co.

Freud, S. ([1905] 2017). *Three Essays on the Theory of Sexuality*. London: Verso.

Freud, S. ([1910] 1957). Leonardo da Vinci and Other Works. In J. Strachey, Ed., in collaboration with Anna Freud. *The Standard Edition of the Complete Psychological Works of Sigmund Freud*, Vol. XI. London: The Hogarth Press and the Institute of Psycho-Analysis.

Freud, S. (1911). Freud's Letter to Jung, 2 November. In *The Freud/Jung Letters: The Correspondence between Sigmund Freud and C. G. Jung (1906–1914)*. Available at https://archive.org/stream/FreudJungLetters/The-Freud-Jung-letters-The-Correspondence-between-Sigmund-Freud-and-C-G-Jung_djvu.txt (accessed 5 September 2019).

Freud, S. (1919). Advances in Psycho-Analytic Therapy. In J. Strachey, Ed., *The Standard Edition of the Complete Psychological Works of Sigmund Freud*. London: Hogarth Press, pp. 157–168.

Freud, S. ([1919] 1955). Lines of Advance in Psychoanalytic Therapy. In L. Strachey (Ed.), *The Standard Edition of the Complete Psychological Works of Sigmund Freud*. Vol. 17. London: Hogarth Press, pp. 157–168.

Freud, S. ([1920] 2010). *Beyond the Pleasure Principle*. Seattle, WA: Pacific Publishing Studio in conjunction with CreateSpace.

Freud, S. ([1921] 2012). *Group Psychology and the Analysis of the Ego*. Greensboro, NC: Empire Books.

Freud, S. ([1927] 2005). *The Essentials of Psycho-Analysis*. Introduction by Anna Freud, translated by James Strachey. London: Vintage Books.

Freud, S. ([1930] 2015). *Civilisation and Its Discontents*. Edited by T. Dufresne, translated by G. C. Richter. Peterborough, ON: Broadview Press.

Freud, S. ([1933] 1953). Lecture 33: Femininity, *New Introductory Lectures in Psycho-analysis*. Standard Edition, Vol. 22. Translated and edited by James Strachey. London: Hogarth Press, pp. 111–134.

Freud, S. and Breuer, J. ([1895] 2004). *Studies in Hysteria*. Translated by Nicola Luckhurst, with an Introduction by Rachel Bowlby. London: Penguin Books.

Fromm, E. ([1941] 1994). *Escape from Freedom*. New York: Henry Holt and Company.

Fromm, E. ([1942] 1980). *The Fear of Freedom*. London and Henley: Routledge and Kegan Paul.

Fromm, E. ([1949] 1986). *Man for Himself*. London: Ark.

Fromm, E. ([1956] 2002). *The Sane Society*. Abingdon: Routledge Classics.

Fromm, E. (1958). *The Mike Wallace Interview: Erich Fromm*. Available at www.youtube.com/watch?v=OTu0qJG0NfU (accessed 24 June 2019).

Fromm, E. (1962). *The Psychology of Nationalism*. Available at www.youtube.com/watch?v=2w4H6hyFf4Y (accessed 25 June 2019).

Fromm, E. (1964). *The Heart of Man: Its Genius for Good and Evil*. New York: Harper and Row.

Fromm, E. (1968). *Erich Fromm Interview with Elionor Fisher*. Available at www.youtube.com/watch?v=AScV6rfc16U (accessed 20 September 2019).

Fromm, E. (1973). *The Crisis of Psychoanalysis*. London: Penguin.

Fromm, E. (1980). *The Heart of Man: Its Genius for Good and Evil*. New York: Harper and Row.

Fromm, E. (1982). *Greatness and Limitations of Freud's Thought: A Revolutionary Study of Genius in Conflict*. London: Sphere Books.

Frosh, S. (1987). *The Politics of Psychoanalysis: An Introduction to Freudian and Post-Freudian Theory*. London: Macmillan Education.

Fulco, A. (1983). Vico and Marx: Human Consciousness and the Structure. In G. Tagliacozzo, Ed., *Vico and Marx: Affinities and Contrasts*. Basingstoke and London: Macmillan, pp. 126–139.

Fullerton, J. (2019). Teenage Girl Kills Herself 'After Instagram Poll' in Malaysia. *The Guardian*, 15 May. Available at www.theguardian.com/world/2019/may/15/teenage-girl-kills-herself-after-instagram-poll-in-malaysia (accessed 12 September 2019).

Gardiner, M. (2000). 'A Very Understandable Horror of Dialectics': Bakhtin and Marxist Phenomenology. In C. Brandist, Ed., *Materialising Bakhtin: The Bakhtin Circle and Social Theory*. Basingstoke: Macmillan, pp. 119–141.

Garfinkel, H. (1986). *Ethonomethodological Studies of Work*. London: Routledge and Kegan Paul.

Gergen, K. J. (1973). Social Psychology as History. *Journal of Personality and Social Psychology*, Vol. 26, No. 2, pp. 309–320.

Goffman, E. ([1961] 1991). *Asylums: Essays on the Social Situation of Mental Patients and Other Inmates*. New York: Doubleday Anchor.

Goldberg, E. and Bougakov, D. (2009). Neuropsychology and A. R. Luria's Concept of Higher Cortical Functions in the Beginning of the 3rd Millennium. In A.-L. Christensen, E. Goldberg and D. Bougakov, Eds, *Luria's Legacy in the 21st Century*. New York: Oxford University Press, pp. 17–22.

Good, P. (2001). *Language for Those Who Have Nothing: Mikhail Bakhtin and the Landscape of Psychiatry*. New York: Kluwer Academic/Plenum Publishers.

Gorman, D. (1992). Joseph Dietzgen. *Radical Chains*, No. 3. Available at https://libcom.org/history/joseph-dietzgen-radical-chains (accessed 5 March 2019).

Gould, S. J. (1996). The Real Error of Cyril Burt: Factor Analysis and the Reification of Intelligence. In *The Mismeasure of Man*. New York: W. W. Norton & Company, pp. 264–350.

Gramsci, A. ([1934] 1999). Americanism and Fordism. In Q. Hoare and G. N. Smith, Eds, *Selections from Prison Notebooks of Antonio Gramsci*. London: Elec-Book, pp. 558–622. Available at http://abahlali.org/files/gramsci.pdf (accessed 29 September 2019).

Granberg, M. (2019). Objective Meaning: The Formation of Self in Mead and Sohn-Rethel. *Acta Sociologica*, Vol. 62, No. 1, pp. 34–46.

Granatella, M. (2015). Imaginative Universals and Human Cognition in 'The New Science' of Giambattista Vico. *Culture & Psychology*, Vol. 21, No. 2, pp. 185–206.

Gray, J. A. (1979). *Pavlov*. New York: Viking Press.

Gregory, C. (2000). Humanism, Self-Actualisation and Holodiction: Psychological Themes in Star Trek. In C. Gregory, *Star Trek: Parallel Narratives*. Basingstoke and London: Macmillan.

Griffiths, L. (2010). Humour as Resistance to Professional Dominance in Community Mental Health Teams. In S. Taylor, Ed., *Ethnographic Research: A Reader*. Los Angeles, CA and London: SAGE in association with the Open University, pp. 213–233.

Griffiths, T. (1970). *Comedians*. London: Faber and Faber.

Guerin, D. (1973). *Fascism and Big Business*. New York: Monad Press distributed by Pathfinder.

Guest, H. S. (2014). Maslow's Hierarchy of Needs: The Sixth Level. *The Psychologist*, Vol. 27, No. 12, pp. 982–983. Available at https://thepsychologist.bps.org.uk/system/files/1214gues.pdf (accessed 25 August 2018).

Gupta, N. (2015). Exploring the Schizoid Defence of the Closet through the Existential-Phenomenology of R. D. Laing. *Journal of Humanistic Psychology*, Vol. 52, No. 2, pp. 170–189.

Habermas, J. (1989). *The Structural Transformation of the Public Sphere: An Inquiry into a Category of Bourgeois Society*. Cambridge, MA: MIT Press.

Hacking, I. (1981). How Should We Do the History of Statistics? In G. Burchill, C. Gordon and P. Miller, Eds, *The Foucault Effect*. Chicago, IL: University of Chicago Press, pp. 181–195.

Haeberle, E. J. (1981). Swastika, Pink Triangle and Yellow Star: The Destruction of Sexology and the Persecution of Homosexuals in Nazi Germany. *Journal of Sexual Research*, Vol. 17, No. 3, pp. 270–287.

Hanon, J. W., Ritchie, M. and Rye, D. R. (2001). Class: The Missing Discourse in Counselling and Counsellor Education in the United States of America. *Journal of Critical Psychology, Counselling and Psychotherapy*, Vol. 1, No. 3, pp. 137–154.

Hanson, J. (2018). *How to Apply Maslow's Hierarchy of Needs to Education*. Available at https://classroom.synonym.com/apply-maslows-hierarchy-needs-education-7771899.html (accessed 24 August 2018).

Harré, R. (2009). *Pavlov's Dogs and Schrödinger's Cat: Scenes from the Living Laboratory*. Oxford: Oxford University Press.

Harré, R. (2012). Methods of Research: Neuroscience and Genetic/Evolutionary Psychology. In R. Harré and F. M. Moghaddam, Eds, *Psychology for the Third Millennium: Integrating Cultural and Neuroscience Perspectives*. Los Angeles, CA and London: SAGE, pp. 37–56.

Harris, B. (1979). Whatever Happened to Little Albert? *American Psychologist*, Vol. 34, No. 2, pp. 151–160.

Harris, B. (1997). Repoliticizing the History of Psychology. In D. Fox and I. Prilleltensky, Eds, *Critical Psychology: An Introduction*. London: SAGE.

Hart, K. E. and Kritsonis, W. A. (2006). A Critical Analysis of John B. Watson's Original Writing: 'Behaviourism as a Behaviourist Views It'. *National Forum of Applied Educational Research Journal*, Vol. 19, No. 3, pp. 1–6.

Hazlitt, W. ([1826] 2004). *On the Pleasure of Hating*. London: Penguin.

Healey, D. (2001). *Homosexual Desire in Revolutionary Russia: The Regulation of Sexual and Gender Dissent*. Chicago, IL and London: University of Chicago Press.

Heaton, J. M. (2015). On R. D. Laing's Style, Sorcery, Alienation. In M. G. Thompson, Ed., *The Legacy of R. D. Laing: An Appraisal of His Contemporary Relevance*. London and New York: Routledge, pp. 47–58.

Hekma, G., Oosterhuis, H. and Steakley, J. (1995). *Gay Men and the Sexual History of the Political Left*. New York: Haworth Press.

Henriques, J., Hollway, W., Urwin, C., Venn, C. and Walkerdine, V. (1984). *Changing the Subject: Psychology, Social Regulation and Subjectivity*. London and New York: Routledge.

Henry, J. (2003). Organisations. *The Psychologist*, Vol. 16, No. 3, p. 139.

Henwood, B. F., Derejko, K.-S., Couture, J. and Padgett, D. K. (2015). Maslow and Mental Health Recovery: A Comparative Study of Homeless Programs for Adults with Serious Mental Illness. *Administration and Policy in Mental Health and Mental Health Services*, Vol. 42, No. 2, pp. 220–228. Available at www.ncbi.nlm.nih.gov/pmc/articles/PMC4130906/ (accessed 24 October 2019).

Hepburn, A. (2003). *An Introduction to Critical Social Psychology*. London: SAGE.

Heuer, G. M. (2017). *Freud's 'Outstanding' Colleague/Jung's 'Twin Brother': The Suppressed Psychoanalytic and Political Significance of Otto Gross*. London and New York: Routledge.

Hill, C. ([1972] 1991). *The World Turned Upside Down: Radical Ideas During the English Revolution*. London: Penguin.

Hill, D. B. (2005). Sexuality and Gender in Hirschfeld's Die Tranvestiten: A Case of the Elusive Evidence of the Ordinary. *Journal of the History of the Sexuality*, Vol. 14, No. 3, pp. 316–332.

Hirschfeld, M. ([1914] 2000). *The Homosexuality of Men and Women*. Introduction by Vern L. Bullough, translated by Michael A. Lombardi-Nash. New York: Prometheus Books.

Hirschfeld, M. (1938a). *Racism*. Translated by Eden and Cedar Paul. London: Victor Gollancz.

Hirschfeld, M. (1938b). *Sexual Anomalies and Perversions: Physical and Psychological Development, Diagnosis and Treatment*. Compiled by Norman Haire. London: Encyclopaedic Press.

Hirschfeld, M. ([1941] 2006). *The Sexual History of the World War*. Honolulu, HI: University Press of the Pacific.

Hobsbawm, E. J. and Ranger, T. O., Eds ([1983] 2012). *The Invention of Tradition*. Cambridge and New York: Cambridge University Press.

Hochschild, A. R. ([1983] 2012). *The Managed Heart: Commercialisation of Human Feeling*. Berkeley and London: University of California Press.

Hoffman, E. (1988). *The Right to be Human: A Biography of Abraham Maslow*. New York: St. Martin's Press.

Holloway, J. (2002). *Change the World Without Taking Power: The Meaning of Revolution Today*. London and Sterling, VA: Pluto Press.

Hollway, W. (1984). Fitting Work: Psychological Assessment in Organisations. In J. Henriques, W. Hollway, C. Urwin, C. Venn and V. Walkerdine, Eds, *Changing the Subject: Psychology, Social Regulation, and Subjectivity*. London and New York: Routledge, pp. 26–59.

Holman, D. (2017). Class. In A. Vossler, C. Havard, G. Pike, M.-J. Barker and B. Raabe, Eds, *Mad or Bad? A Critical Approach to Counselling and Forensic Psychology*. Los Angeles, CA and London: SAGE, pp. 109–122.

Holzkamp, K. (2013). Psychology: Social Self-Understanding on the Reasons for Action in Conduct of Everyday Life. In E. Schraube and U. Osterkamp, Eds, *Psychology from the Standpoint of the Subject: Selected Writings of Klaus Holzkamp*. Basingstoke: Palgrave Macmillan, pp. 233–234.

Hutton, P. H. (1983). Religion and the Civilising Process in Vico and Marx. In G. Tagliacozzo, Ed, *Vico and Marx: Affinities and Contrasts*. Basingstoke and London: Macmillan, pp. 140–150.

Huyanfeng (2011). The Introduction and Dissemination of Behaviourism in Modern China. *International Journal of Business and Social Science*, Vol. 2, No. 3, pp. 127–130.

Intersectionality Score Calculator (n.d.). Available at https://intersectionalityscore.com (accessed 28 December 2019).

Ivinson, G. (2012). Boys, Skills and Class: Educational Failure or Community Survival? Insights from Vygotsky and Bernstein. In Harry Daniels, Ed, *Vygotsky and Sociology*. London and New York : Routledge, pp. 155–174.

Jackson, J. C., Santoro, M. J., Ely, T. M., Boehm, L., Kiehl, A. L., Anderson, L. S. and Ely, E. W. (2014). Improving Patient Care Through the Prism of Psychology: Application of Maslow's Hierarchy to Sedation, Delirium and Early Mobility in the ICU. *Journal of Critical Care*, Vol. 29, No. 3, pp. 438–444.

Jacobitti, E. E. (1983). From Vico's Common Sense to Gramsci's Hegemony. In G. Tagliacozzo, Ed, *Vico and Marx: Affinities and Contrasts*. Basingstoke and London: Macmillan, pp. 367–387.

Jacoby, R. (1997). *Social Amnesia: A Critique of Contemporary Psychology*. New Brunswick, NJ and London: Transaction Publishers.

James, C. L. R. in collab. with Dunayevskaya, R. and Lee Boggs, G. ([1950] 2013). *State Capitalism and World Revolution*. Introduction by Paul Buhle. Oakland, CA and Chicago, IL: PM Press/Charles H. Kerr.

Jennings, J. R. (1983). Sorel, Vico, and Marx. In G. Tagliacozzo, Ed, *Vico and Marx: Affinities and Contrasts*. London and Basingstoke: Macmillan, pp. 326–341.

Johnstone, L. (2003). A Shocking Treatment? *The Psychologist*, Vol. 16, No. 5, pp. 236–239.

Jones, D. (2017). *Applying Maslow to Schools: A New Approach to School Equity*. Available at www.deyproject.org/denishas-blog/applying-maslow-to-schools-a-new-approach-to-school-equity (accessed 24 August 2018).

Jones, E. (1957). *The Life and Work of Sigmund Freud*, 3 Vols. New York: Basic Books.

Jordan, Z. A. (1967). *The Origins of Dialectical Materialism*. Available at www.marxists.org/subject/marxmyths/jordan/article.htm (accessed 24 August 2019).

Kant, I. (1963). *Lecture on Ethics*. Translated by L. Infield. New York: Harper & Row.

Karpov, Y. V. (2005). *The Neo-Vygotskian Approach to Child Development*. Cambridge: Cambridge University Press.

Kazin, M. (2016). Trump and American Populism: Old Whine, New Bottles, *Foreign Affairs*. Available at www.foreignaffairs.com/articles/united-states/2016-10-06/trump-and-american-populism (accessed 15 September 2019).

Kellner, D. (2016). Donald Trump as Authoritarian Populist: A Frommian Analysis. *Logos*. Available at http://logosjournal.com/2016/kellner-2/ (accessed 21 February 2017).

Kenrick, D. T., Griskevicius, V., Neuberg, S. L. and Schaller, M. (2010). Renovating the Pyramid of Needs: Contemporary Extensions Built Upon Ancient Foundations. *Perspectives on Psychological Science*, Vol. 5, No. 3, pp. 292–314.

Khoroshilova, O. (2017). 1917 Russian Revolution: The Gay Community's Brief Window of Freedom. BBC Online, 10 November. Available at www.bbc.co.uk/news/world-europe-41737330 (accessed 12 September 2018).

Kinsella, M. (2014). Reimagining Community in Contemporary Ireland: Lessons from Viktor Frankl's 'Man's Search for Meaning'. *An Irish Quarterly Review*, Vol. 103, No. 409, pp. 60–71.

Kirsner, D. (2015). Laing's The Divided Self and The Politics of Experience: Then and Now. In M. G. Thompson, Ed, *The Legacy of R. D. Laing: An Appraisal of His Contemporary Relevance*. London and New York: Routledge.

Kline, G. L. (1983). The Question of Materialism in Vico and Marx. In G. Tagliacozzo, Ed, *Vico and Marx: Affinities and Contrasts*. London and Basingstoke: Macmillan, pp. 114–125.

Kline, T. (2018). Applying Maslow's Hierarchy of Needs in Our Classrooms. Available at www.changekidslives.org/actions-4/ (accessed 24 August 2018).

Knabb, K., Ed. (2007). *Situationist International Anthology*. Translated by Ken Knabb. Berkeley, CA: Bureau of Public Secrets.

Kovel, J. ([1970] 1984). *White Racism: A Psychohistory*. New York: Colombia University Press.

Kovel, J. (1981). *The Age of Desire: Case Histories of a Radical Psychoanalyst*. New York: Pantheon Books.

Kovel, J. (1984). *Against the State of Nuclear Terror*. Boston, MA: South End Press.

Kovel, J. (1987). *A Complete Guide to Therapy: From Psychoanalysis to Behaviour Modification*. London and Harmondsworth: Penguin.

Kozulin, A. (1990). *Vygotsky's Psychology: A Biography of Ideas*. New York and London: Harvester Wheatsheaf.

Kozulin, A. (2011). Cognitive Aspects of the Transition from a Traditional to a Modern Technological Society. In P. R. Portes and S. Salas, Eds, *Vygotsky in the 21st Century Society*. New York: Peter Lang, pp. 66–86.

Kremer, W. and Hammond, C. (2013). Abraham Maslow and the Pyramid that Beguiled Business. *BBC World Service*, 1 September. Available at www.bbc.co.uk/news/magazine-23902918 (accessed 24 August 2018).

Krueger, J. (2013). Maslow on Creativity: Wisdom or Wishy-Wash? *Psychology Today*, 7 September. Available at www.psychologytoday.com/us/blog/one-among-many/201309/maslow-creativity (accessed 25 August 2018).

Kuhn, T. S. (1970). *The Structure of Scientific Revolutions*. Chicago, IL: University of Chicago Press.

Kurosawa, A., Director (1952). *Ikiru*. Cowboy Pictures.

Kvale, S., Ed (1992). *Psychology and Postmodernism*. London: SAGE.

Lafargue, P. (1883). *The Right to be Lazy*. Translated by Charles Kerr. Available at www.marxists.org/archive/lafargue/1883/lazy/ (accessed 6 September 2019).

Lafrance, M. (2005). The Struggle for True Sex: Herculine Barbin dite Alexina B and the Work of Michel Foucault. *Canadian Review of Comparative Literature*, Vol. 32, No. 2, pp. 161–182.

Laing, R. D. ([1960] 2010). *The Divided Self: An Existential Study in Sanity and Madness*. London: Penguin.

Laing, R. D. (1967). *The Politics of Experience and The Bird of Paradise*. London: Penguin.

Laing, R. D. ([1971] 1999). *The Politics of the Family and Other Essays*. Abingdon: Routledge.

Laing, R. D. (1976). *Do You Love Me? An Entertainment in Conversation and Verse*. New York: Pantheon Books.

Langdridge, D. (2008). Phenomenology and Critical Social Psychology: Directions and Debates in Theory and Research. *Social and Personality Psychology Compass*, Vol. 2, No. 3, pp. 1126–1142.

Langenburg, A. (2017). The Inner Lives of Queer Comrades in Early Soviet Russia. *OpenDemocracy*, 15 December. Available at www.opendemocracy.net/od-russia/artem-langenburg/interview-with-ira-roldugina (accessed 12 September 2018).

Langer, L. L. (1982). *Versions of Survival: The Holocaust and the Human Spirit*. Albany: State University of New York Press.

Längle, A. and Sykes, B.-M. (2006). Viktor Frankl-Advocate for Humanity: On His 100th Birthday. *Journal of Humanistic Psychology*, Vol. 46, No. 1, pp. 36–47.

Lantolf, J. P. (2017). Materialist Dialectics in Vygotsky's Methodological Framework: Implications for Applied Linguistic Research. In C. Ratner and D. N. H. Silva, Eds, *Vygotsky and Marx: Towards a Marxist Psychology*. London and New York: Routledge, pp. 173–189.

Lantz, J. (1998). Viktor Frankl and Interactional Group Therapy. *Journal of Religion and Health*, Vol. 37, No. 2, pp. 93–104.

Larson, C. A. (1979). Highlights of Dr. John B. Watson's Career in Advertising. *The Industrial-Organizational Psychologist*, Vol. 6, No. 3, pp. 3–5.

Lauren, L. (2019). Sickbait: In 30 Seconds I Found Millions of Posts Glorifying Suicide on Instagram. *The Sun*, 24 January. Available at www.thesun.co.uk/fabulous/8264073/suicide-hashtags-dangerous-instagram-social-media/ (accessed 12 September 2019).

Lee, B. (2019). Teen Suicide Rose After Netflix's 13 Reasons Why Aired, US Study Shows. *The Guardian*, 30 April. Available at www.theguardian.com/tv-and-radio/2019/apr/30/teen-suicides-netflix-13-reasons-why-study (accessed 12 September 2019).

Leiman M. (1997). Procedures as Dialogical Sequences: A Revised Version of the Fundamental Concept in Cognitive Analytic Therapy. *British Journal of Medical Psychology*, Vol. 70, pp. 193–207.

Lenin, V. (1916). *The Socialist Revolution and the Right of Nations to Self-Determination*. Available at www.marxists.org/archive/lenin/works/1916/jan/x01.htm (accessed 20 September 2019).

Leon, A. (1946). *The Jewish Question: A Marxist Interpretation*. Available at www.marxists.de/religion/leon/ (accessed 12 September 2019).

Lerro, B. (2017). *Forging Promethean Psychology: Emotional, Sensual, and Imaginational Foundations of Western Psychology*. CreateSpace Independent Publishing Platform.

Levine, B. E. (2009). *Psychiatry's Shock Doctrine: Are We Really OK with Electroshocking Toddlers?* 3 March. Available at www.alternet.org/story/124165/ (accessed 21 July 2019).

Levitin, K. (1982). *One Is Not Born a Personality: Profiles of Soviet Education Psychologists*. Moscow: Progress Publishers.

Levitin, K. (2002). *Karl Levitin Interviews Vladimir I. Lubovsky*. Available at http://luria.ucsd.edu/AudioVideo/DVD_Luria6.mp4 (accessed 26 September 2019).

Lewontin, R. C. (1991). *Biology as Ideology: The Doctrine of DNA*. New York: HarperPerennial.

Linebaugh, P. (2006). *The London Hanged: Crime and Civil Society in the Eighteenth Century*. London: Verso.

Linebaugh, P. and Rediker, M. (2012). *The Many-Headed Hydra: The Hidden History of the Revolutionary Atlantic*. London: Verso.

Linley, P. A. and Joseph, S. (2003). Putting It into Practice. *The Psychologist*, Vol. 16, No. 3, p. 135.

Lonn, M. R. and Dantzler, J. Z. (2017). A Practical Approach to Counselling Refugees: Applying Maslow's Hierarchy of Needs. *Journal of Counselor Practice*, Vol. 8, No. 2, pp. 61–82.

Luria, A. R. (1932). *The Nature of Human Conflicts: An Objective Study of Disorganisation and Control of Human Behaviour*. Translated by W. Horsley Gantt, with a Foreword by Adolf Meyer. New York: Grove Press.

Luria, A. R. ([1972] 2008). *The Man with a Shattered World: The History of a Brain Wound*. With a Foreword by Oliver Sacks. Cambridge, MA and London: Harvard University Press.

Luria, A. R. (1976). *Cognitive Development: Its Cultural and Social Foundations*. Translated by Martin Lopez-Morillas and Lynn Solotaroff, edited by Michael Cole. Cambridge, MA and London: Harvard University Press.

Luria, A. R. (1979). *The Making of Mind*. Cambridge, MA: Harvard University Press.

Luria, A. R. (1987). *The Mind of a Mnemonist: A Little Book about a Vast Memory*. Cambridge, MA: Harvard University Press.

Luxemburg, R. (1915). *The Junius Pamphlet*. Available at www.marxists.org/archive/ewspaper/1915/junius/index.htm (accessed 9 September 2019).

Lynd, S. and Grubacic, A. (2008). *Wobblies & Zapatistas: Conversations on Anarchism, Marxism and Radical History*. Oakland, CA: PM Press.

McDonald, M. and O'Callaghan, J. (2008). Positive Psychology: A Foucauldian Critique. *The Humanistic Psychologist*, Vol. 36, pp. 127–142.

McGregor, D. ([1960] 2006). *The Human Side of Enterprise*. Annotated edn. New York: McGraw-Hill.

Mckenna, T. (2015). The Suicide Forest: A Marxist Analysis of the High Suicide Rates in Japan. *Rethinking Marxism*, Vol. 27, No. 2, pp. 293–302.

McLaughlin, K. (2003). Identities: Should We Survive or Surpass Them? *Journal of Critical Psychology, Counselling and Psychotherapy*, Vol. 3, No. 1, pp. 48–58.

McMullin, R. E. (2000). *The New Handbook of Cognitive Therapy Techniques*. New York: W. W. Norton.

McQueen, H. (2005). *Reading the 'Unreadable' Marx*. Available at www.marxists.org/subject/marxmyths/humphrey-mcqueen/article.htm (accessed 29 August 2019).

Malone, J. C. (2014). Did John B. Watson Really 'Found' Behaviourism? *Behavior Analysis*, Vol. 37, No. 1, pp. 1–12.

Marcus, A. and Menzies, C. (2005). Towards a Class-Struggle Anthropology. *Anthropologica*, Vol. 47, No. 1, pp. 13–33.

Marcuse, H. (1955). *Eros and Civilisation: A Philosophical Inquiry into Freud*. Boston, MA: Beacon Press.

Marinetti, F. T. (1908). *The Founding and Manifesto of Futurism*. Available at www.unknown.nu/futurism/manifesto.html (accessed 14 August 2018).

Marlowe, N. I. (2015). Open Dialogue with R. D. Laing. *Psychosis*, Vol. 7, No. 3, pp .272–275.

Martínez-Roldán, C. M. and Smagorinsky, P. (2011). Computer-Mediated Learning and Young Latino/a Students' Developing Expertise. In P. R. Portes and S. Salas, Eds, *Vygotsky in the 21st Century Society: Advances in Cultural Historical Theory and Praxis with Non-Dominant Communities*. New York: Peter Lang, pp. 162–179.

Marx, K. (1846). *Peuchet: On Suicide*. Available at https://marxists.catbull.com/archive/marx/works/1845/09/suicide.htm (accessed 12 September 2019).

Marx, K. (1860). *Herr Vogt*. Available at www.marxists.org/history/etol/newspape/ni/vol10/no08/marx.htm (accessed 8 August 2019).

Marx, K. ([1867] 1990). *Capital: A Critique of Political Economy*, Vol. I. Translated by Ben Fowkes. Introduction by Ernest Mandel. London and New York: Penguin in association with New Left Review.

Maslow, A. H. (1943). *A Theory of Human Motivation*. Available at https://psychclassics.yorku.ca/Maslow/motivation.htm (accessed 24 August 2018).

Maslow, A. (1962). *Abraham Maslow, Rollo May, Carl Rogers: Existential Psychology I* [wrongly entitled by YouTube as *Existential Psychology II*]. Part I available at www.youtube.com/watch?v=IUI2EayasXU; Part II at www.youtube.com/watch?v=01kkE2xHfgg (accessed 22 August 2018).

Maslow, A. H. (1968). *Towards a Psychology of Being*. 2nd edn. New York: Van Nostrad Reinhold.

Maslow, A. H. (1969). The Farther Reaches of Human Nature. *Journal of Transpersonal Psychology*, Vol. 1, No. 1, pp. 1–9.

Maslow, A. H. (1971). *The Farther Reaches of Human Nature*. New York: Penguin.

Massumi, B. (2015). *Politics of Affect*. Cambridge and Malden, MA: Polity Press.

Mattick, P. (1972). *Critique of Marcuse: One-Dimensional Man in Class Society*. New York: Merlin Herder and Herder.

Mattick, P. (1978). *Anti-Bolshevik Communism*. London: Merlin Press.

Meduza. (2017). Being Gay in Revolutionary Russia: A WWI Veteran's Letter to a Psychiatrist Asking to be Cured of His 'Terrible Vice', 21 August, *Medusa*. Translated by Kevin Rothrock. Available at https://meduza.io/en/feature/2017/08/21/being-gay-in-revolutionary-russia (accessed 13 September 2018).

Megill, A. (1983). Vico and Marx after Nietzsche. In G. Tagliacozzo, Ed, *Vico and Marx: Affinities and Contrasts*. London and Basingstoke: Macmillan, pp. 388–400.

Meisel, P. (1996). The Mad, Mad World of R. D. Laing. *New York Times*, 8 September. Available at www.nytimes.com/1996/09/08/books/the-mad-mad-world-of-r-d-laing.html (accessed 29 July 2018).

Meisel, P. (2017). The Feudal Unconscious: Capitalism and the Family Romance. *October Magazine*, No. 159, pp. 19–36. Available at http://perrymeisel.blogspot.com/2017/09/the-feudal-unconscious-capitalism-and.html (accessed 4 September 2019).

Mentinis, M. (2006). *Zapatistas: Revolutionary Subjectivities and the Chiapas Revolt*. London and Ann Arbor, MI: Pluto Press.

Mentinis, M. (2010). Remember Remember the 6th of December: A Rebellion or the Constitutive Moment of a Radical Morphoma? *International Journal of Urban and Regional Research*, Vol. 34, No. 1, pp. 197–202.

Mentinis, M. (2016). *The Psychopolitics of Food: Culinary Rites of Passage in the Neoliberal Age*. London and New York: Routledge.

Meloni, M., Cromby, J., Fitzgerald, D. and Lloyd, S. (2018). *The Palgrave Handbook of Biology and Society*. London: Palgrave Macmillan.

Melton, A. M. A. and Schulenberg, S. E. (2007). On the Relationship Between Meaning in Life and Boredom Proneness: Examining a Logotherapy Postulate. *Psychological Reports*, Vol. 101, pp. 1016–1022.

Merle, R. (2016). Trump Railed Against Wall Street. His Victory is Going to Be Great for Big Banks, *Washington Post*. Available at www.washingtonpost.com/news/wonk/wp/2016/11/09/trump-railed-against-wall-street-his-victory-is-going-to-be-great-for-big-banks/ (accessed 15 September 2019).

Mildenberger, F. (2007.) Kraepelin and the 'Urnings': Male Homosexuality in Psychiatric Discourse. *History of Psychiatry*, Vol. 18, No. 3, pp. 321–335.

Miller, A. (2008). A Critique of Positive Psychology – or 'The New Science of Happiness'. *Journal of Philosophy of Education*, Vol. 42, No. 3–4, pp. 591–608.

Miller, J. and Miller, J. (1993). *The Passion of Michel Foucault*. Cambridge, MA: Harvard University Press.

Millett, K. (2000). *Sexual Politics*. Urbana and Chicago: University of Illinois Press.

Moghaddam, F. M. (2007). *Great Ideas in Psychology: A Cultural and Historical Introduction*. Oxford: Oneworld Publications.

Moon, K. A. (2007). A Client-Centred Review of Rogers with Gloria. *Journal of Counselling and Development*, Vol. 85, No. 3, pp. 277–285.

Morss, J. R. (1996). *Growing Critical: Alternatives to Developmental Psychology*. London and New York: Routledge.

Mosse, G. L. (1985). *Nationalism and Sexuality: Middle Class Morality and Sexual Norms in Modern Europe*. Madison, WI: University of Wisconsin Press.

Mullan, R. (2017). *Mad to be Normal*. Gizmo Films, Bad Penny Productions, GSP Studios.

Munz, P. (1983). The Idea of 'New Science' in Vico and Marx. In G. Tagliacozzo, Ed, *Vico and Marx: Affinities and Contrasts*. London and Basingstoke: Macmillan, pp. 1–19.

Negri, A. (2017). *Marx and Foucault*. Translated by Ed Emery. Cambridge: Polity Press.

Neher, A. (1991). Maslow's Theory of Motivation: A Critique. *Journal of Humanistic Psychology*, Vol. 31, pp. 89–112.

Neilson, B. and Rossiter, N. (2008). Precarity as a Political Concept, or, Fordism as Exception. *Theory Culture Society*, Vol. 25, No. 7–8, pp. 51–72.

Newman, F. and Holzman, L. (1993). *Lev Vygotsky: Revolutionary Scientist*. London and New York: Routledge.

Nietzsche, F. ([1883–1885] 1997). *Thus Spake Zarathustra*. Ware: Wordsworth.

Nietzsche, F. ([1889] 1997). *Twilight of the Idols: Or, How to Philosophise with the Hammer*. Translated by Richard Polt. Indianapolis and Cambridge: Hackett.

Nightingale, D. J. and Cromby, J. (2001). Critical Psychology and the Ideology of Individualism. *Journal of Critical Psychology, Counselling and Psychotherapy*, Vol. 1, No. 2, pp. 117–128.

Noll, R. (1997). *The Aryan Christ: The Secret Life of Carl Jung*. New York: Random House.

Noys, B. (2015). *Legacies of 'Anti-Psychiatry' and R. D. Laing*, 9 October. Available at www.versobooks.com/blogs/2276-legacies-of-anti-psychiatry-and-r-d-laing (accessed 1 August 2018).

O'Hagan, S. (2012). Kingsley Hall: RD Laing's Experiment in Anti-Psychiatry, *The Guardian*, 2 September. Available at www.theguardian.com/books/2012/sep/02/rd-laing-mental-health-sanity (accessed 12 September 2019).

Oppenheimer, D., Producer (2013). *Encountering Maslow*. Documentary, Harper-Perennial. Available at www.youtube.com/watch?v=9FEwsKcPsKs (accessed 22 August 2018).

Paine, T. (1792). *The Rights of Man*. Available at www.ushistory.org/paine/rights/ (accessed 9 September 2019).

Painter, D., Marvakis, A. and Mos, L. (2009). German Critical Psychology: Interventions in Honour of Klaus Holzkamp. *Theory & Psychology*, Vol. 19, No. 2, pp. 139–147.

Pannekoek, A. (1902). *The Position and Significance of Joseph Dietzgen's Philosophical Works*. Transcribed by Adam Buick. Available at www.marxists.org/archive/pannekoe/1902/dietzgen.htm (accessed 5 March 2019).

Pannekoek, A. ([1948] 2003). *Workers' Councils*. Oakland, CA: AK Press. Available at https://libcom.org/files/Pannekoek%20-%20Workers%27%20Councils.pdf (accessed 29 September 2019).

Pannekoek, A. (1975). *Lenin as Philosopher: A Critical Examination of the Philosophical Basis of Leninism*. With additional notes by Paul Mattick and Introduction by Karl Korsch. New York: Breakout Press.

Panofsky, C. P. (2003). The Relations of Learning and Student Social Class: Toward Re-'Socialising' Sociocultural Theory. In A. Kozulin, B. Gindis, V. S. Ageyev and A. M. Miller, Eds, *Vygotsky's Educational Context in Cultural Context*. Cambridge: Cambridge University Press, pp. 411–431.

Papadopoulus, D. (2009). Klaus Holzkamp's Critical Social Science. *Theory & Psychology*, Vol. 19, No. 2, pp. 161–166.

Parent, A. (2004). Giovanni Aldini: From Animal Electricity to Human Brain Stimulation. *Canadian Journal of Neurological Sciences*, Vol. 31, No. 4, pp. 576–584.

Parker, I. (1994). Discourse Analysis. In P. Banister, E. Burman, I. Parker, M. Taylor and C. Tindall, Eds, *Qualitative Methods in Psychology: A Research Guide*, Buckingham: Open University Press, pp. 92–107.

Parker, I. (1997). *Psychoanalytic Culture: Psychoanalytic Discourse in Western Society*. London: SAGE.

Parker, I. (1998). Against Postmodernism: Psychology in Cultural Context. *Theory & Psychology*, Vol. 8, No. 5, pp. 601–627.

Parker, I. (2005). *Qualitative Psychology: Introducing Radical Research*. Maidenhead: Open University Press.

Parker, I. (2007). *Revolution in Psychology: Alienation to Emancipation*. London and Ann Arbor, MI: Pluto Press.

Parker, I. (2017). *Revolutionary Keywords for a New Left*. Winchester and Washington, DC: Zero Books.

Parker, I. and Burman, E. (1993). Against Discursive Imperialism, Empiricism and Constructionism: Thirty-Two Problems with Discourse Analysis. In E. Burman and I. Parker, Eds, *Discourse Analytic Research: Repertoires and Readings of Texts in Action*. Florence, KY: Routledge.

Pashukanis, E. B. ([1929] 1989). *Law & Marxism: A General Theory*. Translated by Barbara Einhorn, edited and introduced by Chris Arthur. London: Pluto Press.

Paton, M. (2015). R. D. Laing: Was the Counterculture's Favourite Psychiatrist a Dangerous Renegade or a True Visionary? *The Independent*, 30 November. Available at www.independent.co.uk/life-style/health-and-families/rd-laing-was-the-countercultures-favourite-psychiatrist-a-dangerous-renegade-or-a-true-visionary-a6755021.html (accessed 4 August 2018).

Penot, B. (2005). Disavowal. *International Dictionary of Psychoanalysis*. Available at www.encyclopedia.com/psychology/dictionaries-thesauruses-pictures-and-press-releases/disavowal (accessed 4 September 2019).

Penuel, W. R. and Wertsch, J. V. (1995). Vygotsky and Identity Formation: A Sociocultural Approach. *Educational Psychologist*, Vol. 30, No. 2, pp. 83–92.

Peterson-Withorn, C. (2017). The $4.3 Billion Cabinet: See What Each Top Trump Advisor Is Worth. *Forbes*, 5 July. Available at www.forbes.com/sites/chasewithorn/2017/07/05/the-4-3-billion-cabinet-see-what-each-top-trump-advisor-is-worth/#2e699ee55dfc (accessed 7 October 2018).

Pick, D. (1995). Freud's 'Group Psychology' and the History of the Crowd. *History Workshop Journal*, No. 40, pp. 39–61.

Pickering, A. (2015). Laing Beyond Words: Antipsychiatry as Performance. In M. G. Thompson, Ed, *The Legacy of R. D. Laing: An Appraisal of His Contemporary Relevance*,. London and New York: Routledge.

Pilgrim, D. (2002). The Biopsychosocial Model in Anglo-American Psychiatry: Past, Present and Future. *Journal of Mental Health*, Vol. 11, No. 6, pp. 585–594.

Plaut, E. A. and Anderson, K. (1999). *Marx on Suicide*. Translated by E. A. Plaut, G. Edgcomb and K. Anderson. Evanston, IL: Northwestern University Press.

Plekhanov, G. (1907). *Joseph Dietzgen*. Originally published in *Selected Philosophical Works*, Vol. 3. Moscow: Progress Publishers. Available at www.marxists.org/archive/plekhanov/1907/dietzgen.htm (accessed 2 February 2019).

Pocknee, D. (2013). *What Is 'New' about 'New Fordism'?* Available at http://nfo.ricercata.org/writing/what_is_new_about_new_fordism.pdf (accessed 30 September 2019).

Podell, K. (2009). When East Meets West: Systematising Luria's Approach to Executive Control Assessment. In A.-L. Christensen, E. Goldberg and D.

Bougakov, Eds, *Luria's Legacy in the 21st Century*, New York: Oxford University Press, pp.122–145.

Pollard, R. (2008). *Dialogue and Desire: Mikhail Bakhtin and the Linguistic Turn in Psychotherapy*. London: Karnac.

Pompa, L. (1983). Ontological and Historiographical Construction in Vico and Marx. In G. Tagliacozzo, Ed, *Vico and Marx: Affinities and Contrasts*. London and Basingstoke: Macmillan, pp. 62–77.

Powell, R. A., Didgon, N., Harris, B. and Smithson, C. (2014). Correcting the Record on Watson, Rayner, and Little Albert: Albert Barger as 'Psychology's Lost Boy'. *American Psychologist*, Vol. 69, No. 6, pp. 600–611.

Prigatano, G. P. (2009). Neuropsychological Foundations of Human Personality and Luria's Legacy. In A.-L. Christensen, E. Goldberg and D. Bougakov, Eds, *Luria's Legacy in the 21st Century*. New York: Oxford University Press. pp. 62–84.

Pytell, T. (2003). Redeeming the Unredeemable: Auschwitz and Man's Search for Meaning. *Holocaust and Genocide Studies*, Vol. 17, No. 1. pp. 89–113. Available at https://muse.jhu.edu/article/43137#REF104 (accessed 12 September 2019).

Pytell, T. (2016). The Case Against Viktor Frankl: Rollo May's Attacks on Logotherapy. *Psychology Today*, 14 April. Available at www.psychologytoday.com/gb/blog/authoritarian-therapy/201604/the-case-against-viktor-frankl (accessed 11 September 2019).

Rakos, R. F. (2013). John B. Watson's 1913 'Behaviourist Manifesto': Setting the Stage for Behaviourism's Social Action Legacy. *Mexican Journal of Behavioural Analysis*, Vol. 39, No. 2, pp. 99–118.

Ralph, D. (1983). *Work and Madness: The Rise of Community Psychiatry*. Montreal, ON: Black Rose Books.

Ratna, L. (1994). Books Revisited: (A Review of) 'The Divided Self' by R. D. Laing. *British Journal of Psychiatry*, Vol. 165, pp. 420–423.

Ratner, C. (1991). *Vygotsky's Sociocultural Psychology and Its Contemporary Applications*. New York and London: Plenum Press.

Ratner, C. (1993). Contributions of Sociohistorical Psychology and Phenomenology to Research Methodology. In H. J. Stam, L. P. Mos, W. Thorngate and B. Kaplan, Eds, *Recent Trends in Theoretical Psychology: Recent Research in Psychology*. New York: Springer, pp. 503–510.

Ratner, C. (2012). *Macro Cultural Psychology: A Political Philosophy of Mind*. Oxford: Oxford University Press.

Rawlinson, K. (2019). The Comma Touch: Jacob Rees-Mogg's Aides Send Language Rules to Staff. *The Guardian*, 26 July. Available at www.theguardian.com/politics/2019/jul/26/the-comma-touch-jacob-rees-mogg-sends-language-rules-to-staff (accessed 2 August 2019).

Ray, S. (2019). 'We Never Thought He Would Take His Life': 18 Students Kill Themselves after Failing Exams. *The Independent*, 25 April. Available at www.independent.co.uk/news/world/asia/india-student-suicides-failed-exams-telangana-state-school-pressure-a8886551.html (accessed 12 September 2019).

Reddebrek (2018). *Notes on Soviet Attitudes to Homosexuality*. Available at https://libcom.org/blog/notes-soviet-attitudes-homosexuality-03042018 (accessed 10 September 2018).

Reese, H. W. (2013). Influence of John B. Watson's Behaviourism on Child Psychology. *Mexican Journal of Behaviour Analysis*, Vol. 39, No. 2, pp. 48–80.

Reeves, A. and Taylor, P. (2017). Self-Harm and Suicide. In A. Vossler, C. Havard, G. Pike, M.-J. Barker and B. Raabe, Eds, *Mad or Bad? A Critical Approach to Counselling and Forensic Psychology*. Los Angeles, CA and London: SAGE.

Reich. W. (1948). *Listen Little Man!* Translated by Ralph Manheim, with illustrations by William Steig. New York: Orgone Institute Press.

Rexroth, K. (1974). *Communalism: From Its Origins to the Twentieth Century*. New York: Seabury Press. Available at www.bopsecrets.org/rexroth/communalism.htm (accessed 3 September 2019).

Richards, G. (2002). *Putting Psychology in Its Place: A Critical Historical Overview*. London and New York: Routledge.

Ridley, F. A. (1988). *Fascism Down the Ages*. London: Routledge.

Roberts, J. M. (2004). From Populist to Political Dialogue in the Public Sphere: A Bakhtinian Approach to Understanding a Place for Radical Utterances in London, 1684–1812. *Cultural Studies*, Vol. 18, No. 6, pp. 884–910.

Roberts, R. (2010). Madness, Myth and Medicine. *The Psychologist*, Vol. 23, No. 8, pp. 694–695.

Rock, B. and Fonagy, P. (2006). Freud's Influence: Personal and Professional Perspectives. *The Psychologist*, Vol. 19, p. 535.

Rockmore, T. (1983). Vico, Marx, and Anti-Cartesian Theory of Knowledge. In G. Tagliacozzo, Ed, *Vico and Marx: Affinities and Contrasts*. London and Basingstoke: Macmillan, pp. 178–191.

Rogers, C. R. (1953). *Counselling as I See It*. Available at www.youtube.com/watch?v=nl1uOep3pR8 (accessed 10 September 2019).

Rogers, C. R. (1955). Persons or Science? A Philosophical Question. *American Psychologist*, Vol. 10, pp. 267–278.

Rogers, C. R. (1961). *On Becoming a Person: A Therapist's View of Psychotherapy*. Boston, MA: Houghton Mifflin.

Rogers, C. R. (1965). *Carl Rogers and Gloria: Counselling (1965) Full Session*. Available at www.youtube.com/watch?v=24d-FEptYj8 (accessed 10 August 2019).

Rogers, C. R. (1971). Carl Rogers Describes His Way of Facilitating Encounter Groups. *American Journal of Nursing*, Vol. 71, No. 2, pp. 275–279. Available at www.elementsuk.com/libraryofarticles/myway.pdf (accessed 4 September 2018).

Rogers, C. R. (1974a). *Carl Rogers on Empathy: Part 1*. Distinguished Contributors to Counselling Film Series, American Personnel and Guidance Association. Available at www.youtube.com/watch?v=iMi7uY83z-U (accessed 31 August 2018).

Rogers, C. R. (1974b). *Journey into Self*. Video of Group Therapy with Carl Rogers and Richard Farson, directed by Tom Skinner. Available at www.youtube.com/watch?v=_vZCeVB-WVw (accessed 4 September 2018).

Rogers, C. R. (1983). *Carl Rogers: The Conversation*. Presented by Maureen O'Hara. Available at www.youtube.com/watch?v=vNZPVTswrhs (accessed 2 September 2018).

Rogers, C. R. (1985). *The Evolution of Psychotherapy Conference*. Video clip. Available at www.youtube.com/watch?v=6yZ9No6TG6Q (accessed 29 August 2018).

Rogers, C. R. (1989). *The Carl Rogers Reader*. Edited by H. Kirschenbaum and V. L. Henderson. Boston, MA and New York: Houghton Mifflin.

Rose, H. and Rose, S. (2014). *Genes, Cells and Brains: The Promethean Promises of the New Biology*. London: Verso.

Rose, N. (1985). *The Psychological Complex: Psychology, Politics and Society in England, 1869–1939*. London: Routledge and Kegan Paul.

Rose, N. and Abi-Rached, J. M. (2013). *Neuro: The New Brain Sciences and the Management of the Mind*. Princeton, NJ and Oxford: Princeton University Press.

Rose, S. (1994). *The Making of the Memory: From Molecules to Mind*. Toronto, ON: Bantham Books.

Rose, S., Kamin, L. J. and Lewontin, R. C. (1984). *Not in Our Genes: Biology, Ideology, and Human Nature*. Harmondsworth: Penguin.

Rosen, M. (2012). *Dignity: Its History and Meaning*. Cambridge, MA, and London: Harvard University Press.

Ross, K. (2015). *Communal Luxury: The Political Imaginary of the Paris Commune*. London and New York: Verso.

Roth, W.-M., Radford, L. and LaCroix, L. (2012). Working with Cultural-Historical Activity. *Forum: Qualitative Social Research*, Vol. 13, No. 2, Art. 323.

Rugh, P. (2013). Two Years On, Will the Lessons of Fukushima Go Unheeded? occupy.com, 3 November. Available at www.occupy.com/article/two-years-will-lessons-fukushima-go-unheeded#sthash.GV3FAFVx.dpbs (accessed 5 August 2019].

Rühle, O. (1920). *The Revolution Is Not a Party Affair*. Available at www.marxists.org/archive/ruhle/1920/ruhle02.htm (accessed 20 September 2019).

Ryan, F. (2015). *Pratt & Smith: Last Men Hanged in England for Sodomy*. Available at www.petertatchellfoundation.org/pratt-smith-last-uk-men-hanged-for-sodomy/ (accessed 10 September 2018).

Ryan, J. (2017). *Class and Psychoanalysis: Landscapes of Inequality*. London and New York: Routledge.

Ryan, M. (1983). *Womanhood in America*. New York: Watts.

Ryle, A. (1994). Persuasion or Education? The Role of Reformulation in Cognitive Analytic Therapy. *International Journal of Short-Term Psychotherapy*, Vol. 9, Nos 2–3, pp. 111–118.

Sacks, O. (1985). *The Man Who Mistook His Wife for a Hat*. London: Picador Books.

Sacks, O. (1990). *Awakenings*. New York: HarperPerennial.

Samelson, F. (1974). History, Origin Myth and Ideology: 'Discovery' of Social Psychology. *Journal for the Theory of Social Behaviour*, Vol. 4, pp. 217–231.

Scheper-Hughes, N. (1982). *Saints, Scholars and Schizophrenics: Mental Illness in Rural Ireland*. Berkeley, CA: University of California Press.

Scheper-Hughes, N. (2000). The Global Traffic in Human Organs. *Current Anthropology*, Vol. 41, No. 2. Available at http://pascalfroissart.online.fr/3-cache/2000-scheperhughes.pdf (accessed 15 September 2019).

Schulenberg, S. E., Nassif, C., Hutzell, R. R. and Rogina, J. M. (2008). Logotherapy for Clinical Practice. *Psychotherapy Theory, Research, Practice, Training*, Vol. 45, No. 4, pp. 447–463.

Schulenberg, S. E., Schnetzer, L. W., Winters, M. R. and Hutzell, R. R. (2010). Meaning-Centred Couples Therapy: Logotherapy and Intimate Relationships. *Journal of Contemporary Psychotherapy*, Vol. 40, pp. 95–102.

Schulman, M. A. (2015). R. D. Laing: Premature Postmodern Psychoanalyst. In M. G. Thompson, Ed, *The Legacy of R. D. Laing: An Appraisal of His Contemporary Relevance*. London and New York: Routledge.

Scott, S. and Thorpe, C. (2006). The Sociological Imagination of R. D. Laing. *Sociological Theory*, Vol. 24, No. 4, pp. 331–352.

Scribner, S. and Cole, M. (1981). *The Psychological Consequences of Literacy*. Cambridge, MA: Harvard University Press.

Seligman, M. E. P. and Csikszentmihalyi, M. (2000). Positive Psychology: An Introduction. *American Psychologist*, Vol. 55, pp. 5–14.

Şener, Ö. (2013). The Gezi Protests, Polyphony and 'Carnivalesque Chaos'. In Bülent Gökay and Ilia Xypolia, Eds, (2013). *Reflections on Taksim – Gezi Park Protests in Turkey*. Keele: Global Faultlines Publication, pp. 40–43.

Sennett, R. and Cobb, J. ([1972] 1993). *The Hidden Injuries of Class*. London and Boston, MA: Faber and Faber.

Shafer, D. A. (2016). *Antonin Artaud*. London: Reaktion Books.

Shah-Shuja, M. (2008). *Zones of Proletarian Development*. London: OpenMute.

Shapiro, J. (2010). *Contested Will: Who Wrote Shakespeare?*London: Faber and Faber.

Sherlock, R. (2013). Turkey: Taksim Square Protesters in Angry 'Victorious' Carnival. *The Telegraph*, 2 June. Available at www.telegraph.co.uk/news/worldnews/europe/turkey/10094499/Turkey-Taksim-Square-protesters-in-angry-victorious-carnival.html (accessed 21 August 2019).

Shotter, J. (1996). Vico, Wittgenstein, and Bakhtin: 'Practical Trust' in Dialogical Communities. Draft paper for the conference on Democracy and Trust, Georgetown University, 7–9 November. Available at www.massey.ac.nz/~alock/virtual/js.htm (accessed 30 September 2019).

Shotter, J. (2015). Worldly Beings Becoming Human Beings: Differentiations and Articulations within Our Different Ways of Being. *Culture & Psychology*, Vol. 21, No. 2, pp. 231–242.

Shotter, J. and Billig, M. (1998). A Bakhtinian Psychology: From Out of the Heads of Individuals and into the Dialogues between Them. In M. Bell and M. Gardiner, Eds, *Bakhtin and the Human Sciences*. London: SAGE in association with *Theory, Culture & Society*, pp. 13–29.

Shostrom, E. L., Producer and Director (1971). *The Humanistic Revolution*. A presentation by Psychological Films, Santa Ana, CA. Available at www.youtube.com/watch?v=fZqAkH1yQvc (accessed 22 August 2018).

Shulman, A. K. (1991). Dances with Feminists. *Women's Review of Books*, Vol. 9, No. 3. Available at www.lib.berkeley.edu/goldman/Features/danceswithfeminists.html (accessed 30 August 2019).

Sibley, D. (1999). Untouched by Statistics: Representing and Misrepresenting Other Cultures. In D. Dorling and S. Simpson, Eds, *Statistics in Society: The Arithmetic of Politics*. London: Arnold, pp. 89–94.

Simon, H. W. and Billig, M., Eds (1994). *After Postmodernism: Reconstructing Ideology Critique*. London: SAGE.

Simon, L. H. (1983). Vico and Marx and the Problem of Moral Relativism. In G. Tagliacozzo, Ed, *Vico and Marx: Affinities and Contrasts*. London and Basingstoke: Macmillan.

Skeggs, B. (2004). *Class, Self, Culture*. Abingdon and New York: Routledge.

Smith, C. (2004). *Marx and Materialism*. Available at www.marxists.org/subject/marxmyths/cyril-smith/article.htm (accessed 24 August 2019).

Smith, J. R. and Haslam, S. A., Eds (2012). *Social Psychology: Revisiting the Classic Studies*. Los Angeles, CA and London: SAGE.

Sohn-Rethel, A. (1978). *Intellectual and Manual Labour: A Critique of Epistemology*. London and Basingstoke: Macmillan.

Sohn-Rethel, A. (1987). *The Economy and Class Structure of German Fascism*. London: Free Association Books.

Spargo, T. (1999). *Foucault and Queer Theory*. Cambridge and New York: Icon Books and Totem Books.

Stam, H. J. (2006). The Dialogic Self and the Renewal of Psychology. *International Journal for Dialogic Science*, Vol. 1, No. 1, pp. 99–117.

Staughton, L. and Grubacic, A. (2008). *Wobblies & Zapatistas: Conversations on Anarchism, Marxism and Radical History*. Oakland, CA: PM Press.

Steakley, J. D. (1999). Cinema and Censorship in the Weimar Republic: The Case of 'Anders als die Andern'. *Film History*, Vol. 11, No. 2, pp. 181–203.

Steinberg, M. W. (1997). 'A Way of Struggle': Reformations and Affirmations of E. P. Thompson's Class Analysis in the Light of Postmodern Theories of Language. *British Journal of Sociology*, Vol. 48, No. 3, pp. 471–492.

Stenner, P. (2017). Happy Subjects and Humaneering. In E. Andreouli and S. Taylor, Eds, *Advanced Social Psychology, Book 2*. Milton Keynes: The Open University, pp. 79–116.

Stenner, P. and Taylor, D. (2008). Psychological Welfare: Reflections on an Emerging Field. *Critical Social Policy*, Vol. 28, No. 4, pp. 415–437.

Stevens, P. and Harper, D. J. (2007). Professional Accounts of Electroconvulsive Therapy: A Discourse Analysis. *Social Science and Medicine*, Vol. 64, No. 7, pp. 1475–1486.

Stevens, R. (2008). *Sigmund Freud: Examining the Essence of His Contribution*. Mind Shapers Series. Basingstoke and New York: Palgrave Macmillan.

Stoppelman, G. (2000). *Artaud for Beginners*. Illustrated by J. Harmeier. New York and London: Writers and Readers.

Stott, C. J. and Reicher, S. D. (1998). Crowd Action as Inter-Group Process: Introducing the Police Perspective. *European Journal of Social Psychology*, Vol. 28, pp. 509–529.

Stuart, M. (1971). *Willi Wonka & the Chocolate Factory*. Based on a novel by Roald Dahl, starring Gene Wilder. Paramount Pictures.

Sweeney, G. (1997). The King of White Trash Culture: Elvis Presley and the Aesthetics of Excess. In M. Wray and A. Newitz, Eds (1997). *White Trash: Race and Class in America*. New York and London: Routledge, pp. 249–266.

Suchet, M. (2007). Unravelling Whiteness. *Psychoanalytic Dialogues*, Vol. 16, pp. 317–331.

Szasz, T. S. (1979). *The Myth of Psychotherapy*. Oxford: Oxford University Press.

Tagliacozza, G., Ed (1983). *Vico and Marx: Affinities and Contrasts*. London and Basingstoke: Macmillan.

Tajfel, H. (1982). *Social Identity and Intergroup Relations*. Cambridge: Cambridge University Press.

Tanner, R. (2018). *Motivation: Applying Maslow's Hierarchy of Needs Theory*. Available at https://managementisajourney.com/motivation-applying-maslows-hierarchy-of-needs-theory/ (accessed 23 August 2018).

Tateo, L. (2015). Giambattista Vico and the Principles of Cultural Psychology: A Programmatic Retrospective. *Culture & Psychology*, Vol. 28, No. 1, pp. 44–65.

Taussig, M. T. (1980). *The Devil and Commodity Fetishism in South America*. Chapel Hill, University of North Carolina Press.

Taylor, A., Director (2012). *Game of Thrones*, Cersei Lannister, Littlefinger scene. Season 2, episode 1. Distributed by HBO. Available at www.youtube.com/watch?v=sKTc8Chvw5k (accessed 28 September 2019).

Taylor, A. J. P. (1980). *Revolutions and Revolutionaries*. London: Hamish Hamilton.

Taylor, S., Ed (2010). *Ethnographic Research: A Reader*. Los Angeles, CA and London: SAGE in association with the Open University.

Teo, T. (2000). Klaus Holzkamp. In A. E. Kazdin, Ed, *Encyclopedia of Psychology*, Vol. 4. New York: Oxford University Press, pp. 141–142.

Teo, T., Ed (2014). *Encyclopedia of Critical Psychology*. New York: Springer.

The Samaritans (2018). *Suicide: Facts and Figures*. Available at www.samaritans.org/about-us/our-research/facts-and-figures-about-suicide (accessed 14 July 2018).

Thompson, E. P. ([1963] 2013). *The Making of the English Working Class*. London: Penguin.

Thompson, E. P. (1993). *Customs in Common: Studies in Traditional Popular Culture*. New York: The New Press.

Thompson, M. G. (2015). Laing and the Myth of Mental Illness Redux. In M. G. Thompson, Ed., *The Legacy of R. D. Laing: An Appraisal of His Contemporary Relevance*. London and New York: Routledge.

Thomson, A. (2009). *Erich Fromm: Explorer of the Human Condition*. Basingstoke and New York: Palgrave Macmillan.

Tierney, T. F. (2010). The Governmentality of Suicide: Peuchet, Marx, Durkheim, and Foucault. *Journal of Classical Sociology*, Vol. 10, No. 4, pp. 357–389.

Timpanaro, S. (1976). *The Freudian Slip*. London: New Left Books.

Toates, F. (2009). *Burrhus F. Skinner: The Shaping of Behaviour*. Basingstoke and New York: Palgrave Macmillan.

Toates, F. (2010). Understanding Drug Treatment: A Biopsychosocial Approach. In Meg Barker, Andreas Vossler and Darren Langdridge, Eds, *Understanding Counselling and Psychotherapy*. London and Milton Keynes: SAGE and the Open University, pp. 45–75.

Todd, E. (1985). The Value of Confession and Forgiveness According to Jung. *Journal of Religion and Health*, Vol. 24, No. 1, pp. 39–48.

Todd, J. T. (1994). What Psychology Has to Say about John B. Watson: Classical Behaviourism in Psychology Textbooks, 1920–1989. In J. T. Todd and E. K. Morris, *Modern Perspectives on John B. Watson and Classical Behaviourism*. Westport, CT: Greenwood Press, Chapter 5. Available at https://people.emich.edu/jtodd/ToddChapter.pdf (accessed 12 August 2018).

Tolman, C. W. (1989). What's Critical About Kritische Psychologie? *Canadian Psychology/Psychologie Canadienne*, Vol. 30, No. 4, pp. 628–635.

Tolman, C. W. (1994). *Psychology, Society, and Subjectivity; An Introduction to German Critical Psychology*. London and New York: Routledge.

Tolstoy, L. ([1886] 2010). *The Death of Ivan Ilyich and Other Stories*. Translated by Larissa Volokhonsky. London: Vintage Press.

Torn, A. (2012). The Carnival of Kingsley Hall: Alison Torn on the Colourful Case of Mary Barnes. *The Psychologist*, Vol. 25, No. 9, pp. 722–723.

Tougas, K. and Shandel, T., Producers (1989). *Did You Used to be R. D. Laing?* Documentary. Available at www.youtube.com/watch?v=86t5GWB5qRY (accessed 12 September 2019).

Traverso, E. (1995). *The Jews & Germany: From the 'Judeo-German Symbiosis' to the Memory of Auschwitz*. Translated by Daniel Weissbort. Lincoln: University of Nebraska Press.

Trombadori, D. (1991). *Michel Foucault: Remarks on Marx. Conversations with Duccio Trombadori*. Translated by R. James Goldstein and James Cascaito. New York: Semiotext(e).

Tsogas, G. (2012). The Commodity Form in Cognitive Capitalism. *Culture and Organisation*, Vol. 18, No. 5, pp. 377–395.

Tulviste, P. (1999). Activity as Explanatory Principle in Cultural Psychology. In S. Chaiklin, M. Hedegaard and U. J. Jensen, Eds, *Activity Theory and Social Practice: Cultural-Historical Approaches*. Aarhus: Aarhus University Press, pp. 66–78.

Tzara, T. (1918). *Dada Manifesto*. Available at www.391.org/manifestos/1918-dadC-manifesto-tristan-tzara.html#.W3LDr1DPzmZ (accessed 14 August 2018).

Ulman, J. D. (1996). Radical Behaviourism, Selectionism and Social Action. In I. Parker and R. Spear, Eds, *Psychology and Society: Radical Theory and Practice*. London and Chicago, IL: Pluto Press, pp. 81–92.

Vajda, M. (1976). *Fascism as a Mass Movement*. London: Allison & Busby.

Van der Veen, M. (2013). After Fukushima: Revisiting Chernobyl and the Collapse of the Soviet Union. *Rethinking Marxism: A Journal of Economics, Culture & Society*, Vol. 25, No. 1, pp. 121–129.

Vaneigem, R. [J.-F. Dupuis] (1977). *A Cavalier History of Surrealism*. Translated by Donald Nicholson-Smith. Edinburgh: AK Press.

Vaneigem, R. (1994). *The Movement of the Free Spirit*. New York: Zone Books.

Van Elteren, M. (1992). Karl Korsch and Lewinian Social Psychology: Failure of a Project. *History of the Human Sciences*, Vol. 5, No. 33, pp. 33–61.

Vassilieva, J. (2013). Eisenstein/Vygotsky/Luria's Project: Cinematic Thinking and The Integrative Science of Mind and Brain. *Screening the Past*, Vol. 38, pp. 1–16. Available at www.screeningthepast.com/2013/12/eisenstein-vygotsky-luria's-project-cinematic-thinking-and-the-integrative-science-of-mind-and-brain/ (accessed 26 September 2019).

Vice, S. (1997). *Introducing Bakhtin*. Manchester and New York: Manchester University Press.

Vielma, A. J. (2016). Wall Street Basher Trump Loving Goldman Guys for His Team, CNBC. Available at www.cnbc.com/2016/11/30/wall-street-basher-trump-loving-goldman-guys-for-his-team.html (accessed 15 September 2019).

Vološinov, V. N. (1987). *Freudianism: A Critical Sketch*. Translated by I. R. Titunik and edited in collaboration with N. H. Bruss. Bloomington and Indianapolis: Indiana University Press.

Vygotsky, L. ([1962] 1986). *Thought and Language*. Revised and edited by Alex Kozulin. Cambridge, MA: MIT Press.

Vygotsky, L. (1987). Thinking and Speech. In R. Rieber and A. Carton, Eds, *The Collected Works of Lev Vygotsky*, Vol. 1. Translated by N. Minick. New York: Plenum, pp. 5–285.

Wagoner, B. (2012). Learning and Memory. In R. Harré and F. M. Moghaddam, Eds, *Psychology for the Third Millennium: Integrating Cultural and Neuroscience Perspectives*. Los Angeles, CA and London: SAGE, pp. 116–138.

Watson, J. B. (1913). *Psychology as the Behaviorist Views It* (aka *Watson's Behaviourist Manifesto*). Available at https://psychclassics.yorku.ca/Watson/views.htm (accessed 14 August 2018).

Watson, J. B. (1919). *Psychology from the Standpoint of a Behaviourist*. Philadelphia and London: J. B. Lippincott Company.

Watson, J. B. (1920a). Is Thinking Merely the Action of Language Mechanisms? *British Journal of Psychology*, General Section, Vol. 11, No. 1, pp. 169–180. Available at https://doi.org/10.1111/j.2044-8295.1920.tb00010.x (accessed 15 August 2018).

Watson, J. B. (1920b). *Is Thinking Merely the Action of Language Mechanisms?* (Audiobook, published by the Psychology Library, 20 March 2017). Available at www.youtube.com/watch?v=SgilFcV2Bnk (accessed 15 August 2018).

Watson, J. B. (1920c). *Little Albert Experiment* (with original footage, credited to Watson alone). Available at www.youtube.com/watch?v=p3r3NJw2otw (accessed 16 August 2018).

Watson, J. B. (1920d). *Conditioned Emotional Reactions* (Audiobook, a Librivox recording, credited to Watson alone). Available at www.youtube.com/watch?v=p4ZPjSnl7RQ (accessed 8 September 2018).

Watson, J. B. (1924). *Behaviourism*. New York: People's Institute.

Watson, J. B. and Rayner, R. ([1920] 2000). Conditioned Emotional Reactions. *American Psychologist*, Vol. 55, No. 3, pp. 313–317.

Weeks, J. (1975). Where Engels Feared to Tread. *Gay Left: A Socialist Journal Produced by Gay Men*, No. 1, pp. 3–5.

Weeks, J. (1985). *Sexuality and Its Discourse: Meanings, Myths & Modern Sexualities*. London: Routledge and Kegan Paul.

Weeks, J. and Holland, J., Eds (1996). *Sexual Cultures: Communities, Values and Intimacy*. Basingstoke: Palgrave Macmillan.

Weinstock, N. (1989). *Zionism: False Messiah*. Edited and translated by Alan Adler. Introductory interview by Moshe Machover. London: Pluto Press.

Wertsch, J. V. (1985). *Vygotsky and the Social Formation of Mind*. Cambridge, MA and London: Harvard University Press.

Wetherington, L. (2016). *Antonin Artaud: The Asylums and After*. Available at https://jacket2.org/commentary/antonin-artaud-asylums-and-after (accessed 21 July 2019).

White, E. J. (2014). Bakhtinian Dialogic and Vygotskian Dialectic: Compatibilities and Contradictions in the Classroom? *Educational Philosophy and Theory*, Vol. 46, No. 3, pp. 220–236.

White, J. (2006). The Religious Origins of Intelligence Testing. *The Psychologist*, Vol. 19, No. 6, pp. 360–361.

Wickman, S. A. and Campbell, C. (2003). An Analysis of How Carl Rogers Enacted Client-Centred Conversation with Gloria. *Journal of Counselling and Development*, Vol. 3, No. 2, pp. 178–184.

Wikipedia. *2011 Tōhoku Earthquake and Tsunami*. Available at https://en.wikipedia.org/wiki/2011_Tōhoku_earthquake_and_tsunami (accessed 15 September2019).

Wikipedia. *Abraham Maslow*. Available at https://en.wikipedia.org/wiki/Abraham_Maslow (accessed 22 August 2018).

Wikipedia. *Alfred Sohn-Rethel*. Available at https://en.wikipedia.org/wiki/Alfred_Sohn-Rethel (accessed 18 September 2019).

Wikipedia. *Antonin Artaud*. Available at https://en.wikipedia.org/wiki/Antonin_Artaud#cite_note-5 (accessed 19 July 2019).

Wikipedia. *Bolo Tie*. Available at https://en.wikipedia.org/wiki/Bolo_tie (accessed 9 September 2019).

Wikipedia. *Different from The Others*. Available at https://en.wikipedia.org/wiki/Different_from_the_Others (accessed 6 September 2019).

Wikipedia. *Fukushima Daiichi Nuclear Disaster*. Available at https://en.wikipedia.org/wiki/Fukushima_Daiichi_nuclear_disaster (accessed 15 September 2019).

Wikipedia. *Herculine Barbin*. Available at https://en.wikipedia.org/wiki/Herculine_Barbin (accessed 13 September 2019).

Wikipedia. *John B. Watson*. Available at https://en.wikipedia.org/wiki/John_B._Watson (accessed 11 August 2018).

Wikipedia. *Jonathan Leunbach*. Available at https://en.wikipedia.org/wiki/Jonathan_Leunbach (accessed 6 September 2019).

Wikipedia. *Joseph Dietzgen*. Available at https://en.wikipedia.org/wiki/Joseph_Dietzgen#cite_note-3 (accessed 17 September 2019).

Wikipedia. *Kimberlé Williams Crenshaw*. Available at https://en.wikipedia.org/wiki/Kimberlé_Williams_Crenshaw (accessed 15 September 2019).

Wikipedia. *Künstlerkolonie Berlin*. Available at https://de.wikipedia.org/wiki/Künstlerkolonie_Berlin (accessed 19 September 2019).

Wikipedia. *LGBT History in Russia*. Available at https://en.wikipedia.org/wiki/LGBT_history_in_Russia (accessed 13 September 2018).

Wikipedia. *Viktor Frankl*. Available at https://en.wikipedia.org/wiki/Viktor_Frankl#Controversy (accessed 12 September 2019).

Williams, D. I. and Irving, J. A. (2001). Counselling as Western Religion. *Journal of Critical Psychology, Counselling and Psychotherapy*, Vol. 1, No. 1, pp. 3–9.

Williams, R. (1973). Base and Superstructure in Marxist Cultural Theory. *New Left Review* (Nov.–Dec.), No. 82. Available at https://newleftreview.org/issues/I82/articles/raymond-williams-base-and-superstructure-in-marxist-cultural-theory (accessed 4 September 2019).

Wilson, R. (2017). Electroconvulsive Therapy Is Still Being Used Today – with Mixed Results. *Independent Online*, 4 December. Available at www.independent.co.uk/news/long_reads/electroconvulsive-therapy-is-back-but-is-it-worth-the-risk-a8084631.html (accessed 19 July 2019).

Wing, J. K. (1971). Laing and Goffman [a Review of] 'Self and Others' by R. D. Laing. *British Journal of Psychiatry*, Vol. 118, No. 544, pp. 360–361.

Winslow, E. G. (1986). Keynes and Freud: Psychoanalysis and Keynes's Account of the 'Animal Spirits' of Capitalism. *Social Research*, Vol. 53, No. 4, pp. 549–578.

Wolff, C. (1986). *Magnus Hirschfeld: A Portrait of a Pioneer in Sexology*. London: Quartet Books.

Wray, M. and Newitz, A., Eds (1997). *White Trash: Race and Class in America*. London and New York: Routledge.

XinhuaNet (2018). Japan's Suicide Rate Drops for 8th Straight Year in 2017. *XinhuaNet*, 19 January. Available at www.xinhuanet.com/english/2018-01/19/c_136908773.htm (accessed 17 July 2018).

Yates, F. (1966). *The Art of Memory*. Chicago, IL: University of Chicago Press.

Young, J. (2007). *The Vertigo of Late Modernity*. London: SAGE.

Zinn, H. (1999). *A People's History of The United States, 1492-Present*. New York: Perennial.

Zittoun, T. (2015). From Vico to the Sociocultural Imagination. *Culture & Psychology*, Vol. 21, No. 2, pp. 251–258.

Zweig, L. and Bennis, W., Producers (1968). *Being Abraham Maslow*. Documentary, in conversation with Warren Bennis. Available at www.youtube.com/watch?v=sfmo04EZP3o (accessed 22 August 2018).

INDEX

Page numbers in *italics* indicate Figures.

For Product Safety Concerns and Information please contact our EU representative GPSR@taylorandfrancis.com
Taylor & Francis Verlag GmbH, Kaufingerstraße 24, 80331 München, Germany

www.ingramcontent.com/pod-product-compliance
Lightning Source LLC
Chambersburg PA
CBHW050448051126
54379CB00003B/60
* 9 7 8 1 1 3 8 6 1 4 1 1 6 *